The RIGHT and the GOOD

Halakhah and Human Relations

DANIEL Z. FELDMAN

YASHAR BOOKS • 2005

Yashar Ethics Series: Volume II

The Right and the Good
Halakhah and Human Relations

Copyright 2005 by Daniel Z. Feldman

10 9 8 7 6 5 4 3 2 1

Library of Congress Cataloging-in-publication Data

Feldman, Daniel, 1972–
    The right and the good : halakhah and human relations / Daniel Z.
    Feldman.
        p.   cm
    Includes bibliographical references and index.
    (soft cover) ISBN 1-933143-03-7
    ISBN 0-7657-6051-7
    1. Jewish law—Moral and ethical aspects.   2. Interpersonal relations—Religious aspects—
    Judaism   3. Ethics, Jewish
    I. Title
    BJ1286.L3F45   1999
    296.1′8—dc21

For information and catalog write to Yashar Books Inc., 1548 E. 33rd Street,
Brooklyn, NY 11234, or visit our website: www.YasharBooks.com

Dedicated to my parents, Rabbi David and Aviva Feldman, whose every deed and action advocate the ideals described in this book as loudly as all its words.

Table of Contents

ACKNOWLEDGMENTS

With deep gratitude to the *Ribbono Shel Olam*, I humbly tender this work to the reading public.

This book is an updated and expanded version of one published by Jason Aronson in 1999. In the years since, much new literature has come out, and I have attempted to represent some portion of that new material in this version, which is being published by Yashar Books. I extend my sincere thanks to my good friend Rabbi Gil Student, president of Yashar, for this opportunity and for all of his extremely hard work in bringing the book to press. I wish him and Yashar all success and am excited to be a part of this promising new enterprise.

I would like to thank the authors of those works in Hebrew that have been devoted specifically or largely to the topics of this book, which contain among them many citations too numerous and overlapping to identify individually. These works include R. Yisrael Ya'akov Vidavski's *Amirat Shalom K'Hilkhata*; R. David Kog'ah's *Dan L'Khaf Zekhut*;

R. Ya'akov Davidson's *Hilkhot Derekh Eretz*; R. Avraham Tovolsky's *Hizaharu B'Khvod Chaveirkhem, K'tzet HaShemesh B'Gvurato*, and *MiDvar Sheker Tirchak*; R. Hillel David Litwack's *MiDvar Sheker Tirchak, Mishpat Tzedek, Sha'arei Ona'ah*, and *Yisrael HaKedoshim*; R. Joseph D. Epstein's *Mitzvat HaEtzah, Mitzvot HaBayit, Mitzvot HaMusar*, and *Mitzvot HaShalom*; R. Moshe Troyesh's *Orach Meisharim*; R. Tzvi H. Weinberger's and R. Baruch A. Heifetz's *Sefer Limmud L'Hilkhot Bein Adam L'Chaveiro: Lo Tisna Et Achikha BiLvavekha*; R. Yosef Avraham Heller's *Shalom Yihyeh*; R. Shmuel Yudaikin's *Divrei Shalom*; R. Ya'akov Y'chizkiyah Fish's *Titten Emet L'Ya'akov*; R. Betzatel Genchersky's *Darkhei Tzedek*; and R. David Ariav's *L'Reakha Kamokha*.

Over the course of this project, I had the opportunity to witness firsthand many of the things that can go wrong with computers. Thus, I would like to thank the following very patient individuals for technical assistance of all kinds and at all times: Eitan Friedman; Ron Samet; Richard Tannenbaum; Greg Hudis; Stephen Margulies; Dr. Ben Tandowsky; Yoram Heilbronner; Judah Diament; and, of course, for everything, Chaim B. Hollander, Avi Shmidman and Rabbi Benjamin G. Kelsen.

I thank the Mendel Gottesman Library of Yeshiva University for its resources and its staff for its patience and assistance, particularly Ms. Chaya Gordon and Mr. Judah Wohlgelenter.

I would like to thank several good friends who were always available to discuss issues relevant to the content and format of this project, including Rabbi Dr. Yitzchak Schechter, Rabbi Moshe Schapiro, Rabbi Steven Burg, Daniel E. Benovitz, Rabbi Raphael Willig, Rabbi Lavi Greenspan, Rabbi Abraham Shmidman, and Rabbi Meir Yakov Soloveichik. Rabbi Zev Reichman, whom I thanked in the original version, has since become my cousin due to our respective marriages, and our gratitude to him and to Chana is immense, as it is to Zev's parents Rabbi and Mrs. Hershel Reichman.

I am grateful to the entire staff at Jason Aronson Inc. for all their work and encouragement on the first version, in particular Arthur Kurzweil, Pamela Roth and Dana Salzman, who I also thank for her work on this version, as well as Mr. Brian Romer of Rowan Littlefield.

I extend a very special thank you to Mr. Terry D. Novetsky, who with
great patience, insight, graciousness and generosity with his time made
it possible for this version to get to print.

I express my gratitude to all of my *rebbeim*, particularly Rabbi Neil
Winkler and Rabbi Yosef Shurin for their early instruction and influence.
I thank my senior *chevrusas* and mentors Rabbi Baruch Simon and
Rabbi Zvi Sobolofsky for their constant advice and guidance. I am grate-
ful to Rabbi Meir Goldvicht for his support. I thank my *rebbe*, Rabbi
Hershel Schachter, whose *shiurim* I have been privileged to hear for several years, for all of his influence and counsel. Rabbi Dr. Norman
Lamm, chancellor and Rosh haYeshiva of Yeshiva University, took time
from his schedule to offer valued advice for which I am most apprecia-
tive. I thank Rabbi Zevulun Charlop, Rabbi Jacob J. Schacter, and Rabbi
Robert S. Hirt for their advice on this project. Rabbi Mordechai Willig,
whom I have been fortunate to hear *shiurim* from and to draw influence
from for many years in many contexts, graciously agreed to review large
portions of the manuscript, as did Rabbi Yosef Blau, whose comments
and insights are most appreciated. I am grateful also to Rabbi Aharon
Kahn for his comments to a portion of the manuscript. I express my profound gratitude to my *rebbe*, Rabbi Menachem Mendel Blachman of
Yeshivat Kerem B'Yavneh, who has provided insight, instruction, and
support at length from the inception of this project to its conclusion,
including reading almost the entire manuscript. I also acknowledge the
continuing influence of the revered founding Rosh Yeshiva of Kerem
B'Yavneh, Rabbi Chaim Ya'akov Goldvicht, *zatzal*.

I thank Mrs. Bella Wexner *a"h* and, *tibadel l'chaim*, Ms. Susan
Wexner, for their generous sponsorship of the Bella and Harry Wexner
Kollel Elyon at Yeshiva University, in which I was privileged to learn for
four years at RIETS, and to hear shiurim and gain direction from Rabbi
Willig and Rabbi Michael Rosensweig.

I wish to express my appreciation to the administrations of the schools
that currently give me the opportunity to teach Torah under their aus-
pices, including Yeshiva University President Richard M. Joel, Rabbi
Lamm, Rabbi Charlop and the Rabbi Isaac Elchanan Theological
Seminary; Rabbi Michael D. Shmidman and the Stone Beis Midrash

Program of Yeshiva University; and R. Yosef Adler and the Torah Academy of Bergen County in Teaneck, NJ. And to my students at these institutions, I offer my thanks for listening, for challenging me, and helping me to gain a clearer understanding of all I would hope to teach.

I thank my cousins Rabbi Ari and Mindy Marcus and my aunt and uncle Rabbi Meyer and Goldie Fendel for their advice and support at the earliest stages of this project and throughout, as well as my grandmother, Mrs. Miriam Cohen, and my uncles and aunts, Eliot B. Feldman, Drs. Ben and Miriam Landau, and Colin and Ruth Lever, for all they have done. My brother Jonathan and his wife Rachel (and Simcha Leib. Malka, and Esther Leah) and my sister Rebecca are constant and invaluable sources of love and support.

Certainly the most significant events in my life since the first edition came out have been my marriage to Leah, and the birth of our daughter, Adina Ahuva, who bears the name of Leah's beloved grandmother, Rebbitzen Adina Freiberg, *a"h*, who embodied selfless *chesed* and devotion to Torah. I extend my profound gratitude to my father-in-law and mother-in-law, Rabbi Mordechai and Shaindel Feuerstein, together with my grandparents-in-law, Rabbi Chaim Freiberg, and Mr. and Mrs. Moses I. and Shirley Feuerstein, for their warm welcome and cherished support and influence, and to all of the extended family. And to Leah, whose modesty combines with the limitations of language in preventing me from saying a fraction of what should be said, I will only express my gratitude that Adina Ahuva has the role model she has in all the ways of life.

Finally, my deepest appreciation goes to my father and mother, Rabbi David M. and Aviva Feldman, for, quite literally, everything; and in this context, for their constant assistance and guidance on all aspects of this work; for tolerating the more inconvenient details of its production; for their advice, suggestions, insights, and input; and, most importantly, for exemplifying the behavior that is the inspiration for and ideal of this book. It is to them this work is dedicated.

INTRODUCTION

*I*t is not too difficult to find the religious element in the deliberation of the complex issues in the laws of *Shabbat* or in the determination of the *kashrut* of that night's proposed dinner. The rabbi's telephone rings often to summon a response to these questions, where his authority is acknowledged if not assiduously adhered to. Even the less ritually colored concerns of the proper treatment of a patient trapped in an intractable medical condition, or the adjudication of a complicated civil entanglement, at the very least present a clear moral challenge; these situations are hopefully understood by the Torah-observant Jew to fall within the parameters of the vast halakhic framework that guides and inspires existence. In these areas, either the familiar trappings of traditional observance or the ethical conundrums inherent in major life decisions present themselves front and center; the spiritual component thus looms unambiguously as at least a prominent influence, if not the absolute and total motivator for, and arbitrator of, these decisions.

However, even for the committed, conscientious Jew, another vastly important field of *halakhah* is often manifested in a far more subtle manner, a component of Torah law whose latency belies its inestimable significance. It is thus the tragic result that a perception is created that this area is one outside of the purview of *halakhah,* while in reality, nothing could be further from the truth. The day-to-day interactions between people, the treatment of one another in mundane conversation, in walking in the street, in traveling on a bus, or waiting in line to be served in a store are no less the home of *halakhah* than are the activities of the synagogue or the kitchen, the study hall or the hospital bed. Every form of relationship among men, not just monetary but personal as well, not just in the rabbinical court but also across the table at lunch, is the vital concern of Jewish law.

Since the dawn of philosophical investigation, man has struggled to properly establish the guidelines and principles that are to govern the morals and mores of society. Frequently, the aspect of utilitarianism has played a fundamental role in inspiring social theory; a significant portion of the formulations of philosophers has centered on the reality that the world can only maintain itself when certain standards of interaction are upheld.[1] To some, this remains purely a functional necessity; as such, even those theorists who have an extreme view of human liberty ultimately conceded the need for a "social contract."[2] To others, who strove to define a fundamental morality, this truism is then abstracted into a system of ethical values, assuming that that which is contributory to societal health (or "happiness") on the mass level is considered meritorious when practiced by the individual.[3] To some thinkers, this attitude is incorporated into the human psyche, resulting in what has been termed a "moral sense."[4] Philosophers and psychologists debate the extent to which it is possible, if at all, to believe there exists an instinct within the human being that inclines toward moral and ethical behavior beyond immediate self-interest. Even allowing such an assumption, the

---

1. See, for instance, John Stuart Mill, *Utilitarianism,* and Jeremy Bentham, *An Introduction to the Principles of Morals and Legislation.*

2. See, for example, Jean-Jaques Rousseau, *The Social Contract* (1760).

3. Such as, for example, Aristotle, or, differently, Kant.

4. For a recent, extensive exposition of this theory, see James Q. Wilson, *The Moral Sense* (The Free Press, 1993).

ingredients of this attitude are of an imprecise nature, subject to the myriad ideologies that inform the perspectives of the world population.[5]

Nonetheless, lofty ideals of political, philosophical, and psychological theorists cannot ensure that the world community does indeed receive the ethical nourishment necessary to survive. Thus, governments and legal systems have risen throughout history as the primary guardians of personal interaction, regulating those tendencies that threaten the fabric of society.[6] Those values that improve the communal welfare, but whose absence is not destructive, have generally fallen outside the purview of legislative bodies, although social policies of encouragement do exist, particularly in modern times. Despite recent trends in litigation that attempt to translate the most mundane behavior into criminally or civilly actionable terms, the virtues extolled by the great philosophers are nonetheless primarily dependent on the autonomy of the individual.

The purely utilitarian role of the legal and governmental system is one that is found as well in talmudic sources, where, for example, "fear of the government" is credited with saving the world from self-destruction.[7] Indeed, the only active obligation among the seven commandments that are applicable to all of humanity is the establishment of a court system,[8] to regulate the observance of the prohibitive aspects,[9] legislate the elements of civil relationships,[10] and prevent the eruption of

---

5. As William Graham Sumner wrote (*Folkways*, 1906, cited by Wilson), "The mores can make anything right."

6. Note, for example, Thomas Hobbes' *Leviathan*.

7. *Avot* 3:2.

8. *Sanhedrin* 56a, per *Genesis* 2:16

9. See Rambam, *Mishneh Torah, Hilkhot Sanhedrin* 9:10. Note the commentary of R. Eliezer Menachem Mann Schach, *Avi Ezri*, as well as *Har HaMelekh*, and R. Yitzchak Sorotzkin, *Gevurot Yitzchak Al HaTorah* vol. I, #43. See also R. Chaim Sofer, *Responsa Machaneh Chaim*, vol. 2, *Orach Chaim* 22.

10. See Ramban, commentary to the Torah, *Genesis* 34:13 (disputing the above position of the Rambam); see R Avraham diBoton, *Lechem Mishneh*; R. Shlomo of Chelm, *Mirkevet HaMishneh*; and R. Shammai Kehat Gross, *Masa Bnei Kehat* to *Mishneh Torah*; R. Moshe Isserles, *Responsa HaRama* 10; R. Yosef Shaul Nathanson, *Divrei Shaul* to *Genesis*; R. Baruch Epstein, *Torah Temimah*, *Genesis* 18:42; R. Yehoshua Baumol, *Responsa Emek Halakhah* 2:12; R. Ya'akov Etlinger, *Arukh L'Neir* to Sanhedrin; R. Shmuel Greenman, *Chiddushim U'Biurim* to *Sanhedrin* 9; R. Yosef Babad, *Minchat Chinnukh* 37; and R. Naftali Tzvi Yehudah Berlin, *Ha'amek Shealah* 2:3 and *Meromei Sadeh* to *Sanhedrin*. R. Moshe Sofer (*Responsa Chatam Sofer* 6:14) minimizes the practical difference between the positions.

chaos.[11] This function is shared by both the courts within the general society and those that are part of the rabbinic structure. Nonetheless, within the latter system, the administration of justice and order transcends its functional position and fulfills not only a societal need but becomes an expression of God's majesty and the Jew's adherence to His will.[12]

This reality informs every aspect of Jewish morality: that the Jewish system of ethics is not an autonomy, not even the most nobly intentioned one, but a theonomy, instructed in every detail by Divine command. The dealings of the boardroom, the classroom, and the sidewalk are no less directed by holiness and spirituality than are those of the *beit midrash,* the synagogue, or the kitchen. While lamentably, stories appear in the news on occasion implying that this is not obvious to all, and one hears of apparently observant Jews involved in circumstances of financial impropriety or general dishonesty, the vast majority of those committed to *halakhah* are acutely aware that its scope extends far beyond the ritual.

However, just how far beyond that may, unfortunately, not be as well-known. That the wearing of *tefillin* is governed by *halakhah* is obvious, and that the purchase of a car or financing of a house is so regulated is almost as widely understood, despite the rare but well-publicized lapses that may occur. Yet the Torah's influence eclipses that of civil legislation; the line for a bus, the conversation at dinner, and the behavior on the basketball court share equally as the site of religious influence. That the shove one gives another person in order to be served more quickly in the cafeteria, or the comment made moments later when the tray is dropped on the other person's clothes, are subject to their own prohibitions, sometimes comes as a surprise; so, too, that the Torah has a very specific idea of how the victim and the aggressor should deal with each other in the aftermath. These interactions, so mundane and basic, are believed to be a matter of style and personality, immune from interference by any

---

11. See *Chiddushei HaMeiri* to *Sanhedrin.*
12. See *Berakhot* 6a, per *Psalms* 82:1, for example, and *Derashot HaRan, Drush* 11. Note, at length, R. Baruch Rakovsky, *Birkat Avot* 55; R. Shlomo Fisher, *Beit Yishai* 107; and R. David Yitzchak Mann, *Be'er Miriam, Sanhedrin* 9:10. See also the journal *Beit Yitzchak* 28:527–542.

agency. The truth is far different—the voice of *halakhah* is as loud on these fronts as on any other.

The tractate *Avot*, which deals with morals and ethical values, begins with the foundation of all tradition: "Moshe received the Torah at Sinai . . ." The placement is somewhat puzzling; such a basic principle of Judaism belongs at the introduction of the Talmud, rather than in a tractate that comes at the end of the fourth of its six orders. But R. Menachem HaMeiri and R. Ovadiah of Bartenura explain that the organization is most appropriate, for we are given the information when it is most necessary.[13] When studying the laws of the proper blessing on a certain food, or what time to pray, or how to observe *Shabbat*, or how to build a *sukkah*, no reminder is necessary that those laws were given at Sinai; no other source could compel such observance. However, a reminder is needed when encountering the less ritualistic aspects of life; it is then that the interest of religion is less obvious and the Sinaic tradition must be invoked. It must be noted that on further consideration, these commentators appear to be addressing a larger portion of the population than might be assumed. *Avot* is placed sequentially after *Bava Kamma*, *Bava Metzia*, *Bava Batra*, and *Sanhedrin*; these tractates dealt at great length with details of monetary interaction several hundred folios before we are reminded of the Divine revelation. Despite unfortunate exceptions, most Jews do not limit their religious perspectives to overtly ritual activities; it is understood that Torah law is no less encompassing than that of the secular government. Nonetheless, when a tractate says, "Love peace and pursue peace,"[14] "Greet all men with a cheerful countenance,"[15] "Your friend's honor should be as dear to you as your own,"[16] "Whomever the people are satisfied with, God is satisfied with,"[17] and other such statements, even the most committed Jew may often believe he is merely receiving good advice.[18] It is then that it must be emphasized: This, too, is from Sinai.

---

13. See also R. Gedalyah Felder, *Yesodei Yeshurun* to *Pirkei Avot*, pp. 10–11, and R. Yehoshua Segal Daitsch, *Beit HaLachmi, Avot* 1:1.

14. *Avot* 1:12.

15. Ibid., 1:16.

16. Ibid., 2:10.

17. Ibid., 3:10.

18. See also the essay of R. Mordechai HaKohen, "Masekhet Avot BiHalakhah,"

The divinity of these principles was not left for the Oral Torah to explain; many of the regulations governing these day-to-day interactions stem from explicit biblical verses. "You shall not hate your brother in your heart, you shall reprove your fellow and do not bear a sin because of him, you shall not take revenge and you shall not bear a grudge against the members of your people, you shall love your fellow as yourself, I am God,"[19] "In justice shall you judge your friend,"[20] "You shall not oppress your friend,"[21] "Keep far away from falsehood,"[22] "Seek peace and pursue it,"[23] and many other such scriptural passages address themselves directly to everyday interactions.

Some may question the need for the *halakhah* to involve itself in this area; if social conventions and secular laws take up this concern, perhaps the Torah is indeed best focused upon the overtly spiritual. In fact, some authorities[24] attribute the lack of a blessing assigned to interpersonal *mitzvot*[25] to a reflection of this mindset among the populace.[26] Immediately, certain advantages become clear. As R. Natan Gestetner observes,[27] when these behaviors lack the force of *halakhah*, they fall by the wayside

---

printed in the journal *Sinai* 50:133–151; the journal *Torah SheB'al Peh* 4:122–141; and in his *Halakhot V'Halikhot*, pp. 204–227.

19. *Leviticus* 19:17–18.

20. *Leviticus* 19:15.

21. *Leviticus* 25:17.

22. *Exodus* 23:7.

23. *Psalms* 34:15.

24. See, in particular, R. Michael Fisher, *Ateret Mordechai* to *Avot* 1:1, as well as R. Moshe Shternbuch, *Mo'adim U'Zmanim* 2:188.

25. See Rambam, *Mishneh Torah, Hilkhot Berakhot* 11:2, and R. Yosef Karo, *Kesef Mishneh*.

26. See also *Responsa HaRashba* 18; *Responsa Meyuchasot LaRamban* 369; *Abudraham, Sha'ar* 3; Rabbeinu Bachya, *Kad Hakemach, Ot Tzitzit;* R. Menachem Azariah, (*Rama MiPanu*), *Ma'amar HaIttim;* R. Aryeh Leib Heller, *Ketzot HaChoshen*, and R. Yonatan Eibshutz, *Tumim*, to *Choshen Mishpat* 97; R. Meir Dan Plotzki, *Kli Chemdah, Parshat Vayera*; R. Shmuel Yitzchak Hillman, *Ohr HaYashar, Bekhorot* 11a; R. Joseph D. Epstein, *Mitzvot HaMussar*, pp. 230–231; R. Sh'ar Yashuv Cohen, "Mitzvat Ahavat Yisrael B'Halakhah U'V'Aggadah" in the journal *Torah SheB'Al Peh* 36:51; and R. Zalman Goodman in *Beit Abba*, p. 188. Compare also the discussion concerning a blessing on legal proceedings; see *Talmud Yerushalmi, Berakhot* 6:1; R. Tzvi Pesach Frank, *Responsa Har Tzvi, Milei d'Brakhot* 2; and R. Avraham Yehudah Schwartz, *Responsa Kol Aryeh, Orach Chaim* 7.

27. *L'Horot Natan* to *Pirkei Avot* 1:1. See also R. Ya'akov Yehoshua Belcrovitz, *Tiferet Yehoshua*, and R. Baruch Zvi Moskowitz, *Nishba L'Avotecha* to *Pirkei Avot*.

in the face of challenges from economic and other aspects of self-interest.[28] Further, the moral ambiguity present in general society is absent within *halakhah*.[29] However, even these considerations, while not to be underemphasized, are more practical than fundamental.[30]

By involving itself in the details of daily interaction, the *halakhah* brings the Divine Majesty into the streets, the workplace, the cafeteria line. When the restraint in business ethics comes on penalty of imprisonment, it represents perhaps no more than fear of the government; when it stems from a realization of God's Will, it attains a status of holiness. Generosity toward others may be a manifestation of a pleasant personality or a vague notion of "goodness"; within Judaism, such behavior is a basic fundamental of spirituality. The words exchanged upon meeting in the street may be a social convention or an avoidance of awkwardness; in Torah law, these phrases acquire abundant elements of religious achievement. Treating others with respect, love, and kindness is not convention, policy, or personality; it is holiness, it is *mitzvah,* it is the Word of God.

The Ramban, in his commentary to *Chumash,* makes a general observation as to the nature of these commandments in general. Discussing the verse, "and you shall do the right and the good,"[31] the Ramban notes the somewhat vague character of its imperative. Certainly, all behavior should be "right" and "good." The Torah, however, wished to impose the standards of holiness onto man's behavior with the community at large, and to this end several biblical verses, including those mentioned previously, are intended to contribute to the formation of a personality in which every action in the social sphere is influenced by Divine command. Nonetheless, the complexity of life's challenges will inevitably

---

28. See, for example, E. F. Carrit in *Ethical and Political Thinking* (Oxford University Press, 1950), pp. 61–65.

29. See also R. Eliezer Bograd, "HaMusar B'Yisrael Uva'amim," in the journal *Niv Midrashiyah* (winter/spring 1968:96–99). For a recent treatment of this topic from a secular perspective see Jeffrey Stout, *Ethics After Babel: The Languages of Morals and Their Discontents* (Boston: Beacon Press, 1988).

30. See also the discussion of perspectives from the writings of Rabbi A. Y. Kook on this question, by R. Yehudah Shaviv, in the journal *Derekh Eretz Dat U'Medinah,* pp. 215–231.

31. *Deuteronomy* 6:18

result in situations where immediate scriptural instruction is unclear; inclusive of all such circumstances, the Torah exhorts, "you shall do the right and the good." No act that may impact negatively upon another person can be said to be devoid of Sinatic guidance.[32]

Thus, the principles dictating people's behavior with each other have been stamped with the seal of Divine commandment, subject to the commitment and seriousness that this entails. However, it may be that these principles, for certain purposes, carry a severity that not only equals but exceeds that inherent in *mitzvot* in general. A story told, involving R. Yisrael Meir Kagan and R. Yisrael Lipkin, may be instructive in this area.[33] R. Kagan (1838-1933) was the revered author of the authoritative work *Mishnah Berurah* on the *Orach Chaim* section of R. Yosef Karo's code of Jewish law, the *Shulchan Arukh*. However, he was perhaps better known for his treatment of the laws of gossip, *lashon hara*, whose title became his own, *Chafetz Chaim*. This story relates that a certain businessman requested to purchase all of R. Kagan's many books, with the glaring exception of *Chafetz Chaim*. When R. Kagan questioned this, the man admitted that the pressures of his business made it difficult to avoid saying derogatory things about the people he came into contact with, and he would rather not purchase a work whose directives he felt compelled to ignore. R. Kagan prevailed upon him to buy it anyway, relating a comment made to him by R. Lipkin. R. Lipkin (1810–1883), known after his hometown as R. Yisrael Salanter, is famed as the founder of the Musar movement, which popularized the intense study of ethical concepts. When the work *Chafetz Chaim* was completed, R. Lipkin told

---

32. Compare the Ramban's comments to *Leviticus* 19:1. For an analysis of the Ramban's position, see R. Yekutiel Hoffman, "V'Asita HaYashar V'HaTov," in the journal *HaDarom* 62:82–93; Dr. Yehudah Muriel, "HaYashar V'HaTov," in the journal *Sinai* 70:92–99; and R. Eliezer Ben Shlomo, "Birur HaMusag V'Asita HaYashar V'HaTov" in the journal *Niv Midrashiyah* (winter\spring 1968:86–95 in particular, pp. 93–94). Note also R. Yosef Blau, 'Tzadik V'Yashar," in *Beit Yitzchak* 17:55–56. For a practical application and an inquiry into the limitations of this idea, see R. Natan Gestetner, *Responsa L'Horot Natan* 2:100 and 7:127. See also R. Aharon Grossman, *V'Drashta V'Chakarta al haTorah*, vol. 4, p. 574–578. See also footnote 59.

33. This story is related by the author of the work *Erekh Apayim*, in his introduction, as well as in that of R. David Kog'ah to his *Dan L'Kaf Zechut*.

34. *Beitzah* 30a and *Bava Batra* 60b.

its author, "If all you accomplish is to evoke one sigh from one Jew [who becomes aware of the prohibitions and cannot observe them], the work is worthwhile." So, too, R. Kagan told the businessman, he may not believe himself able to adhere to the contents of the book; but if it will at least "evoke a sigh," it is worth the purchase price.

While poetic, R. Lipkin's comment may actually be slightly surprising. While all attempts possible are generally made to educate the populace in the Torah's commandments, if it is known that they will not be observed, the Talmud recommends, "better they be inadvertent sinners than intentional ones."[34] That is, if the education will have no effect on practice, it is perhaps better not to disturb the excuse of ignorance. Therefore, if the *halakhah* has not always preferred knowledge of its laws to the alternative, why would R. Lipkin advocate "evoking a sigh"?

It may be that it is appropriate, for these purposes, to distinguish between commandments that are ritual in nature and those that are given over more readily to human understanding. The Rambam, in his introduction to *Pirkei Avot*,[35] makes such a differentiation in considering to what extent it is desirable that one's instincts correlate automatically with those of the Torah's *mitzvot*. In issues of ritual, it is commendable that one bend one's will to that of the Torah; however, in areas of basic morality, whose underpinnings are readily apprehended by the human psyche,[36] one must strive to develop a perspective that is on its own consistent with the Torah's commandments.[37] This categorization may be relevant here as well. For those *mitzvot* whose themes are beyond us, if practice is not possible, it may be preferable to remain ignorant, as the theory will remain outside the boundaries of comprehension as well, and

---

35. *Shemonah Perakim*, ch. 6.

36. The editors of the journal *Torat HaAdam L'Adam*, R. Tzvi Weinberger and R. Boruch Cheifetz, in the introduction to volume five of that journal (2004) discuss the presumption that interpersonal commandments are more readily understood than commandments between Man and God. In their view, this can be traced to the fact that in an interpersonal commandment, any given human being can be on either side of the equation (in their language, the "robber" or the "robbed"), and thus can relate to both sides; while in reference to a commandment between Man and God, the Divine perspective is unknowable to the human.

37. Note, however, glosses of R. Yaakov Emden to *Shemonah Perakim*; see also R. Shmaryahu Shulman, *Merish BaBirah, Parshat Pinchas*. See as well R. Moshe Miernik, in the journal *Torat HaAdam L'Adam*, vol. 4, pp. 76–7.

nothing will be accomplished. However, in those areas where the rationale is apparent, and the laws, even in theory, will automatically display their contribution to the personality of "the right and the good," even study alone is valuable.[38]

Along these lines, R.Naftali Tzvi Yehudah Berlin[39] comments that while one may not add to the observance of *mitzvot*, this applies to those commandments not given over to immediate understanding; however, these principles of social behavior, readily understandable, are therefore amenable to being added onto through human initiative. Thus, the *Mishnah* says, of personal kindness, that it "has no set measurement,"[40] that is, no limits.

While learning without practicing may thus have some saving grace in this area of *halakhah*, the flip side of the uniqueness of these laws may convey the opposite effect. While God is gracious and merciful and can count good intentions as achieving the same effect as an actual deed, the reality is that human beings are not in the same position and understandably take a result-based perspective to their own suffering. The *Tanakh* tells of Peninah, the other wife of the husband of Chanah, later to become mother of Shmuel the prophet. Apparently a woman of some cruelty, she teased Chanah about her initial barrenness. The Talmud (*Bava Batra* 16a) comments that actually, she had been well-intentioned; she hoped to prod Chanah into more fervent prayer that would eventually provide her with children. R. Chaim Shmuelevitz[41] observes that the Talmud is offering no mitigation of Peninah's guilt. Rather, it is expressing that when dealing with the genuine pain of other individuals, good intentions are no defense; the end result is just as anguishing.[42] As he

---

38. Similarly, see R. Dr. Yechezkel Epstein, "Ahavat Adam BHilkhot Nezikin L'HaRambam," in the journal *Torah SheB'al Peh* 4:37–44. Perhaps for such reasons, some sources seem to imply a preference for these *mitzvot* even in regards to observance; see commentary of Rosh, *Peah* ch. 1, #3, *Mishneh Torah, Hilkhot Geneivah* 7:12, and Tosafot, *Bava Metzia* 20b, s.v. *Issura*. See also R. Eliezer Yechiel Konstat, in the journal *Mevakshei Torah*, vol. 4, #20, pp. 162–163 and pp. 236–7, including the responses of R. Meir Freilich and R. Ilan Greenwald.

39. *Ha'amek Davar*, Deuteronomy 5:30.

40. *Peah* 1:1.

41. *Sichot Musar*, 5732, no. 2.

42. On the reverse situation, positive behavior without benevolent intentions, see *Mitzvot HaMusar*, pp. 229–230.

puts it, if one places a person's arm in an oven, even if one means well, it is no less burnt.[43]

Thus, the equation of effort to accomplishment found in *mitzvot* in general appears absent in regards to interpersonal commandments.[44] The result-oriented nature of these precepts may impact on *halakhah* in a number of ways, requiring their actual physical fulfillment despite excuses. Another example of this is the rule that involvement in one commandment exempts the obligation of seeing to another (*osek b'mitzvah patur min hamitzvah*).[45] While there may be no need to interrupt fulfillment of a mitzvah to attend to another one, many authorities assume this is only true if both are commandments between man and God; however if an interpersonal obligation beckons, the current involvement provides no release.[46]

Further, one must examine in this regard the principle governing a clash between positive and negative commandments, which generally gives precedence to the former (*aseh docheh lo ta'aseh*).[47] Although a negative commandment may step aside when in conflict with a positive one, many authorities assume this would not hold true if the prohibition is an offense against another person.[48] Once again, the practical

43. See also R. Gideon Gilkrov's wide-ranging essay "Chiyuv HaZehirut biKh'vod HaBriyot vi-haEtzot Lkakh," in the journal *Ohr Torah*, vol. 28, no. 7:637–666.

44. See, to this effect, R. Yosef Engel, *Atvan D'Orayta, Klal* 13; R. Moshe Sofer, *Responsa Chatam Sofer, Orach Chaim* 54 (and note also *Choshen Mishpat* 1); R. Avraham Bornstein, *Responsa Avnei Nezer, Orach Chaim* 501; and *Responsa Ma'or HaChaim* 1:19. See also R. Mordechai Carlebach, *Chavatzelet HaSharon al haTorah, Genesis*, pp. 597–598.

45. *Sukkah* 25a.

46. See R. Aryeh Leibush Balhuvar, *Responsa Shem Aryeh, Yoreh Deah* 64, and *L'Horot Natan, Pirkei Avot* 2:1; R. Ovadiah Yosef, *Responsa Yabbia Omer*, vol. 4, *Yoreh Deah* 19 denies any distinction, citing the Meiri, *Shabbat* 9b. In a similar vein, see R. Ya'akov Yechiel Traube, *Responsa Avnei Ya'akov* 42, and R. Tzvi Tannenbaum, *Etz Erez*, 1, 18.

47. *Yevamot* 5a.

48. See, for example, R Moshe Sofer, *Chiddushei Chatam Sofer, Sukkah* 29b and end of *Pesachim*, and *Derashot*, vol. 3, p. 4, in notes; R. Ezriel Hildesheimer, *Responsa R. Ezriel, Shonot* 27; and *Responsa L'Horot Natan* 4:118 and 6:38. Concerning the inverse possibility, however, see R. Mordechai Carlebach, *Chavatzelet HaSharon al haTorah, Genesis*, pp. 197–198.

reality lends these principles priority, even at variance with normal rules.[49]

Even the almost absolute principle of "saving a life overrides everything,"[50] mandating the abrogation of all but three transgressions in a circumstance of risk to life, may find a challenge in this area of *halakhah,* according to a minority view in the Talmud[51] and a suggestion in the Meiri,[52] in reference to theft. Although God will forgive observance of His *mitzvot* if they pose a danger, perhaps the same cannot be said about human beings. However, it must be emphasized that R. Moshe Feinstein[53] observes that this is an inconceivable position for practical purposes; in fact, he even denies it exists as an opinion.

It is possible to assert, though, as emerges from some of the rabbinic discussion on the matter, that both are true. In other words, it is the case that the primacy of life-saving concerns mandates that even theft be commited to save a life. However, unlike commandments between man and God, the theft is not "permitted"; that is, it remains an offense, albeit a necessary one, and the "thief" must repay the value of what he took.[54]

---

49. See also the explanation in R. Shimon Yehudah Shkop, *Chiddushei R. Shimon Yehudah HaKohen, Nedarim,* 1, and see also *Sdei Chemed,* vol. 5, p. 229, and *Responsa V'Darashta V'Chakarta,* vol. 3, *Orach Chaim* 73.

50. *Yoma* 82a.

51. See R. Meir in *Ketubot* 19a, and *Chidushei HaRa'ah,* as well as R Eliyahu of Vilna, *Biur HaGra, Choshen Mishpat* 388:25; *Responsa Chatam Sofer, Choshen Mishpat* 1; and *L'Horot Natan, Pirkei Avot, Peticha* 1:1, 5:5; and commentary to *Avot D'R' Natan,* ch. 8. See also R. Yehudah Shaviv, "Sheker V'Gezel, Yehareg V'Al Ya'avor?" in the journal *Shma'atin* 56/57:47 51. See also R. Yitzchak Shmuel Schechter, *Responsa Yashiv Yitzchak,* 4:23 and 42; R. Shlomo Zefrani, in the journal *Ohr Torah,* vol. 35, #16, p. 89–92; R. Avraham Shea, in the journal *Ohr Yisrael,* vol. 1, #4, p. 146–150; R. Shmuel Eliezer Stern, in the journal *Z'chor L'Avraham,* 5760/1, p. 795–799.

52. In *Chiddushei HaMeiri* and in *Shittah Mekubetzet to Bava Kamma* 81a; note R. Chaim Yosef David Azulai, *Petach Einayim* to *Temurah* 15b. See also *Bava Kamma* 60b, Rashi s.v. *Va-yatzilah* and R. Yaakov Etlinger, *Responsa Binyan Tziyyon* 167 and 168. See as well Dr. Abraham S. Abraham, in the journal *HaMa'ayan,* vol. 20, no. 2:17–25 and the responses of R. Shlomo Zalman Auerbach, R. Eliezer Yehudah Waldenberg, Dr. Leo Levi, and R. Yonah Emmanuel in vol. 20, no. 3:49–54.

53. *Responsa Iggerot Moshe, Yoreh Deah,* vol. 1:214. Note also R. Yehudah Rosanes, *Parashat Derakhim. Drush* 19, and *Responsa Yabbia Omer,* vol. 4, *Choshen Mishpat* 6.

54. As R. Feinstein himself discusses in *Responsa Iggerot Moshe, Choshen Mishpat* 2:63. See also R. Yochanan Shor, in the journal *Beit Aharon V'Yisrael,* vol. 16, #2(92), p. 56–58.

Following this emphasis on results to its logical conclusion may lead one to assume that consequences are the only important element in interpersonal relations, with proper intentions wholly irrelevant. Indeed, this is a possibility raised in some writings, supported by the Talmudic assertion[55] that one who gives charity for personal motivations is "completely righteous."[56] However, we have already established that this area of Jewish law is one where the underlying theme of the commandment is even more accessible than usual, with a concomitant emphasis on integrating the value represented into one's personality; thus, it seems difficult to assert that anything less that an integrated package of intent and practice is the desired goal.

In any event, it appears that the status of these ethical principles as a *mitzvah* is not only genuine but in many cases applied more stringently than other *mitzvot*. Whatever the conclusion, the process is the same; the rules of the sidewalk and the marketplace are evaluated in a light as bright and as focused as those of the synagogue and the kitchen. A cliche of introductions is to claim "not enough has been written about this subject." In this instance, I hope to prove the opposite, that the concerns of the rabbinical giants in this field have consumed much paper and ink and have occupied a place in talmudic thought no less prominent than the more identifiably "religious" concepts, and to convey the message that *Shabbat, kashrut,* and *tefilah* are not alone at the forefront of rabbinic involvement. The great talmudic sages represent, as they have throughout the generations, the ideal of the Torah personality, a synthesis of

---

55. *Pesachim* 8a. See R. Shmuel Landau, *Ahavat Tziyon*, #10, citing his father, author of *Noda B'Yehudah*; R. Yitzchak Elchanan Spector, introduction to *Responsa Nachal Yitzchak*; and R. Ovadiah Yosef, *Responsa Yabbia Omer,* 6, *Yoreh Deah* 29 and *Anaf Etz Avot* to *Pirkei Avot,* 2:20, who discusses an even more extreme case, where the donor not only had ulterior motives, but didn't know at all that charity was being given.

56. See R. Avraham Loftiber, *Zera Avraham,* 62:2, and R. Shimon Gabel, *Kli Golah, Yevamot* 62a; and note an extreme formulation in R. Meir Dan Plotzki, *Kli Chemdah, Parshat VaYechi* 3 and R. Shmaryahu Shulman, *Merish BaBirah, Parashat VaYechi,* s.v. *v'atem,* explaining the *Ohr HaChaim, Genesis* 50:20 against the question of *Responsa Beit Yitzchak, Yoreh Deah* 1:8:8, and see also R. Mordechai Carlebach, *Chavatzelet HaSharon al haTorah, Genesis* pp. 725–726. For a treatment of this topic from a different perspective, see R. Ben Zion Kriger, in the journal *Techumin,* vol. 24, p. 314–324, and note also, in the journal *Torat HaAdam L'Adam,* vol. 4: R. David Ariav, pp. 113–5, and R. Mordechai Elefant, pp. 148–149.

devoted attention to the relationship between man and God and man and man, and their writings display this in all its glory.

To this end it must be emphasized that this is not a work of practical *halakhah,* and it would not be my place to offer one. In fact, it is just the opposite; it is hoped that by displaying a fraction of a portion of the vast analysis of these topics, their intricacy and complexity will become apparent, and the rote execution of these behaviors will receive the attention it deserves. If a possible situation of embarrassing another is recognized as more comparable to a concern of desecration of the *Shabbat* than as a matter of "personal style," and thus is evaluated with the proper gravity, this work will have served a purpose. The reader who would like a more detailed understanding of the significance of the names cited, historically, biographically, and within the structure of *halakhah,* is advised to turn to the bibliography. As far as practice, it must be stressed that proper *psak* (halakhic ruling) demands not just the sources but a serious analysis of their relative weight, authority, and precise scope, combined with an experienced and trained intuition. Thus, this work makes absolutely no claims in this area but rather hopes to place these concerns within their proper context. It is also hoped that the sources provided will both prompt and facilitate further examination of these issues, as well as of those tangential topics that arise.

Another category that this work does not claim is that of a *musar* text, a genre of literature containing ethical instruction and exhortation. That is certainly not my place, either, and, therefore, this is not a work of moral lectures. As such, the many talmudic and midrashic statements emphasizing the importance of these concepts, but not adding new points of law, are largely absent here, as are relevant stories and other lore. However, it is not unreasonable to aspire that studying the details of these principles will impact on practice; in fact, this was a favored method of the aforementioned driving force of ethical analysis, R. Yisrael Lipkin (Salanter), who wrote:[57] "in encountering a law that is relevant to himself, one should learn the concept from its sources . . . and this

---

57. *Iggeret HaMusar,* and *Ohr Yisrael,* ch. 7, p. 54. See, at length, R. Joseph D. Epstein's introduction to both *Mitzvot HaMusar* and *Mitzvot HaBayit.* A similar sentiment is expressed by R. Avraham Yeshaya Karelitz in his *Emunah U'Bitachon* 3:3, and cited in the introduction to R. Betzalel Genchersky, *Darkhei Tzedek.*

method leads to the soul acquiring the idea in order to observe it, perhaps more [effectively] than introspection in issues of fear of Heaven."[58] This is a personal goal of my own, in the sense that it is hoped that involvement in this work will influence my own behavior. If the reader feels the same way, to perhaps more successful results, how much the better.

Further, the above cited words of the Ramban, concerning "the right and the good," which inspired the title of this work, motivates much of its content as well. It emerges from the Ramban's comments that the interpersonal commandments are meant to seep into the consciousness, to create a personality that is founded upon those principles and capable of functioning in sync with their core values. As with the position of the Rambam noted above, it becomes incumbent upon the Jew who is serious about his Judaism to not only learn the rules but to delve into their underlying reasons, logical structures, and conceptual frameworks, in order to further the process of incorporating these values into the personality. Such study may indeed be of the core obligation of "you shall do the right and the good."[59]

R. Avraham Yellin, author of the work *Erekh Apayim*, a collection of the laws pertaining to anger, makes a similar point in his introduction. Even those who do not read his book will nonetheless notice to their surprise that a topic believed to be minor and simple, such as anger, can serve as the subject of an entire book. This awareness will result, hopefully, in a greater attention to the relevant details (or, at the very least, "evoking a sigh"). So, too, it is hoped that a presentation of some of the myriad relevant sources, even if they are not examined, will be of value.

This work does not concentrate on topics of monetary or civil law, which are found in the volume of the *Shulchan Arukh* entitled *Choshen Mishpat*. Those laws require many more volumes and indeed have received much attention not only in Hebrew but in English as well.

---

58. In this vein, it may also be that R. Lipkin's advice to R. Kagan, recounted above, was motivated by the hope that practice would indeed be affected.

59. Indeed, a booklength treatment of the Ramban's comments, with this very goal, was recently published, containing writings of the late *Rosh Yeshiva* of Yeshivat Chevron—Knesset Yisrael, R. Simcha Mordechai Ziskind Broide, entitled *Sam Derekh: HaYashar VeHaTov* (Otzar HaPoskim, Jerusalem, 2004, edited by R. Yaakov Yehudah Zilberlicht).

Rather, our concern here is with those basic principles of everyday inter-action, before and after any monetary transactions. Further, this work focuses on those precepts that are applicable in all situations, rather than those directed at specific individuals, such as respect for parents and the like. Many of these *holakhot* are collected by R. Avraham Gumbiner, author of the classic work *Magen Avraham* to the *Shulchan Arukh,* in his comments at the end of the laws of *Massa U'Mattan,* or "business."[60] From these concepts, only a handful are discussed here (the *Magen Avraham* lists more than thirty-five). Even those topics that are discussed here may be only parts of more extensive subjects; for example, our dis-cussion of honesty does not include *geneivat da'at* or improper measure-ments in business.

In the Rambam's Mishneh Torah, many of these concepts are included within the section entitled "*Hilkhot Deiot*" or, roughly, "*Laws of Dispositions.*" R. Ya'akov Davidson[61] comments on the appropriateness of this heading. Many halakhic questions depend on the ascertaining of the facts of a situation and their understanding thereof; for example, a ques-tion in *kashrut* may necessitate determining certain facts of animal anatomy or chemistry. Unlike other areas of *halakhah,* however, the topics discussed here can be affected by an individual's personality, opinions, and sensitivities. The reaction one will have toward a comment or a gesture can determine whether it is recommended, allowed, or unequivocally condemned.[62] Truly, these concerns are governed by "the laws of dispositions."

This, too, contributes to a goal of this work. While it will not define the parameters of *halakhah,* it will hopefully call attention to those aspects of the reality, the *metziut,* that must be determined in order to properly observe the related precepts. Absent such evaluation, very often one's relationship toward another person must be treated as carefully as food from an unknown source. Just as the latter would not be eaten

---

60. *Orach Chaim* 156.

61. *Hilkhot Derekh Eretz,* ch. 175.

62. A similar comment can be found in the work *Yad K'tannah, Deiot,* 7:34 in explanation of the reality that so many of these crucial topics often find only tan-gential treatment in the works of halakhic codification. Compare, as well, R. Moshe Miernik, in the journal *Torat HaAdam L'Adam,* vol. 4 , pp. 66–72.

without ascertaining its *kashrut,* so, too, every effort must be made to understand the background, attitudes, and perspectives of the individual being dealt with. Otherwise—and this is especially true in light of R. Shmuelevitz's aforementioned observation that misdirected good intentions provide no defense in this area—one must tread very carefully indeed.

Beyond their importance in and of themselves, an extra level of significance is bestowed on these concepts by the laws of sanctification and desecration of God's Name. The Talmud states[63] "'And you shall love God your Lord'[64]—that God should become beloved through you. That one should learn Scripture, and Talmud, and serve Torah scholars, and that his dealings with people should be pleasing to them; then what do the people say of him? 'Joyous is his father who taught him Torah, joyous is his *rebbe* who taught him Torah, woe to those who have not learned Torah. This individual, who learned Torah, see how pleasant his ways are, how perfect are his actions.' Of such a person, the verse says,[65] 'And He said to me, you are My servant, Israel, in whom I glory.'"[66] The Talmud then proceeds to describe, God forbid, the reverse situation. By careful devotion to specifically those ideals that are shared by the Torah and general society, where in truth the Torah blazed the trail, the majesty of Judaism is most perfectly displayed.

One note: Some of the issues discussed here have been considered in some sources to be inapplicable to one whom the Talmud categorizes as "wicked" (*rasha*). Whether or not this is the case, such exceptions will not receive much mention here, as it will be the assumption of this work, in accordance with the position of several great pillars of *halakhah,* among them R. Avraham Yeshayah Karelitz[67] and other prominent authorities,[68] that this label is largely inapplicable in the present age; that

---

63. *Yoma* 86a.

64. *Deuteronomy* 6:5.

65. *Isaiah* 49:3.

66. See also R. Yitzchak Hecht, *Responsa Sha'arei Kodesh* 2:137.

67. *Chazon Ish, Yoreh Deah, Hilkhot Shchitah* 2:16 (the context is somewhat different, but the principle is relevant).

68. This view is found as well in *Marganita Tava* (#17), citing Maharam Lublin (based on the impossibility of rebuke in modern times; see chapter 12, pp. 182–183). *Marganita Tava* is a work by R. Yonatan Voliner, published by R. Yisrael

the circumstances of modern influences, social values, and temptations have mitigated the responsibility of even the most inveterate of sinners.[69] Rather, to use R. Karelitz's words, it is the obligation of all to "draw them back with the ropes of love, and stand them in the ray of light as much as possible." Thus, while it is not the function of this work to rule on halakhic matters, it will be presumed, following the guidance of the wide range of contemporary authorities, that the behaviors discussed here must be extended equally to all.

The importance of these concepts granted, the sweeping nature of a comment in the Talmud is still surprising. Discussing certain enactments that were instituted for the sake of *darkhei shalom,* "ways of peace," the Talmud adds,[70] "the entire Torah is also for the sake of *darkhei shalom.*" While certainly much of the Torah's concerns are focused in this area, it appears to be somewhat of an exaggeration to give *shalom* such a commanding place among the Torah's objectives. In this regard, an observation of R. Meir Dan Plotzki[71] is illuminating. He writes that while this

---

Meir Kagan (*Chafetz Chaim*) in the back of his book *Ahavat Chesed.* As to whether R. Kagan himself endorsed this view, see R. David Ariav, *L'Reakha Kamokha,* vol. 2, p. 63, *Nir L'David,* #116.

69. See R. Shlomo Wahrman, in the journal *HaDarom,* vol. 63:78–82, and in his *Orot HaShabbat* 13 (see also *She'erit Yosef* 2:7 and *Orot HaShabbat* 12); R. Sha'ar Yashuv Cohen, in the above cited article in *Torah SheBe'al Peh,* pp. 53–57; R. Ephraim Moshe Korngut, *Ohr Yechezkel,* pp. 99–103; R. Joseph D. Epstein, *Mitzvot HaShalom,* pp. 292–297; R. Avraham Tobolsky, *Hizharu Bikhvod Chaveirkhem,* pp. 116–119; R. Moshe Tzuriel in the journal *HaMa'ayan* 17:4 (compare though, the response of R. David Betzalel Klein, *Responsa Tehilot David* 2:70; his opinion seems to be in the distinct minority); R. Shimon Gabel, *Sofrei Shimon, Berakhot* 31a; R. Moshe Aharon Teichman, in *Har HaMelekh,* vol. 6, *Hilkhot Deiot* 6:3, pp. 157–168; and R. Avraham Sherman, in the journal *Techumin,* vol. 1:317–318. Note also R. Avraham Yitzchak HaKohen Kook, *Ma'amarei HaRa'ayah,* p. 92, and R. Shmuel Halevi Vosner, *Responsa Shevet HaLevi,* vol. 5, *Kuntres HaMitzvot* 51. Note *Sefer Mitzvot Katan* 17, who assumes that the status is relevant only to one who has rejected rebuke, which may be impossible to effectively administer in modern times (*Arakhin* 16b). See also R. Natan Gestetner, *Natan Piryo, Bava Metzia,* p. 292. For earlier authorities who indicate a lenient attitude toward modern transgressors, see R. Yaakov Etlinger, *Responsa Binyan Tziyyon HaChadashot* 23; R. Akiva Eiger, *Responsa* 96; and R. Chaim Ozer Grodzinski, *Responsa Achiezer* 3:25.

70. *Gittin* 59b. Note also *Bamidbar Rabbah* 11:7 and *Tanchuma, Tzav* 3.

71. *Kli Chemda, Parshat ViZot HaBerakhah* 4:4. See also *Sefer Charedim,* ch. 7.

statement certainly addresses the state of relationships among men, it cannot be overlooked that there are various types of harmony and disharmony. Some discord refers to interpersonal strife; however, another type of conflict is the inner contradiction, the constant battling of conscience and temptation, of desire and commitment. Each and every *mitzvah* in the Torah is devoted to smoothing friction of some sort, whether it be on the streets or in the soul; or whether it be the jarring disharmony of one striving to accomplish in the eyes of God while neglecting his fellow, or the devoted citizen who is uninterested in a relationship with the Divine. It is the genuinely unified personality, however, who is thus in all his actions a sanctification of God's Name, and this is the ultimate *shalom*. May we all be blessed, truly, with *shalom*.

ONE

Emotional Homicide: Embarrassing Others

I. A Shocking Severity

The halakhic correlation between emotional and physical assault is perhaps most starkly conveyed by a talmudic passage concerning first King David and then Tamar, the daughter-in-law of Yehudah.[1] The King, weathering the aftermath of his involvement with a woman of questionable marital status,[2] cries to the heavens about the humiliation he suffers at the hands of his detractors. Even when involved in the study of unrelated issues of ritual impurity, they shift the attention to the incident with thinly veiled legal inquiries. "David," they taunt, "what

---

1. *Bava Metzia* 59a; see also *Sanhedrin* 106a.
2. See, however, *Shabbat* 56a and Tosafot, *Bava Metzia* 59a, s.v. *Noach*.

manner of death befalls him who has relations with a married woman?"
David's retort is quick to turn the tables on these verbal attacks. "He is
executed with strangulation, and then receives a portion in the world to
come; however, one who shames his fellow in public has no portion in
the world to come."[3] The Talmud derives a principle from this tale, in
the name of Rava: "Better for one to have relations with a possibly married woman than to shame his fellow in public."

The text continues with a reference to the earlier trial of Tamar.[4]
Twice widowed from sons of Yehudah, she was accused of being unfaithful to his family, to which she maintained an obligation to marry into a
third time, in keeping with the laws of *yibbum*. Unbeknownst to the
court, which stands ready to execute her, the father of her unborn child
is actually Yehudah himself. Tamar refuses, however, to save herself by
explicitly volunteering this information, an act that would surely humiliate Yehudah. This noble act of near-sacrifice prompts the derivation of
another halakhic principle: "Better for one to hurl himself into a fiery
furnace than shame his fellow in public."[5]

---

3. On his response, see R. Tzadok HaKohen of Lublin, *Tzidkat HaTzadik* 238.

4. *Genesis* 38.

5. This also appears in *Berakhot* 43b, *Sotah* 10b, and *Ketubot* 67b. It should he
noted, however, that Tamar's actions posed a problem to many commentators, as
they seem to transcend the limits of even the most meritorious behavior. It is one
thing to require martyrdom rather than resorting to embarrassing another; can it
really be suggested, however, that a defendant on trial for his life may not exoner-
ate himself if it necessitates casting a shadow on another? R. Zechariah Stern,
Responsa Zecher Yehosef (vol. I, Tahaluchot HaAggadot, ch. 13), suggests that Tamar's
assessment of the situation was that she would not be believed if she attempted to
incriminate Yehudah and thus felt the humiliation would accomplish nothing and
was not justified. This notion is similarly entertained by R. Shlomo Zalman
Auerbach (*Responsa Minchat Shlomo* 7), who adds the factor that she herself
brought about the situation by misleading Yehudah in the first place; nonetheless,
he rejects both ideas and maintains that a complete understanding of Tamar's
silence remains elusive. See also R. Ya'akov Moshe Feldman, *Meshivat Nefesh* to
Torah Temimah, Genesis 38:29, and R. Yehoshua Ehrenberg, *Responsa D'var Yehoshua*
3:24. See also R. Asher Weiss, *Minchat Asher Al haTorah, Genesis,* 53:3, who suggests
that Tamar only behaved as she did because she had reason to be sure that Yehudah
would respond as he did. R. Natan Gestetner observes further (*L'Horot Natan* to
Pirkei Avot) that living in pre-Sinaitic times, Tamar was not technically Jewish, and,
according to many, only Jews are obligated in martyrdom. Hence, her behavior
must be viewed as an act of unusual piety, perhaps explaining the Rambam's reluctance to codify it as a precept, as discussed later. See also R. Yehudah Herzl Henkin,

The first principle, from the King David story, finds little mention in later halakhic sources.[6] This is not surprising as the precise conflict of values dealt with, adultery and avoiding humiliating others, is not a frequent one in human experience. It is the second principle, mandating the sacrifice of one's life before that of another's dignity, which commands more significant rabbinic attention. The *Rif* includes this in his compilation of halakhic conclusions from the tractate *Bava Metzia*, apparently indicating its acceptance as normative, and he is not alone among medieval authorities. The authors of the *Tosafot*[7] question the absence of humiliating others among the talmudic list of those transgressions requiring martyrdom, such as murder, idol worship, and sexual immorality.[8] They respond by limiting this list to those prohibitions explicitly mentioned in the Torah, a standard that embarrassing others apparently does not fulfill. The very question, however, is predicated on the assumption that humiliating others does indeed require the ultimate sacrifice in its avoidance.[9] Joining this group is Rabbeinu Yonah, who in his classic ethical treatise *Sha'arei Teshuvah*,[10] rules that

Responsa B'nei Banim (1:43), who deals at length with other issues concerning Tamar. See also the *Pri Megadim*'s *Teivat Gomeh*; R. Yosef Chaim Sonnenfeld, *Responsa Salmat Chaim* 953–954; R. Yaakov Etlinger, *Responsa Binyan Tziyyon* 1:172; and R. Ovadiah Yosef, *Responsa Yabbia Omer*, vol. 6, *Yoreh Deah* 13:14, who discusses in great detail the question of martyrdom and non-Jews, as well as R. Yitzchak Sorotzkin, *Gevurot Yitzchak* 1:61; R. Yosef Roth, *Siach Yosef* 2:12:3; R. Yekutiel Yehudah Halberstam, *Responsa Divrei Yatziv, Yoreh Deah*, 51; R. Yitzchak Yedidiah Frenkel, *Derekh Y'sharah* 2:28 (as well as his discussion of many of the details of this prohibition); and R. Shimon Gabel, *Sofrei Shimon, Berakhot* 43b. See also R. Meir Shapiro's *Responsa Ohr HaMeir* 22 for a discussion of Tamar's status. Note also R. Yoav Yehoshua Weingarten, *Chelkat Yoav, Kava D'Kashyata* 10. See also R. Mordechai Carlebach, *Chavatzelet HaSharon al haTorah, Genesis*, p. 597–598, and R. David Ariav, *L'Reakha Kamokha*, vol. 3, *kuntres habiurim* 9.

6. See R. Moshe Feinstein, *Dibrot Moshe* to *Bava Metzia*. R. Feinstein also observes that David, in his comparison, did not mean to imply that repentance is not effective for one who has humiliated another, only that the additional requirement to obtain the forgiveness of the victim contributes a level of difficulty. See R. Chanokh Henakh of Sassov, *Ein Chanokh* to *Avot* 3:11, and R. Yisrael Frankforter, *Da'at Yisrael, Hilkhot Deiot* 6:8.

7. *Sotah* 10b, s.v. *Noach.*

8. *Pesachim* 25a, *Sanhedrin* 74a.

9. See R. Yitzchak Ze'ev Soloveitchik, *Chiddushei HaGriz* to *Sotah.*

10. *Sha'ar* 3:139. See R. Avraham Erlanger, *Ma'or HaSha'ar* to *Sha'arei Teshuvah.*

this prohibition takes precedence over self-preservation. The *Sefer Ohel Moed*[11] echoes this position. It should also be noted that the passage concerning Tamar is not the only Amoraic source to discuss risking one's life to avoid embarrassing another. The *Midrash*[12] contains an opinion that Yosef was in danger of being killed by his brothers when he exposed himself to them without his guards; nonetheless, he preferred this to the possibility that they would be humiliated in front of strangers.[13]

The Meiri, however, is clearly not of this mind, for in his talmudic commentary (*Berakhot* 43b and *Sotah* 10b) he interprets the talmudic comment to be *derekh he'arah* and *derekh tzachut*—that is, not to be understood as practically authoritative. Similarly, a perusal of the Rambam's *Mishneh Torah* uncovers no requirement for martyrdom in this instance. The great commentator to the *Shulchan Arukh*, the *Pri Chadash*, in his glosses to *Mishneh Torah*,[14] does cite the position of *Tosafot* as authoritative and apparently feels the Rambam to be in consonance with this view; furthermore R. Shlomo Zalman Auerbach, in his *Responsa Minchat Shlomo* (no. 7) writes "with the exception of the Meiri, all *rishonim* have interpreted the statement in accordance with its literal meaning." Nonetheless, the Rambam's complete omission is generally taken to be significantly indicative of his position.[15] R. Yehudah Herzl Henkin adds the *Sefer HaChinnukh*,[16] R. Yehudah HaChasid,[17] and the *Menorat HaMa'or*[18] to the list of those who view the phrase figuratively.[19]

---

11. *Sha'ar Reishit Chokhmah, Derekh Shlishi Netiv* 3, cited in *Responsa B'nei Banim* 1:43.

12. *Tanchuma, Parshat Vayigash.*

13. See *Gevurot Yitzchak* 1:61. See also the discussion in R. Baruch Simon, *Imrei Baruch, Genesis, Vayigash* 1.

14. *Mayim Chaim, Hilkhot Yesodei Ha Torah* 5:2.

15. See also R. Binyamin Auerbach, *Nachal Eshkol* to *Sefer HaEshkol*, vol. 2 p. 118, and R. Ephraim Greenblatt in *Otzerot Yerushalayim*, vol. 92, p. 1470.

16. Number 240. This represents R. Henkin's reading of the *Chinnukh's* phrase *derekh azharah*. The footnotes in the *Minchat Yerushalayim* edition, however, take the opposite understanding, linking the *Chinnukh's* position with that of Rabbeinu Yonah.

17. Quoted in the commentary of the *Ba'al HaTurim* to the Torah.

18. *Ner 2, Klal 5*, part 2, who considers the notion to be non-obligatory advice.

19. *Responsa B'nei Banim* 1:41.

What emerges, then, is a dispute among *rishonim,* with the *Rif,* the *Tosafot,* and Rabbeinu Yonah taking the Talmud at face value and obligating self-sacrifice before shaming another, and the Meiri and the Rambam apparently unwilling to allow so drastic a notion into practical *halakhah.* R. Yehudah Leib Graubart felt that this difference of opinion could be paralleled to another dispute, at least as far as *Tosafot* and the Rambam were concerned.[20] The *Tosafot,* in their commentary to *Avodah Zarah,*[21] are of the position that although martyrdom is obligatory in only a limited number of instances, one may voluntarily sacrifice himself for any *mitzvah* if he deems it appropriate. The Rambam, however, in his *Mishneh Torah,*[22] explicitly excludes such an option.[23] Such preexisting points of view can certainly dictate the understanding one brings to a phrase such as "better for one to hurl oneself into a fiery furnace rather than shame his fellow in public." To the authors of the *Tosafot,* who recognize voluntary self-sacrifice for all commandments, such a singling out for humiliating others must mean an obligatory martyrdom. Accordingly, they rule in *Sotah* that this commandment should theoretically be listed among those precepts that demand precedence for them over self-preservation. Alternatively, the Rambam, who generally recognizes no permissibility of self-sacrifice absent an obligation, can interpret the unique teaching of this text to be the one such instance. Hence, no obligation is mentioned in *Mishneh Torah,* for the Rambam views humiliating others as a transgression that allows, but does not mandate, self-sacrifice. Indeed, another eminent commentator, *P'nei Yehoshua,*[24] analyzes the intent of the text as to whether it refers to an option or an obligation.[25]

---

20 *Responsa Chavalim BaN'imim* 1:12:6 (*sugyot*). See also R. Shimon Gabel, *K'li Golah, Berakhot* 43b, and R. Mordechai Carlebach, *Chavatzelet HaSharon al haTorah, Genesis,* pp. 597–598.

21. 27b, s.v. *Yakhol.*

22. *Hilkhot Yesodei HaTorah* 5:1.

23. The *Nimmukei Yosef* to *Yevamot* takes a middle position, allowing voluntary martyrdom only for leaders of a generation who feel the circumstances are appropriate. See *Kessef Mishneh, Hilkhot Yesodei HaTorah* 5:4. See also R. Yitzchak Ohlboim, *Sh'eilat Yitzchak* 3:106, and R. Ephraim Oshry, *Responsa Mima'amakim* 5:14.

24. *Bava Metzia* 59a.

25. The *Menorat HaMa'or, Ner* 2, *Klal* 5, part 2, seems to view it as an option. See also *Responsa P'nei Maivin,* vol. 2, p. 166, quoting the *Binyan Shlomo.*

II. Humiliation as Murder: A Literal Comparison?

Nonetheless, it seems clear that a concern more fundamental to the local issue informs this dispute among the *rishonim*. The Talmud, earlier in this same passage (58b), identifies the logic relevant to its conclusions. One who shames his fellow in public, we are told forcefully, is as if he shed blood. We are even provided with physiological evidence of this moral relationship; when one is embarrassed, *azil sumaka v'ati hivara,* the features lose their red color and turn white;[26] thus, the talmudic term for humiliation, *halbanat panim,* "whitening the face."[27] While this does seem to contradict empirical observation, as an embarrassed individual, blushing, is normally red-faced, R. Ovadiah of Bartenura offers an explanation.[28] At first, an embarrassed individual reddens in the face, as he initially experiences rage at what has occurred. However, once he fails to provide a satisfactory response, his concern turns inward to an internal sense of worry, and the blood leaves his face, resulting in the whitening of the face. The *Midrash Shmuel*[29] quotes, in the name of R. Menachem L'Beit Meir, a description that will be familiar to anyone who has ever been truly embarrassed. "One who is humiliated, his face first turns red, and then turns white, because due to the magnitude of the shame, his 'soul flies away,' as if it wanted to leave the body . . . once the blood returns to its source, the face turns white, like someone who has died . . ."[30] Nonetheless, some texts do contain the emendation "reddening the face" instead.[31]

---

26. The *Kad HaKemach* (no. 5) points out that this is also found in the verse in *Isaiah* (29:22): "No longer will Yaakov he ashamed, no longer will his face be whitened."

27. Indeed, R. Moshe Rosmarin (*D'var Moshe* to *Pirkei Avot* 3:11) analyzes whether attaining the biological response is intrinsic to the violation of the prohibition. R. Y. H. Henkin, *Responsa B'nei Banim* 1:41, assumes that the response is definitely not necessary and adduces many proofs to that effect.

28. *Avot* 3:11.

29. *Pirkei Avot* 3:15.

30. See also *Magen Avot* 3:11, for a more extensive description, including a reference to "those knowledgeable in medical matters." According to *Mosby's Medical Dictionary*, blushing is "commonly the result of dilation of superficial small blood vessels in response to heat or sudden emotion."

31 See *Tosafot Yom Tov* and *Machzor Vitri* and several of the citations in the *Midrash Shmuel*. See also *Midrash Tehillim* 52:4, where it is explained that Doeg was referred to as *edomi,* the "red one," because his superior scholarship embarrassed David.

The question, then, becomes the evaluation of this comparison between homicide and humiliation. If humiliation is indeed equal to murder in the absolute sense of the word, it is readily understandable that it must be avoided even at the cost of one's own death, as is clearly established as the rule for murder. The Talmud[32] challenges one who would slay another to save himself: "How do you reason that your blood is redder than his?" If humiliation is truly shedding of blood, one who wishes to do so to preserve his own life must answer to the same objection.[33]

This issue, then, serves as an analytical prerequisite to any question of martyrdom. How are the Talmud's words to be taken? Is humiliation indeed equivalent to murder in all respects, to any and every extent?[34] Or, rather, is the phrase a homiletical device, worded to convey the intense severity of the prohibition[35] but never meant to be equated with murder to the fullest sense of its ramifications? R. Shlomo Zalman Auerbach offers an example of the second possibility. The Talmud states, "He who steals from his friend the value of a *prutah* is as one who takes his life from him,"[36] and yet no authority has recommended following this comparison through to its logical conclusions. Also along these lines, R. Tzvi Ashkenazi comments in another instance of the talmudic usage of the Hebrew *k* at the beginning of a word to suggest a comparison, as is the case here, humiliation being called *k'sh'fikhat damim,* "like" murder. In that instance, he writes, the similarity is less than absolute.[37] R. Yaakov Etlinger concurs, noting that were this not the case, an individual who disrespects the festivals would be treated with the severity of an idol worshiper, as is the implication of the Talmud in *Makkot* (23a).[38] R. Moshe Shick, however, conveys by implication a differing approach

---

32. *Sanhedrin* 74a.

33. See, however, R. Reuven Grozovsky, *Chiddushei R. Reuven, Yevamot* 32.

34. See, in this light, *Responsa Besamim Rosh* 11.

35. See R. Yitzchak b. Sheshet, *Responsa HaRivash* 171, who observes that the Talmud frequently uses extreme language in order to convey the gravity of a prohibition.

36. *Bava Kamma* 119a.

37. *Responsa Chakham Zvi* 77.

38. *Responsa Binyan Tziyyon* 172, although he will ultimately conclude stringently in this instance, as discussed below.

to this generalization.[39] Apparently the *rishonim* struggled on this point, with consequent implications for their positions on martyrdom.[40]

Accordingly, Rabbeinu Yonah, cited earlier as obligating self-sacrifice in his *Sha'arei Teshuvah,* identifies embarrassing others as *avak r'tzichah,* an equivalent derivative subcategory of murder, in his commentary to *Pirkei Avot* (3:11).[41] Concurring in later generations are the *Pri Megadim* (in his *Mattan S'kharan Shel Mitzvot*[42] and *Teivat Gomeh*), the *Responsa Ohr David* (14:1), the *Chiddushei Maharakh* (*Hilkhot Yesodei Ha Torah,* ch. 5), the *Responsa Binyan Tziyyon* (173 and 175), and R. Avraham Piotrokowski.[43] Rabbi Yaakov Emden, in his commentary to Pirkei Avot (3:15), cites the position of Rabbeinu Yonah without expressing disagreement. The Alshikh, commenting on the Torah, interprets the verse "he who spills blood of a person, in a person (*shofeikh dam ha-adam ba-adam*), his blood shall be spllled"[44] as referring to one who humiliates another, incurring an internal spilling of blood. "Do not be surprised," he warns, "that one can deserve capital punishment even though he has not actually ended a life, for has not a person's face been created in the image of God, and without which he would be comparable to an animal; therefore, he who whitens the face, where the image of God resides, is deserving of death for he has blemished the site of the image of God." R. Shlomo Aviner[45] goes as far as to impute literal significance to the designation of homicide, citing a medical authority of the opinion that the physiological effects of humiliation may indeed contribute to a shortened lifespan.

Consequently, later authorities lined up to takes sides on the martyrdom issue. R. Ya'akov Etlinger concluded that in his view the majority

---

39. *Responsa Maharam Shick, Yoreh Deah* 347, 348.

40. See, however, R. Natan Gestetner's differing analysis of the position of *Tosafot* in his *Responsa L'Horot Natan* 8:2, cited later, as well as that of R. Y. H. Henkin (*Responsa B'nei Banim*), quoting R. Naftali Tzvi Yehudah Berlin (*Meromei Sadeh* to *Sotah*) and the *Mishnat Avraham* to the *Sefer Chasidim* 946. See also R. Aharon Soloveichik, *Parach Mateh Aharon, Mada,* p. 30.

41. Note, though, the commentary *Zeh HaSha'ar* to *Sha'arei Teshuvah.*

42. *Chakirah* 5, where he uses the term *abizrayhu dish'fikhat damim.* See also R. Avraham Erlanger, *Birkat Avraham, Pesachim* 25a.

43. *Piskei Teshuvah* 74, in footnote, at length.

44. *Genesis* 9:5.

45. *Am K'Lavi,* vol. 1 p. 305.

position indeed forbids humiliating another even at the expense of one's life.[46] R. Ovadiah Yosef[47] considers the issue and does not appear to offer an explicit conclusion.[48] However, it seems to be the currently accepted position that although a number of earlier sources obligate self-sacrifice, the existence of significant dissent on the topic precludes the practical implementation of such a principle. This follows the analysis of the *Beit Yosef*,[49] who states the principle that the presence of any dispute on a question of martyrdom prevents it being put into practice.[50] R. Yehudah Herzl Henkin also investigates this issue to a lenient conclusion, feeling this to be the position of the vast majority of *rishonim* and noting that martyrdom is not mandated by any of the works of halakhic codification.[51]

Further, even if theoretically martyrdom was called for, the variability present in all real life situations makes it impossible to put such policy into practice. The unpredictability of the other's reaction and sensitivities make actual self-sacrifice unfeasible. R. Pinchas Levinson[52] notes that the concept is phrased in the Talmud, atypically, as a matter of "preference." This is to signify that it is reflective of the assumption that the victim would equate humiliation with his own death; however, as there always exists a possibility that this is not true, one may not allow oneself to be physically killed to avoid the embarrassment.[53] Thus, what

---

46. *Responsa Binyan Tziyyon* 172 and 173. See also R. David Rozenberg, *Responsa Minchat David* 2:79, and *Responsa D'var Yehoshua*, vol. 2.

47. *Responsa Yabbia Omer* vol. 6, *Yoreh Deah* 13.

48. Although some assume that he rules stringently, see Dr. Abraham S. Abraham, in the journal *HaMa'ayan*, vol. 20, no. 2:17–25, and R. David Barda (who advances the argument to disagree), in *Ohr Torah* 24:50, and R. Avraham Dori's response in 24:93. A stringent approach also is implied in R. Yosef's commentary to Pirkei Avot, *Anaf Etz Avot* 3:15.

49. *Yoreh Deah*, 157. See, however, *Siftei Kohen* 157:1.

50. See also *Responsa Shevet HaKehati* 1:164, who cites many of the stringent opinions noted earlier, before concluding that actual martyrdom may not be implemented. See also R. Shlomo Yehudah Leib Levitan, *Responsa Yeriot Shlomo* 41.

51. *Responsa B'nei Banim* 1:43. See also *Minchah Chareivah*, *Sotah* 10a. Note also the extensive discussion of R. Aharon Buaran, in the journal *Torat HaAdam L'Adam*, vol. 2, p. 81–96, particularly in reference to the issue of martyrdom in the instance of a dispute.

52. In the journal *HaPardes*, vol. 39, no. 4:16–20 (29), and continued in vol. 39, no. 6:16–17 (42).

53. In regard to the varying and subjective nature of humiliation, see R. Yaakov Davidson, *Hilkhot Derekh Eretz*, ch. 140.

emerges is a theoretical equation that conveys a tremendous seriousness inherent to the prohibition but that would in no situation actually allow the martyrdom to be put into practice.

Among those dismissing the martyrdom requirement as inconceivable is R. Asher Weiss, who further posits that any measure taken in the furtherance of justice is immune from the taint of the prohibition of humiliation. Building on a comment of R. Yaakov Emden,[54] he observes that all attempts to obtain justice involve placing a defendant or suspect in an embarrassing position, and yet no one would entertain the notion that all such endeavors are impossible. He acknowledges, of course, that within such activities, every effort should be taken to reduce embarrassment, while that concern does not necessitate waiving the needs of jurisprudence.[55] A similar approach is found in the responsa of R. Yosef David Weiss of Antwerp,[56] who is emphatic on the need to minimize the humiliation when possible, and also to exclude punitive measures from this dispensation, as those are only available to a Bet Din and not to an individual.[57]

The definition of the relationship between humiliation and murder as a homiletic comparison or, more severely, as an absolute equation apparently lies below the surface of other halakhic discussions as well. R. Shlomo Kluger, commenting on the *Shulchan Arukh*,[58] records a surprising and, as he acknowledges, unprecedented ruling concerning the obligation to rescue one whose life is in danger. While it is understood that such an obligation does not attach itself at the cost of one's own life,

---

54. Glosses to *Bava Metzia* 24a.

55. *Minchat Asher al haTorah, Genesis* 53. Of course, this approach further calls into question the decision of Tamar, as discussed earlier; R. Weiss addresses this at length in his essay.

56. *Responsa VaYa'an David* 3:106.

57. R. Y. D. Weiss has no sympathy for a principal who humiliated a parent, claiming it impossible to run an educational institution without occasionally doing so; he writes, "one who stands to open a necessary institution to teach children in the path of Torah and fear of Heaven, and on the other hand knows that he will humiliate his fellow in public even once in his life (not in a permissible instance), better that he not open the institution, for one who humiliates his fellow in public has no portion in the World to Come." The circumstances of the incident are not given in the responsum.

58. *Chokhmat Shlomo* to *Choshen Mishpat* 427:1.

R. Kluger extends this notion further, maintaining that a person need not save another's life if he himself will consequently endure humiliation. Emotional death, humiliation, would seem in his analysis to possess a genuine equivalency to physical death. R. Meir Dan Plotzki, in his work *Kli Chemdah,*[59] writes extensively to refute this notion. More recently, R. Shlomo Zalman Auerbach rejected this ruling, noting that "it is impossible to compare self-inflicted humiliation to embarrassing others."[60] R. Auerbach's son-in-law, R. Zalman Nechemiah Goldberg, in an independent article[61] critiques R. Kluger's reasoning and notes that a logical conclusion of his argument would be that one may not save his own life if it would be undignified to do so. Joining in disagreement with the position of R. Kluger are R. Aryeh Leib Grosnas,[62] R. Avraham Yafeh-Shlesinger,[63] and R. Raphael Silber.[64]

III. Violating the Sabbath, and Other Implications

However, R. Auerbach's opposition to this innovation does not necessarily imply a rejection of the absolutist understanding of the humiliation/

---

59. *Parshat Ki Teitze*, 6.

60. *Responsa Minchat Shlomo* 7. This particular phrasing leaves room to speculate as to the precise nature of R. Auerbach's objection, as it would seem from his language that he considers the distinction between self-inflicted humiliation and that aimed at another to be the significant issue (indeed, the Talmud does state, "one cannot compare embarrassment by one's own hand to embarrassment at the hands of others [*Ta'anit* 15b]") rather than arguing with the very literal reading of the equation between embarrassment and death. In fact, as will be noted later, it may be that R. Auerbach himself approves of such an understanding. Rather, it may be that he considered the severity of the offense to be based not merely on the damage incurred by the victim but also by the egregious nature of the verbal aggression directed from one party to the other. It should also be noted that the precise logic of R. Kluger's ruling actually derives itself from sources other than those dealing with humiliation, specifically the laws of *k'vod habriyot*, of maintaining human dignity, and the interaction of this concept with the imperative to return lost property, extending, of course, to endangered life. However, R. Yisrael Meir Lau, in his *Responsa Yachel Yisrael* (1:77) independently considers an identical ruling, in that case dealing directly with the laws concerning humiliation. Similarly, this notion is dealt with briefly by R. Shlomo Abraham, *Divrei Shlomo* 8.

61. In the journal Tzohar ("*Ohel Baruch*" volume, pp. 328–331).

62. *Responsa Lev Aryeh* 42.

63. *Responsa Be'er Sarim* 3:4:6.

64. *Marpei L'Nefesh* 2:44:13. Note also the challenge of Shalom Tzvi Mussbaum, *Sanhedrei K'tannah*, pp. 49–51.

murder comparison. R. Auerbach, until his death considered one of the leading halakhic authorities in the world, authored an extensive discussion, published in his *Responsa Minchat Shlomo* (no. 7) as well as other places,[65] of the principles regulating the suspension of the laws of *Shabbat* in order to save a life. Toward the end of this discussion, he expresses considerable difficulty with the accepted assumption that one may not violate the *Shabbat* to avoid humiliating another person just as one would to save that person's life. He acknowledges that there certainly are some differences between embarrassment and death, disagreeing as he does with the aforementioned opinion of R. Kluger and noting further that no one would ever suggest that it is permissible to kill someone who attempts to embarrass him, claiming self-defense. Nonetheless, he still considers the comparison to be of sufficient weight to warrant, at least upon initial consideration, pushing off considerations of *Shabbat*. R. Auerbach expends great effort to explain this discrepancy between theory and practice, offering at one point to allow passive and rabbinical violations of the Shabbat in accordance with the laws of *k'vod habriyot,* maintaining human dignity. He ultimately is unsatisfied in this struggle, concluding "the issue continues to need a definitive decision." R. Yosef Roth[66] observes that the purpose of violating *Shabbat* in instances of mortal danger is the preservation of physical life and does not stem from the severity of the crime of murder. Therefore, even if humiliation is equated absolutely with homicide, it does not necessarily follow that superseding the *Shabbat* is called for.[67] Interestingly, R. Shimon Pollack does seem prepared to consider leniencies in the laws of *Shabbat* if humiliation is the alternative.[68]

---

65. See the journals *Moriah* (3:3–4) and *Torah She B'al Peh* (vol. 141), and *Mazkeret Moshe: Sefer Zikaron L'Moshe Efrati* pp. 24–56.

66. *Siach Yosef,* vol. 2, 11:3. See also R. Mordechai Carlebach, *Chavatzelet HaSharon al haTorah,* Genesis pp. 605–607, where it is suggested that requiring martyrdom to avoid embarrassing another is an extension of claiming that one has no right to protect one's self at the expense of another's life or dignity; this logic is not transeferable to the instance of violating the Sabbath to save another. However, further on (pp. 607–608) he acknowledges that this analysis is inconsistent with the language of Rabbeinu Yonah.

67. Nonetheless, linking embarrassment to death may still indicate such a conclusion, if both are to be avoided with equal concern.

68. *Responsa Shem MiShimon* 1:16.

R. Natan Gestetner, in his responsa,[69] considers another issue relevant to evaluating the comparison. A *kohen* who has killed someone is
prohibited from partaking in the priestly blessing, the *birkat kohanim*.[70]
Would a *koh* who embarrasses others be similarly excluded?
R. Gestetner proceeds to analyze the issue, noting the earlier question of
martyrdom to avoid shaming others. He concludes leniently citing a sup-
porting implication in the *Responsa Ralbach*,[71] finding the comparison to
be less than total. He concurrently advances a technical argument, prov-
ing that even were the severity of humiliation equivalent to (or worse
than, as he notes in the name of the *P'nei Yehoshua*) homicide, this *kohen*
would nonetheless not be excluded; the category is limited to physical
murder, as indicated by Talmud, citing the verse, "your hands are filled
with blood."[72] The identical conclusion is reached in a responsum by
R. Shmuel Wosner.[73] Nonetheless, R. Baruch Weiss, in an independent
analysis of the issue in his book-length treatment of the laws of *birkat
kohanim*,[74] reaches a stringent conclusion and forbids such a *kohen* from
partaking in the blessing.

This position may perhaps be shared by the authors of the *Tosafot* to
Masekhet Arakhin. The Talmud suggests that among other transgressions,
murder is atoned for through the priestly vestments.[75] The *Tosafot*[76] deal
with this statement in light of the contradictory statement earlier that the
murderer will suffer bodily afflictions for his sins. They reconcile these
ideas by interpreting the text dealing with the priestly vestments as

---

69. *Responsa L'Horot Natan* 8:2.

70. *Berakhot* 32b, and *Shulchan Arukh, Orach Chaim* 128:35. See, at length,
R. Yitzchak Fishberg, *Nesiat Kapayim*, pp. 186–194.

71. Number 117, referred to in the *Magen Avraham, Orach Chaim* 128:153.
The Ralbach considers the instance of a *kohen*, guilty of many offenses, repeatedly
humiliating others among them. However, in evaluating his status for the purposes
of *birkat kohanim*, he does not take the embarrassments into account.

72. *Isaiah* 1:15, brought in *Berakhot* 32b; see *Tosafot, Yevamot* 7a, s.v.
Sheneamar, who explain that hands used for murder cannot then be effective in
prayer. Although a similar conclusion might he reached as to the appropriateness of
a mouth that has embarrassed another being used to pronounce the prayer, this is
nonetheless not explicitly within the text.

73. *Responsa Shevet HaLevi* 8:172.

74. *Birkhot Horai* 23:12:9.

75. *Arakhin* 16a, citing *Genesis* 37:31.

76. S.v. *ha d'ahani ma'asav*.

referring not to actual murder, but rather to embarrassing others in public. The implication is clearly that while humiliating others is symbolically identified as murder, one is not to take this usage literally.

Another issue to which this concern is relevant is taken up by R. Yisrael Meir Lau, formerly the Ashkenazic Chief Rabbi of Israel.[77] One normally possesses the privilege, if one so wishes, of allowing another to impinge on one's rights, known as *mechilah*. May one permit another to embarrass him? If humiliation is an interpersonal offense with a severity comparable to murder, yet not in actuality equal to murder, then its gravity would not necessarily preclude an option of *mechilah*. However, if the comparison to bloodshed is taken literally, one must consider the fact that no individual has the right to permit himself to be murdered in weighing this question.[78]

The assumption that the identification with murder is not absolute is taken by R. Ya'akov Reischer.[79] He raises the issue of a non-Jew, subject to the seven Noahide laws, which include, of course, murder. R. Reischer maintains that in defining these laws, the umbrella of murder as universal prohibition does not extend to include embarrassing others among its restrictions and punishments. While humiliating others is compared to homicide, he admits, this does not indicate genuine equivalence.[80]

IV. Losing One's Portion in the World to Come

It is interesting to note that this question of how to evaluate the Talmud's comparison seems to be reflected consistently in other comments of the previously cited *rishonim*. King David's retort to his tormentors included the admonishment that one who shames others in

---

77. *Responsa Yachel Yisrael* 75.

78. See also the discussion in R. Elyakim Dvorkes, *B'Shvilei HaParshah*, p. 93.

79. *Responsa Shvut Ya'akov* 1:164.

80. See, however, the dissenting opinions in R. David Ariav, *L'Reakha Kamokha*, vol. 3, section 2, ch. 1 *Nir L'David* 133. A further analysis of the status of non-Jews vis-a-vis these prohibitions is offered by R. Shalom Martzbuch in the memorial volume *MiPri Yadeha*, pp. 223–228. Note also the innovative approach of R. Yekutiel Yehudah Halberstam, *Responsa Divrei Yatziv, Yoreh Deah* 51, where it is suggested not only that the prohibition is applicable to non-Jews but that, for technical reasons, the comparison to homicide is even more literal.

public forfeits his eternal reward. This notion is in fact stated authoritatively a number of times in the Talmud.[81] Commentators offer several possibilities to explain the basis for such a severe condemnation.

As noted earlier, Rabbeinu Yonah views humiliating others to be a subcategory of murder, necessitating martyrdom, in his *Sha'arei Teshuvah* and in comments to *Pirkei Avot*. His explanation of the penalty incurred maintains the integrity of this position. He reasons that he who publicly shames others logically shares the punishment of a murderer, who in theory also deserves to be stripped of his portion in the world to come. However, the murderer actually has an advantage in this area. He has committed a crime that is universally acknowledged as horrendous, and society instantly will register its complete rejection of his actions. Consequently, he will recognize the gravity of his misdeed and will repent fully. Having done so, he will continue to bear the responsibility for his actions on the temporal plane but will ultimately achieve atonement, and the eternal punishment will be suspended. However, a person who embarrasses others, although spiritually he is equivalent to a murderer, may never reach such a realization. Society will not rebuke him comparably, if at all, and in his own mind he has committed no serious transgression. Thus, the repentance effected by the shedder of blood will not be undertaken by him who humiliates his fellow, and the eternal punishment will not be suspended.[82]

The Rambam offers a different rationale, and once again it is one consistent with his previously noted position. In his commentary to the Mishnah[83] he observes that shaming others does not appear to be a prohibition that one would intuitively associate with such a severe punishment as losing one's portion in the future reward. However, the action is indicative of the nature of its protagonist. One who would regularly[84] engage in such behavior, writes the Rambam, can only be one of low character and underdeveloped morality, an individual whose behavior in

---

81. *Bava Metzia* 58b and *Avot* 3:11.

82. *Sha'arei Teshuvah*, *Sha'ar* 3:141.

83. *Sanhedrin*, ch. 10:1.

84. The source and logic behind the Rambam's assumption that the penalty is only for one who commits this transgression "regularly" is discussed in R. Moshe Feinstein, *Responsa Iggerot Moshe, Orach Chaim* vol. 5, 20:14.

general will inevitably result in spiritual condemnation. Thus, the Rambam, who declined to impose martyrdom to avoid humiliating others, apparently feeling the homicide/humiliation comparison to be nonliteral, is here loyal to that position. In his view the transgression itself did not earn the punishment, but rather revealed a personality who will prove himself in other ways to be deserving of such.[85]

The *P'nei Yehoshua*, in his commentary to *Bava Metzia* (59a), suggests another basis for this notion. There is a widely held assumption that one who commits suicide, at least in the absence of certain mitigating conditions, forfeits his portion in the world to come.[86] Nonetheless, the Talmud states that it is preferable to hurl oneself into a fiery furnace before shaming another. It must be, writes the *P'nei Yehoshua,* that embarrassing others carries a punishment at least as severe as suicide, or else the latter would not be a preferable option. This explanation is slightly difficult to understand, however, as a person who is halakhically compelled to sacrifice his life cannot readily be considered as one who has committed a transgression of suicide. This objection is raised at length by R. Binyamin Aryeh Weiss.[87]

The *Iyyun Ya'akov* (*Bava Metzia* 59a), commenting on the Talmud's statement that it is preferable to have relations with a possibly married woman rather than humiliate another person, highlights another aspect of this transgression. In his opinion, martyrdom is an option rather than an obligation, a recommendation based on the severity of the punishment. This penalty is greater than that for adultery, as the Talmud implies, because adulterous tendencies are a normal part of human makeup and a source of great temptation. Humiliating others, however, is not an innate human tendency, and thus its egregiousness is not mit-

---

85. See also *Menorat HaMa'or* 58 and *Nachal Kedumim, Parshat Kedoshim.*

86. R. Yosef Shaul Nathanson (*Yad Shaul* to *Yoreh Deah* 345) questions this assumption, claiming that it is not explicitly stated in any talmudic sources. The *Pardes Yosef* (*Exodus* 20:13) goes to lengths to provide such a source. See also *Even Ya'akov* 1 of the *Tzitz Eliezer*, Rabbi Eliezer Yehudah Waldenberg, and R. Yosef Schwartz, *Ginzei Yosef* 13:2. R. Ovadiah Yosef assumes this to be the implication of *Gittin* 57b (*Yabbia Omer* 6:Y.D.:13:14). See also, at length. R. David Shperber, *Responsa Afarkasta D'Anya,* 4:370.

87. *Responsa Even Y'karah, Mahadurah Tinyana* 96. It seems from the *P'nei Yehoshua's* language, it should be noted, that he is sensitive to this difficulty.

igated by the realities of mortal weakness.[88] The author of the *Midrash Eliyahu* notes a further manner in which humiliation is more severe than murder: physical death occurs once and is over with, while the emotional pain lasts and reverberates.

The *P'nei Yehoshua* (*Bava Metzia* 58b) offers another possibility, this time in the name of the *Tosafot Yom Tov,* citing the *Midrash Shmuel.* One who embarrasses another and strips away his sense of dignity violates his *tzelem Elokim,* his creation in the image of God, as noted earlier in the name of the Alshikh. It is this Divine image that is the basis for the soul. One who has displayed a disregard for this image, therefore, undermines his own conception of a soul.[89] The *Sefer Tikkunei Teshuvah* expresses a similar notion, ruling that one who humiliates others must fast as atonement and that acquiring the forgiveness of the injured party is not sufficient.[90] This builds on the assumption that there exists here more than an interpersonal crime, but rather an attack has been committed against God Himself through the vehicle of the Divine image. This is a concept that has groundings in midrashic sources. R. Tanchuma, in a discussion of the severity of humiliating others, is quoted as remarking, "Know: whom are you disgracing? 'In the image of God he was created!"[91] Further, the Talmud[92] derives significant halakhic principles from the verse "He who mocks the poor blasphemes his Creator."[93]

V. The Role of the 'Public'

As the prohibition of embarrassing others is generally referred to as "humiliating others in public," halakhic authorities turn their attention

---

88. Compare the comments of R. Avraham Bornstein, *Responsa Avnei Nezer, Even HaEzer* 57.

89. See also *Chiddushei Aggadot* of the Maharal of Prague, *Gittin* 56b, as well as *Bava Metzia* 59a, and *Be'er Avot* to *Pirkei Avot* of R. Menachem Mendel Frankel-Teomim, R. Moshe Outz Meri, *Ahavat Shalom* to *Pirkei Avot*, and *Torat Chaim, Bava Kamma* 90a.

90. Note also the language of the *Orchot Tzadikim* (*Sha'ar HaTeshuvah*): "He who humiliates another, this is his penitence: he must appease him, and fast forty days or more, and afflict himself every day, and confess all of his days."

91. *Bereishit Rabbah* 24:8. See also *Sanhedrin* 58b. Note *Tomer Devorah*, ch. 2.

92. *Berakhot* 17a.

93. *Proverbs* 17:5.

to the definition of "public," and then to the question of whether the presence of the public is an indispensable element of the prohibition. While the term *b'rabbim*, in public, is often taken to signify a group of ten, many assume that for the purposes of this transgression three people constitute an audience. This was the opinion of the *Pri Megadim* in his *Mattan S'kharan Shel Mitzvot*, cited approvingly by the *Responsa Binyan Tziyyon*. In this generation, R. Ephraim Greenblatt ruled accordingly,[94] noting the opinion of the Gerrer Rebbe, the Sefat Emet, in his commentary to *Pirkei Avot*. R. Binyamin Yehoshua Zilber concurs, explaining that the main concern is exposing the humiliation to public knowledge, a task generally assumed to be accomplished once three people know about it. He concludes that this group of three may include both the victim and the perpetrator of the embarrassment, thus in actuality necessitating only one witness.[95] He then notes an additional difference between this "public" and that normally utilized in *halakhah*. While a minyan for the purposes of, for example, prayer, requires ten men, in this instance, certainly no distinction is made between male and female, as all are equally forbidden this behavior.[96]

Even if the definition of "public" is reduced from ten or more to three, or perhaps one additional party, many authorities held that even this number was not necessary for the prohibition to take effect. The *Pri Megadim* rules accordingly,[97] citing the language of the Rambam that it is forbidden to embarrass a fellow Jew, "and all the more so in public." This is also the opinion of the *Kol Bo* (67) and the *Sefer Yereim*,[98] and, later, R. Yisrael Meir haKohen Kagan.[99] The first Lubavitcher Rebbe, in his *Shulchan Arukh HaRav*, acknowledges that this may not be the implication of Rashi[100] but writes that it is certainly the opinion of the

94. *Responsa Riv'vot Ephraim* 6:453:2.
95. *Responsa Az Nidbaru* 8:63.
96. A similar ruling is made by R. Yosef Engel, who notes that a minyan for the purposes of sanctifying God's name may include women (*Gilyonei HaShas* to *Sanhedrin* 74a). Alternatively, see *Minchat Chinnukh* 295/296 and *Responsa Chakal Yitzchak* 44. Note also R. Yehudah Yerucham Leib Perlman, *Ohr Gadol* 1.
97. *Eshel Avraham, Orach Chaim* 156.
98. Number 37, 38; he does, however, distinguish between private and public humiliation in the area of requisite intent.
99. *Chovat HaShmirah* 14.
100. *Arakhin* 16b, s.v. *upanav mishtanin*. Note also his commentary to the Torah, *Leviticus* 19:17.

Rambam and the *Sefer Mitzvot Gadol*;[101] further, in the *Torat Kohanim*, the *Midrash* does not even contain the words "in public."[102] R. Y. H. Henkin proves at length that the prohibition is in effect even in private and suggests based on the text of the Rambam and the Tur[103] that the word *b'rabbim*, meaning "in public," should be amended slightly to read *b'dvarim*, meaning "verbally."[104] However, the *Sefer Mitzvot Katan* (126) does require an audience.[105]

Several authorities suggest an intriguing possibility.[106] It is conceivable that the prohibition exists in full force, regardless of the presence or absence of an audience. However, in order to incur the condemnation discussed in the Talmud, such as forfeiting one's portion in the world to come as well as the exhortation toward martyrdom, the transgression must be committed in public. This possibility requires further explanation.

VI. A Two-tiered Prohibition

R. Shimon b. Tzemach Duran, the Tashbetz, notes that in the process of humiliating another, one commits two distinct transgressions, evolving from two different passages in the Talmud.[107] The first is the topic of the talmudic text cited earlier (*Bava Metzia* 58b), *ona'at d'varim*, "verbal" oppression, subsumed within the biblical prohibition, "a man shall not oppress his friend."[108] Verbal oppression is a larger category,

---

101. Prohibition 6.

102. See also R. Raphael Silber, *Marpei L'Nefesh* 344:7.

103. *Choshen Mishpat* 420.

104. Along these lines, compare *Makkot* 24a and *Midrash Tehillim* 17.

105. See also *Responsa Sha'ar Ephraim* 65; *L'Horot Natan* to *Pirkei Avot* 3:11; and R. Avraham Dori, *Ohr Torah* 24:93.

106. See, for example, R. Shammai Kehat Gross, *Responsa Shevet HaKehati* 1:361; R. Yitzchak Kolitz, in *Torah SheB'al Peh*, vol. 36, pp. 41–44; and R. Pinchas Levinson in *HaPardes*, ibid.

107. *Magen Avot*, *Avot* 3:15.

108. *Leviticus* 25:17; see *Bava Metzia* 58b. There is a difference of opinion as to whether this prohibition and its monetary correlate, *ona'at mamon* (generally manifested by significant overcharging in sales), are to be counted as one prohibition or two. R. Sa'adiah Gaon (prohibition 85, see commentary of R. Yerucham Perlow) counts one, while those who count two include the Rambam (*Sefer HaMitzvot* prohibition 259); R. Moshe of Coucy (*Sefer Mitzvot Gadol*, prohibition 171); *Sefer Mitzvot Katan* (no. 122); R. Eliezer of Metz (*Sefer Yereim* 51 and 259, and *Yereim HaShalem* 127 and 180); and the *Sefer HaChinnukh* (338). R. Yosef Chaim

comprising any damage inflicted upon a person (including a child)[109] that is not physical or monetary but rather emotional.[110] The Talmud cites several examples of this, such as falsely raising the hopes of a merchant one has no real consideration of patronizing;[111] reminding a repentant individual or a convert of his past behavior; telling someone his misfortunes are a result of his misdeeds; perpetrating a painful practical joke; causing a sudden fright to another;[112] and, of course, embarrassing another individual.[113]

Further, it need not actually be verbal.[114] R. Eliezer of Metz[115] included even displaying a displeasing countenance in this category. The *Sefer Chasidim* (972) contains a striking example: while it is generally accepted that one must take great care in publicly challenging a lecturer to avoid embarrassing him,[116] the *Sefer Chasidim* suggests that the mere presence of a superior scholar at a presentation of a lesser speaker, while commendable as an act of modesty, is intimidating and thus forbidden.

Sonnenfeld is asked about an interesting aspect of the relationship between these prohibitions in his *Responsa Salmat Chaim* 840.

109. See *Bava Kamma* 86b; *Mishneh Torah, Hilkhot Deiot* 68; *Sefer HaChinnukh* 338.

110. See, however, *Responsa Mahari Basan* (#25), who posits that the prohibition is specifically addressed to offense that is expressed under the pretext of innocent or laudatory commentary, and is thus deceptive in nature; this view is disputed by R. Boruch Moshe Kubin in the journal *Torat HaAdam L'Adam*, vol. 4, pp. 206–210.

111. See R. Aharon Walkin, *Saviv LiReav* to *Sefer Yereim* 51:2. Analyses of this aspect of the prohibition appear in R. Menahem Zilber, *Shut Moznei Tzedek*, 3, *Choshen Mishpat* 26; and, in the journal *Torat HaAdam L'Adam*, vol. 4, R. Boruch Moshe Kubin (pp. 206–210) and R. Yitzchak Oshinsky (pp. 215–218).

112. See *Bava Kamma* 91a; Rambam, *Sefer HaMitzvot* 251; *Shulchan Arukh, Choshen Mishpat* 420:32.

113. The Rambam in the *Mishneh Torah* (*Hilkhot Mekhirah* 14:12–14) lists another example not found in this passage, that is, asking someone a question he definitely will not he able to answer. See *Ohr Sameach; Kiryat Sefer*; R. Avraham Price, *Mishnat Avraham* to *Smag*, prohibition 171:2; and R. Aharon Yehudah Grossman, *V'Darashta V'Chakarta*, p. 298.

114. Note the examples given, as well as the *Chafetz Chaim's Chovat HaShemirah* (14), which discusses letters and gestures. For a detailed discussion of nonverbal offenses in this area, see R. Joseph D. Epstein's *Mitzvat HaEtzah*, pp. 301–310.

115. *Sefer Yereim* 51.

116. See, for example, *Moed Katan* 5a and *Chullin* 6a; note the discussion in R. Hillel David Litwack's *Sha'arei Ona'ah*, pp. 11–15.

R. Yaakov Emden[117] raises objections to this conclusion.[118] The *Responsa Keren L'David* (18) includes disturbing one's sleep (*gezel sheinah*) within this prohibition.[119]

Thus, all humiliation is subsumed under the umbrella of verbal oppression, as it inflicts emotional pain.[120] R. J. David Bleich[121] notes another common element to the examples in the Talmud; all the instances display a lack of regard for the value of the other individual.[122] The Talmud displays an exquisite sensitivity to the potential of even an accidental misplaced word to cause great anguish: "To one whose relative has been hanged, do not say, 'hang this fish.'"[123] This attitude is also evidenced by countless enactments of the Rabbis designed *sh'lo l'vayesh*, "not to embarrass."[124] It would seem that no reason exists to distinguish between private and public violations of this prohibition.

---

117. In comments printed in *Sh'eilat Ya'avetz*, vol. 2, *Mafteichot, Chiddushei Gefe"t* 75; see *Mekor Chesed* to *Sefer Chasidim*.

118. The *Sefer Chasidim* himself would certainly admit to a level of subjectivity in this situation; compare his own comments earlier (963).

119. A detailed discussion of that offense, together with many other issues included in *ona'at devarim*, appears in R. Yaakov Yeshaya Bloi, *Pitchei Choshen*, vol. 4, ch. 15, #3. See also R. Boruch Moshe Kubin in the journal *Torat HaAdam L'Adam*, vol. 4, pp. 210–214.

120. In fact, it would seem that monetary oppression should also he included; see R. Moshe Shick, *Maharam Shick al Sefer HaMitzvot* 64, and R. Eliyahu Bakshi Doron, *Responsa Binyan Av* 3:59:4. On humiliation as a primary example, see R. Moshe Chaim Lutzatto, *Mesilat Yesharim*, ch. 11.

121. In the journal *HaDarom* 35:140.

122. Note also R. Elyakim Shulsinger, *Mei Kama* to *Smag*, prohibition 171. R. Shaul Gabbai, in the journal *Torat HaAdam L'Adam*, vol. 4, pp. 203–205, suggests that a proper definition would not include all types of anguish but only that which specifically exploits the disadvantaged status of the victim.

123. *Bava Metzia* 59b. See also *Kallah Rabbati* 2 and *Hizharu Bikhvod Chaveirkhem* 6:19. Note, as well, R. Yechezkel Landau, *Dagul MeRevavah*, *Choshen Mishpat* 420, citing Maharam MiRotenberg, and R. Moshe Troyesh, *Orach Meisharim* 5:4.

124. See *Bikkurim* 3:7; *Shabbat* 3b, 34b, 104a; *Pesachim* 82a; *Ta'anit* 9a, 26b; *Moed Katan* 27a; *Sotah* 32b and 40a; *Sanhedrin* 11a; *Mishneh Torah, Hilkhot Shabbat* 30:11, *Hilkhot Berakhot* 7:10; *Beit Shmuel, Even HaEzer* 34:2; *Prishah, Maharshal*, and *Taz*; *Hizharu Bikhvod Chaveirkhem*, pp. 169–171; *Responsa Chatam Sofer, Orach Chaim* 196; and R. Moshe Dov Wolner, *Responsa Chemdat Tzvi*, 2:23. See also *Mekor Chesed* to *Sefer Chasidim* (139:1), who also observes how many of these enactments are specifically to protect the honor of sinners; see also *Tosafot Yom Tov* to Pesachim, ch. 3.

Further, the Talmud elsewhere[125] notes another relevant transgression. The Torah obligates every individual to take upon himself the spiritual well-being of his fellow, exhorting, "You shall surely rebuke your friend."[126] However, lest one think this project should be pursued even if it results in "changing the color of his face," the Talmud is quick to cite the end of the verse: "and you shall not bear iniquity because of him." The warning is not to allow the fulfillment of this commandment to simultaneously cause a transgression of humiliating another.[127] It would then appear to go without saying that one without the religious motivation of rebuke is certainty admonished to take care in his treatment of others;[128] this is similar to the prohibition of striking another, which is derived from the warning to the administrator of the penalty of lashes, "forty times you shall hit him, do not exceed this." If in the midst of a biblically sanctioned punishment a prohibition against additional lashes still exists, how much more so when there is no such setting.[129]

If the prohibition of verbal oppression addresses the hurt feelings and emotional scarring caused by embarrassment, another element of the offense yet remains to be covered by "you shall not bear iniquity because of him." In addition to the pain felt by the humiliated individual, there

---

125. *Arakhin* 16b.

126. *Leviticus* 19:17.

127. While there are instances that allow limited embarrassment of others for the purposes of spiritual chastisement, the laws of rebuke are complex and beyond the scope of this discussion, and no less an authority than the *Chazon Ish* questioned their precise applications in modern times, citing such phrases as "R. Elazar B. Azariah said: I would be shocked if there is anyone in this generation who knows how to properly rebuke," which appears in this talmudic text, and "just as there is a *mitzvah* to say that which will be heard, there is also a *mitzvah* not to say what will not he heard" (*Yevamot* 65b). R. Eliyahu Bakshi Doron, the former Sephardic Chief Rabbi of Israel, in his *Responsa Binyan Av* (3:4) explains the comment of the Talmud that rebuke must he given "even one hundred times" to refer to the tone that must be taken. Even at the outset, rebuke must he offered in such a manner that even upon repeated attempts it will not be resented. In any event, considering the attendant prohibitions, this undertaking must he dealt with using the utmost consideration and deliberation. Note also R. Uri Langer, *Ohr HaMitzvot* 302/303. See also chapter 12, footnote 99.

128. See, for example, *Smag*, prohibition 6; *Sefer Yereim* 95; *Kiryat Sefer*, *Deiot*, ch. 6; and *Margoliyot HaYam* to *Sanhedrin* 99a, 22.

129. This logic is stated explicitly in such early authorities as the Rambam (*Hilkhot Deiot* 6:8); the *Smag* (*lavin*, 6); and the *Yereim* (195).

is the completely separate component of the stripping away of human dignity, the lowering of status within society. In this respect, it would seem more likely that the degree of publicity attendant to the incident would have a direct effect on the severity of the offense.[130] This follows along the lines of the aforementioned comments of the Alshikh, the *Tikkunei Teshuvah,* and the *P'nei Yehoshua*; the Divine image, the source of human dignity, has been compromised. Along these lines as well, R. Shalom Martzbach[131] suggests that one may waive one's right to be protected against verbal oppression in its base form, but not if humiliation is involved, as this offends the Divine image. This violation is to a great extent defined by the presence of a community in which to bear the disgrace, and thus it is understandable that the greatest level of condemnation should be reserved for those who would inflict humiliation in such a setting.

As R. Elyakim Dvorkes observes,[132] the relevance of a prohibition of humiliation even when attempting to perform a positive commandment is not limited to the obligation of rebuke. To this end he cites two examples. The Talmud is explicit in criticizing those who would give charity if that resulted in the humiliation of the recipient; in one place, repeating the exhortation that it is preferable to enter a fiery furnace, and relating that Mar Ukva chose just such a hiding place rather than be caught by his beneficiary.[133] Further, R. Dvorkes cites the Maharsham as harshly condemning an anonymous and misguided individual who, in his enthusiasm for the opportunity to recite the blessing on an unusual creation, pronounced this blessing in the presence of a human being he considered in that category. In humiliating that person, the individual "converted *mitzvah* into murder, and through his great thoughtlessness lost, with his *mitzvah,* his portion in the World to Come." Similarly, some

---

130. However, such a distinction is perhaps not supported by the language of the *Pri Megadim,* who writes "even alone with the individual, one violates the prohibition of 'you shall not hear iniquity because of him.'" Nonetheless, the previously cited wording of Rashi, particularly as cited by the *Shulchan Arukh HaRav* (and note also *Marpei L'Nefesh* 3:44:7) does imply that this prohibition attains particular significance in public.

131. In *MiPri Yadeha,* pp. 223–228.

132. *B'Shvilei HaParshah,* p. 92–93.

133. *Ketubot* 67b; see also *Berakhot* 6b and *Chagigah* 5a.

precedent exists to allow one to suspend personal stringencies in dietary restrictions when the goal is to prevent embarrassment of a guest.[134]

This distinction is perhaps implicit in the words of the *Menorat HaMaor*, who divides his treatment of the prohibitions concerning shaming others into two parts. In the first,[135] he writes: "Whoever says, in front of his fellow, intentionally, things that will cause his fellow embarrassment when he hears them, and whitens his face, due to the humiliation that he feels, and the fact that he believes that all who are present know that these things are against him," has committed a transgression that is equal to spilling blood. Here the focus is on the pain caused to the victim, perhaps reflective of the prohibition of verbal oppression. In the second part,[136] there is a slightly different emphasis: "and one who says in public things that are against the honor of his fellow, and that this is something that it is clear that those who are present are aware it is being said about him, and this is something serious in the eyes of man, concerning such a 'whitening' it is better for one to be killed, and even burnt, rather than whiten his fellow's face in public." In this instance, reference is made to the destruction of the dignity of the afflicted party, possibly the intended beneficiary of the protection of "you shall not bear iniquity because of him," and it is here that the *Menorat HaMa'or* emphasizes that it is preferable to be killed rather than allow oneself to trample over this injunction.[137]

Similarly, Rabbeinu Yonah's language also supports such an approach. Later in *Sha'arei Teshuvah*[138] he writes: "If a man shall remind his friend, in private, of the misdeeds of his ancestors, he violates that which is written in the Torah, 'a man shall not oppress his friend.' And if he shall humiliate him concerning his ancestor's actions in front of others, concerning this our Rabbis have said, 'those who embarrass others in public descend to *gehinnom* and do not rise up' (*Bava Metzia* 58b)." R. Yerucham Fishel Perlow[139] assumes that the latter

---

134. See *Shulchan Arukh, Orach Chaim* 168:5, and *Responsa Shevet HaKehati* 6:288. For another case, see R. Yosef David Weiss, *Responsa VaYa'an David* 3:122.

135. *Ner 2, Klal* 8:57.

136. Ibid., 58.

137. The *Ohel Moed* does state, however, that even in private, martyrdom is advocated over shaming another.

138. *Shaar Shlishi* 214.

stricture is a reference to "you shall not bear iniquity."

R. Perlow does, however, explain the position of R. Sa'adiah Gaon in his *Sefer HaMitzvot* (prohibition 56) differently. In his view, R. Sa'adiah Gaon considers the distinction between the two prohibitions to lie in the fact that while verbal oppression implies some level of malice, the instance of "you shall not bear iniquity" is unique in that one who is rebuking another presumably has his best interests at heart. Nonetheless, the prohibition is in effect, and R. Sa'adiah Gaon feels it is particular to the instance of rebuke.

It should be noted that in light of this, even if the assessment of Rashi's opinion that an audience is necessary for "you shall not bear iniquity" is correct, there appears to be no reason to assume this would hold true for the prohibition of verbal oppression. Thus, it follows that to humiliate someone even in private is prohibited according to all authorities, at the very least on the strength of one prohibition if not two.

Additionally, the prohibition of "you shall not bear iniquity" would appear to contain the further egregious element of an internal moral contradiction. One who undertakes the task of rebuking another, with the mindset of setting him on the straight and narrow, and yet he himself, at that very moment, is violating a serious prohibition, certainly strikes a dissonant chord. This is highlighted by the words of the Rambam and the *Sefer HaChinnukh,* who observe that while it is at times permissible to embarrass a person for the purposes of rebuke,[140] this is limited to offenses against God; but for offenses among men, it is better to avoid embarrassment. This notion emphasizes the incongruity of exhorting an individual to be mindful of his friend's honor at the very moment his own is being impinged on by the rebuker. This is sharpened by the position of the *Minchat Chinnukh,* who maintains specifically that offenses against the one rebuking should be overlooked rather than embarrassing another, but crimes against a third party should not be. This further underlines the element of the lack of respect shown to the subject of rebuke undermining a simultaneous exhortation to respect the one rebuking.

The *Chinnukh* concludes his discussion of the prohibition of humili-

---

139. Commentary to *Sefer HaMitzvot* of R. Sa'adiah Gaon, prohibition 56.
140. See footnote 68.

ating others by noting that there is no punishment of lashes for this offense, in spite of its biblical status, as it is a non-physical crime, although he does end with the ominous phrase "many messengers exist for the Almighty to exact payment from those who violate His wishes." The Mordechai, however, does mandate lashes for the transgression of verbal oppression.[141] This opinion is also considered in the responsa of R. Meir of Rothenberg.[142] The *Chiddushei Anshei Shem* raises the objection of the nonphysical nature of the offense[143] and concludes that the reference is to the rabbinical version, *makkot mardut*, which may actually be applied more severely.[144] The Rama[145] cites this interpretation of the Mordechai.[146] Monetarily, however, the Talmud excludes verbal embarrassment from the reparations associated with personal injury.[147] In either case, R. Shlomo Luria[148] rules that the lashes can be commuted to a monetary fine; whether such fines are paid to the victim or to charity is a matter of some dispute.[149] The Rosh recommends excommuni-

---

141. *Bava Metzia* 4:306, see also *Shiltei Giborim*.

142. *Responsa Maharam Rothenberg* 785.

143. As does the *Responsa Lechem Rav* 6; the *Biur HaGra* (*Choshen Mishpat* 420:49); *Knesset HaGedolah, Orach Chaim* 39; and R. Shlomo Luria, *Yam Shel Shlomo, Bava Kamma* 8:49 and 57. Note the explanation of R. Chaim Chizkiyahu Medini, *Sdei Chemed, ma'arekhet halamed, Klal* 12. R. Yosef Epstein (*Mitzvot HaShalom*, pp. 185–186) and R. Ya'akov Hoffman (*Kovetz Torani of Kollel Zikhron Shneur*, vol. 6, pp. 28–33) suggest that the Mordechai's position is based on the fact that it is possible at times to violate this prohibition with an action, either by physically humiliating another, or, if one assumes that monetary and verbal oppression share the same prohibition, by engaging in the former. See also R. Zalman Uri in the journal *HaPardes*, vol. 35, no. 5:21–22 (45).

144. See also *Darkhei Moshe, Choshen Mishpat* 228.

145. *Choshen Mishpat* 420:38. See *Be'er Heitev*.

146. Note, however, R. Chaim Beneviste, *Kenesset HaG'dolah*, who observes that the language of the Mordechai is not easily amenable to this interpretation. An extensive analysis of the position of the Mordechai by R. Ya'akov Hoffman can be found in the journal *Kitrei Eliezer* (5763, p. 334–338. See also p. 338–340, where the author lists other principles relevant to this prohibition).

147. *Bava Kamma* 91a. See Rosh 8:4. The *Shulchan Arukh*, apparently concerned that this will be misinterpreted as a basis for leniency, writes: "Even though one who embarrasses someone verbally is not subject to having to pay reparations, it is a tremendous transgression, and it is only an evil fool and one of haughty spirit who insults and embarrasses others and whoever verbally embarrasses a decent member of the Jewish people has no portion in the world to come" (*Choshen Mishpat* 420:39). This language appears in *Mishneh Torah, Hilkhot Chovel U'Mazik* 3:7.

148. *Yam Shel Shlomo, Bava Metzia* 8:49.

cating one who humiliates others,[150] and the Rambam notes that latitude is granted to a rabbinical court to take punitive and preventative action as they see fit.[151] Special consideration is given if the humiliated party is a Torah scholar.[152] R. Tzvi Lifshitz, writing in the halakhic journal *Techumin*,[153] undertakes an extensive discussion of financial penalization of those who embarrass others in modern times.[154]

R. Moshe Sofer, the *Chatam Sofer,* rules in a fascinating manner concerning an incident of verbal oppression.[155] The case concerned a man, *shochet* of the community, who played a practical joke on an individual who was known to value greatly the mitzvah of *milah*. The shochet told this man that he had had a boy and that the man was invited a few days hence to perform the honors. After traveling several hours to the *brit,* the man was greatly disappointed to find that the *shochet* had actually had a girl and had merely played a cruel game with him. The *Chatam Sofer* was asked whether this *shochet* should be removed from his position. While he allows the *shochet* to keep his job, the *Chatam Sofer* excoriates him at length and finally levels on him a fine of ten gold coins, a sum prescribed by the Talmud as a penalty to be paid to one who has had performance of a mitzvah "stolen" from him.[156]

The logic of the *Chatam Sofer's* ruling is illuminating. It does not seem indicated that he felt the man deserved to be compensated equally for a nonexistent *mitzvah* in the manner he would have been had there actually been a *milah* to perform. Rather, it would appear that his evaluation was as follows: The man was willing to make a significant journey on the

---

149. See *Responsa Mahari Veil* 147 and *Responsa Chatam Sofer, Choshen Mishpat* 181.

150. *Bava Kamma* 8:14.

151. *Mishneh Torah, Hilkhot Chovel U'Mazik* 3:5. The positions of the Rambam and the Rosh are both recorded in *Shulchan Arukh, Choshen Mishpat* 1:5 and 420:38.

152. *Mishneh Torah, Chovel U'Mazik* 3:6; note the *Maggid Mishneh's* citation of the *Talmud Yerushalmi, Bava Kamma* 8:6. See *Shulchan Arukh, Choshen Mishpat* 1:5.

153. Vol. 37, p. 381.

154. See also R. Ezra Basri, *Responsa Sha'arei Ezra* 3:326; R. Ephraim Moshe Korngut, *Ohr Yechezkel,* pp. 360–363; and R. Yosef Shalom Elyashiv, *Kovetz Teshuvot* 2:129.

155. *Responsa Chatam Sofer* 176.

156. *Chullin* 87a.

assumption that he would be rewarded with a *mitzvah*. As no such mitz-vah exists, he has a right to the monetary value of that prize for which he agreed to undertake this trip, a value represented in the Talmud by ten gold coins.

These efforts notwithstanding, a quotation from the Talmud[157] makes clear the futility of attempting to ever completely rectify the damage wrought by the humiliation of others. "R. Yochanan said in the name of R. Shimon B. Yochai, greater is the transgression of verbal oppression than that of monetary oppression, for in reference to one the Torah says, 'and you shall fear your God' and in reference to the other it does not say 'and you shall fear your God.'[158] R. Elazar said, one is against an individual himself, and one is against an individual's money. R. Shmuel B. Nachmeni says, one is subject to repayment; the damage caused by the other can never be repaid."[159]

---

157. *Bava Metzia* 58b; see also *Mishneh Torah, Hilkhot Mekhirah* 14:18.

158. See commentary of Maharsha.

159. For analysis of the nature of this irreparability, see R. Natan Gestetner, *Natan Piryo, Bava Metzia*, p. 291.

TWO

A Rose by Any Other Name: Derogatory Nicknames

I. The Theory: Two Aspects

The civil codes that exist and have existed throughout world history are centered largely on rectifying damage inflicted upon person or property. Verbal offenses are often included, to the extent that they carry a broader impact, such as libel and defamation of character. It is assumed, however, that the spoken word, to the extent to which it is contained at that, is beyond legal redress. "Sticks and stones may break my bones, but words will never hurt me," goes the adage, and the law generally shares this indifference. The right to be referred to in casual conversation as one wishes is therefore not a right actionable in court or even recognized in constitutions. This is yet another area, then, in which Torah laws transcend those of society at large. "Three descend to *gehinnom* and do not rise up," states the Talmud, and concluding the list, after the adulterer and he who humiliates others in public: "one who creates a derogatory nickname for his fellow."[1]

The Talmud continues to note that the second category, humiliating others, would seem to include the third: addressing others in an insulting manner would apparently be a detail of the broader category of embarrassing another. To this, the distinction is offered, "even though he has become used to the name."[2] Rashi adds, "He has already become accustomed to that that they refer to him as such, and his face is not whitened, nonetheless he intends to humiliate him."[3] Some suggest that the latter detail comes to indicate that there is no difference between one who creates the sobriquet and one who perpetuates its usage.[4] R. Yisrael Yosef Rappaport[5] suggests that the severity of the second instance is due to the negative intent, regardless of the result.[6] Thus, there emerges a dually tiered prohibition in regards to creating a new name for another. To the extent that he bears humiliation, that larger transgression is certainly violated; and further, even once the burning embarrassment that accompanies the initial labeling is passed, a separate prohibition remains operative.

It might be possible to suggest that these two prohibitions are reflective of two disparate elements present in the distortion, or complete fabrication, of an individual's nomenclature. The aspect of humiliation is self-evident and is treated as such in the Talmud. Addressed in a manner beneath his dignity, the recipient of such name-calling is subject to a profound degradation. As such, the extensive body of ethical and legal liter-

---

1. *Bava Metzia* 58a.

2. The phrase used, *dash bei,* is defined, in another context, by the *Responsa Terumat HaDeshen* (25) as having endured a thirty-day period; see *Shulchan Arukh, Orach Chaim* 128:30 and *Orach Meisharim* 5:6.

3. See Maharsha, and R. Natan Gestetner, *Natan Piryo, Bava Metzia,* p. 291, who assumes some level of embarrassment must be present; the questions raised, however, may be addressed by the theory below.

4. See, for example, R. Yosef Cohen, *Sefer HaTeshuvah, Hilkhot Teshuvah* 3:14. See also R. David Ariav, *L'Reakha Kamokha,* vol. 3, sec. 2, ch. 2, *Nir L'David* 136.

5. *LiTeshuvat HaShanah, Hilkhot Teshuvah* 3:14.

6. See also R. Avraham Erlanger, *Birkat Avraham, Bava Metzia* 58b.

ature governing the embarrassment of others steps back not an inch in encountering this behavior.

However, the offense does not end there, as is clear from the Talmud's delineation; the singling out of this transgression from the latter category of humiliation is to instruct on this element. Beyond embarrassment, a further level of emotional violation is present. A person's name is his connection to his sense of identity, to his awareness of his own existence as an independent individual. Indeed, the rabbinical sages considered names to be deeply indicative of one's inner character. R. Meir gleaned information about those he met from the meanings of their names, and R. Yose suffered for failing to do this.[7] In a less spiritual sense, the name serves to identify to the individual himself his very essence. To be deprived of this name is to become disenfranchised from the reality of being a unique creation; it is to stand bereft of any evidence of individuality. The resulting alienation is profound; it clearly impacts differently than humiliation in other forms, yet apparently in as devastating a manner. The fact that the initial sense of embarrassment has abated is thus inconsequential, and a degradation all its own remains.[8]

II. The Issue of Intent

It is perhaps for this reason that the halakhic authorities found it necessary to give serious attention to the question of whether even a neutral, or possibly a laudatory, designation is also to be outlawed. In fact, the very word used talmudically to indicate a nickname, *kinnui*, contains an interpretational ambiguity. *Tosafot*[9] offer two possible definitions of the term, similar sounding words that result from variant texts. The first text provides *shem shafel*, that is, a "low" name, one bereft of dignity and respect, consistent with those designed to humiliate. The second definition, however, is not inherently pejorative: *shem tafel*, a secondary

---

7. *Yoma* 83b.

8. R. J. David Bleich, in an article in the journal *HaDarom* 35:140, suggests somewhat differently, that beyond the aspect of humiliation is the element of the user relating to the subject with an attitude of disrespect, a transgression regardless of the subject's reaction. Similarly, see R. David Rosenthal, *Divrei Yosher* to *Pirkei Avot* 3:11.

9. *Nedarim* 2a, s.v. *Kol Kinuyyei.*

name. Whether the quality of being secondary, while not necessarily being insulting, is enough to forbid the name is as stated the topic of some discussion.

Nonetheless, it should be noted from the outset that the Talmud does use the adjective *ra,* "bad," in formulating the prohibition. Thus, the basis to question this ingredient deserves some analysis. At first glance, it might relate to the reality that the offensiveness of any name is subjective; what might be intended as affectionate may be received as a verbal assault. This reasoning is present in the writings of R. Shraga Feivel Shneebalg, to an additional degree. He considers the possibility of a name acceptable to its subject, but considered slighting by the general populace.[10] His inclination is toward stringency, apparently feeling that the reality of the degradation that ensues transcends the victim's reduced appreciation of the potential in this area.[11]

However, there exists another aspect to the nonjudgmental nickname, in line with that stated previously. The loss of identity that accompanies the deprivation of one's given nomenclature does not distinguish between artificial names that are endearing and those that are contemptuous. Thus, it might be suggested that even innocent nicknames are to be restricted, as the focus is not as much on the acceptability of the new designation as it is on the abandonment of the original one. *Tosafot*[12] considers it an appropriate expression of extra piety to avoid even innocuous nicknames, possibly following this reasoning, as R. Moshe Troyesh comments,[13] "additional affection is displayed when using the actual name." Additionally, he suggests that R. Zeira, who attributed his long life to this stringency, was concerned that the usage of any artificial

---

10. *Responsa Shraga HaMeir* 6:6:2.

11. See also the ruling of R. Mordechai Eliyahu in his *Bein Adam L'Chaveiro* (p. 23), where he prohibits any name with even a minor degrading implication, even if the intent is innocent.

12. *Megillah* 27b, s.v, *v'lo.* The *Tosafot* are coming to explain why R. Zakkai attributed his long life to not using nicknames, when this is apparently required behavior anyway. R. Moshe Mordechai Shteger, *Bearot Mayim* to *Megillah,* suggests he was careful even when not in the presence of the subject; note the discussion following.

13. *Orach Meisharim* 5:6.

name could result in a derogatory one being tolerated. The Meiri[14] probably goes the furthest, in that he interprets the Talmud's condemnation of nicknames to apply even when the subject has no objection.

Alternatively, the grounds to be lenient are also significant; a name that is not hurtful to its designee may become a welcome aspect of his dignity, and a reference as such becomes not significantly different from the utilization of the name given in infancy. Indeed, the adjective of "bad" is adopted in the phrasing of the *Shulchan Arukh*,[15] as it is in the Talmud. As such, Rashi[16] does not seem to be concerned at all by inoffensive nicknames,[17] although the words of the Rambam[18] are inconclusive. This position explains the apparent usage of such terms in various places in the Talmud.[19]

R. Ya'akov Davidson[20] offers a parallel from another area of *halakhah* to display the severity attached to a derogatory appellation. Both a bathhouse and a lavatory may not be prayed in. However, a bathhouse that has not yet been used for that purpose, but merely has been designated as such, does not yet attain this status.[21] This is not the case, however, with the lavatory; merely labeling a room as such renders it unfit for prayer.[22] R. Yisrael Meir Kagan[23] explains the distinction, based on the Talmud,[24] as stemming from the fact that the lavatory is more distasteful. This reflects an unfortunate reality: the more degrading a designation, the greater the ease with which it attaches itself to its target. The same is certainly true of people.

---

14. *Bava Metzia* 58b.

15. *Choshen Mishpat* 228:5.

16. See *Kessef Mishneh, Hilkhot Teshuvah* 3:14.

17. See also R. Moshe Rosmarin, *D'var Moshe to Pirkei Avot* 3:154.

18. *Mishneh Torah, Hilkhot Deiot* 6:8; *Hilkhot Teshuvah* 3:14. See *Orach Meisharim* and R. Menachem Krakowski, *Avodat Melekh*.

19. See, for example, *Bekhorot* 58a, *Ketubot* 79a, *Kiddushin* 58a, and *Chullin* 110a. A lengthy discussion of incidences in the Talmud that seem at variance with this prohibition, and reconciliations of that difficulty, appears in R. David Ariav, *L'Reakha Kamokha, Kuntres HaBiurim* 6. Note also *Responsa Chavvot Yair* 152.

20. *Hilkhot Derekh Eretz*, ch. 63.

21. *Shulhan Arukh, Orach Chaim* 84:1.

22. *Orach Chaim* 83:2.

23. *Mishnah Berurah* 84:2.

24. *Shabbat* 10b.

R. Aharon David Grossman[25] discusses the tendency of Rashi to be
lenient on this point, as indicated previously by his language, *nitkavein
l'hakhlimo,* "he intended to humiliate him." The implication is that not
only is a benign nickname permissible, but that the operative factor is the
intent of the user, and therefore even a name with negative possibilities
may not be out of the question it the intentions are innocent. This is evidenced by Rashi's position elsewhere, in commenting on the Talmud's
identification of R. Yose as *"hachorem."*[26] To the authors of *Tosafot,*[27]
wary of any nickname, this had to be a reference to the city that he came
from. To Rashi, however, the term indicates "sunken nostrils," as defined
elsewhere in the Talmud.[28] The lack of offensive intent apparently renders such a designation acceptable. Support for such reasoning can also
be found in the *Shittah Mekubetzet,*[29] where the definition of the commonly used term *shin'nena* is given as "having big teeth."[30] However, the
latter may be more consistent with good health[31] and thus distinguished
from Rashi's *hachorem.* Thus, the element of intent is crucial.

This is taken up similarly by R. Yosef Chaim ibn Eliyahu, the *Ben Ish
Chai,* in his responsa.[32] He concludes simply that "the matter is judged
according to the time and the era, and according to the feelings of the
people, and if their practice is to take offense at this or not."[33] The
responsum deals with a case similar to that of *hachorem,* and thus it is
surprising that the *Ben Ish Chai* does not adduce that talmudic text as a
proof. R. Grossman suggests therefore that the case in the Talmud
involved using the name as identification when the subject was not present, and thus is of limited relevance to the *Ben Ish Chai*'s analysis, which
concerns addressing the individual in this manner. Thus, it is possible
that the following formulation is appropriate: in the individual's pres-

---

25. *Responsa V'Darashta V'Chakarta, Choshen Mishpat* 12.
26. *Menachot* 37a.
27. s.v. *R. Yose Hachorem.*
28. *Bekhorot* 43a.
29 *Ketubot* 14a.
30. This is also the definition provided by the *Arukh* (*Erekh Sheyn*).
31. See *Ketubot* 111b.
32. *Responsa Torah L'Shmah* 421.
33. Note *Bekhorot* 44a. See also *Sefer Sha'ar Shimon Echad* 3:74.

ence, the most significant concern is the subject's sensitivity to the name, as the *Ben Ish Chai* writes, and for third-person references, the central issues are the inherent nature of the name and the intent of the user, as Rashi indicates. Along these lines, R. Moshe Drei[34] is lenient concerning a name used in jest, that the subject does not object to, providing also it is not used regularly. R. Troyesh observes, from the fact that humiliation was considered by the Talmud to be an integral part of this transgression, that the primary evil is in using the name in the individual's presence. However, it seems from *Tosafot*[35] that even references in the absence of the designee pose a problem.

The issue of identification is central to the analysis of R. Avraham Binyamin Silverberg.[36] He deals with a situation in which a person's name is insufficient to distinguish him from being confused with others, and therefore his acquaintances wish to attach a physically descriptive, but not derogatory, term to his name. He adduces midrashic proof[37] to his conclusion that this is certainly permissible.[38]

Further, a distinction might be drawn between names that are neutral and those that are complimentary. Of the latter, the authors of the *Tosafot*[39] felt that laudatory names are permissible, concluding as such that it is acceptable to refer to an individual using only the name of his family. R. Grossman adds, however, that in modern society, to do so without some kind of title is often considered disrespectful. This is already hinted at in the *Midrash*[40] where it is related that King David felt humiliated that he was referred to as "Son of Yishai" rather than by his given name.

The sensitivities that lie within the human being are multileveled and beyond the range of being easily perceptible. The boundaries set by the

---

34. In the journal *Ohr Torah* 24:157.

35. *Pesachim* 112a, s.v. *Tzivah*.

36. *Responsa Mishnat Binyamin* 23.

37. See *Midrash Rabbah, Exodus* 2.

38. As he observes, the facts specific to his discussion actually result in the proposed nickname being a type of blessing; the individual's name was Chaim, and as he was tall, they wished to call him *Chaim Arukhim*—translatable both as "Tall Chaim" (ungrammatically) or "long life."

39. *Ta'anit* 20b, s.v. *B'hakhinoti*.

40. *Bamidbar Rabbah* 18:13.

halakhic authorities to the creation of nicknames necessitate that a thorough attempt to grasp the depths of these sensitivities precede the utilization of these appellations. Absent such analysis, this behavior is fraught with interpersonal risk of the first order.

CHAPTER

THREE

Better to Stand on a Box: Honoring Oneself at the Expense of Others

An oft-told tale, usually said of R. Yisrael Salanter, describes the rabbi coming upon two children quarreling. The subject of their heated dispute was which of the two boys was the taller. In a final act of desperation, one child pushed the other to the ground, and, standing over him, proclaimed, "There, now I am the taller one!" R. Yisrael helped the defeated child to his feet and then said to the aggressor, "There was no need to push him to the ground to prove that you were taller—all you had to do was stand on a box!"

In *halakhah*, the sage's words represent more than just good advice; they actually state the letter of the law. The child's attempt to undermine the other in order to solidify his own status constitutes an action called *mitkabbed biklon chaveiro*—drawing honor through the humiliation of one's fellow—and it receives unreserved condemnation in the Talmud and afterward. While R. Nechunia Ben HaKaneh attributed his long life to his absolute and total avoidance of such behavior,[1] statements of greater intensity are found twice in the Rambam's *Mishneh Torah*.[2] He who would glorify himself at another's expense is not only to be criticized; he "has no portion in the world to come." This additional level of condemnation is grounded in the Jerusalem Talmud[3] and the *Midrash*.[4]

The discrepancy between the Babylonian Talmud, which seems to consider refraining from this conduct a source of merit, and the Jerusalem Talmud and the Rambam, who treat the matter with significantly greater severity, is questioned by R. Shmuel Yitzchak Hilman[5] and by the author of the *Yad HaK'tannah*.[6] While the latter sources excluded the *mitkabbed biklon chaveiro* from the world to come, this crime is absent from listings in the Babylonian Talmud of offenses deserving such punishment.[7] R. Ya'akov Davidson[8] assumes that there is a dispute between the two Talmuds, and later between the Rambam and the author of the *Shulchan Arukh*,[9] as to the level of prohibition involved.

R. Shmuel Yudaikin[10] suggests that the various references deal with different levels of involvement. One act of self-glorification through another's humiliation is not in itself an act worthy of deprivation of the eternal reward, as are other transgressions included in the aforementioned listing. However, repeated employment of this technique of

---

1. *Megillah* 28a.

2. *Hilkhot Deiot* 6:3, *Hilkhot Teshuvah* 3:13.

3. *Chagigah* 2:1. See commentary of R. Yeshaya Pick to *Peirush Mishnayot* of the Rambam, *Sanhedrin* 10:1; R. Akiva Eiger, *Chiddushim* to *Shulchan Arukh*, *Orach Chaim* 156; R. Adoniyahu Kraus, *Adnei Yad HaChazakah*; and R. Yisrael Avraham Abba Berger, *Yad Yisrael* to *Mishneh Torah*.

4. *Bereishit Rabbah* 1:5.

5. *Ohr HaYashar*, *Chullin* 37b.

6. *Hilkhot Deiot*, ch. 5, *Mada*, *Aseh* 3:4.

7. See *Sanhedrin* 90a.

8. *Hilkhot Derekh Eretz*, chs. 182 and 183.

9. As evidenced by his comments in *Kessef Mishneh*, *Hilkhot Teshuvah* 3:14. See R. Pinchas Breuer in the journal *VaY'lakket Yosef*, vol. 6, no. 99, in footnote.

10. *Divrei Shalom* 5:26.

advancement is indicative of a severely deficient personality, one who is unlikely to have merited everlasting paradise. This notion is explicit in the Rambam's formulation.[11]

Further, another distinction must be noted. The example offered in the Rambam differs markedly in severity from that indicated in the Talmud. The Rambam[12] describes the *mitkabbed biklon chaveiro* as a person who displays his superiority to others as an expression of his own value, so that his fellow's disgrace is his honor. However, in the Talmud's instance, we find much less malicious intent. R. Nechuniah Ben Hakaneh was inspired to his meritorious standard of behavior by R. Huna, who refused to let R. Chana bar Chanilai carry the former's luggage in the streets of the latter's hometown. His reasoning was, since such work was not his normal responsibility, to engage in it at this time would represent a lowering of his dignity, and R. Huna felt that to benefit in any way from such a situation would constitute *mitkabbed biklon chaveiro*.

Thus, there emerge two levels of *mitkabbed biklon chaveiro*. When this behavior is undertaken purposefully, with the goal of deprecating another in order to reap comparative glory, the conduct is certainly prohibited and receives unanimous condemnation. However, any gain derived from another's disgrace or misfortune, albeit not premeditated, smacks of the spirit of this transgression. Thus, the avoidance of such profit earned a long life for R. Nechuniah Ben HaKaneh. It is perhaps in this vein that R. Ben Zion Ouziel[13] considers (but ultimately concludes against) the possibility that deriving medical knowledge from the study of deceased individuals is contrary to this principle. Similarly, R. Binyamin Yehoshua Zilber[14] considers whether the prohibition is applicable only if the inferior other is explicitly offered in comparison, or perhaps it is enough that the contrast is made apparent in a nonverbal manner. He concludes that both are forbidden, but only the former case earns the punishment mentioned previously.

---

11. See *Peirush Mishnayot, Sanhedrin* 10:1.
12. *Hilkhot Teshuvah* 4:4.
13. *Responsa Mishpetei Ouziel*, vol. 1, *Yoreh Deah* 28.
14. *Responsa Az Nidbaru* 8:63.

The author of the *Sefer Teshuvah MeAhavah*[15] observes that two distinct elements seem to exist within this prohibition. First, there is the aspect of deriving honor from this inappropriate source. It might be that this explains the reference to this tendency within the context of reward and punishment; as this individual draws his value only by siphoning off of others, his merit fails to reflect positively on him in any significant manner.[16] Further, there is also the obligation to treat others in a manner that would be desirable to the protagonist (*v'ahavta l'reakha kamokha*), which is lacking by definition in the *mitkabbed biklon chaveiro*.

Further, the element of humiliation is not to be discounted and may be fundamental to the severity of the punishment. On this point, a relevant dispute concerns whether or not the disgraced individual need be present for the prohibition to take force, at least in its most absolute sense. The Rambam states explicitly that the victim is absent, a factor that falsely gives the impression that no serious offense has been committed. R. Chaim Vital,[17] however, assumes he is in attendance.[18] R. Reuven Margolios, in his commentary to the *Sefer Chasidim,* writes that this factor determines the severity of the prohibition.[19]

The exhortation to avoid glorification at the cost of another's disgrace imposes a tremendous burden of sensitivity into the approach one must take toward functioning within a social framework. R. Yeshayahu Berlin, in his introduction to his work on R. Achai Gaon's *Sheiltot, She'eilat Shalom,* writes that in his analysis of Torah issues, he always strove to find support for positions he tended to disagree with, to make certain to steer clear of this pitfall. Similarly, perhaps showing more concern than can be expected, R. Shneur Zalman Dov Anusishky[20] deletes the name of an authority with whom he plans to disagree in one responsum, for fear of appearing to be *mitkabbed biklon chaveiro*. This vigilance, practiced in all interactions of daily life, would undoubtably prove rewarding.

---

15. *Hilkhot Teshuvah* 4:4.
16. See a similar suggestion in R. M. M. Frankel, *Be'er Avot, Pirkei Avot* 4:1.
17. *Sha'arei Kedushah*, part 2, *sha'ar* 8.
18. See also R. Avraham David Wahrman, *Milei D'Chasiduta*, p. 34.
19. *Mekor Chesed*, to *Sefer Chasidim* 19.
20. *Responsa Matzav HaYosher* 6.

FOUR

All's Fair in Love and Peace: Instigating and Perpetuating Disputes

I. The Lesson of Korach

History has proven time and again what should be self-evident, that a harmonious environment within society is the most conducive to a productive and successful culture. Within *halakhah*, however, the role of peace is infinitely more significant. Rabbinic authorities agree from the outset that both negative and positive commandments are devoted to this ideal; it is the identity of the specific *mitzvot*, however, that occupies much halakhic debate.

In the aftermath of the rebellion of Korach, the Torah guards against a repeat of the events in the form of an injunction not to "be like Korach and his followers."[1] To many authorities[2] this constitutes an absolute prohibition against instigating and perpetuating disputes. This interpretation is found in the Talmud,[3] although the Rambam[4] assumes this to be an *asmachta*, a rabbinically assigned allusion, rather than the actual meaning of the verse, which is a predictive warning[5] as opposed to a prohibition. The technical phrase is *l'hachzik b'machloket*; R. Baruch Epstein[6] translates this as "allowing a dispute to take root." R. Joseph D. Epstein[7] explains similarly, thus applying the prohibition equally to the instigator of the dispute and the one who continues it.[8] R. Zalman Nechemiah Goldberg[9] takes into account the entire context of the biblical source, including Moshe's behavior, in interpreting the commandment. He thus suggests it includes not only avoiding the initiation of a dispute, but, if necessary, sending a message of apology or dispensing with one's own honor in order to effect a reconciliation, regardless of where the fault lies.[10]

R. Achai Gaon, in his formulation of the prohibition,[11] emphasizes that contentious behavior will result in hatred among men. Building on

---

1. *Numbers* 17:5.

2. Included among these are R. Shlomo ibn Gabirol, Rabbeinu Yonah (*Sha'arei Teshuvah*, *Sha'ar* 3:58), R. Shimon ben Tzemach Duran, the Bahag, the *Sefer Mitzvot Gadol* (prohibition 156) and the *Sefer Mitzvot Katan* (132). See *Sefer Charedim*, chs. 24, 42, and *Chafetz Chaim*, *Lavin* 12. Note R. Yoav Yehoshua Weingarten, *Responsa Chelkat Yoav* 2:20.

3. *Sanhedrin* 110a.

4. *Sefer HaMitzvot, Shoresh* 8.

5. The prediction concerns the nature of the punishment that will befall the querulous individual; apparently, the affliction of *tzara'at* is appropriate (as the Talmud in *Sanhedrin* continues), rather than being swallowed into the Earth, as befell Korach. This is based on the *Midrash Tanchuma*. See Rashbam, *Bava Batra* 122a, and *Torah Temimah*, *Numbers* 17:6. See also R. Meir Simchah of Dvinsk, *Meshekh Chokhmah*, and R. Mordechai Gifter, *Pirkei Torah*, to *Parshat Korach*.

6. *Torah Temimah*, *Numbers* 16:16.

7. *Mitzvot HaShalom*, pp. 122–124.

8. Note also R. Avraham Erlanger, *Ma'or HaSha'ar*, pp. 130–131.

9. In the journal *Moriah*, vols. 169/170:62–72. See also R. Avraham Y. Ehrman, *Kodesh Yisrael*, #25.

10. See also R. Zvi Shpitz, *Mishpetei HaTorah*, 1:95.

11. *Sheiltot D'Rav Achai Gaon, Parshat Korach* 131.

this, R. Reuven Margolios[12] suggests that the prohibition is actually a protective injunction on behalf of the prohibition against hatred.[13]

The Ramban[14] understands the verse to forbid specifically challenging the institution of *kehunah*, as Korach did.[15] R. Shalom Dov Ber Wolpe[16] notes that the Ramban's point seems valid; as Korach's behavior was, in fact, heretical, why should a prohibition named after him be interpreted only as referring to quarreling? Rather, he suggests, the descent starts with dispute; the transgressions that come afterward are a direct result.

II. Disputes for the Sake of Heaven?

If the events concerning Korach are to be taken as paradigmatic of forbidden dispute, it is necessary to understand the significance of this reference.[17] The *Mishnah* in *Pirkei Avot*[18] contrasts arguments that are nobly fought for "the sake of Heaven" with those that are not. The former category is represented by the halakhic debates of Hillel and Shammai; Korach and his disciples symbolize the latter.[19] R. Bachya[20] writes that even the negative designation is reserved only for disputes concerning issues of Torah relevance;[21] all other quarrels are relegated to a category of even less repute, that of the behavior of a *kesher r'shaim*, a "band of evildoers."[22] R. Ovadiah of Bartenura defines the difference

---

12. *Margoliyot HaYam* to *Sanhedrin*, 110a, 6. Note also *Ha'amek She'eilah* to *Sheiltot*, and *Kodesh Yisrael* at length.

13. See R. Yosef Engel, *Gilyonei HaShas* to *Sanhedrin*, and see also R. Yehudah Shaviv, in the journal *Shma'atin*, no. 100, pp. 318–322.

14. Glosses to the Rambam's *Sefer HaMitzvot*, and additional prohibitions. See also R. Eliezer of Metz, *Sefer Yereim* 357, and *Toafot Re'em*.

15. See also *Marganita Tava* to *Sefer HaMitzvot*, who understands the translation of the verse as per Yonatan Ben Uziel to agree with the Ramban. See also R. Chaim Yosef David Azulai, *Petach Einayim* to *Sanhedrin*. As to whether or not other religious appointments are included, see *Mitzvot HaShalom*, p. 126.

16. Introduction to *Yedaber Shalom* to *Mishneh Torah*. See his comments, at length, pp. 19–34.

17. See also R. Moshe Blau, *Mishnat Moshe* to *Sanhedrin*.

18. 5:17.

19. See *Pardes Yosef, Leviticus* 1:1.

20. Commentary to *Pirkei Avot*.

21. Along similar lines, see *Responsa HaRivash HaChadashot* 33.

22. *Sanhedrin* 26a.

as motivation: a dispute for the "sake of Heaven" is inspired by a quest for the truth, while its alternative is fueled by a love for victory. Along those lines, R. Yehudah Assad[23] interprets the meaning of the statement in the *Mishnah* that the noble dispute will "last forever" while the other "will eventually be nullified." As the latter is not a search for truth, the protagonist realizes it will not have lasting impact but does not care, as the quarreling itself serves his purposes.[24] The author of the *Yad HaK'tannah*[25] suggests a litmus test to determine the proper categorization:[26] "when one finds in his heart no ulterior motive, and will experience no happiness, no sadness, and no glory, and not any personal benefit to one's self,"[27] only then is there a possibility that the confrontation is "for the sake of heaven." Even so, such an analysis is extremely difficult to self-administer in a completely honest fashion; as R. Yonatan Eibshutz observes,[28] every controversy inspires its protagonist with the impression of noble motives. R. Naftali Tzvi Yehudah Berlin,[29] abstracting the issue to the general one of transgressions undertaken for noble causes, imposes two criteria to justify such an undertaking: the disputant must derive no personal benefit from the

---

23. *Chiddushim* to *Parshat Korach*.

24. See also R. Avraham Shmuel Binyamin Sofer, *Ketav Sofer Al Ha Torah* to *Parshat Korach*.

25. *Deiot*, ch. 10, *mada ot* 42.

26. See also *Ma'or VaShemesh, Parshat Korach*.

27. This last criterion may emerge from a careful reading of the *Mishnah*. Many commentators (see, for example, *Tosafot Yom Tov*) note that the examples given are phrased "Hillel and Shammai" and "Korach and his followers." As the first lists the two sides of the dispute, a more appropriate rendering would be "Korach and Moshe." Many commentators explain that the phrasing is indeed accurate; the members of the band of Korach were not truly united, but rather each was out for his own glory. Even among themselves, there was fighting; this component of self-interest, the quarreling of "Korach and his followers," is emblematic of a dispute not for the sake of Heaven. See R. M. M. Frankel, *Be'er Avot to Avot*; R. Elimelekh of Lisensk, *Noam Elimelekh*, and R. Pinchas of Koritz, *Imrei Pinchas*, cited in *Ma'aseh Avot*; R. Chanokh Zundel, *Etz Yosef*, and R. Baruch Tzvi Moskowitz, *Nishba LaAvotekha* to *Avot*, at length. For an interesting variation, see R. Aharon b. Yehudah HaLevi, *Chasdei Avot*. An alternate interpretation of the language of the Mishnah can be found in R. Boruch D Povarsky, *Bad Kodesh al HaTorah*, vol. 2, p. 179, where it is suggested that Moshe is left out of the formulation because the fight itself was one-sided; Korach was attacking him, and not vice versa.

28. *Ye'arot D'vash*, vol. 2, *drush* 8.

29. *Responsa Meishiv Davar* 2:9.

argument, and a careful cost-benefit evaluation must be undertaken. R. Eibshutz adds that an indication of the nature of the dispute is the manner in which the combatants treat each other outside of the context of the disagreement.[30] R. Hirsch Meisels[31] notes the fact that almost by definition, the prohibition of perpetuating dissent is not mitigated by the belief of either party that truth is on his side.[32] R. Yechezkel Landau, one of the greatest authorities of the eighteenth century, went as far as to comment,[33] "in our times, one does not find a dispute for the sake of Heaven."[34] Along these lines, R. Natan Gestetner[35] finds the example of Hillel and Shammai to be significant; they are indicative of the level necessary to wage such a battle. Nonetheless, the assumption that proper motivation provides some justification for respectful disagreement, even in later generations, must be allowed as the basis for basic discussions in the development of *halakhah*. As Rabbeinu Asher wrote,[36] albeit several centuries ago, "Whom do we have greater than Rashi, who enlightened our eyes with his commentary, and [nonetheless] his own descendants, Rabbeinu Tam and R. Yitzchak, [prominent authors of the *Tosafot*] argued about him, and contradicted his words; for it is a Torah of truth, and no favor is shown to any man." However, even such noble disagreements carry risks; accordingly, R. Eliyahu Ragoler[37] warns of the dangers inherent in even a "dispute for the sake of Heaven."

III. Further Sources Obligating Peace

In addition to, or instead of, the Korach model, other sources have been offered in condemnation of disharmony.[38] The Torah earlier[39] warns

---

30. See also R. Ovadiah Yosef, *Anaf Etz Avot* to *Pirkei Avot*, 5:17.
31. *D'var Tzvi* to *Responsa Mekadshei HaShem* 2:16.
32. See also *Chamra V'Chayai* to *Sanhedrin*, citing R. Yonatan.
33. *Responsa Noda B'Yehudah, Mahadurah Kamma, Yoreh Deah* 1.
34. See also *Pardes Yosef, Leviticus* 26:3.
35. *L'Horot Natan* to *Pirkei Avot*.
36. *Responsa HaRosh, Klal* 55:15.
37. *Responsa Yad Eliyahu* 2:25.
38. A discussion of these sources is found in R. Yosef Avraham Heler's *Kuntres Shalom Yihyeh*, ch. 1.
39. *Exodus* 23:2.

against "responding to a grievance by yielding to the majority to pervert [the law]."[40] R. Shlomo ibn Gabirol[41] understands this, in the spirit of King Solomon's words[42] "do not speedily go out to a quarrel," as an exhortation against joining a conflict, for "without wood, the fire goes out."[43] R. Shimon R. Tzemach Duran includes this in his enumeration of the *mitzvot*.[44]

Prior to engaging in warfare, the Jewish nation is commanded,[45] "*v'karata aleha l'shalom*—you shall call out to it [the city to be battled] for peace." While in essence, most authorities understand this commandment to be operative only in regards to actual warfare between nations,[46] it is nonetheless taken as indicative of an attitude and priority within the Torah's central goals and considerations.[47]

R. Yeshayahu Horowitz[48] suggests that the verse prohibiting the kindling of fire on *Shabbat*[49] be understood in a more expansive manner than is conventional. In his interpretation, the forbidden fire is not just actual flames but the emotional conflagration fueled by disputation. Thus, querulous behavior on the *Shabbat* day incurs additional levels of violation.[50]

---

40. In the Talmud (*Sanhedrin* 32a, 36a), this verse is used differently; see *Mitzvot HaShalom*, pp. 160–163.

41. *Azharot* 24; see *Sefer Charedim* 24:29.

42. *Proverbs* 25:8.

43. Ibid., 26:20.

44. *Zohar Rakia*, prohibition 24.

45. *Deuteronomy* 20:10.

46. For a discussion of this *mitzvah*, see R. Yitzchak Yedidiah Frenkel, *Derekh Y'sharah* 1:51, R. Yehudah Heschel Levenberg in *Kovetz Nehorai*, vol. 2: *Sefer Zikaron L'R. Yosef Chaim Shneur Kolter*, pp. 266–272, and in his *Imrei Chein* to *Deuteronomy*, 26; R. Mordechai HaKohen, in the journal *Machanayim*, no. 121, pp. 34–52, and in the journal *Torah SheB'Al Peh*, vol. 21: R. Shmuel Baruch Verner, pp. 52–59, and R. Sh'ar Yashuv Cohen, pp. 74–81.

47. See, for example R. Yaakov Etlinger, *Minchat Ani*; R. Chaim Kasar, *Ketz HaMizbeach* to *Deuteronomy*; Dr. Avraham Arzi, in *Machanayim*, no. 123, p. 28–33; and R. Yitzchak Raphael, *Torah SheB'Al Peh*, vol. 21, pp. 9–11.

48. *Shnei Luchot HaBrit, Parshat Vayakhel*.

49. *Exodus* 35:3.

50. See also R. Chaim Yosef David Azulai, *Moreh B'Etzba* 64:152.

The verse in *Psalms*[51] mandates, "seek peace, and pursue it (*bakesh shalom v'rodfehu*)." The *Sefer Charedim*[52] considers this instruction to seek peace to be an obligation *midivrei kaballah,* "from tradition."[53] This designation is used for commandments that are biblical, but post-penta-teuchal.[54] Although these obligations are actually rabbinical, as they do not trace back to Sinai, their scriptural grounding may give them a higher status, thus, for certain purposes, these precepts would be treated as biblical.[55]

The significance of peace being "sought" and "pursued" is high-lighted by the *Midrash,*[56] which states "the Torah was not concerned that one pursue *mitzvoth* . . . but, as for peace, 'ask for (seek) peace' in its place, and 'pursue it' in another place." R. Shneur Zalman of Liady, the first Lubavitcher Rebbe,[57] derives from this comment that *shalom* com-mands higher priority than *mitzvot*. The Satmar Rebbe, R. Yoel Teitlbaum,[58] makes a similar observation, noting that the *Midrash* is indicating that harmony should be pursued even if it means the loss of

---

51. 34:15

52. 35:19; see also 12:57.

53. The *Menorat HaMaor* (*Ner* 6, *K'al* 2, *Chelek* 1, *Perek* 2) also believes this verse to contain a *mitzvah midivrei kaballah,* but considers the subject to be *shalom* in the sense of greetings rather than in the sense of a state of peace.

54. Other examples include the fasts of Tishah B'Av, Shiva Asar B'Tamuz, Asarah B'Tevet, and Tzom Gedalyah (*Zechariah* 8:19); the *mitzvot* of Purim (*Esther* 9:21–22); and Kavod and Oneg Shabbat (*Isaiah* 58:13).

55. This is the often cited opinion of R. Aryeh Leib of Metz, *Turei Even,* *Megillah* 5b, s.v. *Chizkiyah*; see also *Turei Zahav, Orach Chaim* 687:2, citing Rabbeinu Tam; *Sdei Chemed,* vol. 2, pp. 63 and 258; R. Meir Simchah of Dvinsk, *Ohr Sameach, Berakhot* 3:9; R. Yerucham Ciecanaowitz, *Responsa Torat Yerucham* 3:26 and 3:82; R. Yisrael Meir Lau, *Responsa Yachel Yisrael* 46; and the Veroyer Rav (author of *Sha'arei Torah*) in the journal *Kerem Shlomo,* vol. 36, no 4, pp. 9–11. However, many earlier authorities disagree; see Ran, *Megillah* and *Ta'anit*; R. Yechezkel Landau, *Responsa Noda B'Yehudah, Mahadurah Tinyana, Yoreh Deah* 146, citing Rambam, and Rashi, *Mikvaot* 6:7, and *Teshuvot HaMeyuchasot L'Ramban* 263. See also *Mishnah Berurah,* 692:15, citing *Pri Megadim,* and R. Baruch Weiss, *Birkhot Horai* 23:11.

56. *Bamidbar Rabbah* 39:27 and *Tanchuma, Chukkat* 22; see also *Vayikra Rabbah* 99.

57. *Shulchan Arukh HaRav, Orach Chaim* 156:2.

58. *Responsa Divrei Yoel* 54.

another *mitzvah*.[59] The *Avot D'Rabbi Natan*[60] interprets the verbs used in the verse to say that *shalom* must be actively imported to those places where it is lacking.[61] R. Yaakov Etlinger[62] writes that while the verse "you shall call out to it for peace" is directed toward removing conflict, the verse of "seek peace and pursue it" commands an active effort toward a positive sense of peace.

In addition to any specific injunction against strife, R. Yisrael Meir Kagan[63] enumerates a host of other transgressions that are likely to be violated when an atmosphere of contention persists. Among these are causeless hatred, malicious gossip, anger, verbal oppression, humiliation of others, taking revenge, bearing a grudge, cursing others, attempting to deprive another of his livelihood, and desecration of the Divine Name.[64] Thus, engaging in conflict is fraught with dangers, both direct and indirect.[65]

IV. Overriding Prohibitions for the Sake of Shalom

In light of these perils, certain unusual dispensations exist. In the Talmud Yerushalmi,[66] R. Shmuel b. Nachmani quotes in the name of R. Yonatan that it is permissible to spread negative information about those who perpetuate strife, citing scriptural support.[67] This is codified

59. R. Shlomo Zalman Friedman (*Zivchei Shlomo*, pp. 154 and 360) offers a homiletical explanation of why this is so. When a person does not have the opportunity to perform a *mitzvah*, he is not obligated to "pursue it" because he is not held responsible for an opportunity not afforded him. This is true, however, only because others in the Jewish nation are attending to this *mitzvah*, and he shares in their merit. This vicarious fulfillment is only possible through the harmonious unity of the Jewish people; when this link itself is missing, it must be actively revived, for nothing else can perform that function. A similar comment is made by R. Shimon Gabel, *Kli Golah*, *Bava Batra* 99a. See also the journal *VaY'lakket Yosef*, vol. I, no. 56.

60. 12:6.

61. See also R. Eliyahu of Vilna, *Mirkevet Eliyahu*, *Avot* 3:12, per *Hosea* 1:9.

62. *Minchat Ani*.

63. *Shemirat HaLashon*, ch. 15.

64. On this last aspect, see R. Shmuel Landau in *Responsa Noda B'Yehudah*, *Mahadurah Tinyana*, *Yoreh Deah* 29; *Chasdei David* to *Tosefta*, *Eiruvin*; and *Mitzvot HaShalom*, p. 133.

65. See also *Mitzvot HaShalom*, pp. 314–320.

66. *Peah* 1:1.

67. *1 Kings*, 1:14. On this derivation, see R. Avraham Price, *Mishnat Avraham* to *Smag* 10:9:4.

by several authorities.[68] However, as R. Akiva Eiger[69] explains, this is only allowed for the purposes of silencing the dispute. When this is not possible, the laws of *lashon hara* are unchanged.[70] Even when leniencies are operative, strict guidelines still govern their employment, as specified by R. Yisrael Meir Kagan.[71] The need to stifle those who would engender discord is displayed also by those authorities who rule that honor, such as standing up in their presence, should not be accorded to these individuals, even when it is otherwise indicated.[72]

The maintenance of harmony is thus recognized as a paramount value; consequently, conflicts with other halakhic values will at times be decided in favor of *shalom*. The most well-known of these instances is found in the Talmud,[73] where we are told that God Himself allowed His Name to be erased (as part of the procedure in which the guilt or innocence of a possibly adulterous wife is determined) in order to advance the cause of peace. The extrapolation of this passage to wider application depends on an accurate delineation of the nature of the prohibition being overridden. On the surface, erasing God's Name appears to be an outright biblical prohibition.[74] After discussing the destruction of

---

68. See *Sefer Mitzvot Gadol*, prohibition 10; *Sefer Mitzvot Katan* 8; *Hagahot Maimoniot, Hilkhot Deiot* 7:3; and *Magen Avraham, Orach Chaim* 156. See also R. Shimshon Chaim Nachmani, *Zera Shimshon, Parshat Korach* 9.

69. *Gilyon HaShas* to *Talmud Yerushalmi*.

70. See also *Machatzit HaShekel, Orach Chaim* 356; R. Yonatan Shteif, *Mitzvot Hashem*, vol. 2, p. 30; R. Mordechai Lichtenstein, *Mitzvot HaLevavot* 2:21; R. Meir Dan Plotzki, *Kli Chemdah, Parshat Metzora* 1; and R. Dror Binyamin Sandler, in the journal *Torat HaAdam L'Adam*, vol. 4, pp. 194–195. Note the additional limitations recorded by R. Avraham David Wahrman, *Milei D'Chasiduta*, p. 36, and see *Imrei Yehosef* to *Sefer Mitzvot Katan*. See, however, *Ma'or HaSha'ar*, p. 130.

71. *Chafetz Chaim, Hilkhot Lashon Hara* 8:8. R. Kagan also notes that this dispensation is not found in the codes of the Rambam, the Rosh, or the Rif. An extensive analysis of the concept can be found in R. Chaim Shlomo Abrahams, *Birkhat Shlomo*, 21.

72. *Iyyun Yaakov* to *Ein Yaakov, Gittin* 31a, and *Mitzvot HaLevavot*.

73. *Shabbat* 116a, *Sukkah* 53b, *Nedarim* 66b, *Makkot* 11a, and *Chullin* 141a. See R. Fischel Avraham Mael, *Shivtei Yisrael*, pp. 184–191.

74. As to the prohibition of erasing God's Name in general, see R. Yosef Babad, *Minchat Chinnukh* 437; R. Yitzchak Hecht, *Responsa Sha'arei Kodesh* 1:91–148; R. Chaim Ya'akov Arieli, *Be'er Ya'akov* to *Shevuot* 42; R. Simchah Rosenberg, *Heikhal Simchah* 17; *Torat Ze'ev, Zevachim* 41; *Minchat Eliyahu* to *Hilkhot Tefilin*; R. Eliyahu Kushelevsky, *Ner LaMa'or*, pp. 130–136; R. Yitzchak Yedidiah Frenkel, *Derekh Y'sharah* 1:16; R. Yosef Teomim, in the journal *HaPardes*, vol. 22, no. 825–28

idolatry, the Torah warns, "You shall not do so unto the Lord your God."[75] The Talmud[76] understands this to be an explicit prohibition against the erasing of the Divine Name. Thus, it may be assumed that the aforementioned erasure proves that the pursuit of harmony justifies the violation of Torah prohibitions.[77] In addition, it is the position of R. Shneur Zalman of Lublin[78] and others that positive commandments are operative as well, further affecting the range of the dispensation. However, the Rama, in his responsa,[79] slows this procedure somewhat in ruling that the injunction is only transgressed when destructive intent is present; erasure with a constructive purpose does not constitute a violation of a prohibition.[80] Along these lines, R. Avraham Bornstein, the Sochatchover Rebbe,[81] and R. Yechezkel Landau[82] allow erasing that serves the purpose of any *mitzvah*.[83] R. Yehudah Loew of Prague, the Maharal,[84] makes an observation that provides a more self-contained purpose to the Rama's reasoning. The word *shalom* designates not only "peace," but also itself serves as a form of God's Name.[85] The Maharal understands the relationship to be not only semantic but conceptual as well. Thus, the advancement of peace is itself a perpetuation of God's

---

(55); R. Avraham Shitrit, *Responsa Be'ero Shel Avraham*, vol. 1, 29; R. Avigdor Neventzal, *B'Yitzchak Yikarei* 43; the journal *Otzerot Yerushalayim*, vol. 31, p. 492, and vol. 32, p. 503; and R. Shlomo Wahrman, *She'erit Yosef* 4:59. In particular reference to the erasure mentioned in connection with the adulterous wife, see R. Tzvi Domb, *Responsa Imrei Tzvi* 82:6.

75. *Deuteronomy* 12:4.

76. *Makkot* 22a.

77. Indeed, R. Plotzki, *Kli Chemdah*, ibid., traces the aforementioned dispensation to speak *lashon hara* about those who spread discord to this passage.

78. *Responsa Torat Chesed*, *Orach Chaim* 4.

79. *Responsa HaRama* 100:10.

80. See R. Avraham Teomim, *Responsa Chesed L'Avraham, Mahadurah Tinyana*, *Yoreh Deah* 43; R. Yitzchak Shmelkes, *Responsa Beit Yitzchak*, *Orach Chaim* 10:5; and R. Shlomo Zalman Braun, *Shearim Metzuyanim B'Halakhah*, *Nedarim* 66b and *Chullin* 141a.; R. Yekutiel Halberstam, *Responsa Divrei Yatziv*, *Yoreh Deah* 177.

81. *Responsa Avnei Nezer*, *Orach Chaim* 35.

82. *Responsa Noda B'Yehudah, Mahadurah Tinyana*, *Yoreh Deah* 181.

83. Note, however, R. Aryeh Pomerantzik's *Emek Brakhah, Issur Mechikat HaShem* 1, citing *Gittin* 19b, *Hagahot Maimoniot, Hilkhot Yesodei HaTorah*, ch. 6, in the name of the *Re'em; Beit Yosef, Yoreh Deah* 276 in *Bedek HaBayit*; and *Turei Zahav* and *Siftei Kohen*, ibid.

84. *Netivot Olam, Netiv HaShalom*, ch. 1.

85. *Shabbat* 10a.

Name; in a very direct sense, this deletion was an "erasing for the purpose of correcting," not merely constructive in general, but conducive to the local concept of preserving God's Name.[86] R. Yitzchak Sternhill[87] observes that this is indeed the position of the Maharal elsewhere in his halakhic writings, that such erasing is permissible.[88]

Nonetheless, despite his delimited reading of the talmudic passage, the Rama earlier in his responsa[89] does allow the violation of certain prohibitions for the sake of peace.[90] The *Responsa Mitzpeh Aryeh*[91] suggests that all violations are permitted for the sake of *shalom* with the exception of those that impact on marital status. R. Chizkiyahu di Silva,[92] however, limits these leniencies to issues of convention, forbidding the abrogation of even rabbinical laws. Rashi[93] implies that that which may be done in the service of peace is that which "appears prohibited." R. David b. Zimra, the Radbaz,[94] adds that one who acts stringently in a matter of undetermined permissibility, where the general practice is to be lenient, may not do so in any public manner for fear of sowing discord. However, R. Shimon b. Tzemach Duran[95] was of the opinion that the instance in the Talmud of erasing God's Name is a unique one, biblically ordained (*gezerat hakatuv*) and particular to its own concerns; thus, no wider application may be derived, not for the

---

86. Note a similar approach in the footnote to *Responsa Eretz Tzvi*, 1:23. In general, a larger issue exists as to the permissibility of destroying holy objects for the purpose of their reconstruction or replacement, or for any other *mitzvah*; see the discussions of the *Responsa Torat Chesed* and the *Responsa Avnei Nezer* cited earlier; and *Responsa Radbaz* 596; *Responsa Rama MiPanu* 336; *Responsa Divrei Yoel* 6; R. Tzvi HaKohen Zesherovsky, *Minchat Tzvi* #437; *Responsa Sha'arei Kodesh* 1:117–8; R. Chanokh Henokh Singer, in *HaPardes*, 27:4, pp. 15–16 (24); and R. Lipman David Shovaks in the journal *Har HaMor* 8:17–21.

87. *Kokhvei Yitzchak* 1:16.

88. Note, however, his comments in *Gur Aryeh, Deuteronomy.*

89. *Responsa HaRama* 11. See also his words in *Yoreh Deah* 228:21. Note also R. Raphael Silber, *Marpei L'Nefesh* to *Bereshit*, p. 127, and the objection of R. Moshe Teitlbaum, *Yismach Moshe* to *Parshat Mishpatim*; see R. Shmaryahu Shulman, *Merish BaBirah* to *Parshat Naso.*

90. See *Kli Chemdah*, ibid.

91. *Even HaEzer* 50.

92. *Pri Chadash, Orach Chaim* 496:7.

93. *Berakhot* 54a, s.v. *V'Omer.*

94. *Responsa HaRadbaz* 4:1368.

95. *Responsa HaTashbetz* 1:2.

laws of preserving peace nor for the laws of obliterating the Divine Name. Centuries later, this claim was echoed by R. Aryeh Pomerantzik[96] who explicitly disputes the words of the Rama in his earlier responsum.

Whatever the precise specifications, halakhic decisors have manifestly incorporated this concern into their deliberations. Setting the standard is the Rambam,[97] who closes his discussion of the laws of Chanukah with these comments: "If one has yet to light the candle for his household [according to most, the *Shabbat* candles][98] and also the Chanukah candle; or the candle for his household, and kiddush for *Shabbat*, the candle of his house takes precedence, for the sake of a peaceful household (*mishum sh'lom beito*), for the Name is erased in order to make peace between a man and his wife; great is peace, for the entire Torah is given to make peace in the world, as it says, 'Its ways are ways of pleasantness, and all of its paths are peace.'"[99] Although this precedence shown to the candles of the household, based on the relationship to *sh'lom beito*, is found in the Talmud,[100] the Rambam elaborates significantly, joining the concept to that of the erasing of God's name. R. Avraham Friedlander[101] suggests that this is to indicate not merely preference to *shalom* but absolute prioritization. For example, not only should limited funds be spent on candles rather than on wine for *kiddush*, as candles represent *shalom*, but even if one has already purchased wine for *kiddush* but cannot afford candles, the wine must be sold in favor of the candles. R. Menachem Mendel Schneersohn,[102] the seventh Lubavitcher Rebbe, explains that the Rambam is not claiming that the

96. *Emek Brakhah, Issur Mechikat HaShem* 4.
97. *Mishneh Torah, Hilkhot Megillah V'Chanukah* 4:14.
98. See *Ritva* to *Shabbat* 23b, and R. Yosef Engel, *Gilyonei HaShas* citing *Responsa Halakhot K'tanot* 2:181.
99. As will be noted, this is based on a statement in the Talmud. However, many scholars observe that the Rambam's phrasing adds a dimension not necessarily contained in that text; see R. Natan Gestetner, *Responsa L'Horot Natan* 1:14; R. Yissakhar Shlomo Teichtal, *Responsa Mishnat Sakhir* 2:215; R. Ya'akov Nissan Rosenthal, *Mishnat Ya'akov*, vol. 1, pp. 39–40; and R. Yirmiyahu Leow, *Divrei Yirmiyahu, Chanukah* 4:14.
100. *Shabbat* 23b. See *Kokhvei Yitzchak* 1:1 and 1:2, at length.
101. In *Har HaMelekh* to *Hilkhot Chanukah*.
102. In the journal *HaMa'or*, vol. 50, no. 6:311.

Shabbat candles are more important than Chanukah candles or than *Kiddush*; in fact, their rabbinical origin would place them on equal or lesser footing than the latter *mitzvot*. Rather, the result of the fulfillment of this *mitzvah*, *shalom*, is more all-encompassing than the others. This is evidenced by the Rambam's concluding his words by noting that "the entire Torah is given to make peace . . ." As this is the case, showing precedence to the cause of peace is consistent with the goals of all *mitzvot*, and thus the course of action that will reap the most spiritual benefit.

This sensitivity has continued into the later generations. R. Yosef Patzanofsky[103] relates that R. Chaim of Volozhin recommended dispensing with a controversy concerning a slaughterer suspected of not properly inspecting an animal's lung, observing that inspection of the lung is a rabbinical requirement, while strife is a biblical prohibition.[104] R. Yisrael Pesach Friedlander weighs this aspect heavily in considering whether a *brit* may be held later in the day, in spite of the requirement that it be held as early as possible.[105] Preserving harmony factors heavily in several responsa of R. Ezra Basri: to allow a flagrant sinner to remain in place as cantor of a congregation;[106] to assign to a *mitzvah* performed in a contentious manner the invalid status of *mitzvah haba'ah ba'aveirah*, a commandment fulfilled through a transgression;[107] and to be factored among those elements that may justify the charging of minor forms of interest (*avak ribbit*).[108] R. Baruch HaLevi Epstein[109] suggests that even according to the rejected position in the Talmud that a Torah scholar is not permitted to waive his honor, he may do so for the purposes of peace.[110]

---

103. *Pardes Yosef*, *Leviticus* 26:3.

104. It is interesting to note that in recording this incident, R. Patzanofsky attaches it to yet another biblical verse, "I will provide peace in the land" (*Leviticus* 26:6). On that verse see Ramban; Ibn Ezra; and R. Pinchas Katz, *Ish MiBeit Levi* to *Leviticus*.

105. *Responsa Avnei Yoshpe*, *Yoreh Deah* 126.

106. *Responsa Sha'arei Ezra* 1:5.

107. Ibid., 19.

108. Ibid., 52.

109. *Torah Temimah*, *Numbers* 16:16.

110. See also *Mitzvot HaShalom*, p. 585, and R. Moshe Rosmarin, *D'var Moshe*, *Avot* 1:42.

The Talmud states[111] that one should not enter into prayer while under the influence of any of a number of improperly conducive emotions, among these anger and contentiousness. In light of this and of the previous passage, the Radbaz[112] points out that in choosing a synagogue, and a seat within the synagogue, the ability to get along with the surrounding congregants must be taken seriously into account.[113] He even goes as far as to consider, although prefacing with an apprehensive *lulei d'mistafina*, "were that I were not afraid," that praying at home without a *minyan* is preferable to joining one that will lead to an experience of disharmony. R. Yehoshua Tzvi Michel Shapiro[114] endorses the overall concept, while disagreeing with the last detail; he infers that this is also the position of R. Yonatan Eibshutz[115] and assumes that the Radbaz, too, would agree for practical purposes.

V. The Peacemaker

As has been noted, peace is not only maintained by force of prohibition but is also to be actively promoted. The *Sefer Mitzvot Katan*[116] includes making peace between people as part of his definition of the commandment of loving one's fellow; the *Mishnah*[117] assumes it to be a basic act of kindness. The role of peacemaker is an exceedingly valuable one. In this light, R. Shammai Kehat Gross[118] observes that by rights, one who fulfills this role should be paid; however, since this is not the custom, no such remuneration can be expected. Earlier authorities consider the possibility of pronouncing a blessing on performing this function.[119] The call to serve this function is a universal one, extending

---

111. *Berakhot* 30b.

112. *Responsa Radbaz* 3:472.

113. See also R. Betzalel Stern, *Responsa B'Tzel HaChokhmah* 4:19:7, citing *Mesadder Chillukim V'Shittot* 53.

114. *Kuntres Imrot T'horot*, ch. 12.

115. Comments printed in *Sefer Halakhah Achronah* and *Kuntres Hara'ayot* in *Sefer HaPardes*, p. 8b.

116. Number 8, see *Mitzvot HaShalom*, pp. 545–559, where peacemaking as a commandment is discussed at length.

117. *Peah* 1:1.

118. *Responsa Shevet HaKehati* 3:310.

119. See *Responsa HaMeyuchasot L'Ramban*, 169 and *Abudraham, sha'ar* 3; see *Mitzvot HaShalom*, p. 551.

beyond the Jewish community. Rabbeinu Yonah[120] recommends that every town take the measure of appointing individuals entrusted with the role of peacemaking, sensitive people schooled and talented in the art of appeasement and brokering reconciliation.[121]

VI. The Prohibition of Lo Titgod'du

Another prohibition that bears relevance to the maintenance of communal harmony is that of *lo titgod'du*, "you shall not cut yourselves [in anguish over a lost relative]."[122] The Talmud[123] perceives a dual meaning in this phrase,[124] referring not only to physical cutting but condemning as well the creation of *agudot agudot*, separate and distinct groups within the community.[125] Whether this is to be taken as an actual interpretation of the text, or rather a rabbinically assigned allusion (*asmachta*), is a matter of some dispute.[126] R. Tzvi Zesherovsky[127]

---

120. *Iggeret HaTeshuvah.*

121. See also R. Chaim Ozer Grodzinski, *Responsa Achiezer*, vol. 2, *Yoreh Deah* 19.

122. *Deuteronomy* 14:1.

123. *Yevamot* 14a.

124. As to the grammatical aspect of this derivation, see *Chiddushei HaRashha* to *Yevamot*, and R. Shmuel HaLevi, *Ramat Shmuel.*

125. Whether the word "groups" is used precisely, or whether perhaps even one person with divergent practices presents a problem, is the subject of a question posed to R. Yosef Chaim Sonnenfeld in *Responsa Salmat Chaim* 883. See also R. Aryeh Leib of Metz, *Turei Even*, *Megillah* 2a, in *Avnei Shoham* (and note objection of R. Yehonatan Elishberg, printed in the journal *Moriah*, nos. 239/220:305); R. Yosef Rosen, *Responsa Tzofnat Paneach* (Dvinsk 5700), *Even HaEzer* 61; and R. Shimon Gabel, *Kli Golah* to *Yevamot*. The possibility that the prohibition is directed only at those who instruct others in halachic practice is considered in R. Yisrael Yosef Bronstein, *Avnei Gazit*, pp. 332–333.

126 On the former position, see *Kessef Mishneh, Hilkhot Avodat Kokhavim* 12:14; *Responsa Me'il Tzedakah* 49; *Eishel Avraham (Pri Megadim)* 493:6; *Responsa Meishiv Davar* 3:37:5; and *Sdei Chemed, Klalim, Ma'arekhet Halamed, Klal* 78; and R. Yehudah Leow, *Gur Aryeh* to *Deuteronomy*; on the latter, *Sefer HaMitzvot L'HaRambam*, prohibition 45; *Mayim Chaim* to *Mishneh Torah*; R. Chaim Yosef David Azulai, *Sha'ar Yosef* to *Horayot* 7b; R. Eliyahu Mizrachi to *Deuteronomy*; and *Torah Temimah* to *Deuteronomy*. On both, see *Mitzvot HaShalom*, pp. 129–131; *She'erit Yosef* 4:42; R. Yisrael Yosef Bronstein, *Avnei Gazit*, pp. 324–326. R. Moshe Feinstein, *Responsa Iggerot Moshe, Orach Chaim*, vol. 4, no. 34, assumes the prohibition is biblical.

127. *Minchat Tzvi* 467.

observes that there is a thematic connection between the two prohibitions derived from this verse, self-mutilation in mourning and communal fracture. The linkage is suggested by the beginning of the verse, "You are children to the Lord your God." The Jewish people realize that as children of God, all that occurs is ultimately for the best; thus, there is no reason to grieve in a drastic, inappropriate manner.[128]

So, too, the Father of the Jewish people would be anguished by unnecessary division among His children. The latter version of the prohibition is stated in relevance to halakhic practice: "Abaye said... such as two rabbinical courts within one city, one ruling like *Beit Shammai* and one like *Beit Hillel*; . . . Rava said, like one rabbinical court in a city, half of the court ruling like *Beit Shammai* and half like *Beit Hillel*."[129]

The *rishonim* present varying perspectives on the essence of this prohibition.[130] Rashi,[131] and many others, identify the problem as giving the appearance that the Jewish people are governed by two Torahs, that each group possesses its own body of *halakhah* not shared by the other. This is problematic for several reasons, one of which is that it presents an idolatrous image. Also, as R. Shmuel Landau[132] observes, blatant divisions among Jews create a desecration of God's Name.[133] The Rambam,[134] however, seems to understand the motivation to be avoiding the conflicts that inevitably arise when separate groups are formed, at odds with each other. This is also the position of the *Sefer HaChinnukh*.[135] R. Naftali Tzvi Yehudah Berlin[136] observes that Rashi's understanding appears more consistent with the discussion in the

---

128. A similar understanding of this part of the prohibition is found in R. Yitzchak of Volozhin, *Peh Kadosh* to *Deuteronomy*.

129. As to whether or not there is a distinction between biblical and rabbinical principles in regards to this prohibition, see R. Yisrael Y. Piekarski, *Even Yisrael* to *Yevamot*.

130. See *Keren Orah*, *Yevamot* 33a, s.v. *Megillah Nikra'it*, who identifies these two positions within a disagreement in the Talmud. See also R. Yaakov Wehl, *Ikvei Aharon Pesher Davar*, *Yevamot* 6.

131. *Yevamot* 14a, s.v. *El Hatam*.

132. In his father's *Responsa Noda B'Yehudah*, *Mahadurah Tinyana*, *Yoreh Deah* 29.

133. See *Chasdei David* to *Tosefta*, *Eiruvin*, and *Mitzvot HaShalom*, p. 333.

134. *Mishneh Torah*, *Hilkhot Avodat Kokhavim* 12:14.

135. *Mitzvah* 467. See also *Responsa HaRadbaz Lil'shonot HaRambam* 27.

136. *Responsa Meishiv Davar* 1:17.

Talmud, where this objection is raised in relation to the various dates established for the reading of *Megillat Esther* in different cities. Grounded in an inherent difference in the status of the cities, this variation is unlikely to evoke controversy; however, a case could be made that it does give the appearance of two Torahs.[137]

The Ritva[138] comments on the talmudic derivation in a manner amenable to both reasons. The interpretation is suggested by the beginning of the verse: "You are children to the Lord your God." All of Israel is children to one God, as opposed to that which may be indicated by multiple Torahs, or by a divided nation.

As R. Berlin observes further, if the central concern is the appearance of two Torahs, then following the logic mentioned earlier, divergences in matters of custom should not pose a problem, as it is accepted as a matter of course that different people have different customs.[139] However, if the fear is the risk of conflict, it is an unfortunate reality that issues of custom are not immune from this danger.[140] Accordingly, the Rambam and the *Sefer HaChinnukh*, mentioned previously as proponents of the latter rationale, do apply the prohibition to issues of custom,[141] as does R. Moshe of Coucy.[142] The *Magen Avraham*[143] also appears to agree

---

137. See also R. Ya'akov Feldberger, in the journal *Am HaTorah* vol. 2, no. 7:20–25.

138. 13b, s.v. *Vi'Akati*.

139. Note also R. Berlin's comments in his *Ha'amek Davar* to *Chumash*.

140. See *Responsa Maharshdam, Yoreh Deah* 356; R. Shlomo Wahrman, *She'erit Yosef* 4:42; and the journal *HaPardes*, vol. 7 no. 64:25–27; R. Menachem Krakowski, *Avodat Melekh*, to *Hilkhot Avodat Kokhavim*; R. Avraham Erlanger, *Birkat Avraham, Pesachim*, p. 329; R. Elyakim Shlezinger, *Responsa Beit Av* 93; R. Alon Avigdor, *Adnei Paz* 29; R. Yechezkel Sarna, in *Kovetz Nehorai L'Zekher Nishmat R. Meir Kotler*, p. 91–102; R. Yaakov Aharon Rothman, *Sefer Zikkaron Beit Abba*, p. 255; R. Avraham Yeshayah Savitz, *Be'er Avraham* pp. 104–106; R. Aharon Soloveichik, *Parach Mateh Aharon, Mada*, pp. 172–173; R. Yitzchak Ralbag, in the journal *Torah Sh'b'al Peh*, vol. 41, pp. 91–95; R. Yisrael Yosef Bronstein, *Avnei Gazit*, pp. 329–332; and R. Yosef Roth, *Siach Yosef* 22. For a wide-ranging discussion of this and all aspects of the prohibition, see R. Yaakov Zev Smith in the journal *HaMetivta* 5749:235–273.

141. See also *Ohalei Tam* in *Tumat Yesharim* 170, and the Rambam's *Responsa Pe'er HaDor* 151.

142. *Sefer Mitzvot Gadol*, prohibition 62.

143. *Orach Chaim* 493.

with this position.[144] R. Naftali Tzvi Yehudah Berlin[145] observes that despite the obligation to adhere to personal custom, derived from "Do not abandon the Torah of your mother," this prohibition overwhelms that imperative.[146] This question bears great relevance to issues of communal prayer.[147]

---

144. The *Magen Avraham*'s comments are somewhat ambiguous; the above reflects the understanding of R. Moshe Sofer, *Responsa Chatam Sofer* 6:1, and R. Yitzchak Weiss, *Responsa Minchat Yitzchak* 8:57. However, see *Eishel Avraham* of the Butchatcher Rav 493; R. Netanel Weill, *Korban Netanel, Yevamot* 9:4; and R. Shalom Mordechai Shwadron, *Da'at Torah*. See also R. Shilo Raphael, in the journal *HaDarom* 20:30–32.

145. *Meromei Sadeh, Yevamot* 14a.

146. See also R. Shaul Yisraeli, "HaChiyuv Limnoa MiMachloket K'ikkaron Mancheh BiKeviut HaHalakhah," in the journal *Torah SheB'Al Peh* 23:32–38.

147. See R. David b. Zimra, *Responsa HaRadbaz* 3:474 and 534; R. Yosef Karo, *Responsa Avkat Rokhel* 32; R. Shlomo Kluger, *Responsa U'Bacharta BaChaim* 24 and *Responsa HaElef L'kha Shlomo* 45; *Responsa Meishiv Davar*; R. Ephraim Greenblatt, *Responsa Riv'vot Ephraim* 2:44; *Responsa Avnei Yoshpe* 117; R. Moshe Turetsky, *Yashiv Moshe*, p. 10 (rulings of R. Yosef Shalom Eliashiv); R. Aharon Grossman, *Responsa V'Darashta V'Chakarta*, vol. 1, *Orach Chaim* 21; and R. Moshe Tzuriel, in the journal *Sha'alei Da'at* 7:101–106. In regards to wearing *tefillin* on Chol HaMoed, about which there are differing halakhic opinions, see *Shulchan Arukh, Orach Chaim* 33:2 and Rama, *Eishel Avraham* (Buchatch) ibid.; *Responsa HaBach HaChadashot* 42; *Responsa Maharsham* 3:359; *Responsa HaAlshikh* 59; R. Chaim Yehudah Leib Litwin, *Responsa Sha'arei Deah, Tinyana* 7; R. Moshe Teitlbaum, *Responsa Heishiv Moshe* 31; R. Shmuel Leib Taback, *Responsa Teshurat Shai* 486; *Responsa Beit Yitzchak, Yoreh Deah* 2:88; *Responsa Zikhron Yehudah* 115; *Responsa Beit Lechem Yehudah* 110; R. Yissakhar Berish of Bendin, *Responsa Divrei Yissakhar* 4; R. Chaim Elazar Schapiro, *Sefer Ot Chaim V'Shalom* 31; *Responsa Menuchat Moshe* 90; R. Meir Leibush Malbim, *Artzot HaChaim* 31; R. Mordechai Ze'ev Ettinger, *Magen Giborim* 31; R. Shmuel Ehrenfeld, *Responsa Chatan Sofer* 427; R. Mordechai Winkler, *Responsa Levushei Mordechai, Tinyana, Orach Chaim* 423; R. Hillel Posek, *Responsa Hillel Omer, Orach Chaim* 320; R. Shmuel Abuhab, *Responsa D'var Shmuel* 322; R. Akiva Sofer, *Responsa Da'at Sofer*, vol. 3, *Orach Chaim* 2; R. Shimshon Morpugo, *Responsa Shemesh Tzedakah* 90:15; R. Yosef Schwartz, *Responsa Ginzei Yosef* 32:2, and in the journal *VaY'lakket Yosef: Tzofnat Pa'aneach*, p. 2; *Sefer Mishnat Chasidim*; R. Avraham Strok, *Ohr Avraham* 4; and R. Moshe Feinstein, *Responsa Iggerot Moshe, Orach Chaim*, vol. 4, no. 34 (see also no. 305:5, as well as his words in the memorial volume *Mevakshei Torah* for R. Shlomo Zalman Auerbach, vol. 2, pp. 461–5). The majority of these forbid a situation in which, in one synagogue, some wear *tefillin* on Chol Hamoed and some do not; although some are lenient. R. Moshe Shternbuch (*Responsa Teshuvot V'Hanhagot* 2:31, and note also 2:80) tends toward leniency based on his suggestion that the responsibility of *lo titgod'du* is to bring the matter before a *bet din* for final decision; as no modern court is

R. Yechiel Yaakov Weinberg, in a lengthy responsum[148] that includes a critique of R. Berlin's position, concludes that while *lo titgod'du* is indeed limited to matters of actual law, there exists an additional prohibition, specifically addressed to customs, that prohibits differentiated behavior in situations of potential strife, thus mandating adherence to *minhag hamakom*, "the custom of the place."[149] This prohibition is a formidable one that R. Weinberg gives much attention to.

Returning to *lo titgod'du*, R. Chaim Mordechai Roller[150] suggests that a distinction exists between long-standing, established customs and those more recent and less entrenched. Some authorities considered the variant customs of *Ashkenazim* and *Sefardim* to be so well-known and acknowledged as to be untouched by this prohibition.[151]

Along these lines, many *rishonim*[152] suggest that a mitigating factor present in the multiple options for *Megillah* reading is the fact that no side believes the other is acting in an incorrect or prohibited manner, rather according to a prearranged and understood differentiation. It would appear that the primary concern is thus the fear of discord; if each side recognizes the other's right to act in a different manner, this consideration is nullified. This guideline is adopted by R. Yosef Chaim Sonnenfeld in his responsa,[153] as well as by others.[154] Accordingly,

---

empowered to decisively rule on a question such as this, no prohibition pertains. For an interesting perspective on some of the basic positions see R. Ya'akov Davidson, *Hilkhot Derekh Eretz*, ch. 24. Note R. Chaim Leib of Krakow, *Chayyei Aryeh* 9, cited in *Sdei Chemed, Ma'arekhet Chol Hamoed*, #16, who does not apply the prohibition to issues of disputed halakhic ruling.

148. *Responsa Seridei Eish*, Vol. 2 (new editions), *Yoreh Deah* 11 and 12.

149. See *Pesachim* 50b–52b, and *Yerushalmi Pesachim* 4:1.

150. *Responsa Be'er Chaim Mordechai* 4.

151. Those lenient on this point include R. Mordechai Benet, *Parashat Mordechai, Orach Chaim* 4, and *Em HaRo'im, Ma'arekhet Lamed*; see R. Moshe Halberstam, *Responsa Divrei Moshe* 35. However, see also *Responsa Chatam Sofer* 6:1; *Pe'at HaShulchan, Hilkhot Eretz Yisrael* 3:32; R. Moshe Mintz, *Responsa Maharam Mintz* 15; and R. Moshe Shick, *Responsa Maharam Shick, Orach Chaim* 43. See, as, well, R. Yitzchak Hershkowitz , *Responsa Divrei Ohr* 9.

152. This position is expressed by the Ritva, *Megillah* 2a; the Rosh; the Meiri, *Yevamot* 14a; the *Maharam Galanti*, in *Divrei Mordechai, Kuntres Gedulat Mordechai* 6, cited in *Sdei Chemed*, vol. 4, p. 60.

153. *Responsa Salmat Chaim* 874–882.

154. See, for example, R. Aharon Rosenfeld, *Responsa Minchat Aharon*, vol. 2, *Hilkhot Sukkah* 88.

R. Yehudah Leib Litwin[155] and R. Yechiel Michel Epstein[156] rule that for issues that are not halakhically indispensable, this prohibition is not a concern.[157]

Similarly affected by this evaluation is a situation in which the entire population agrees to allow two modes of practice. The consensus would apparently obviate concerns of strife, but the appearance of two Torahs would still be a danger. The latter position is considered normative by some,[158] while others disagree.[159]

Further, if the issue is disharmony, it may become less problematic if one or both of the parties is unaware of the divergency. So, too, if the variation is not obvious; thus, leniency is more easily conceivable for actions done in silence.[160] R. Yehudah Lansdorfer,[161] however, forbids multiple practices in the same area even when not simultaneous to each other; apparently, his concern is more with the appearance of two Torahs. A similar position is held by R. Aryeh Leib of Metz.[162]

Of course, as R. Moshe Halberstam[163] observes, it is very possible that both proposed rationales for the prohibition are accepted as *halakhah*. If this is indeed the case, then the stringencies of both would be operative; effort must be taken to avoid any differentiation that risks either causing a conflict or giving the appearance of two Torahs.[164]

R. Halberstam's son-in-law, R. Mattisyahu Deutsch, independently adopts a similar perspective in his responsa,[165] but suggests a distinction that affects the above mentioned discussion in reference to customs.

---

155. *Sha'arei Deah* 2:7, cited in R. Yitzchak Sternhill, *Kokhvei Yitzchak* 3:7:2.

156. *Arukh HaShulchan, Orach Chaim* 551:22.

157. See also R. Avraham Shmuel of Wolkowysk, *Livnei Binyamin, Ma'arakhah* 45.

158. See R. Shneur Zalman of Liadi, *Shulchan Arukh HaRav, Orach Chaim* 493:7, and R. Elazar Kahanov, *Responsa Zikhron Betzalel* 22

159. See R. Avraham Strok, *Ohr Avraham* 4.

160. See *Responsa Meishiv Davar*; R. Yosef Shaul Nathanson, *Responsa Shoel U'Meishiv, Mahadurah Talitai* 1:247; *Yam Shel Shlomo, Yevamot* 3:10; *Responsa Avnei Nezer, Orach Chaim* 29; and *Responsa Iggerot Moshe, Orach Chaim* 2:94.

161. *Responsa Me'il Tzedakah* 50.

162. *Turei Even* to *Megillah* 19a, in *Avnei Shoham*.

163. *Responsa Divrei Moshe* 35.

164. R. Halberstam uses this reasoning to reconcile a difficulty in the rulings of the Rama (*Orach Chaim* 493:3).

165. *Responsa Netivot Adam*, 5.

Granted, adopting a dual stringency approach would forbid divergence in customs, as the risk of conflict is present, even if the "two Torahs" concern is not. However, in the case of long established customs that have become identified with a particular group, the entrenched nature of these customs will eliminate any basis for dispute. Thus, such divergence should be permitted, even within an enclosed area, as neither risk is present.

To support his point, R. Deutsch cites *Responsa Emek haTeshuvah* (112), who posits that the prohibition of *lo titgod'du* is only binding on individuals who are empowered to act differently; in other words, are not bound by any preexisting and established practice. Such a distinction would thus exempt the situation discussed by R. Deutsch.[166]

In any case, it appears that at least the Rambam, if not others, finds this prohibition to be the source for the Torah's opposition to conflict.[167] R. Avraham Sherman[168] suggests that the Rambam prefers this as a source to the aforementioned possibilities because, as interpreted by the Talmud, it indicates that the prohibition is applicable even when the quarreling centers on matters of *halakhah*. R. Moshe Weinberger[169] proposes that inherent in this prohibition is an obligation to attempt, through dialogue, a consensus that will eliminate the need for any divisions.

The multiplicity of sources offered to serve as the fundamental prohibition of disharmony, or the imperative of spreading peace, by their variation belie their true implication, which is in actuality an imposing unity of opinion. The unhesitating dedication of rabbinic thinkers toward locating the precise scriptural authority for this principle displays the almost instinctual realization that communal strife is wholly incompatible with a society defined by Torah values. In such a light, halakhic authorities, while ever cognizant of the multiple factors comprising the complexity present in all of life's challenges, continue to place these concerns at the forefront of rabbinic responsibility.

---

166. It should be noted, though, that this suggestion appears incompatible with the Netziv's words cited earlier.

167. See R. Yechezkel Sarna in *Kovetz Nehorai*, vol. 1, pp. 91–102.

168. In the journal *Ohr HaMizrach*, nos. 130/131:272–280.

169. In the journal *HaMetivta* 5756:181–185.

CHAPTER

FIVE

More than the Best Policy: Honesty

I. The Admonition Toward Honesty

Honesty, known as "the best policy," often serves as the hallmark of the respectable citizen, and its quality is frequently used interchangeably with that of all adherence to demands of social morality. Of course, within *halakhah*, truth is no less valued; indeed, it is the very "seal of God."[1] Along with peace and justice, it is one of the pillars that support the world's existence.[2]

---

1. *Shabbat* 55a; note also *Talmud Yerushalmi, Sanhedrin* 1:1. See also Maharal of Prague, *Netivot Olam, Netiv HaEmet*, ch. 2, and R. Yitzchak Hecht, *Responsa Sha'arei Kodesh* 2:75.
2. *Avot* 1:18.

The best-known biblical admonition toward honesty is phrased in a unique manner. The Torah warns,[3] "Stay far away from falsehood." While it is certainly a phrase that commands attention, this passage lacks the terminology normally utilized in formulating prohibitions.[4] This unusual element has prompted some discussion as to the precise scope of the verse. On the one hand, the strength of the language used perhaps suggests a transgression of particular severity;[5] on the other hand, the lack of a standard prohibitive phrase may be significant. In the major passage in the Talmud[6] that interprets this verse, most of the application is given to the context of courtroom proceedings; the application in general life is left unclear.[7] Other talmudic texts, however, do cite this verse in condemning general dishonesty.[8]

Many early authorities did assume a prohibition to be in effect, or at least a positive commandment to speak the truth. The *Sefer HaChinnukh*[9] interprets the verse as a prohibition and attributes its unusual language to "its great revulsion."[10] The *Yad HaK'tannah*[11] explains the talmudic discussion of courtrooms as representing an extreme violation of the injunction, and it is no less applicable in normal circumstances. Many, such as R. Moshe of Coucy,[12] assume that while the commandment is

---

3. *Exodus* 23:7.

4. While the verse "You shall not lie to one another" (*Leviticus* 19:11) is phrased as a standard prohibition, this is generally taken to refer specifically to swearing falsely in monetary manners (*Bava Kamma* 105b). See, however, R. Shneur Zalman Dov Anusishky, *Responsa Matzav HaYosher* 6, who notes that "a verse cannot leave its simple interpretation," and thus a general injunction against lying must be included here as well.

5. See, for example, *Sefat Emet al haTorah*, *Shoftim*, 5639; note the comments of R. Mordechai Babad, *Minchat Machvat* 2:35.

6. *Shevuot* 31b.

7. See, for example, R. Ya'akov Ariel, *Responsa B'Ohalah Shel Torah*, vol. 1, *Even haEzer* 79:4.

8. *Yevamot* 65b, *Ketubot* 17a, *Tanna D'Bei Eliyahu*, ch. 3. R. Yaakov Emden, *Sh'eilat Ya'avetz* 1:5, apparently considers this evidence conclusive.

9. *Mitzvah* 74.

10. See also *Pele Yoetz* ("*sheker*"); *Mesilat Yesharim* (ch. 11); and *Piskei Teshuvot* (Vol. 6, p. 325).

11. *Deiot*, ch. 10. See also R. Naftali Tzvi Yehudah Berlin, *Harchev Davar* to *Exodus*.

12. *Sefer Mitzvot Gadol*, positive commandment 107; see also R. Moshe Chaim of Klein-Varden, *Brit Moshe* to *Sefer Mitzvot Gadol*. It should be noted that some

indeed biblical and does refer to a private citizen telling the truth, this takes the form of a positive imperative rather than a prohibition.[13] In nonlitigious contexts, the source prohibiting lying is cited by many as a verse in *Psalms*,[14] "The speaker of falsehoods shall not stand before my eyes."[15] The non-Pentateuchal level of authority may become the basis for leniency in those instances when lying is permitted.

Whatever the precise nature of command, most of these authorities emphasize that false statements are unacceptable in all forms, even those that may be considered harmless, in that no other individual is affected in a negative way by the dishonesty.[16] One notable exception to this group is R. Eliezer of Metz,[17] who does focus the prohibition on those lies that impact negatively on other people.[18] Nonetheless, R. Avraham Abba Schiff[19] observes that even R. Eliezer of Metz would acknowledge that all dishonesty is prohibited at least on a rabbinical level. However,

---

room exists to question whether the *Sefer Mitzvot Gadol* indeed focuses on the private citizen or on the courtroom; see R. Ezriel Cziment, *Mitzvot HaMelekh*, positive commandment 177, and R. Yerucham Perlow's commentary to *Sefer HaMitzvot* of R. Sa'adiah Gaon, vol. I, p. 156:3. See also, in the journal *VaY'lakket Yosef*, vol. 6: R. Akiva Lindenfeld, 2; R. Moshe Kenig, 46; and R. Asher Anschel Jungreiss, 21, and in the footnote.

13. See also *Sefer Mitzvot Katan* 227; *Sefer Charedim, Mitzvot HaTeloyot BaPeh*; *Zohar Harakia*; *Sefer Chasidim* 1060; Rabbeinu Yonah, *Avot* 1:8 (although he understands the specific source differently), and note the implications of *Shulchan Arukh, Yoreh Deah* 402:12 and *Responsa HaRama* 11. See also R. Hillel David Litwack, *MiDvar Sheker Tirchak*, pp. 42–43, and note his citations of *Ma'alot HaMidot, Ma'alat Hatemimut*; R. Yehudah Rosanes, *Derekh Mitzvotekha*, pt. 2; R. Moshe Chaim Lutzatto, *Mesilat Yesharim* 11; R. Yisrael Meir Kagan, *Chafetz Chaim, Petichah*, Esi'in 13; R. Ya'akov Etlinger, *Arukh L'Neir* to *Yevamot* 65b; R. Ya'akov Emden, *Chiddushim* to *Gittin* 14a; and R. Ya'akov Gesuntheit, *Tiferet Ya'akov* to *Chullin* 94a.

14. 101:7; see *Sotah* 42a.

15. See R. Moshe Troyesh, *Orach Meisharim*, p. 67.

16. Note R. Ya'akov Greenwald, in *VaY'lakket Yosef* 6:56.

17. *Sefer Yereim* 235. Note R. Aharon Walkin, *Saviv LiRe'av* to *Sefer Yereim*.

18. An analysis of this position by R. Yehoshua Ehrenberg can be found in *Responsa D'var Yehoshua*, vol. 1, *mafteichot v'hosafot* 19. As R. Ehrenberg observes, the passage in *Ketubot* that R. Emden endorses is reflective of the opinion of *Beit Shammai*, whose view is not accepted; and the normative opinion of *Beit Hillel* is presented in *Massekhet Kallah Rabati* (ch. 10) in a manner supportive of the view of R. Eliezer of Metz.

19. *Toafot Re'em* to *Sefer Yereim*. Note also the somewhat unclear comments of R. Shmuel Zanvill Zotler, in *VaY'lakket Yosef*, 6:113.

R. Yerucham Fishel Perlow,[20] a proponent of this more restricted, victim-based understanding, questions the existence of even a rabbinical injunction.[21] Rather, such lying is to be considered a "repugnant trait" (*middah megunah*).

II. The Nature of the Prohibition of Dishonesty

In order to understand the scope of the prohibition in regards to this issue, it may be relevant to consider the nature of the transgression. Many authorities[22] observe that there seem to be two views one can take toward this injunction. From one perspective, the concept can be understood to be primarily a function of personal character; that is to say, that dishonesty is generally inconsistent with a genuine religious personality.[23] In this light, the focus is not the offense committed against another individual when one is not honest, but rather the inner corruption irrelevant to any harmful effects. In this spirit, one can understand the language of *tirchak*, "stay far away"; rather than being geared toward a specific act of lying, the message is that dishonesty is extremely harmful to the soul, in and of itself. In fact, R. Eliezer Friedman[24] suggests that *tirchak* requires avoiding being one who hears lies, not just avoiding being the one who tells them. Conversely, it might be possible to suggest that if this is the case, damage that another person incurs through lack of full disclosure, but without being actually lied to, will be the domain of many other prohibitions, but not this one. Nonetheless, even within this understanding, it is still just as possible that all manners of deception, no matter how indirect, are included within this commandment.[25] So, too, as a matter of personal integrity,

---

20. Commentary to *Sefer HaMitzvot* of R. Sa'adiah Gaon, positive commandment 22.

21. See also R. Avraham Erlanger, *Ma'or HaSha'ar* 3:181.

22. See, for example, R. Eliezer Yehudah Waldenberg, *Responsa Tzitz Eliezer* 15:12; R. Shimon Gabel, *Kli Golah* to *Gittin* 14a and *Sofrei Shimon* to *Berakhot* 43b; R. Aharon Yosef Rosen, *Iyyim BaYam* to *Ketubot* 21; and, at great length, *Responsa Matzav HaYosher* 5 and 6.

23. See *Sukkah* 46b, where honesty is dealt with in reference to setting an example for one's children; see also R. Yosef Chaim Sonnenfeld, *Responsa Salmat Chaim* 847, and R. Kenig in *VaY'lakket Yosef*.

24. *Ateret Yirmiyahu* to *Exodus*.

25. See R. A. Chenakh Leibowits, *Chiddushei HaLev* to *Exodus*.

it makes no difference who is the one being lied to; any false statement will impinge on this commandment.[26] Thus, even a lie spoken as a joke, with innocent intentions, may still be forbidden, provided actual deception is occurring and the truth is not self-evident.[27]

Alternatively, the prohibition could be understood primarily in light of the interpersonal crime, warning against hurting another individual through dishonesty. If that is the case, then the actual expression of a false statement, as opposed to a mere omission of the truth or the like, is of little consequence. As long as an individual has been harmed by a diminished exposure to the truth, this prohibition has been transgressed. Indeed, one is forbidden not only to report falsely on the past or the present, but even making a neutral statement about the future, if the speaker has no plans to fulfill its content, is forbidden.[28] According to the Ramban and R. Zerachiah HaLevi, this is derived as well from "stay far away from falsehood."[29]

An issue that may be affected by determining the nature of the offense is the question of whether it is possible to reverse the violation of the falsehood prohibition. If one assumes that the sin is one of poor character traits, and the very utterance of a lie is thus forbidden, then it might be suggested that telling the truth afterward does little to repair the damage. However, if the offense is defined as a crime against another person who is misled, correcting the false impression may indeed nullify the violation, as R. Shammai Kehat Gross writes.[30] In either event, it is understood that one is obligated to inform an individual one has lied to of the truth.

Thus, the appearance of the word *tirchak* in the biblical verse has prompted many theories as to its practical significance. If, as it seems, the intent is to either go beyond or fall short of the standard prohibition

---

26. See *Sofrei Shimon*; however, see also R. Meir Dan Plotzki, *Kli Chemdah* to *Parshat Yitro*.

27. See R. Yisrael Meir Kagan, *Sefat Tamim*, and R. H. D. Litwack, *MiD'var Sheker Tirchak*, pp. 46–47. Note also R. Aharon Grossman, *Shut V'Darashta V'Chakarta*, vol 3, *Yoreh Deah* 49.

28. *Bava Metzia* 49a.

29. See also *Sefat Tamim*, ch. 6.

30. *Responsa Shevet HaKehati* 3:299. See also *Titten Emet L'Ya'akov, Responsa* 52.

that would have been indicated by a formulation such as "do not lie," it consequently becomes necessary to determine the intent and parameters of such language. To begin with, the Talmud, speaking in a courtroom context, describes twelve practices designed to insure complete honesty within the proceedings, all of which are traced to this verse.

One measure of the extra severity the phrase may connote is suggested by the *Orchot Tzaddikim*.[31] It is not enough merely not to lie; rather, one must take extra action to ensure that one does not speak falsehood even inadvertently. Therefore, one should put his dealings into writing, so that the records will prevent even accidental misstatements.

Along these lines is a discussion as to undetermined situations (*safek*). Normally, when dealing with a biblical prohibition, one must act stringently if one is not in possession of all the facts necessary to ascertain the proper course of action.[32] However, according to the Rambam, this is in itself a rabbinical concept, and on a biblical level, prohibitions apply only in situations in which the violation is definite.[33] Nonetheless, the Munczaczer Rebbe, R. Chaim Elazar Schapiro,[34] as well as R. Baruch Frankel-Teomim,[35] writes that when it comes to falsehood, the unique phrasing of the verse suggests that one take care that even an undetermined situation be avoided if falsehood is a possibility.[36]

R. Zalman Sorotzkin[37] suggests that the word *tirchak* is added in recognition of the fact that for certain purposes, such as the spreading of peace, one is permitted to alter the truth. Nonetheless, the objectionability of dishonesty makes such an eventuality highly undesirable. Thus, the Torah recommends that one "stay away," that is, strive to avoid a situation that will make falsehood necessary, even though, in such a situation, it then becomes tolerated. Further, if such a situation

---

31. *Sha'ar HaEmet.*
32. *Avodah Zarah* 7a.
33. The Rambam's position is evident from several places in his *Mishneh Torah*; see *Shev Shmat'ta* 1. For a book-length treatment of this topic, see R. Avraham Binyamin Veiroshab, *Ahavat Avraham.*
34. *Responsa Minchat Elazar* 3:18.
35. *Hagahot* to *Turei Even, Megillah* 20.
36. See also *Kokhvei Yitzchak*, vol. 2, *Kuntres Acharon* 19.
37. *Oznayim L'Torah* to *Exodus.*

arises, one should then make an effort to minimize the falsehood to whatever extent possible.[38]

One manner in which the responsibility for honesty is greater than one may assume is found in the writings of R. Yehudah HaChasid.[39] One may feel that one is honest if one represents the truth to the best of one's knowledge. Nonetheless, one should not make statements such as "Go to so-and-so and he'll tell you as I have said." As the response of the other person is not in one's control, one cannot say with confidence that this is the case, even though one's experience may strongly indicate that it is so. R. Reuven Margolios[40] supports this assertion with a similar concept found in the *Shulhan Arukh*.[41]

Similarly, R. Yehudah HaChasid[42] notes an increased sensitivity toward evoking falsehood in others. To this end, he recommends that if an individual is found in low spirits and gives no indication he wishes to share his troubles, he should not be pressed on the issue, as he will feel compelled to provide a false explanation. Along these lines, R. Moshe Sofer[43] writes that although actions that are causative rather than direct (*grama*) are normally exempt from penalty on a biblical level, the word *tirchak* makes falsehood an exception to this rule.

Thus, the vast majority of authorities assume that dishonesty is prohibited not only in speech but in writing as well.[44] This seems to be

---

38. For more on this, see chapter VI.

39. *Sefer Chasidim* 1060.

40. *Mekor Chesed* to *Sefer Chasidim*.

41. *Yoreh Deah* 215:3; see *Siftei Kohen*, citing *Bayit Chadash*.

42. *Sefer Chasidim* 1062.

43. *Responsa Chatam Sofer, Even HaEzer* 20.

44. This is related somewhat to a larger question, throughout *halakhah*, as to the equation, or lack of equation, of written words to speech (*k'tivah k'dibbur*). On this, see R. Akiva Eiger, *Responsa* 29–32; R. Moshe Sofer, *Responsa Chatam Sofer* 6:19; R. Avraham Shmuel Binyamin Sofer, *Responsa K'tav Sofer, Yoreh Deah* 106 and 136; R. Shimon (Eiger) Sofer, *Responsa Hitor'rut Teshuvah*, in several places; R. Shmuel Engel, *Responsa Maharash Engel*, vol. 1, *Yoreh Deah* 61; *Responsa Divrei Malkiel* 6:60; R. Avraham Yehuda Schwartz, *Responsa Kol Aryeh, Orach Chaim* 11; R. Baruch Epstein, *Torah Temimah, Exodus* 18:7, *Numbers* 5:121, *Deuteronomy* 21:144 and 25:135; R. Yoav Yehoshua Weingarten, *Responsa Chelkat Yoav*, vol. 1, *Mahadurah Tinyana* 19; R. Shlomo Heiman, *Chiddushim, Hosafot Chadashot* 2; R. David Sikili, *Responsa Kiryat Chanah David*, vol. 1; R. Chaim Mordechai

clearly implied or stated in *Tosafot*[45] and R. Meir HaLevi's *Yad Ramah*.[46] Nonetheless, there exists a small minority of those who feel that the specific prohibition is focused on speech, largely based on a comment of R. Shmuel Eidels (known as the Maharsha).[47] However, many authorities[48] emphasize that the Maharsha's comments were made only in the context of something that gives a misleading impression (*mechzi k'shikra*) rather than outright dishonesty. Thus, no extrapolations toward lying in writing may be made and such behavior is forbidden.

Along these lines, R. Yehudah HaChasid[49] writes that even a nodding or shaking of the head in a manner that creates a false impression is prohibited.[50] He traces this actually to a different verse,[51] "You shall have correct scales, correct weights, correct dry measure, and correct liquid measures." The last term, in Hebrew, is *hin tzedek*; the Talmud[52] reads

---

Ya'akov Gottlieb, *Responsa Yagel Ya'akov, Orach Chaim* 10; R. Yosef Chaim Sonnenfeld, *Responsa Salmat Chaim* 49; R. Natan Gestetner, *Responsa L'Horot Natan* 7:77; R. Shlomo Gross, *Responsa Mishnah Shleimah* 560; *Responsa Halakhah L'Moshe* 2:106; R. Yosef Nechemiah Kernitzer, *Chiddushei R. Yosef Nechemiah* 70; R. Yechiel Michel Leiter, *Responsa Darkhei Shalom* 19; R. Menachem Mendel Schneebalg, *Responsa Siftei Ani* 115; R. Moshe Natan Nota Lemberger, *Responsa Ateret Moshe* 204; R. Yerucham Ciecanowirz, *Responsa Torat Yerucham* 1:15; R. Simchah Elberg, *Shalmei Simchah* 1:61; R. Shraga Feivel Shneebalg, *Responsa Shraga HaMeir* 8:20:3; R. Moshe Shternbuch, *Responsa Teshuvot V'Hanhagot* 2:40; R. Avraham Yafe-Shlesinger, *Responsa Be'er Sarim* 252:1; R. Shmuel Greenberger, *Responsa Merkachat Besamim* 17; R. Avraham Binyamin Silverberg, *Responsa Mishnat Binyamin* 58; R. Shammai Kehat Gross, *Responsa Shevet HaKehati*, vol. 1, and 3:248; and R. Menachem Genack, in the journal *Ohr HaMizrach*, 48:1/2, pp. 28–31.

45. *Bava Batra* 94b, s.v. *Hakhi* and *Megillah* 9a, s.v. *Vayishlach*.

46. *Bava Batra* 172a, s.v. *Amar Lehu*. See R. Litwack, p. 46.

47. *Chiddushei Aggadot LaMaharsha, Bava Batra* 15. See his citation in R. Shalom Mordechai HaKohen's *Da'at Torah, Orach Chaim* 156; see also *Sefer HaMidot* of R. Nachman of Breslov, *Emet* 5 (compare, however, *Ha'arot* of R. Natan of Breslov). For an innovative interpretation of the Maharsha's comments, see R. Yitzchak Sternhill, *Kokhvei Yitzchak* 3:2:8 and 9.

48. *Sefer Chasidim* 47 and 1058.

49. See R. Meir Dan Plotzki, *Kli Chemdah, Parshat V'Zot HaB'rakhah*; *Titten Emet L'Yaakov* 8; *Responsa Tzitz Eliezer*, ibid.; and *Sofrei Shimon* to *Berakhot*. See also R. Yehudah Assad, *Responsa Yehudah Ya'aleh, Yoreh Deah* 316.

50. Note a similar comment in R. Elchanan Wasserman, *Kovetz Shiurim*, vol. 2, *Mikhtavim*, p. 84.

51. *Leviticus* 19:36

52. *Bava Metzia* 49a.

this into Aramaic as *hein tzedek,* or "correct yes," thus declaring, "Your 'yes' must be correct, and your 'no' must be correct." Nonetheless, R. Chaim Yosef David Azulai[53] questions the application of this passage to nonverbal communication. To this end, R. Reuven Margolios[54] adduces evidence from the Talmud[55] and *Shulchan Arukh*[56] toward the principle *remiza k'dibbur,* or "indicating is as speech."[57] Nonetheless, this may not be necessary if one assumes all manners of conveying falsehoods to be by definition included in the relevant prohibitions.

In sum, Rabbeinu Yonah[58] lists nine categories of perpetrators of prohibited falsehood, some of which appear in similar listings of the Rambam[59] and the *Yad HaK'tannah,*[60] who offer somewhat different groupings. This list includes: (1) one who through dishonesty causes a financial loss to another, primarily represented by swearing falsely in court; (2) a falsehood that does not directly harm another, but creates a situation in which this is likely, such as dishonestly drawing a person into confidence; (3) one who does not actually cause another's money to be lost, but take steps that will prevent another from profiting appropriately; (4) one who relates events in an inaccurate or false manner, but on a topic that will not impact negatively on the listener in any way; (5) one who makes a promise to another, with the intent of reneging; (6) one who promises sincerely, but later does not live up to his commitments;[61] (7) one who unjustly tries to secure the gratitude or good opinion of another (*geneivat da'at*);[62] (8) similar to the last item,[63] one who takes

---

53. *Brit Olam* to *Sefer Chasidim.*

54. *Mekor Chesed* to *Sefer Chasidim.*

55. *Yerushalmi, Gittin* 7:1.

56. *Orach Chaim* 307:22 and *Choshen Mishpat* 235.

57. See also R. Yosef Engel, *Gilyonei HaShas* to *Yerushalmi, Moed* 128.

58. *Sha'arei Teshuvah, Sha'ar* 3:178–186. See R. Avraham Y. Ehrman, *Kodesh Yisrael* #24, for a lengthy analysis of these categories consistent with the above discussion.

59. *Peirush HaMishnayot* to *Pirkei Avot.*

60. *Deiot,* ch. 10.

61. See *Bava Metzia* 49a; *Yerushalmi, Bava Metzia* 2:2; *Yoreh Deah* 258:12. See also R. Moshe Karelitz, *Ohr Chadash* to *Sha'arei Teshuvah.*

62. See *Chullin* 94a. See also *Mishneh Torah, Hilkhot Deiot* 2:6 and *Peirush Mishnayot* to *Keilim* 2:7. See *Zeh HaSha'ar.*

63. On the difference between the two, see *Ma'or HaSha'ar.*

praise for qualities not actually possessed; and (9) similar to item number 4, but the speaker gets some pleasure out of his dishonesty, though in a nonmonetary fashion.[64]

Integrity of speech, action, and attitude stands at the forefront on the list of attributes of the committed citizen and certainly the devoted Jew. While the challenges to honesty come in multiple forms, the call to resist these challenges is constant and emblematic of the halakhic ideal. It behooves every Jew to spare no effort in ensuring that all his words and deeds are stamped with "the seal of God."

---

64. On the issue of number 9 being considered more excusable than number 4, see R. Shmuel David Katz Friedman, *Milei D'Chasiduta*, p. 37.

SIX

Not to Be Brutally Honest: Lying for the Sake of Peace

I. Talmudically Endorsed Falsehoods

The inability of human beings to dictate the circumstances of their lives must inevitably lead, on occasion, to an irreconcilable clash between even the most resolutely respected principles. While truth, "the seal of God,"[1] stands at the inviolate center of the Jewish value system, the necessities of a peaceful existence often challenge a total adherence to this ideal. The Talmud's cognizance of this reality is revealed by a passage dealing, initially, with the brothers of Yosef.[2] The brothers, fearing Yosef's revenge for having sold him into slavery many years earlier, now

---

1. *Shabbat* 55a.
2. *Yevamot* 65b.

that their father Ya'akov had passed away, tell him that their father had instructed him to forgive them.[3] This was not actually the truth, yet the Talmud sanctions their behavior. "R. Ilai says in the name of R. Elazar ben R. Shimon, it is permitted to alter the truth for the sake of peace."

This powerful notion is then taken even further. "R. Natan says, it is a *mitzvah* to do so." The source for this is a story concerning the prophet Shmuel, sent to anoint David as king over Israel. Shmuel is aware of the negative reaction this will evoke in King Shaul, and after inquiring about this, is instructed by God to claim that he is actually on his way to bring a sacrifice.[4] R. Yaakov Etlinger[5] observes that this would seem actually to be a case of preservation of life, as Shmuel had put it, "How can I go? Shaul will hear and will kill me." If that was the case, it is an already established principle that almost all precepts of the Torah, including certainly the injunction against lying, may be violated to save a life. He suggests that Shmuel was not in any physical danger, because "messengers performing a *mitzvah* are not harmed,"[6] as the Ritva observes. R. Moshe Troyesh advances this concept in a fascinating manner in his *Orach Meisharim*. Shmuel had no reason to fear for his life, for certainly God, having specifically sent him on this mission, would protect his life. However, God's manner is not to interfere with human emotions, and therefore Shaul's disgruntlement was inevitable. It was thus only for the purpose of preserving peace that God commanded Shmuel to lie. R. Yechiel Moshe Epstein[7] takes a different approach, which perhaps further emphasizes the message. True, God could have intervened to save Shmuel's life; nonetheless, He specifically chose this method in order to teach that it is appropriate to lie for the sake of peace.

---

3. *Genesis* 50:16–17.

4. *1 Samuel* 16:2.

5. *Arukh L'Neir* to Yevamot.

6. *Pesachim* 8a. The assumption is that the opinion of R. Nehorai (*Nazir* 66a) is authoritative, that this principle is applicable even in the instance of a significant likelihood of danger (*shekhiach hezeika*). See R. Yisrael Meir Lau, *Responsa Yachel Yisrael* 1:39. Going in a different direction, see R. Shlomo Zalman Braun, *Shearim Metzuyanim B'Halakhah* to *Yevamot*.

7. *Be'er Moshe* to *Samuel* (p. 357).

The Talmud concludes by going one level further. Having been told first that it is permissible to lie to preserve peace, and then that it is required, we then read, "The house of R. Yishmael taught, great is peace, for even the Holy One, blessed be He, changed the truth for it." The reference is to Sarah's comment, after hearing that she would have a child, that this was unlikely, as her husband Avraham was elderly.[8] In relating the discussion to Avraham, God only reported that Sarah was skeptical because of her own advanced age.[9]

II. Theories Explaining the Dispensation

The Rama, in his responsa (number 11), discusses these ideas. In his view, this passage is merely reflective of a host of examples of instances in which we are permitted to compromise religious values for the sake of peace. The prohibition of "keep far away from falsehood,"[10] formidable as it indeed is, must bow to the cause of harmony.[11]

In analyzing the issue, many authorities[12] observe that there seem to exist at least two possible methods of explaining these concepts, one of which is represented by the Rama's words. The verse in the book of Zechariah (8:19) identifies two of the pillars of God's world: "And truth and peace are beloved." It appears that these two values are equivalent, sharing jointly the role of ultimate ideals. In the event of an irreconcilable conflict, one of these must be sacrificed. This is consistent with the Rama's discussion: in order to uphold peace, truth at times must be jettisoned.[13] The first Lubavitcher Rebbe, R. Shneur Zalman of Liady,[14]

---

8. *Genesis* 18:12.

9. *Genesis* 18:13.

10. *Exodus* 23:7.

11. See also R. Moshe Teitlbaum, *Yismach Moshe, Parashat Kedoshim*, and R. Shmaryahu Shulman, *Merish BaBirah, Parshat Naso*.

12. See, for example, R. Joseph Epstein, *Mitzvot HaShalom*, pp. 570–579; R. Aharon Yosef Rosen, *Iyyim BaYam* to *Ketubot* 2:1; R. Yehoshua Ehrenberg, *Responsa D'var Yeshoshua*, vol. 1, *mafteichot v'hosafot* 19.and R. Yisrael Meir Lau, *Responsa Yachel Yisrael* 1:39 (also printed in the journal *Torah SheB'Al Peh* 21:88–100).

13. See also R. Meir Dan Plotzky, *Kli Chemdah, Parshat Metzora* 1.

14. *Shulchan Arukh HaRav* 156:2.

writes, basing himself on the *Midrash*'s[15] interpretation of a verse,[16] "Since peace is greater than all the commandments . . . it was permitted to alter the truth for the sake of peace."

However, it may be possible that another explanation exists. It may be that the prohibition of engaging in falsehood is defined to a certain extent by the intent of the speaker. Lying, as forbidden in the Torah, would thus refer to that falsehood that is perpetrated for the purposes of achieving some personal gain at the expense of honesty. If, alternatively, one's aim is the venerable search for peace, this falsehood may never have fallen within the realm of the Torah's injunction. Thus, the previously mentioned comments of the Talmud are to be taken to mean that when one alters the truth in the pursuit of harmony, his actions do not bear the stigma of *sheker*, of falsehood, in the eyes of the *halakhah*. In fact, R. Eliezer of Metz[17] was of the opinion that the only type of falsehood prohibited by the biblical verse is that which results in harm to another.[18]

R. Avraham Weinfeld, author of *Responsa Lev Avraham*, feels strongly that this is the case, and suggests that even the above-cited words of the Rama are mistakenly attributed to him and are in reality the words of his questioner. He thus rules that one who has spread malicious, but true, information about another, in violation of the prohibition of lashon hara, is permitted and actually obligated to lie in order to mitigate the effects of his transgression.[19] Joseph D. Epstein[20] suggests an even more direct formulation. The prohibition of falsehood is rooted in its destructive impact; when the intent is to preserve harmony, the action is the complete opposite of the prohibition.[21]

---

15. *Midrash Rabbah, Chukkat* 19:27.

16. *Psalms* 34:15

17. *Sefer Yereim* 235.

18. See also R. Yitzchak Shmelkes, *Beit Yitzchak al HaTorah, Parshat B'ha'alotekha* 144, and R. Shmuel Zanvil Zotler, in the journal *VaY'lakket Yosef*, vol. 5., #113.

19. Published in the journal *Torat HaAdam L'Adam*, vol. 5, pp. 142–146.

20. *Mitzvot HaShalom*, p. 579.

21. See also R. Ya'akov Ariel, *Responsa B'Ohalah Shel Torah*, vol. 1, *Even haEzer* 79:4.

The Ritva states as much, commenting on the well-known position of *Beit Hillel* that one should compliment the beauty of a bride regardless of empirical evidence to the contrary.[22] The comparison is offered: "One who has made a purchase at the market, should the other praise the merchandise in front of him, or criticize it in front of him?"[23] The Ritva explains the relevance, noting that "whatever is done for the methods of peace (*darkhei shalom*), the prohibition 'keep far away from falsehood' does not apply to this." This is, indeed, a quite tenable reading of the Talmud's intent. *Beit Hillel's* ruling is objected to by *Beit Shammai* on the strength of "keep far away from falsehood," to which the marketplace reference is a response, ending with the advice, "One's opinion should always be palatable to the populace."[24] The implication is that the prohibition of falsehood has been deemed irrelevant in this instance.[25] The alternate viewpoint is expressed by R. Yeshayahu Horowitz,[26] who writes, "If it is possible to create a situation where the other party will be appeased without deception, then 'keep far away from falsehood.'"

III. Dispensation or Obligation?

In this vein, one could explain two of the points of view presented in the Talmud, assuming they are at odds with each other. Is the alteration of truth in the service of peace an option, or an actual obligation? If the first possibility just described is correct, it can be understood that this notion represents a permissible option rather than a mandatory course

---

22. *Ketubot* 16b.

23. See the discussion of R. Yitzchak Menachem in the journal *Ohr Torah*, vol. 28, p. 46.

24. Rashi comments, "to do to every individual as that individual wishes." The Rambam codifies this in *Mishneh Torah, Hilkhot Deiot* 6:1 and *Hilkhot Yesodei HaTorah* 5:11. R. Avraham Yitzchak HaKohen Kook (*Tov Roei* to *Ketubot* 17a) derives from the Rambam's language that this is an aspect of sanctification of God's Name.

25. See, however, *Turei Zahav, Even HaEzer* 65:1, who understands the comparison as a reflection on human speech patterns, adduced to indicate that in such situations general language is often used, and thus the comments at the wedding are not to be taken as actually false, merely non-specific.

26. *Shnei Luchot HaBrit, Amud HaShalom*, p. 15:4; see *Orchot Tzaddikim, Sha'ar Sheker*, and R. Yosef Avraham Heller, *Shalom Yihyeh*, ch. 13.

of action. Truth and peace are to be taken as equals, as the verse in *Zechariah* indicates, and when they clash irreconcilably, one must bow to the other.[27] By necessity, one or the other must be given precedence. "It is permitted to alter the truth for the sake of peace," and thus choose harmony as the prevalent ideal, but it is also permissible not to, ascribing priority instead to truth.

Alternatively, if the prohibition of *sheker* is not applicable to one who is bending the boundaries of honesty in the pursuit of peace, then such alterations must be understood as compulsory and not optional. If the injunction against lying is not in effect, then there can be no excuse for being lax in bringing about peace. Only one choice remains: "It is a *mitzvah* to do so."

The *rishonim* apparently took sides on whether this is to be viewed as mandatory or optional. The Talmud[28] states that one of the qualities of a rabbinical scholar is that he is expected to be resolutely honest in all things. However, there are three areas in which he is permitted to fudge the truth without damaging this reputation.[29] These are listed as modestly denying knowledge of a specific talmudic tractate;[30] preserving the privacy of the marital relationship;[31] and concealing the identity of one

---

27. As to which should ideally take preference, truth or peace, see R. Moshe Shick, *Maharam Shick al Pirkei Avot*, who comments that the *Mishnah* (1:18), which states, "Rabban Shimon b. Gamliel says, the world stands on three things, on truth, on justice, and on peace," is worded in order of priority; see also R. Yisrael Shepansky, *Ohr HaMizrach* 15:51, who advances the argument against this position. Along those lines, the *Iyyim BaYam* quotes a Chasidic insight (which is also noted by R. Zalman Sorotzkin, *Oznayim LaTorah*, *Genesis* 50:15): Truth is the seal of God (*Shabbat* 55a), but *Shalom* is the Name of God (*Shabbat* 10a); the seal is representational, while the name actually descriptive. See also R. Chaim David HaLevi, *Aseh L'kha Rav* 4:62 (Also printed in the journal *Shma'atin* 102:29–40).

28. *Bava Metzia* 23b.

29. See, at length, R. Hillel D. Litwack, *MiDvar Sheker Tirchak*, pp. 57–63. As to whether or not only scholars are allowed these dispensations, see R. Ya'akov Yechizkiyah Fish, *Titten Emet L'Ya'akov*, *Responsa* 1.

30. This follows Rashi's interpretation of what is meant by usage of the word *masekhet*. See also *Sefer Chasidim* 1061. On the general issue of lying for the sake of modesty, see *Titten Emet L'Ya'akov*, *Responsa* 12. Note also the dispute between the *Taz* and the *Magen Avraham* concerning one who piously adopts a voluntary fast, and wishes to deny it to others; see the treatment of this topic in R. Chaim Shlomo Abrahams, *Birkhat Shlomo* 42.

31. Again, Rashi's reading or the word *puraya*; see Maharsha for a completely different interpretation.

who has provided him with hospitality, so that that individual not be besieged with requests.[32] The *Nimmukei Yosef*[33] questions the absence of the pursuit of peace among this list. He explains, in the name of the Rif, that the topic of this passage is only those areas in which a scholar has the option to distort the truth if he wishes. Dishonesty for the sake of harmony does not belong here, because that is an obligation and not merely discretionary, says the Rif, citing R. Natan's aforementioned position.[34] The Rosh, in his code,[35] also cites all the positions in the Talmud, apparently allowing R. Natan's opinion to be viewed as conclusive.

However, this does not appear to be the position of the Rambam. In his *Mishneh Torah*[36] he records the exemptions from the scholar's requirements of honesty related in the Talmud, and with this he lists the pursuit of peace. Concerning all four of them, he writes, "This is permissible." Elsewhere in *Mishneh Torah* he writes merely that a scholar "does not alter the truth in his speech, not adding or subtracting, except for matters of peace and the like."[37] The Rambam seems to understand this principle as a mere dispensation and not a compulsory action.[38]

It would follow, then, that the Rif understands peace to be a principle that transcends the necessity for honesty, not falling within the grasp of its obligations and prohibitions. Accordingly, it is the only choice in the event of a conflict. The Rambam, however, took the prohibition of falsehood to be in effect here, too, and thus truth and peace are arranged as opposing equals. As such, the option exists of selecting either value, with the election of truth as laudable as that of harmony.

---

32. See Rashi, 24a, s.v. *B'ushpiza*, and R. Moshe Feinstein, *Dibrot Moshe, Bava Metzia* 31. On the issue of lying to protect others from added exertion, see *Titten Emet L'Ya'akov*, p. 20.

33. *Bava Metzia* 13a in the pages of the Rif.

34. That this is indeed the position of the Rif also appears evident from his code in *Yevamot* 21a, *Bidapei HaRif*. See *Chafetz Chaim, Hilkhot Issurei Rekhilut, Klal 1, Be'er Mayim Chaim* 14.

35. *Yevamot* 6:21.

36. *Hilhot Gezeilah V'Aveidah* 14:13.

37. *Hilkhot Deiot* 5:7.

38. See R. Yehoshua Falk, *Drishah, Choshen Mishpat* 262, as well as his *Sefer Me'irat Einayim*.

IV. Blatant Dishonesty vs. Misrepresentation

The Rambam's language is indicative of another inclination consistent with this reasoning. His choice of words, particularly "adding or subtracting," suggests that outright lying is inadvisable; rather, one is to merely allow a slight compromise to the veracity of his statements. The tension between the two titans of the Jewish value system makes difficult the complete rejection of one in service of the other. As the Rambam seems to recognize a binding prohibition of falsehood, to whatever extent honesty can be preserved it is imperative to do so.[39] It is instructive, in this light, that the Talmud uses the word *l'shannot*, "to alter the truth," rather than *l'shaker*, "to lie."

It may be that this reluctance to sanction blatant dishonesty is shared by the Ramban. In his commentary to the Torah, he brings this perspective to God's modified report to Avraham of his wife's comments. He stresses that God's version was inherently true, as Sarah's intent was to express concern as to the stage of life they both shared, and the inclusion of Avraham in this consideration was merely omitted in the interest of harmony.[40] Likewise, the *Ohr HaChaim* has difficulty ascribing outright falsehood to the Source of all truth, noting that Sarah's main concern had been her own maturity, with her reference to Avraham's age an afterthought emphasizing the magnitude of the promised miracle.[41] Whether his comments are reflective of a general attitude toward the balancing the truth with harmony, or instead a specific sensitivity to the integrity of God's word, is arguable.

R. Moshe of Brisk, in his commentary to the *Shulchan Arukh*, *Chelkat M'chokeik*,[42] shows unambiguous preference for avoiding blatant dishonesty. In explicating the *Shulchan Arukh*'s ruling in favor of calling every bride beautiful, he notes that this is not to allow explicitly denying

---

39. See also R. Ya'akov of Dubno, *Ohel Ya'akov*, *Parshat Emor* (cited in R. H. D. Litwak, *MiDvar Sheker Tirchak*, p. 54) and *Titten Emet L'Ya'akov*, *Responsa* 14.

40. See also R. Moshe Sofer, *Responsa Chatam Sofer* 6:59, and R. David Shperber, *Responsa Afarkasta D'Anya* 3:154.

41. See also R. Yosef Yehudah Leib Sorotzkin, *Meged Yosef*, Genesis 18:13; R. Nisan Hameiri, *Nitzanei Nisan* ibid., 18:12; R. Dov Berish Meisels, *Binyan David al haTorah*, *Parshat VaYechi*, p. 269, #65.

42. *Even HaEzer* 65:1.

an obvious blemish, as this is a complete falsehood.[43] Rather, he should merely state that she is *na'ah*, "pleasant," and allow the listener to introduce his own interpretation. For example, R. Yehoshua Falk suggests the phrase may be taken to mean "pleasant in her actions."[44] In support of his position, the *Chelkat M'chokeik* refers to *Tosafot*.[45] However, upon examination the authors of the *Tosafot*, in two separate comments on this text, appear to be saying just the opposite. Their recommendation of merely leaving the negative unsaid is explicitly attributed to *Beit Shammai*, the implication clearly being that *Beit Hillel*, the prevailing opinion,[46] allow even outright falsehood. Further, the language of the *Shulchan Arukh* also conveys that impression, permitting "saying that she is *'na'ah'* . . . even if she is not *'na'ah.'*"[47] Also, the *Avot D'Rabbi Natan* relates stories in which Aharon HaKohen blatantly falsified facts in order to spread peace.[48]

This variance of thought seems to mirror the considerations named earlier. If one understands the prohibition of falsehood to be irrelevant in face of the pursuit of harmony, perhaps no limitations should be put upon the appropriate utilization of dishonesty. Alternatively, if the injunction maintains its force regardless of good intentions, deference to its weight would mandate that outright lying be avoided wherever possible. This is also the preference shown by R. Yisrael Meir Kagan in his *Chafetz Chaim*.[49]

V. Further Possible Ramifications

R. Yitzchak Sternhill[50] offers an interpretation of the dispute between *Beit Hillel* and *Beit Shammai* that also reflects these possibilities. In

---

43. See also *Tiv Kiddushin* to *Even HaEzer*.

44. *Prishah, Even HaEzer* 65, cited in *Be'er Heitev* and *Beit Shmuel*.

45. *Ketubot* 17a, s.v. *kallah k'mot sh'hi* and *y'shabchenu b'einav oh yignenu b'einav*.

46. The *Chelkat M'chokeik* himself clearly states that the ruling of the *Shulchan Arukh* is recorded to show opposition to the opinion of *Beit Shammai*.

47. See *Shittah Mekubetzet, Ketubot* 17a.

48. See commentary of R. Ovadia Bertenura to *Avot* 1:12.

49. *Hilkhot Issurei Rekhilut* 1:8; however, he does note that blatant falsehood is permissible when necessary.

50. *Kokhvei Yitzchak* 1:16.

actuality, it is surprising that *Beit Shammai*, who presumably also agree to the significance of peace, do not also allow lying about the bride for its sake. Rather, it must be that they, too, would sanction dishonesty if necessary to avoid disharmony; however, in this instance, the lying serves to preemptively strengthen harmony, which is not actually threatened, rather than combat discord. While that is certainly also a laudable project, it is not enough to justify violating the prohibition of *sheker*. However, *Beit Hillel* are willing to go further and allow dishonesty as long as it contributes to the cause of peace, even if it is not absolutely necessary.[51] This explanation thus attributes to *Beit Hillel* a position that dishonesty in the service of harmony is not really prohibited and is thus actively recommended, while *Beit Shammai*, believing the prohibition to still be in effect, suspend it only when no other option exists.[52]

This sensitivity is present also in the understanding of R. Yosef Chaim ibn Eliyahu of the permission of the scholar to dishonestly claim ignorance of a specific tractate. He observes that "knowledge" is multilayered, and even the most accomplished scholar can state with candor that he does not truly possess knowledge of any subject. Once again, reluctance is encountered toward allowing blatant falsehood.[53]

Along these lines, R. Avraham Yitzchak HaKohen Kook[54] quotes an opinion that one who has fallen prey to temptations of dishonesty in the past should not take advantage of this dispensation.[55] However, he him-

---

51. A different explanation of the position of *Beit Shammai*, and of the point of departure for *Beit Hillel*, suggested by R. Shlomo Zalman Auerbach, can be found in the journal *M'vakshei Torah*, (vol. 5, issue 25, p. 243.

52. A similar explanation is found in R. Joseph D. Epstein, *Mitzvot HaShalom*, p. 577; however, compare his *Mitzvot HaBayit*, p. 412. See also R. Hillel D. Litwak, *MiDvar Sheker Tirchak*, p. 55 and *Titten Emet L'Ya'akov*, p. 130. For a different analysis of the dispute between *Beit Hillel* and *Beit Shammai*, see R. Yechiel Moshe Epstein, *Be'er Moshe* to *Leviticus*, pp. 435–437. Note as well R. Yehoshua Aryeh Leib Hoshki, *Lev Aryeh* to *Parshat Ki Teitze* 22. See, at great length, R. Shneur Zalman Dov Anusishky, *Responsa Matzav HaYosher* 5 and 6. An extensive, and innovative, treatment of this passage by R. Nachum Yitzchak Broide appears in the journal *Moriah*, vol. 23:6–9, p. 246–256.

53. *Responsa Rav Poalim*, vol. 3, *Choshen Mishpat* 1.

54. *Tov Roei* to *Ketubot*.

55. The *Degel Machaneh Ephraim*, *Parshat Beha'alotkha*, attributes a similar position to the Rav of Polnoa.

self disagrees, noting that altering the truth in these situations is an obligation, and thus this is not an appropriate area for such stringencies.

The presence of the stigma of falsehood, regardless of circumstances, is evident in an unusual suggestion of R. Moshe Sofer.[56] Speaking of the necessity to maintain a clean body while wearing *tefillin*, R. Sofer notes that this refers not just to physical cleanliness but also to the spiritual. Such being the case, one should not utter falsehoods with *tefillin* on. R. Sofer adds that this is true even if the misrepresentation is in the service of peace, apparently assuming that the status of falsehood is still evident.

Such considerations are manifest in the ruling of R. Eliyahu of Lublin. In his responsa,[57] he prescribes the limitation of the previously mentioned dispensation to occasional usage and warns against allowing the formation of a habit.[58] His opinion seems also to reflect the burden of the falsehood prohibition, circumstances notwithstanding, and consequently asks for discretion in allowing its compromise.[59]

VI. Lying and the Effect on Children

It is important to note that even if the position of R. Eliyahu of Lublin is not accepted, the concern of not allowing permissible lying to affect the respect for honesty and integrity is a serious one. This is in particular an issue when children are involved. As sensitivity to their education is paramount, this may even override the motivation of keeping the peace.

In this vein Rabbi Dr. Aaron Levine has written[60]: "One aspect of the father's *hinnukh* responsibility to his son is a duty to habituate him in

---

56. *Chiddushei Chatam Sofer*, *Shabbat* 49a.

57. *Responsa Yad Eliyahu* 61 and 62.

58. See also R. Shlomo Luria, *Yam Shel Shlomo*, *Yevamot* 46. R. Rafael Williger, in the journal *Torat HaAdam L'Adam*, vol. 5, pp. 147–164, assumes a similar position to be normative and thus writes that lying is only permitted when certain restrictions are met; see his article for details.

59. See also *Merish BaBirah*, *Parshat Kedoshim*.

60. In the journal *Tradition*, vol. 36, no. 1, Spring 2002; see also his *Case Studies in Jewish Business Ethics* (Hoboken, New Jersey: Ktav Publishing House Inc., Yeshiva University Press, 2000), pp.19–32.

truth telling. The standard of truth telling set for *hinnukh* stands on a higher level than the standard set for the adult world. This principle can be derived from R. Zeira's dictum that it is prohibited to break a promise to a child because by so doing you habituate a child to lie (*Sukkah* 46b).[61] Let's take note that it is sometimes permissible to break a promise made in good faith. One circumstance obtains when A commits himself to confer B with a largess. Provided A made his commitment in 'good faith,' his subsequent retraction is not unethical. Given the considerable expense involved, B presumably never relied on the promise and hence A's retraction did not dash B's expectations (*Arukh ha-Shulchan, Choshen Mishpat*, 204:9.) Another qualifying circumstance obtains when A and B reach verbal agreement in a transaction. Before they get around to legally consummate their transaction the price of the article goes up (down). Here it is not regarded as unethical for the disadvantaged party to renege on the deal. (ibid 204:8).

"Given that the breaking of a promise is sometimes permissible, why does R. Zeira state his dictum in absolute terms without qualification? What must be inferred therefore is that one *may never break a promise to a child*. Given the child's immaturity, he (she) will not appreciate and understand fully the rationale for why the retraction is morally acceptable. Relatedly, the boundaries between morally acceptable and morally unacceptable retraction will be blurred as far as a child is concerned. Since it is morally unacceptable to break a promise to a child, prudence demands that an adult should avoid, as much as possible, making promises and threats to children.

"Because the *hinnukh* duty requires a higher standard of truth telling, the *darkhei shalom* license should not apply in a *hinnukh* setting. Explicitly taking this position is R. Nahum Yavrov: Ordinarily, if K knocks on D's door without an appointment, D is under no obligation to see him. Moreover, D's privacy right puts him under no duty to inform K what he is doing at that time and/or why he does not wish to see him. Informing K, through a member of the household, that he is 'unavailable' runs, however, the risk of insulting K. If K were important enough,

---

61. Note, as well, *Piskei Teshuvot*, vol. 6, p. 326, and, in the journal *VaY'lakket Yosef*, vol. 6, #2 , #21 and #46.

D would surely interrupt whatever he is doing and give *K* an audience. With the aim of avoiding friction with *K*, *D*, according to R. Shelomo Z. Auerbach (Jerusalem, 1910–1995, quoted by R. Yaakov Yehezkel Fish, *Titen Emet L'Yaakov* 5:24), should therefore inform *K*, through a member of the household, that he is not home. Since the latter response avoids a strain in relationships it constitutes a permissible lie and is therefore an application of the *darkhei shalom*. Addressing himself to this issue, R. Nahum Yavrov (contempt, Israel, *Niv Sefatayim* 3:32, *hiddushim*, 57–58.) posits that this instruction should not be made in the presence of a child, and certainly one should not use a child to deliver the untruth to the unexpected stranger. To be sure the untruth is a permissible lie, but any involvement of a child here will habituate him (her) to lie. R. Yavrov bases his ruling on R. Zeira's dictum.

"While truth must operate on a higher plane in the world of *hinnukh* compared to the adult world, some amount of intersection with the adult standard of honesty must be admissible. This is so because *hinnukh* is religious training not just for an ideal world but for the real world as well. In the real world an individual will assuredly encounter many instances where the use of some form of untruth will be the only means to end, mitigate or avoid strife and discord. Recall R. Yavrov's strictures regarding allowing a child even to *witness* the delivery of an untruth to an unexpected caller. But R. Yavrov himself points out variations of the case where the use of a lie by a child would be permissible. A case in point occurs when the father is sleeping and the child assesses that if he tells the unexpected caller the truth, the caller will expect the child to wake up his father. Suppose, however, the child assesses that his father would not want to be awakened to meet the unexpected caller. Here, the only way to avoid strife is for the child to tell the unexpected caller that his father is not home.

"Relatedly, in the instance where children are involved in a scuffle, a child is permitted to make use of lies as a means of ending the discord among his playmates. (R. Shelomo Zalman Auerbach and R. Yosef Shalom Elyashiv, quoted in *Titten Emet l'Yaakov*, op. cit., 5:10.)

"The thrust of the above discussion leads to the proposition that the use of permissible lies has some place in the world of *hinnukh*. But its main place should be in the theoretical realm. In this regard, parents and teachers should stress that the use of permissible lies is only a second best solution to real world problems.

"Conscientious efforts to inculcate truth and integrity as positive values works to bring the adult world closer to the pristine world of *hinnukh*. This is so because the task of promoting integrity and truth as a positive value challenges parents and educators to come up with creative solutions to ending strife and discord without the use of lies and deceptions. It challenges them also to avoid circumstances that would be a natural setting for permissible lies and permissible broken promises, even to the extent of changing their life style. The dividend society reaps from this type of *hinnukh* is that each successive generation of youth enters the adult world with a new burst of moral energy and society moves to a higher and higher standard of integrity."[62]

Further in his writings, Rabbi Levine introduces another area affected by concerns similar to those of R. Eliyahu of Lublin: "Collective bargaining provides another setting for the *darkhei shalom* principal. Consider that if negotiations reach an impasse, a lie on the part of one side may avert a strike and bring on a settlement. Because the lie promotes peace, it should be permissible on the basis of *darkhei shalom*.

"Coming into the session, however, with prepared lies and deception with the aim of springing them loose when and if circumstances warrant is illegitimate. Such a stratagem amounts to a deliberate plan to use deception to achieve monetary gain. Irrespective if the plan is actually implemented or if its use is halakhically valid, the fact remains that the training, readiness and preparation per se to use lies and deceptions acclimates one to lie and therefore debilitates the character. Moreover, if success as a negotiator is to some degree predicated on the honing of the skill in artful lying, the practitioner faces the long run danger that his profession will develop for him 'an acquired taste' for lying. These stratagems should therefore be prohibited on the basis of 'They have taught their tongue to speak lies, they weary themselves, etc. (*Jeremiah* 9:4).' If lies and deception have any legitimacy in a collective bargaining session

---

62. Note also a similar point in R. Simchah Rabinowitz, *Piskei Teshuvot*, vol. 6, ch. 156, p. 326.

it would only be as a spontaneous reaction to the situation at hand with the motive being to avert a strike."

VII. The Controversial Position of the *Sefer Chasidim*

This motivation of minimizing the incidence of falsehood has likewise been attributed to R. Yehudah HaChasid, author of the *Sefer Chasidim*, whose words[63] are cited authoritatively by the *Magen Avraham*.[64] He deals with a person who is approached with a request for money and, not wishing to relinquish any, yet hoping to avoid subsequent argument, decides to claim he has no money. Upon initial consideration, the pursuit of peace should allow such an inaccurate representation of his financial situation. Nonetheless, the *Sefer Chasidim* takes a stringent stand, legislating that such license is given only to a person who would lie about events that have taken place in the past. However, realities of the present and plans for the future are still confined within the restraints of total honesty. Hence, his current solvency is not an appropriate area for obfuscation.

This innovative ruling has garnered many challenges, among them that of R. Chaim Yosef David Azulai,[65] who notes an apparently contrary implication in the *Shulchan Arukh*.[66] A false oath intended to represent the past is treated with greater severity than an unfulfilled oath declaring intentions for the future. The suggestion is that falsifying the past is a greater transgression than misrepresenting the future. If anything, the focus of the *Sefer Chasidim* should be inverted, allowing dishonest representations of the future but not the past.

R. Yosef Patzanovsky offers the possible logic for the *Sefer Chasidim*'s opinion, citing the accompanying commentary of R. Reuven Margolios, *Mekor Chesed*. As suggested previously, the rabbis sought to limit the implementation of this principle.[67] If dispensation were granted for

---

63. 426.

64. *Orach Chaim* 156. See also R. Moshe Sofer, *Responsa Chatam Sofer* 6:59.

65. *Brit Shalom* to *Sefer Chasidim*. See also the commentary of R. Avraham David Wahrman to that work, *Milei D'Chasiduta*, p. 124.

66. *Choshen Mishpat* 344.

67. Similarly, R. Chaim Mordechai Roller, *Responsa Be'er Chaim Mordechai*, vol. 3, *Orach Chaim* 6, considers, and rejects, the possibility that the dispensation is

falsehoods concerning the future or the present, rampant misuse is easily imaginable. Any lie can be supported with the claim that it will potentially prevent some impending disruption of harmony. Restricting the rule to situations in the past ensures a limited usage that will not compromise the value of honesty in a fundamental manner. Hence, R. Azulai's objection is to be answered, as the relative severity of broken oaths is irrelevant to the present concern, which is restraining the incidences of even well-intentioned falsehoods.

Many authorities[68] note a basic textual difficulty with the notion of the *Sefer Chasidim*. As described previously, the Talmud attributes the source of the mitzvah to lie for the sake of peace to God's instructions to Shmuel concerning the anointing of David. As this was then a future event, how is it possible to deny that such instances are also within the relevant dispensation?[69] One approach to this problem may be to assume that if the *Sefer Chasidim* is concerned with limiting the usage of falsehoods, he consequently believes that dishonesty in the service of harmony is an option rather than an obligation. The story of Shmuel was brought in support of the position that such dishonesty is a *mitzvah*; if the *Sefer Chasidim* disputes this conclusion, perhaps he likewise rejects this text as a source, and thus does not incorporate it into his vision of the *halakhah*.[70]

Alternatively, R. Margolios offers the interpretation of R. Shmuel Eidels to this text.[71] In actuality, God commanded Shmuel to perform two missions: to bring a sacrifice and to anoint David. His instructions were to respond, upon being asked where he was going, that his journey

---

limited to falsehoods about which the truth will never be revealed. However, R. Shimshon Chaim Nachmeni, *Toldot Shimshon*, *Pirkei Avot* 1:12, endorses this and several other strict limitations.

68. See *Elyah Rabbah* and *Pri Megadim*, *Orach Chaim* 156, and *Responsa Lev Chaim* 15.

69. R. Chanoch Padwa rejects the limitation of the *Sefer Chasidim* on the strength of this and other challenges (*Responsa Cheishev HaEphod* 1:59). See also, in the journal *VaY'lakket Yosef*, vol. 9, #40 and #87.

70. God's instructions to Shmuel may then be understood as protecting his life, rather than harmony, as posited above.

71. *Chiddushei Aggadot L'Maharsha*, *Yevamot* 65b. This interpretation is also found in the Ritva and the Meiri.

was for the purpose of offering a sacrifice, and to omit his other function. Thus, his obfuscation was centered on the question of what task he had set out to perform, the commencement of his traveling being an event in the past.[72]

R. Azulai also notes the three instances in which a rabbinical scholar is permitted dishonesty. To disavow knowledge of a given tractate is to misrepresent a present situation. R. Azulai's solution appears to be the reclassification of this permission. He observes that the goals served here are that of modesty. The implication is that the rules would be different than those governing the service of peace. The *Responsa Lev Chaim* points out that such a reassignation is appropriate only according to Rashi's understanding.[73] *Tosafot*,[74] however, understand all of the three examples to be derivatives of the dispensation for the pursuit of harmony; their separate listing is merely a reflection of their more frequent occurrence. R. Yehoshua Falk[75] suggests a merger of the positions of Rashi and *Tosafot* in noting that all concerns of Torah and its commandments, such as modesty, are matters of peace; "For its ways are ways of pleasantness, and all its paths are peace."

R. Nachum Yavrov, in his work *Niv S'fatayim*, contends that R. Azulai's understanding is not really a reclassification of this concept, but rather is consistent with the previously mentioned approach to the *Sefer Chasidim*'s position. Just as limiting the dispensation to past events will prevent its abuse, so, too, the sages of the Talmud were confident that misrepresentations for the purpose of modesty would not lead to problems. Thus, allowing such license would not contradict R. Yehudah HaChasid's central concern.

The understanding of the Rambam[76] presents an additional complication to the position of R. Yehudah HaChasid. His interpretation of the word *masekhta* in the Talmud is not that a scholar has the right to plead ignorance to a particular tractate, as the other *rishonim* understand.

---

72 This is also consistent with considerations of avoiding outright dishonesty, as discussed above. See *Mekor Chesed*.

73 *s.v. b'masekhet.*

74 *s.v. b'ushpiza.*

75 *Drishah, Choshen Mishpat* 262.

76. *Mishneh Torah, Hilkhot G'zeilah V'Aveidah* 14:13.

Rather, the instance is that of a scholar who is currently involved in the study of a tractate but wishes to avoid inquiries in that area of learning. The concern, assumes R. Avraham De Boton in his *Lechem Mishneh*, is the personal embarrassment he would experience were his knowledge to prove lacking.[77] As protection, he is permitted to pretend his current activities are in another tractate. In the Rambam's picture, the subject of deception is certainly a present reality. Accordingly, the *Responsa Lev Chaim* assumes the Rambam is at variance with R. Yehudah HaChasid. R. Ya'akov Y. Fish[78] identifies a similar position within the words of the Ramban.[79]

Yet another issue raised is that of the talmudic passage concerning the praises of the bride. Once again, this seems to address an issue in the present. The *Niv S'fatayim* repeats his theory, noting that apparently, if the Rabbis of the Talmud instituted such a practice, they necessarily felt that such restricted usage would not engender misuse.

It seems possible to suggest an alternative formulation of the position of R. Yehudah HaChasid, one that can readily accommodate all of these objections. It could be that R. Yehudah HaChasid was of the view that dishonesty in the service of peace is a concession in the face of two irreconcilable ideals, rather than a blanket suspension of the laws of falsehood. Accordingly, one is only permitted to avail himself of this option if no other route exists to avoid disharmony. If, however, a third choice exists, allowing the avoidance of both lying and evoking strife, this option must be taken. This is relevant to the specific case dealt with by the *Sefer Chasidim*. A person confronting a request for money that he does not wish to honor, in spite of having the funds, faces three choices. He can refuse, instigating conflict; he can misrepresent his financial situation, avoiding tensions; or, he can comply with the request, which is neither

---

77. On the subject of lying to avoid embarrassment, note Rashi, *Kiddushin* 44; *Responsa HaRosh* 82:1; R. Tzvi Ashkenazi, *Responsa Chakham Tzvi* 44; Rashi; *Avodah Zarah* 58a, s.v, *d'mi*; and *Tosafot*, s. v. *ikla*; and *Orchot Chaim* 56; as well as R. Moshe Ze'ev Zoger, *Responsa VaYashev Moshe* 71; *Responsa Maharsham* 7:152; R. Yitzchak Shmuel Schechter, *Responsa Yashiv Yitzchak* (5:34) and *Titten Emet L'Ya'akov, Responsa* 6 and 17.

78. *Titten Emet L'Ya'akov, Responsa* 14.

79. Commentary to *Genesis* 42:33.

dishonest nor disharmonious. As the prohibition against falsehood is still in effect, in R. Yehudah HaChasid's opinion, as long as the third choice exists, one cannot ignore it and claim to have been forced into dishonesty, as that is not the only way to preserve the peace.[80]

If this is true, one can understand the *Sefer Chasidim*'s distinction between misrepresenting the past versus the present and the future. The differentiation is not merely a way to limit potential usages of the dispensation to alter the truth. Rather, it addresses the issue of whether the circumstances pitting truth against peace are immutable or not. If the situation is a reality cemented in past events, no longer subject to adapting its elements to avoid conflicting values, then dishonesty is the only route to peace and is permitted. If, however, a level of control over the circumstances still exists, and the conflict can be bypassed, that must be the path taken. The distinction is thus, are the circumstances defined in the past and no longer subject to alteration, or can perhaps actions in the present and future contribute to preserving harmony and obviate the need for dishonesty? This interpretation can perhaps be supported by the words of R. Shneur Zalman of Liady, who writes,[81] "It has only been said that one may alter the truth for the sake of peace, in reference to relating events that have already occurred."[82] The emphasis is on the incontrovertibility of the situation, more than on the entire discussion dealing with events of the past.

If such an approach is granted, these objections are all readily reconciled with the *Sefer Chasidim*'s position. God's preference of David over Shaul was a reality beyond Shmuel's control. The instances in which a scholar may misrepresent his studies all indicate situations defined in the past, whether it be the scholar's erudition to date, as the understanding of most *rishonim*, or his initial embarking on his current curriculum, as the Rambam. So, too, the bride's attractiveness is not subject to being improved by the revelers at her wedding.

---

80. A similar interpretation is perhaps implied in R. Hillel D. Litwack, *MiDvar Sheker Tirchak*, p. 56.

81. *Shulchan Arukh HaRav, Orach Chaim* 156:2.

82. R. Shneur Zalman goes on to question, however, whether or not this is indeed the conclusion for purposes of practical *halakhah*.

In any event, the assumption that the *Sefer Chasidim*'s position reflects that he understands the dispensation to be merely the lesser of two evils, consistent to both of the previously mentioned approaches, is implicit in the writings of R. Nachman Kahana, the Spinka Rav. Citing the aforementioned statement of the Ritva that the prohibition of *sheker* is inoperative when in conflict with peace, he comments that the Ritva is in opposition to the *Sefer Chasidim*.[83] R. Shalom Mordechai Shwadron[84] rules as well against the *Sefer Chasidim*, and the general acceptance of this stringency is somewhat of a question.[85]

It would appear that Rabbeinu Yonah also feels that the prohibition of falsehood remains active even in these extenuating circumstances. In his *Sha'arei Teshuvah*[86] he enumerates nine levels and types of dishonesty.[87] Rabbeinu Yonah contends that of these categories, only the fourth, misrepresenting facts in a nonharmful manner, is suspended in the pursuit of peace.[88] It would seem, then, that the injunction of falsehood remains prohibited, and only bows to harmony as a result of irreconcilable conflict. Thus, only the aspect of falsity itself is overridden, but not any of the other elements that are present in the other categories.[89]

---

83. *Orchot Chaim* 156.

84. *Responsa Maharsham* 7:152; note as well R. Padwa's position, cited above.

85. See R. Litwack, p. 56.

86. *Sha'ar* 3:178–186.

87. See chapter 5, page 69.

88. This restriction is also found in *Yad HaK'tannah, Hilhot Deiot*, ch. 10. See also R. Avraham Erlanger, *Ma'or HaSha'ar* 3:181. In regards to the fifth category, making promises, see *Shulchan Arukh HaRav, Orach Chaim* 156:2, and R. Yosef Avraham Heller's *Shalom Yihyeh*, ch. 13.

89. Interestingly, in regards to *geneivat da'at*, the questioner of R. Yosef Chaim Sonnenfeld, *Salmat Chaim* 843, takes the opposite approach, assuming that *geneivat da'at* for the sake of peace is more easily excusable than is general falsehood. So, too, it seems that R. Shammai Kehat Gross is based on an authority differing from Rabbeinu Yonah in his *Responsa Shevet HaKehati* 3:252. He deals with an individual who has collected charitable funds to be disbursed among needy Torah scholars, who is concerned that a specific scholar may feel insulted if he received funds he knew to come from charity. R. Gross allows the first individual to claim that the money is a gift out of his own pocket, even though this will earn him undeserved gratitude, a violation of *geneivat da'at*. He contends that the prohibition of *geneivat da'at* is inactive here, for, as an extension of the prohibition of falsehood, it is deferred for the sake of peace. R. Anusishky, *Responsa Matzav HaYosher* 6, also advances the case against Rabbeinu Yonah's limitation.

VIII. Further Applications

Ironically, it may be suggested that the more constricted understanding of this dispensation, that it is the lesser of two evils rather than a complete abrogation of the prohibition of falsehood, may recommend a more expansive application in some sense. If the pursuit of peace is powerful enough to overwhelm the injunction against lying, as expounded at length by the Rama in his responsum noted earlier, it may also be that it is likewise effective in overwhelming other precepts of the Torah when necessary.[90] Alternatively, if the principle is enacted only because it utilizes a loophole in the laws of falsehood, there is no basis to extrapolate to other areas of Jewish law.[91]

R. Shimon Greenfield[92] considers the case of a woman who, in her youth, had given birth under circumstances less honorable than those in which she now chooses to live. Currently married, she has just borne her husband's first son. The husband, unaware of the more unsavory aspects of his wife's past, enthusiastically awaits performing the *mitzvah* of *pidyon ha-ben*. Is the husband to be informed that it is not necessary, irrespective of the substantial damage that will be incurred to marital harmony? Or, is a sham religious ceremony to be countenanced? R. Greenfeld, cognizant of the imperative to maintain peace looming large, allows the pseudo-ritual, while providing advice on the avoidance of the transgression of pronouncing an unwarranted blessing. R. Ovadiah Yosef,[93] in a similar instance, goes as far as to allow the blessing. R. Yosef's eventual successor in the Israeli Sefardi Chief Rabbinate, R. Eliyahu Bakshi-Doron, discusses yet another case in his *Responsa Binyan Av*.[94] A similar issue concerns the unjustified insertion of the phrase *betulta da*, signifying a virgin, into the public reading of a *ketubah* at a wedding.[95]

---

90. See *Chullin* 141a.

91. A related inquiry may be the reverse issue of falsehood for other situations of religious challenge; see R. Litwack, pp. 61–62, and *Titten Emet L'Yaakov*, *Responsa* 6.

92. *Responsa Maharshag* 3:65.

93. *Responsa Yabbia Omer*, vol. 8, *Yoreh Deah* 32.

94. 2:54.

95. See *Responsa Tashbetz* 3:178; R. Akiva Eiger, *Gilyon HaShas*, *Ketubot* 21b; *Responsa Maharsham* 7:152; R. Moshe Feinstein, *Responsa Iggerot Moshe*, *Even*

The parameters of *shalom* have also met with some expansion in halakhic literature. Several authorities consider the instance of a judge, whether in the rabbinical court or otherwise, who foresees a perversion of justice emanating from the body on which he sits, owing to his being in the minority. If he will abstain from voting, pleading ignorance, more judges will have to be added, improving the odds for a just verdict. R. Yonatan Eibshutz and R. Ya'akov of Lisa[96] allow such a maneuver,[97] although the *Responsa Beit Ya'akov* does forbid it. As R. Ya'akov Reisher[98] observes, "Proper justice is peace"; he further adds that this conforms to the spirit of the talmudic dictum "One should always train himself to say 'I don't know,'"[99] albeit apparently homiletically. R. Yosef Chaim ibn Eliyahu[100] states further, "to uphold the banner of Torah—there is no greater *shalom* than this." [101] He adduces proof from the Talmud[102] that protecting the reputation of the rabbinical court may theoretically be justification for some falsehood. However, practically speaking, he concludes against it, wary of the opinion the populace may form of such behavior. Additionally, protecting a bereaved individual from learning the news in an unduly harsh manner has been considered to fall within the rubric of *shalom*.[103]

Often the complexities of a mature religious existence preclude an easy satisfaction of all fundamental tenets simultaneously. The careful balancing of conflicting pillars of the halakhic value system remains one of the foremost challenges of the dedicated Jew. One reality, however,

---

HaEzer 101, and *Orach Chaim* 4:118; R. Moshe Shternbuch, *Responsa Teshuvot V'Hanhagot*, 3:660; and R. Yitzchak Shmuel Schechter, *Responsa Yashiv Yitzchak*, vol. 2, *Even HaEzer*, 33.

96. *Urim V'Tumim* and *Netivot HaMishpat*, respectively, to *Choshen Mishpat* 12.

97. See *Mekor Chesed* for ramifications of this to the aforementioned position of the *Sefer Chasidim*.

98. *Responsa Shvut Ya'akov* 138.

99. *Berakhot* 4b.

100. *Responsa Torah L'Shmah* 371; see also 364.

101. See also R. David Shperber, *Shut Afarkasta D'Anya* (3:154) who considers the question of whether a judge can be misleading in his examination of witnesses in order to extract the truth.

102. *Rosh Hashanah* 20a.

103. *Responsa Shvut Ya'akov* 2:99. See also *Titten Emet L'Ya'akov, Responsa* 11.

remains undisputed: the role of pursuing and maintaining a peaceful existence as a paramount priority of the Torah's vision, "Its ways are ways of pleasantness, and all of its paths are peace."

CHAPTER

SEVEN

Burying—And Lending— the Hatchet: Vengeance and Grudges

I. The Biblical Prohibition of Revenge

Fundamental considerations of personal justice and fairness naturally inform the attitudes that comprise basic human instinct. A minimal element of reciprocity is prominent among the standards demanded of cordial interpersonal relationships. The golden rule of "Love your neighbor as yourself" is a biblical imperative, but is at the same time entirely consistent with a pragmatic social philosophy. What challenges primary sensibilities, however, is to be obligated in a standard of behavior toward

97

others that is benevolent, regardless of having suffered an equal measure of malevolence at the hands of these same others.

Nonetheless, such a response lies as the cornerstone of a dual prohibition in the Torah. Sharing the same verse as the commandment to love
one's neighbor are the twin transgressions of *nekimah* and *netirah*: "You
shall not avenge (*lo tikom*) nor bear any grudge (*lo titor*) against the members of your people."[1] While the word "avenge" may invoke images of
violent vigilantism, the Talmud informs us of the significantly more
mundane nature of the two injunctions,[2] and as to the distinction
between them.[3] An individual, wishing to borrow his neighbor's sickle,
is rebuffed. The next day, the offending neighbor is now himself at need
and asks the rejected party to lend him his scythe. If the latter were to
obey his natural instinct to refuse, noting the treatment he himself
received, he would be in violation of *nekimah*, of revenge. Further, over-
coming his initial inclination does not suffice. If he cannot also resist the
temptation to add, "I am not like you," as he hands over the scythe, he
flouts the injunction of *netirah*, of bearing a grudge.

In fact, the picture of the merciless vigilante is not only overblown but
wholly irrelevant. The Talmud specifies that the entire scope of these
prohibitions is limited to monetary matters rather than including
offenses of a more personal nature. Nonetheless, we are warned against
acting on this differentiation, as the Talmud repeats the passage that also
appears elsewhere.[4] "Those who are insulted and do not insult in return;
who hear their humiliation, and do not retort; perform in love and happiness, in spite of affliction; about such individuals the verse proclaims:
'Let them that love him be the as the sun when it comes out in its
might.'"[5]

The Talmud does allow the exception of an offended Torah scholar
who is duty bound to protect a source of honor that transcends personal

---

1. *Leviticus* 19:18.

2. Indeed, the *Taz* (*Yoreh Deah* 228:13) identifies these prohibitions as being
among those that most of the world regularly violates.

3. *Yoma* 23a.

4. *Shabbat* 88b and *Gittin* 26b.

5. *Judges* 5:31.

considerations,[6] even with a ferocity compared to a snake.[7] Nonetheless, even this dispensation is modified to mean the scholar will only "take it to heart,"[8] and not protest if another comes to his defense.[9] Further, if his pardon is requested, the Talmud offers the recommendation: "One who forgives offenses done to him, all his transgressions are forgiven."[10]

II. Philosophical Theories in Explanation of the Prohibition

The author of the *Yad HaK'tannah*[11] reflects that the underpinnings of these transgressions seem counterintuitive not only to human nature but also to the otherwise established trends of *halakhah*. Biblical law

---

6. See also *Shabbat* 63a, and *Chiddushei Maharsha*. Note the extensive discussion as to what a Torah scholar may forgive in R. Avraham Tovolsky's *K'tzet HaShemesh B'Gvurato*, pp. 72–74.

7. Note the understanding of R. Meir Simchah HaKohen of Dvinsk, *Ohr Sameach*, *Hilkhot Talmud Torah*, 1:2, and see R. Reuven Melamed, *Ohr HaTeshuvah* to *Sha'arei Teshuvah*, 3:58. Many commentators suggest that the meaning of "vengeance like a snake" lies in a snake's relationship to enjoyment. As he eats only tasteless dirt, he gets no joy out of eating; so, too, a Torah scholar's vengeance must be purely for the honor of Torah, and he must feel no personal satisfaction. (Alternatively, just as the snake injects venom with no benefit to himself, so, too, the scholar feels no gain from the negative response.) See R. Heschel of Krakow, *Chanukkat HaTorah*, p. 36b; R. Chaim Yosef David Azulai, *Petach Einayim*, *Yoma* 23a; R. Tzvi Hirsch of Abironav, *D'var Tzvi*, *Orach Chaim* 156; R. Avraham Weinfeld, *Responsa Lev Avraham* 128; and, at greater length, R. Zalman Sorotzkin's *Einayim L'Torah* to *Leviticus*. R. Yosef Patzanovsky (*Pardes Yosef*, *Leviticus* 19:17) takes it a step further; a snake who bites and poisons someone in reality weakens himself (*Avodah Zarah* 30b). So, too, a true Torah scholar will not only not enjoy avenging his honor, it will cause him anguish as well. R. Yonatan Eibshutz offers a similar interpretation, with an additional twist, in his *Tiferet Yehonatan* to *Leviticus*. For a general discussion of this and other types of "permitted" revenge, see R. Eitan Weissman, in the journal *Shma'atin*, vol. 37, 141–142, pp. 156–167.

8. On this, see commentaries of R. Yehudah Zak and R. Isaac Stein to *Sefer Mitzvot Gadol* 13.

9. See Rashi, s.v. *D'nakit b'libei*. Note also commentary of Meiri to *Yoma*.

10. The phrase is actually *ma'avir al midotav*, literally, "passes on his measurements." Rashi (*Rosh Hashanah* 17a) explains, one who does not take care to evaluate the exact degree to which another anguishes him, rather dispenses with such evaluations ("measurements") and goes on his way... so, too, the Heavenly judgment does not take care to precisely evaluate his misdeeds, and leaves him alone. For a homiletic approach to interpreting this phrase, see *Responsa Eretz Tzvi*, vol 2. p. 395.

11. *Hilkhot Deiot*, ch. 7, *Lo Ta'aseh* 4 and 5.

imposes numerous punitive measures intended to allow its transgressors to incur the damage they directed at others. A thief repays not only the principal but a final total of double the value (*kefel*), a monetary loss reflective of that he attempted to impose on another. Not only does a person who wounds another pay compensation, but even a person who unsuccessfully attempts to wreak some type of havoc through the mechanism of false testimony (*eid zomem*) bears himself the burden of that havoc in legal retaliation. The implication is clear; the *halakhah* recognizes not only the recovery of actual losses but also the imposition of penalties correspondent to the degree of intended malevolence. As the Torah is itself replete with such methods of treating the misanthropist in the manner he displayed towards others, it seems incongruous that here we find no such recompense permitted.

The *Yad HaK'tannah* notes, in this light, that it is not insignificant that the Talmud chooses as its example the seemingly trivial subject of neighbors lending, or refusing to lend, property to each other. These prohibitions are specifically geared toward occurrences of everyday life, events in the annals of interpersonal relationships that arouse annoyance and irritation rather than physical harm or destruction of property. In the case of the latter, the Torah has assigned responsibility and ordered restitution, recognizing that the world will not function properly if matters of such gravity are not addressed. However, of that which remains, we are told almost by default to forgive and forget. Were every minor incident taken to heart, allowed to evolve into a full-blown feud, the consequences to a harmonious existence would be disastrous. The prohibitions against *nekimah* and *netirah*, then, serve to alleviate the malevolent tensions that too often arise from the most banal of daily disagreements.[12]

The essential triviality of the vast majority of human conflicts is a theme that resonates in the works of the Rambam. In his *Mishneh Torah*, having recorded the prohibition against *nekimah*, he adds: "And even though no punishment of lashes is incurred for this transgression, it is a bad attitude in the extreme; rather, it is appropriate for one to forgive offenses done to him in all matters of this world, for it is all, to those who

---

12. Note R. Avraham Price, *Mishnat Avraham* to *Sefer Mitzvot Gadol*, prohibitions 11:1.

understand, things of vanity and triviality and not worthy of avenging." He concludes, "This is the proper attitude that enables the settlement of the world[13] and the interaction of individuals one with the other."[14]

In his *Sefer HaMitzvot*, the Rambam uses the following words to describe the injunction against *nekimah*. "We are enjoined not to avenge one against another, and that is, that one should commit an action, and the other shall not deviate from searching after him until he has paid him back for his bad act, until he has done to the other as he has done to him."[15] The Rambam's focus, in interpreting the prohibition, seems to be on the act of aggression directed against the other as retribution for his refusal to provide assistance. The explanation is thus provided by the aforementioned rationale found in *Mishneh Torah*; that is, that earthly disputes on the whole do not merit the discord that an expression of vengeance will engender.

It thus appears that in the Rambam's view, the emphasis of this prohibition is on the offense perpetrated against the one who refused to lend the property, more so than on the mindset encouraged by such behavior.[16] Although he does discuss the attitudinal aspects in *Mishneh Torah*, this can be understood more as the conceptual underpinnings of the prohibition than its central concern. It is not irrelevant in this light to note the Rambam's words in his *Guide to the Perplexed*, in which he explains that those laws codified in the *Hilkhot Deiot* section of *Mishneh Torah* are geared toward improving personal qualities, giving order to and enhancing the relationships among men.[17] The initial formulation of the prohibition, as it appears in *Sefer HaMitzvot*, certainly seems to

---

13. The Mahari Chagiz, in his *Tzror HaChaim*, brings to this phrase *yishuv ha'aretz* the unusual interpretation of *yishuv Eretz Yisrael*, "the settlement of the land of Israel." R. Moshe Greenes (*Karan P'nei Moshe, Parshat Chayyei Sarah*, p. 34), observes that the Talmud (*Yoma* 9b) attributes the destruction of the Temple to baseless hatred; as the prohibitions of *nekimah* and *netirah* deter hatred, this indeed contributes to the resettlement of the land of Israel.

14. *Hilkhot Deiot* 7:7.

15. Prohibition 304.

16. Note R. Joseph D. Epstein's discussion in his *Mitzvot HaMussar*, pp. 135–147, in which he investigates this question of the focus of the prohibition being on the action or its effect on attitude.

17. *Moreh Nevukhim* 3:35.

center on the action taken against the victim of the vengeance more than on the intellectual effect on the perpetrator.[18] Nonetheless, it remains possible that the Rambam was fundamentally concerned with the accompanying frame of mind, yet felt that halakhic relevance comes only when this attitude is evidence by an observable action.[19]

The Rambam's emphasis of behavior over thought in this instance is further supported by comments concerning the corollary prohibition against *netirah*. Again in *Mishneh Torah*, he writes, ". . . one should erase the matter from his heart and not remember it, for as long as he bears a grudge, he may come to avenge; therefore, the Torah was concerned about *netirah*, until it is erased from the heart and not remembered at all."[20] *Netirah*, the purely mental partner of the more active *nekimah*, is apparently prohibited only, or at least primarily, because of its likelihood to lead to the latter.[21] R. Avraham Altshnili[22] and R. Hillel David Litwack[23] suggest that this formulation may impact on the *halakhah*; if the original aggressor has passed away and can no longer suffer *nekimah*, there may be no danger in bearing a grudge against him. Whether such a notion would be generally accepted is questionable.[24]

---

18. Toward an analysis of the relationship between this particular prohibition and its accompanying impacts on attitude in the writings of the Rambam, see the numerous references to this concept in R. Isadore Twersky's *Introduction to Mishneh Torah*, as well as R. Binyamin Ze'ev Benedict's *HaRambam L'lo Stiyah Min HaTalmud*, pp. 232–246.

19. See R. Nachum Rabinowitz's *Yad Peshutah* to *Deiot*. This touches upon the question of the relevance of this prohibition to that of *Lo tisna et achikha b'l-vavekha*—"You shall not hate your brother in your heart" (*Leviticus* 19:17). See again R. Epstein's discussion.

20. *Hilkhot Deiot* 7:8.

21. The great nineteenth-century talmudist R. Yosef Engel included in one of his works, the *Sefer Lekach Tov* (*Klal* 8), an essay investigating whether or not any biblical prohibitions were issued purely or primarily to safeguard other biblical prohibitions, a function more commonly associated with rabbinical injunctions (*Yevamot* 21a, *Avot* 1:1). He proceeds to list seventeen such instances; however, *netirah* as protection for *nekimah* is not among them. R. Moshe Sofer of Erlau does include this among his own independently compiled list (*Responsa Yad Sofer* 26, the fifth of nine such concepts. R. Yochanan Sofer, in his *Ittur Sofrim* to the *Responsa Yad Sofer*, adds ten more items to the list.).

22. *Har HaMelekh*, vol. 3, pp. 203–208.

23. *Yisrael HaKedoshim*, pp. 50.

24. As to the ability of the status of "safeguard," ascribed to a biblical law, to affect the parameters of this law, note R. Nachum Weidenfeld's comments in his

In this light, another aspect of the Rambam's position can be considered. As noted previously, the Talmud distinguishes between personal (*tza'ar haguf*) and monetary offenses in delineating the boundaries of this prohibition. As R. Yosef Babad and others observe, the Rambam makes no mention of an exemption of personal offenses from the strictures of these injunctions.[25] This omission has prompted much rabbinic discussion.[26]

The Rambam's license to dismiss a ruling of the Talmud, if he indeed does so,[27] may stem from at least two possibilities. The midrashic *Sifra* parallels the Talmud's passage in *Massekhet Yoma* for the most part as related previously, but omits the distinction between monetary and personal offense. It may then be that a dispute exists between the Talmud and the *Sifra*, with the Rambam siding with the *Sifra*. Alternatively, the Rambam's son, R. Avraham, in his responsa, displays a different text of the Talmud, distinguishing not between personal and monetary offenses but between worldly matters (*milei d'alma*) and attacks against the Torah itself (*milei d'orayta*),[28] a differentiation consistent with the Talmud's dispensation for a Torah scholar to avenge the honor of the Torah. It is possible that the Rambam also had this text, as R. Nachum Rabinowitz considers.[29] The Ritva also shows evidence of having this reading in his comments to *Massekhet Rosh Hashanah*.[30]

Thus, if the Rambam does indeed opt for a source that recognizes no dispensation for personal offenses, it may be that this is consistent with his overall perspective on the prohibition of *nekimah* and *netirah*. The

---

Responsa Chazon Nachum (92), in which he argues against such interpretations. Compare, however, the sources cited in *Sefer Y'kara De'Chaim* pp. 281–287.

25. *Minchat Chinnukh* 241.

26. See, among others, R. Aharon Soloveichik, *Parach Mateh Aharon, Madda*, pp. 89–90; R. Elyakim Krumbein, in the journal *Techumin* (6: 292–304); R. Dov Ber Zuckerman, in *Shittah Mekubetzet L'Minchat Chinnukh* (241); and R. J. D. Epstein's aforementioned discussion in *Mitzvot HaMussar*.

27. Beyond the range of interpretations possible within the *Mishneh Torah*, R. Altshnili, writing in the omnibus *Har HaMelekh*, suggests the Rambam in *Mishneh Torah* reverses the position he expresses in *Sefer HaMitzvot* and does in fact acknowledge a distinction.

28. *Responsa R. Avraham Bno Shel HaRambam*, Paris, p. 103.

29. *Yad Peshutah* to *Hilkhot Deiot*.

30. 17a, s.v. *Amar Rava*.

focus of the prohibition is to encourage the dismissal of all insults and malfeasances, or at least those not actionable in court, in order to prevent society's descent into a state of constant petty squabbling. As such, both material and personal offenses are best forgotten.

This position is even more consistent within the view of the *Sefer HaChinnukh,* whose language more clearly omits any distinction among the types of offenses susceptible to these prohibitions.[31] For his part, the rationale underlying the injunctions stems from a larger philosophy of life's vicissitudes. The misfortunes that befall an individual should be understood as a divine response to his own behavior. Therefore, it is inappropriate to hold anyone else responsible for his misfortunes, regardless of how their actions or inactions appear to be directly related.[32] R. Yehudah HaChasid displays a similar attitude.[33] If this is to be one's perspective, there indeed remains little room to distinguish within the nature of the malevolence.[34]

This perspective might perhaps be of value in explaining a verse in the Torah. In the context of warning of Divine punishment for the failings of the Jewish people, the passage states (*Leviticus* 26:36), "They will flee as one flees the sword; and they will fall, but without a pursuer." This verse has posed much difficulty for commentators. How does the absence of a pursuer intensify the punishment? Is it not preferable to be without one?

With the *Sefer HaChinnukh's* view in mind, it might be suggested that the verse refers to the psychological relief one obtains from the ability to blame all of his misfortunes on some human "pursuer." When it is possible to do so, it allows the sufferer to forestall any introspection into the causes of his suffering, as all is the responsibility of the pursuer. However, when there is no obvious malefactor, it becomes necessary to look within for spiritual explanations: in the context of Divine punishment, a most appropriate response.

---

31. *Mitzvah* 240 and 241.

32. See also *Pele Yoetz* 50; note, as well, *Reponsa V'Darashta V'Chakarta,* Vol. 3, *Choshen Mishpat* 10–11.

33. *Sefer Chasidim* 183.

34. See also R. Aharon David Goldberg, *Shirat David* to *Leviticus.*

The more inclusive positions of the Rambam and the *Sefer HaChinnukh* (as well as the Ritva, with his variant text) are at odds with the significant number of authorities who do consider the Talmud's distinction to be authoritative. Among these are the *Sefer Mitzvot Gadol*,[35] Rabbeinu Yonah,[36] R. Eliezer of Metz,[37] the Meiri,[38] and *Tosafot*.[39] This creates a clash that R. Yisrael Meir Kagan felt to be irreconcilable; he thus considers it an unresolved point of biblical law, which must be treated stringently.[40] R. Ya'akov Nissan Rosenthal suggests that a relevant factor is whether or not the aggrieved individual has been apologized to or not. If he has, then it is forbidden to seek any vengeance even in personal matters, while in monetary matters it is prohibited in either case.[41] R. Avraham Yitzchak HaKohen Kook posits that the Rambam and the *Sefer HaChinnukh* agree that the prohibition does not apply in its purest form to personal offenses; however, since it is nonetheless discouraged and poor conduct generally, they saw no need to explicitly recommend it.[42] Further, he suggests that the focus in the literature on monetary matters is a concession to human weakness, as people often find personal attacks impossible to ignore.[43]

---

35. Prohibition 12.

36. *Sha'ar* 3:38; see Rabbi Krumbein's article for an interpretation of Rabbeinu Yonah's words, as well as a more extensive listing of these authorities and an analysis of their positions.

37. *Sefer Yereim* 40–41.

38. *Yoma* 23a.

39. *Bava Metzia* 71a and *Kiddushin* 28a, according to the reading of R. Shlomo Luria, *Yam Shel Shlomo, Bava Kamma*, 8:44.

40. *Petichah* to *Chafetz Chaim, Be'er Mayim Chaim* 8–9. See also R. Chaim Yosef David Weiss's *Responsa V'Ya'an David* 261:2. See also R. Avraham Y. Ehrman, *Kodesh Yisrael* #18.

41. *Mishnat Ya'akov, Deiot*, 7:7.

42. *Mitzvot Ra'ayah*, p. 96.

43. Ibid, p. 98. See also R. Yosef Epstein (*Mitzvot HaShalom*, p. 164). The notion that human nature dictates that many find it impossible to remain silent in the face of an *ad hominem* attack is a factor for some understanding toward those who respond "in the heat of the moment"; see *Responsa HaRivash* 216; *Shittah Mekubetzet, Ketubot* 14b; *Shulchan Arukh, Yoreh Deah* 228:28; *Yam Shel Shlomo, Bava Kamma* 2:26, on related positions in other areas of *halakhah*.

R. Eliezer of Metz's position seems to differ significantly from that of the Rambam and of the *Sefer HaChinnukh*.[44] In his *Sefer Yereim*, he explains the reasoning that would limit *nekimah* and *netirah* to monetary matters. The surrounding verses in the Torah deal with issues such as theft, charitable donations, prompt compensation of workers, and the like. It would follow, then, that this is likewise the theme of *nekimah* and *netirah*. Even when one does not receive such treatment himself, he is no less obligated to maintain a policy of generous and gracious behavior toward others.

Thus, the focus is somewhat different; the concern is not so much on the act of vengeance, but rather on allowing an insufficient motivation to diminish one's charitable performance.[45] This is stated clearly in the *Sefer Reishit Chokhmah*, citing the *Midrash L'Olam*: "One should always perform acts of kindness, even to one who has treated him badly, and not avenge or take a grudge... and this is the way of holy Jews." In this light, the Talmud's choice of example is extremely precise; the instance of refusing to lend a tool very specifically identifies the parameters of the law. The prohibition deals with withholding assistance, as in the example; and it is limited to nonpersonal, nonactionable offenses, as in the example. The two aspects are related, as the transgression is passive in nature, its scope is more naturally limited to the absence of a service than inclusive of a response to a personal attack. The latter, provoking an active reply, would fall outside the definition of these prohibitions.

R. Pinchas HaLevi Horowitz, in his commentary to the Torah, interprets the relevant verse in a manner consistent with R. Eliezer of Metz's approach.[46] The complete phrase forbids avenging from or bearing a grudge against *b'nei amekha*, "the members of your nation." Often, the Talmud interprets a reference to the Jewish nationality of the subject to be a requirement that he adhere to behavior consistent with the standards of the nation—*oseh ma'aseh amkha*.[47] Among these Jewish qualities is the aspect of *gemilat chasadim*, expressions of kindness.[48]

---

44. See also R. Raphael Yosef Chazan, *Responsa Chikrei Lev, Yoreh Deah* 80.
45. See R. Moshe Chaim Luzzatto's discussion, *Mesilat Yesharim* 11.
46. *Panim Yafot* to *Leviticus*.
47. See, for example, *Bava Batra* 4b.
48. *Yevamot* 79a.

Therefore, one who declines to help out another might be considered in betrayal of Jewish values and not himself worth of receiving kindness. Nonetheless, the Talmud advises an awareness that whatever traits may be lacking in this particular individual, he remains a part of the nation of *gomlei chasadim* and must be treated as such.[49] Thus, the focus of the transgression is the withholding of kindnesses more than the act of vengeance itself. A somewhat similar sentiment is expressed by R. Moshe Alshikh.[50]

An additional perspective may be gleaned from the words of the Jerusalem Talmud.[51] There, taking vengeance on another Jew is compared to retaliating against one's hand for damage done to one's foot. As all of the Jewish people comprise one unified entity, can it be productive for one part to extract vengeance from the other?[52]

III. Possible Halakhic Ramifications of the Theories

R. Yosef Patzanofsky[53] cites from the work *Siftei Tzadik* (number 7) a halakhic discussion that may serve as a test case for these positions. An individual notices that another person turns down requests from a third party to lend property. Is he permitted to deny this man his own property, considering that his reluctance comes not from personal vengeance, as he never suffered himself, but from an objective evaluation that this man does not deserve his assistance? Perhaps the Rambam and the *Sefer HaChinnukh* would incline toward leniency, as he is not actually taking revenge. However, in the view of R. Eliezer of Metz that this is not sufficient to justify withholding assistance, it may not be relevant who the original victim was.[54] Similarly, R. Hillel David Litwack[55] considers the

---

49. *Ketubot* 8b. See also the *Sefer HaMitzvot* of *Maharam Shick* (#243).

50. *Torat Moshe* to *Leviticus*.

51. *Nedarim* 9:4. See also *Pardes Yosef* to *Leviticus*.

52. See R. Yehudah Horowitz, *Imrei Yehudah*, *Leviticus*, and *Da'at Chokhmah U'Mussar* 2:1.

53. *Pardes Yosef* to *Leviticus*.

54. A lengthy analysis of the question of revenge or grudge bearing by a third party, by the editorial board of the journal *Torat HaAdam L'Adam*, appears in volume 4 of that journal (pp. 261–82).

55. *Yisrael Kedoshim*, p. 50.

case of one who commits an act of vengeance, but for technical reasons, the effects never reach the original offender. If the focus is the treatment of the other individual, perhaps there is room to suggest that despite the attempt, the transgression has not been violated. However, if the concern is the act of vengeance, it would seem no distinction should be made. Similarly, any act of revenge that somehow is beneath the notice of the subject would be subject to similar considerations.[56]

IV. The Relationship of Grudge-Bearing to Revenge

Whatever understanding is adopted of the prohibition of *nekimah*, it may be that the accompanying injunction of *netirah* is to be interpreted somewhat differently.[57] While it does appear from the Rambam that *netirah* exists to prevent the occurrence of *nekimah*, the *Yad HaK'tannah* states emphatically that this is not the case. Rather, it stands independently as a transgression of its own, in force regardless of the possibility of *nekimah*.

R. Avraham Yitzchak HaKohen Kook expresses a position completely reverse to the one just mentioned.[58] The concern is really the feelings engendered by the act of vengeance, a highly negative character trait. Allowing one to take revenge, *nekimah*, or even to mention the possibility, *netirah*, strengthens this attitude; thus, the prohibitions are designed to prevent the accompanying mindset.[59] Hence, the actions are prohibited to prevent the attitudes, rather than the other way around.

This need for classification prompts the investigation of several issues within the prohibition of *netirah*. First among these is the relationship of the two prohibitions; or more directly, consideration of the fact that one who imposes vengeance on another is motivated to do so by the bearing of a grudge. As this is the case, it must be determined if it is ever possi-

---

56. R. David Ariav (*L'Reakha Kamokha*, p. 291, *Nir L'David*, 25) considers it obvious that such a situation would involve a violation of the prohibition of *nekimah*.

57. For a thorough analysis of the positions in relation to this prohibition, see R. Elchanan Adler, in the journal *Beit Yitzchak* 25:306–318.

58. *Mitzvot Ra'ayah*, p. 96.

59. See Ramban's commentary to the Torah, *Deuteronomy* 6:14.

ble to violate *nekimah* without first violating *netirah*;[60] and if not, the necessity for a separate prohibition for *nekimah* is called into question. Further, as R. Natan David Shapira[61] observes, it would appear that for *nekimah* to apply, there should be a correlation in severity between the act of vengeance and the original offense; while *netirah*, not involving any action, would have no such requirement.

R. Aryeh Leib of Metz[62] makes an interesting observation prompted by a detail in the Talmud's language. In illustrating the prohibition of *nekimah*, the example given is refusing to lend a scythe after being denied a sickle. In the example given of *netirah*, the order is reversed; a sickle is grudgingly handed over after being refused a scythe.[63] R. Aryeh Leib suggests that both are part of one story. First Reuven denied a sickle to Shimon, who responded by withholding his scythe. Afterwards, when Shimon needed the sickle again, Reuven acquiesced, but not without bearing a grudge. It is this act of *netirah* that is given particular significance, in that it follows an act of *nekimah* and perpetuates this cycle.[64]

R. Yerucham Perlow writes that a distinction must exist, for otherwise R. Sa'adiah Gaon, in his listing of the *mitzvot*, would count these two prohibitions as only one of the six hundred and thirteen commandments.[65] He suggests that transgressing *nekimah* may involve less acrimony than to violate *netirah*. An individual may have a policy of not lending out his property, not out of dislike for his neighbors but out of fear of the effects of wear and tear on his tools. However, if another

---

60. R. Yisrael Meir HaKohen, for one, seems to feel that by the time an act of revenge has taken place, both prohibitions will have been transgressed; see *Chafetz Chaim, Petichah*, and *Lavin* 8–9. See also R. Shmuel Aharon Rabin, *Tosefet Ahavah* to *Sefer Yereim* 40:1.

61. In the journal *Torah SheB'Al Peh*, vol. 36, pp. 116–120.

62. *Gevurot Ari* to *Yoma* 23a, s.v. *Eizo Netirah*.

63. See also the Ritva's commentary concerning this difference, as well as *Siftei Chakhamim* to *Leviticus* 19:17.

64. See also R. Shmaryahu Shulman's *Merish BaBirah* to *Parshat Kedoshim*. Compare also R. Yisrael Ya'akov Kanievsky, *Kehilot Ya'akov, Makkot* 16 (in older editions), who considers whether or not an act of *netirah* has taken place if it is motivated by some separate offense.

65. *Biur* to *Sefer HaMitzvot LeRasag*, prohibition 53.

individual would lend something to him, he would calculate that the benefit he gleans would outweigh the risks involved in returning the favor. Despite the absence of malice, R. Perlow considers the refraining from also lending to those who do not provide him with such services as a violation of *nekimah*.

It might be that the Ra'avad disagrees with this, for in his commentary to the *Midrash*[66] he observes the apparent incongruity of the initial refusal to lend being considered innocent, while the identical behavior, in response, is stigmatized with a prohibition. He explains that the first party may be reluctant to lend for economic reasons, with no malicious feelings whatsoever. The second, however, is motivated by vengeance, and it is there that the transgression lies. The implication is that if his motives are primarily economic, it would not be forbidden.

It should be noted, however, as observed by the Steipler Gaon, R. Yisrael Yaakov Kanievsky,[67] that the Ra'avad's language contains an interesting implication. One might infer that, were the original refusing party to have had malicious feelings, he too would have been in violation of *nekimah*. If that were indeed the case, and the Steipler does not reach a conclusion on the matter, it would expand the definition of *nekimah* to include not only those "reciprocating" a previously refused favor, but even one who declines help for any unjustifiable[68] feeling of dislike.[69]

In any case, R. Shammai Gross seems to feel differently from R. Perlow in a responsum dealing with a man who wishes to absent himself from his friend's celebration of a joyous event on the grounds that this man was not in attendance at his own such occasion.[70] He then proves that this thinking is evident in a ruling of the Rama citing the Mordechai.[71] The suggestion is then made that perhaps it is for this

---

66. *Peirush HaRa'avad, Torat Kohanim, Parshat Kedoshim*.

67. *Kehilot Yaakov* (original 10 volume edition, vol. 10, #54).

68. In contrast with the previously mentioned hypothetical of the *Siftei Tzadik*, where the potential lender may feel justified in withholding kindness from a morally unworthy recipient.

69. See as well the discussion in R. David Ariav, *L'Reakha Kamokha*, p. 287, *Nir L'David* 17.

70. *Responsa Shevet HaKehati* 3:325.

71. *Choshen Mishpat* 312:9. The ruling concerns a man who rents a house to his friend and states explicitly that he does so only out of his friendship with the

reason that the Talmud provides the example of lending property as opposed to money. As money is spent and then must be raised again to repay the loan,[72] external fears are more likely to induce reluctance to lend money. Property, however, that is returned itself carries less risk and thus abstention from loaning it out is more likely due to antipathy than to financial concern, and thus more likely the focus of the transgression of *nekimah*. This position is concurred to by R. Shimon Greenfeld,[73] who then explains the inclusion in the biblical verse of the phrase, "I am God," often taken as a warning that God knows one's innermost thoughts. There, as one's intent is relevant to defining an action as permitted or forbidden, this phrase is appropriate. Also agreeing are R. Avraham Weinfeld[74] and R. Moshe Shternbuch.[75]

To R. Perlow, however, *nekimah* can be violated even if the considerations are of an economic nature. *Netirah*, on the other hand, requires a sustained feeling of offense, and in fact lending the property, despite not having that courtesy extended to him when he was in need, may actually strengthen this feeling and engender an actual hatred.

R. Shlomo Luria, in his commentary to the *Sefer HaMitzvot*, suggests another distinction. Noting a slight difference in the formulation of the two prohibitions as found in the Rambam and the *Sefer Mitzvot Gadol*, he writes that *nekimah* applies only between two "friends," while *netirah* applies to "any one of Israel." *Nekimah* is limited to acquaintances, because refraining from helping the other out, in spite of their friendship, will appear vindictive; however, to a stranger, economic considerations may be at play. R. Perlow writes that the variation in language is insufficient basis for such a ruling, especially considering their joined presentation in the biblical verse.[76]

---

latter. Subsequently, after discord erupts between them, he has the right to evict him. The *Taz* objects that this seems to be a form of vengeance.

72. See *Kiddushin* 47a.

73. *Responsa Maharshag* 2:53.

74. *Responsa Lev Avraham* 128.

75. *Responsa Teshuvot V'Hanhagot* 1:832.

76. See R. Menachem Krakowski's *Avodat Melekh* (*Deiot*, 7:7), which offers another explanation of the variance in language; see also R. Moshe Shick, *Maharam Shick al Sefer HaMitzvot* 243.

VI. Silent Grudges of the Heart

Another important issue in *netirah*, also significant toward establishing its own independent parameters, is whether the grudge must be expressed, as it is in the story in the Talmud, or whether it is enough that it is felt, as Rashi comments on that same Talmudic passage, "for the matter is preserved in his heart, and he has not distracted himself from it."[77] This question would also become relevant to *nekimah* if it is assumed that vindictive intent is necessary. The *Dina D'Chayai*[78] suggests that this is the distinction that necessitates both prohibitions; *netirah* can be violated mentally while *nekimah* is purely active. It seems also from Rabbeinu Yonah[79] and the *Sefer HaChinnukh* that *netirah* can be violated mentally. Rav Kook was of the opinion that mere thought cannot be considered within the range of transgressions; while in his opinion, noted earlier, the attitude is the entire goal of the prohibition, nonetheless, the Torah does not govern attitudes directly.[80] Even if one assumes that an expression of the grudge is required, it might not be necessary for it be to verbal: the classic ethical treatise *Mesilat Yesharim* (ch. 11) implies that even an angry glare or an unenthusiastic response of assistance may be sufficient.[81] R. Yisrael Meir Kagan, however, felt that an unverbalized intent is enough for both prohibitions. R. Perlow discusses this issue further to clarify the positions of the early authorities. R. Shmuel Baruch Werner, considering the deleterious effect of grudges as indicated by the prohibition, suggests that the reverse situation might then be equally prohibited. That is to say, one who has performed acts of kindness toward another, and is then disappointed by a lack of reciprocation, should perhaps be encouraged to overcome this emotion, as the consequences of the growing resentment may be equivalent to those resulting from a grudge over an active grievance.[82]

---

77. s.v. *Eini.*

78. Prohibition 11.

79. *Sha'arei Teshuvah, Sha'ar* 3:38. See also R. Avraham Erlanger, *Ma'or HaSha'ar* and *Zeh HaSha'ar.*

80. This is an idea quoted frequently in the name of R. Joseph B. Soloveitchik; see *Al HaTeshuvah*, pp. 41–43, and *Shiurim L'Zekher Abba Mari Zal* 2:182–196.

81. As to whether this would constitute actual *netirah* or merely discouraged behavior, see R. David Ariav, *L'Reakha Kamokha*, p. 283, *Nir L'David* 8.

82. Memorial Volume for R. Shmuel Boruch Werner, pp. 110–111.

Concluding with a query of R. Patzanovsky may be instructive as to the spirit of these laws. Suppose a man is faced with two simultaneous requests for the same object, one from an individual who had previously denied him assistance. In that he can only help one of them, is there any reason he must opt for the one who had denied him use of his property? One's initial reaction would be that while the unhelpful individual is biblically protected against vengeance, he certainly does not deserve preferential treatment. However, upon further analysis, it is remembered that the Talmud mandates physical assistance (*t'inah u'preikah*) be rendered to an enemy before a friend, in order to attempt to mitigate the existing animosity.[83] Such reasoning is certainly relevant here as well, and R. Patzanovsky reaches no decision in the matter.[84]

The differences of personality and policy that threaten to undermine harmony in society are manifold. An excessive meditation on any real or imagined offense can soon deteriorate to a full-blown hatred, regardless of the pettiness of its source. The Torah, ever cognizant of this reality, warns us not once but twice to eliminate absolutely all such disastrous tendencies from consideration. The promise of the *Sefer HaChinnukh* beckons: "The prohibition of 'Do not avenge' contains great purpose: to put quarreling to rest, and to remove conflict from the heart of people, and once there is peace among men, God, blessed be He, will make peace with them."

---

83. *Bava Metzia* 32b.

84. See also R. Ari Cohen, in the journal *Techumin*, vol. 19, p. 89, and note as well his extensive treatment of many of the subjects of this chapter, pp. 67–90.

EIGHT

See No Evil:
Favorable Judgments
of Others

I. "With Justice Shall You Judge . . ."

To actively control judgment is a profound challenge. The evaluative component a person brings to his experiences and to the events that he witnesses is largely automatic and instinctual, the sum of his knowledge and attitudes instantly joining to register an opinion immediately following any stimulus. The prejudices and biases, loves and hates, and previous positions espoused by an individual give body to the estimation he forms of his surroundings. To be asked to subvert this process, to mindfully reroute the courses of one's thought processes to a conclusion colored by an outside agenda, however honorable, runs counter to natural human tendency.

Nonetheless, the *halakhah* requests just such a departure from customary evaluational procedures. We are instructed by the Torah[1] *B'tzedek tishpot et amitekha*—"With justice shall you judge your friend." The Talmud[2] gives focus to the intent of this phrase: *Hevei dan et chaverkha l'khaf zekhut*—"Judge your friend favorably." The neutral, dispassionate voice of objectivity so prized in jurisprudence is insufficient in daily interactions. This imperative to impose a positive bias on one's judgment, presented as it is as Talmudic interpretation of a verse, appears to be a biblical mandate.[3] Some authorities, however, noted that the implication of other Talmudic sources[4] was that this behavior constituted meritorious conduct more than an absolute obligation.

Further, the verse has another interpretation, a warning to judges to give equal attention to both sides in a dispute; in addition, the imperative for a qualified individual to take up the judicial mantle, when necessary, is also included. Which is to be considered the primary, and perhaps the focal, reading of the verse may be a matter of some disagreement. The Meiri[5] felt that judging others favorably is only hinted at in the verse, rather than its main imperative. The *Sefer Charedim*, however, considers generous personal evaluation to be the verse's primary concern, and lists it twice.[6] This appears also to be the opinion of Rabbeinu Yonah[7] and R. Yehudah HaChasid.[8]

The Rambam in his *Sefer HaMitzvot*[9] gives the three understandings equal weight; however, in *Mishneh Torah*[10] he records only the equal treatment of litigants as an obligation.[11] R. Yerucham Fishel Perlow sug-

---

1. *Leviticus* 19:15.
2. *Shevuot* 30a.
3. See R. Shimon (Eiger) Sofer, *Responsa Hitor'rut Teshuvah* 1:69.
4. See *Shabbat* 127b and Avot 1:6.
5. *Shevuot* 30a.
6. Ch. 1, *Mitzvot Aseh Hat'luyot Balev* 30 and 46.
7. *Shaarei Teshuvah* 3:218; see *Chafetz Chaim, Hilkhot Lashon Hara, Klal 3*, in *Be'er Mayim Chaim*.
8. *Sefer Chasidim* 31.
9. Positive commandment 177.
10. *Hilkhot Sanhedrin* 21:1.
11. See R. Meir Tzvi Bernfeld's *Responsa Sofer HaMelekh* 4.

gests that the Rambam changed his mind between the two works[12] and ultimately came to view the focal imperative to be addressed to judges, with private citizens exercising generous evaluation of others a praiseworthy character trait.[13] The reconciliation of these divergent tendencies is relevant to the details of this concept.

II. Guidelines for Judgment

An oft-quoted saying relates that while one is required to judge others favorably, "one is not obligated to be a fool." The generosity of opinion that is mandated or advised does not constrain an objective individual to put himself at risk, materially, spiritually, physically, or otherwise, by turning a blind eye and a deaf ear to obvious evidence of wrongdoing. Thus, this principle applies itself in differing manners to various instances and individuals. Prominent among those who established the levels of categorization are Rabbeinu Yonah,[14] and, centuries later, R. Yisrael Meir Kagan.[15]

One who is known to be righteous, solid in reputation, and engages in behavior that is known to be exemplary[16] has earned the benefit of the doubt in subsequent actions. If his conduct is apparently innocent, or even if it indicates equally in both directions, it must be assumed that he is free of guilt. According to many authorities, an individual deserves the advantage of his meritorious past automatically, without need of the

---

12. *Biur* to *Sefer HaMitzvot* of R. Sa'adiah Gaon, *Aseh* 97.

13. See *Mishneh Torah, Hilkhot Deiot* 5:7, and *Peirush HaMishnayot, Avot* 1:6.

14. *Sha'arei Teshuvah* 3:218, and *Peirush* to *Pirkei Avot* 1:6. Concerning Rabbeinu Yonah's words, see R. Avraham Erlanger, *Maor HaSha'ar* to *Sha'arei Teshuvah*, and R. Chaim Pardes, *Ashdot HaPisgah* to *Parshat Kedoshim*. See also the lengthy analysis of R. Yechiel Neuman in the journal *Torat HaAdam L'Adam* (vol. 5, pp. 199–214).

15. *Chafetz Chaim, Ese'in, Klal* 3:7.

16. The Rambam (*Peirush HaMishnayot* to *Avot*) refers to a "famous man of righteousness and good actions," while Rabbeinu Yonah's language in *Sha'arei Teshuvah* is less demanding, implying that a majority of positive behavior is sufficient to enter an individual into this category. However, in his *Peirush* to *Avot*, his wording resembles that of the Rambam. See R. David Kog'ah's *Dan L'Khaf Zekhut*, p. 10, footnote 7, and R. Hillel David Litwack's *Mishpat Tzedek*, p. 27, footnote 8. Whether "righteousness" refers to one's behavior overall, or just in the area in question, is discussed by R. Avraham Y. Ehrman, *Kodesh Yisrael* #23.

principle of *dan l'khaf zekhut*,[17] which comes into play only when an evaluation is necessary.[18] Further, even in an instance when likelihood is on the side of wrongdoing, his history earns him the assumption of rectitude. His reputation serves him in good stead beyond this, as well; if he has committed a definite transgression, indisputable as to its facts, his history entitles him to the assumption that he has repented and maintains his praiseworthy status. This is based on a statement of the Talmud:[19] "If you have seen a Torah scholar transgress at night, do not think badly of him the next day... for he has certainly repented by then."[20] R. Yeshayahu Horowitz[21] adds that it must be assumed that the scholar had committed the sin for an unknown but laudable motive. In general, an isolated display of a negative character trait should be assumed an aberration.[22]

The next category is populated by the average citizen, who strives to make a productive contribution to society and to lead a meritorious life, but occasionally is known to fall prey to temptation. Such an individual is subject to a greater degree to having the circumstances dictate his evaluation, although they are colored greatly by the imperative of *dan l'khaf zekhut*. If the indication is that the behavior is innocent, it unquestionably must be assumed that that is the case. If morally opposite interpretations are equally feasible, it is still appropriate to assume virtuousness.[23]

If it appears that the behavior was indeed illicit, it is not prohibited to

---

17. See Rabbeinu Yonah, commentary to *Avot*, and *Sha'arei Teshuvah*, *Sha'ar* 3:218, and commentary *Zeh HaSha'ar*, and R. Binyamin Yehoshua Zilber's *Responsa Az Nidbaru* 2:75.

18. On the difference between basic entitlement to benefit of the doubt as a matter of fairness and the added element of generosity in judgment, see R. Yitzchak Hutner's *PachadYitzchak* to *Rosh Hashanah*, *Ma'amar* 14:11–12.

19. *Berakhot* 19a.

20. R. Hutner (*Pachad Yitzchak, Iggerot U'ktavim* 38) assumes that this privilege is extended only to Torah scholars, in contrast even with righteous, but unlearned individuals; for all others, only actions not yet known to be improper are subject to meritorious assumption under the base principle.

21. *Shnei Luchot HaBrit, Sha'ar HaOtiyot* 20; see *Mishpat Tzedek*, p. 27, footnote 8.

22. *Chafetz Chaim, Klal* 4:38 in *Be'er Mayim Chaim*.

23. See *Meiri, Shabbat* 127, s.v. *Vechain Ma'aseh*.

believe this is the case, although it is still praiseworthy to remain unde-cided in the matter. It is, of course, forbidden to inform anyone else of his belief, should he conclude that the suspect is guilty; the laws of *lashon hara*, malicious gossip, continue to apply, assuming no danger is posed to a third party.[24]

An individual of unknown character is assumed to belong to this cat-egory.[25] R. Kagan suggests[26] that it is on this point that the issue of the status of the obligation plays a role. When someone has an established reputation, biblical law requires that he be judged in accordance with this reputation, with a generous tilt. However, when the subject is of undetermined virtue, the favorable slant on his evaluation is an admirable practice, but not obligatory.[27]

However, if the person in question is known to be unprincipled, blindly ignoring his laxity of standard or outright immorality could endanger one's own status, be it moral, physical, or financial. Thus, it is permitted, perhaps even recommended, to assume that current activities are consistent with his past, even if the impropriety is not evident or indi-cated. Unconfirmed gossip is insufficient to enter someone into this cat-egory, even after it has infiltrated the generally utilized conduits of public information.[28]

The ideal treatment of this last group is a matter of disagreement. To some authorities, among them Rabbeinu Bachya[29] and a student of the Rambam,[30] it remains an honorable endeavor to search for an exculpa-tory interpretation. However, others, such as Rabbeinu Yonah[31] and the Meiri, maintain that it is appropriate and advisable to disdain this indi-vidual and his behavior.[32]

---

24. See *Chafetz Chaim, Klal* 3:5 and 10:1.

25. See *Tosefot Yom Tov*'s analysis of *Peirush Mishnayot L'HaRambam, Yoma* 1:5.

26. *Chafetz Chaim, Petichah* to *Ese'in* 3, in *Be'er Mayim Chaim*.

27. The halakhic relevance of one's own familiarity with the individual in ques-tion is grounded in *Masekhet Kallah Rabati*, ch. 9; see *Mishpat Tzedek*, p. 27, foot-note 7. See also R. Moshe Rosmarin, *D'var Moshe* to *Pirkei Avot*.

28. *Chafetz Chaim* 1: *Klal* 7:3, 4.

29. Commentary to *Avot*.

30. *Sefer HaMussar Al Avot*.

31. *Peirush* to *Proverbs* 21:12 and to *Avot*.

32. See also R. Avraham Grodzinski, *Torat Avraham*, pp. 156–157.

III. Theories Behind the Obligation

The key to interpreting this debate may lie in determining the goal of judging others favorably. One aspect of evaluating others positively is the sense of goodwill that is evoked through the exercise of this principle. R. Shlomo Luria[33] notes that this behavior is fundamental to the preservation of harmony in society.[34] The attempt to bestow a generous estimation on others minimizes the grounds for animosity and strife and thus contributes to the maintenance of the noncontentious community,[35] as well as the realization of the imperative of "loving one's neighbor."[36] R. Eliezer of Metz,[37] in fact, considers judging unfavorably to be a violation of "You shall not hate your brother in your heart."[38]

R. Yehoshua Leib Diskin[39] suggests another motivation. A fundamental factor in the avoidance of sin is the embarrassment associated with iniquity. Believing that society on a whole adheres to a higher standard is essential to maintaining this attitude. Thus, it is necessary to assume that the behavior of one's social group is exemplary; this is the aim of the obligation to be *dan l'khaf zekhut*. Similar thinking is evident earlier in the writings of the Meiri,[40] who notes that one who suspects others will lose respect for society as a whole and will immunize himself against their good influence. This is perhaps the reasoning behind R. Binyamin Yehoshua Zilber's position[41] that the entitlement to favorable judgment is one that the beneficiary has no right to waive; it is not his prerogative to weaken the stigma that wrongdoing is branded within society. R. Moshe Teitlbaum[42] suggests another rationale that may have

---

33. *Responsa Maharshal* 64.

34. The *Sefer Charedim* (chs. 12, 54) writes that this principle is fundamental to advancing the goals of "Seek peace, and pursue it" (*Psalms* 34:15).

35. See R. Chanokh Zundel, *Etz Yosef* to *Pirkei Avot*.

36. See *Yesod V'Shoresh HaAvodah, Sha'ar Avodat HaLevi*, ch. 8; R. Moshe Yechiel Elimelekh of Libertov, *VaYomer Moshe, Parshat Kedoshim*; and, at length, R. David Kronglass, *Sichot Chokhmah U'Musar*, pp. 70–76.

37. The implication of *Sefer Yereim* 39.

38. *Leviticus* 19:17.

39. *Responsa Maharil Diskin*, end of *Psakim*, and *Chiddushei Maharil Diskin Al HaTorah, Leviticus*.

40. *Chibbur HaTeshuvah, Meishiv Nefesh, Ma'amar* 1:4.

41. *Responsa Az Nidbaru* 12:4.

42. *Yismach Moshe* to *Pirkei Avot*.

similar practical ramifications: to whatever extent one assumes others' behavior to be respectable, one minimizes the desecration of God's Name that results from sin.

IV. Possible Halakhic Ramifications

The range of motivations possible within this imperative may also play a role in determining an issue considered by R. Joseph D. Epstein.[43] Assuming righteousness in another manifests itself in a variety of ways. On one level, it expresses itself in the behavior one shows to the individual in question; on a more basic, but perhaps more intellectually challenging level, it may obligate convincing oneself, internally, that the suspect is innocent. Thus, the precise focus of this commandment requires analysis. If R. Diskin's theory of social stigma is to be adopted, then the emphasis is apparently based on the inner evaluation, regardless of any outward manifestation; Rashi's language of "suspicion"[44] indeed carries this connotation. However, if the concern is the effect such feelings impose upon social harmony, the outer expressions may be the central concern, although a case could be made that this equilibrium is disrupted by condemnation both explicit and internal.

Another ramification, also raised by R. Epstein, may be the instance of a suspected individual who has expressed his lack of concern as to how he is judged. If R. Diskin's reasoning is the controlling element, then the suspect's disregard for his rights in this matter is not of relevance. However, if evaluating others favorably is to be understood as an act of kindness and friendship from one to another, as is perhaps the implication of the Talmud,[45] it is more easily conceivable that this privilege may be waived.

A further ramification may be whether this generosity must be extended as well to individuals who are deceased, an issue raised by R. Hillel David Litwack.[46] While this can no longer impact directly on social interaction, at least as far as the subject himself is concerned, communal standards may still be affected.

---

43. *Mitzvot HaMussar*, pp. 214–216.
44. *Shevuot* 30b.
45. See *Shabbat* 127b and Rashi, as well as *Rashi* to *Peah* 1:1.
46. *Mishpat Tzedek*, p. 32.

R. Ezriel Ciment[47] suggests that this dual objective is instructive toward understanding R. Kagan's distinction cited previously, that of the subject who is known earning an obligation of favorable judgment, and the unfamiliar individual receiving such treatment as a matter of admirable practice but not as an imperative. The twin goals of this ideal reap profit in two directions. The first is advantageous to the suspected individual; by assuming his innocence in order to preserve a harmonious society, his respected status is upheld. This expresses itself as an obligation toward a member of the community of known repute.

The second element is concerned more about the effect on the one evaluating than on the subject; to assume righteousness on the part of the population as a whole, for this purpose, is meritorious behavior rather than an absolute commandment and does not distinguish between recognized and unrecognized subjects.

Another issue relevant to the above question concerns whether one is obligated to employ favorable judgment when the issue is not one of religious merit, but rather of conforming to personal preference. For example, one who might take umbrage at another's not joining in his family event; should one assume the absence was attributable to unavoidable factors? If the obligation is one of maintaining societal standards, it would seem to be limited to issues of moral and spiritual rectitude; if, however, it is directed at avoiding communal friction, any matter that may cause conflict would fall within its purview.[48]

Another issue that may be affected concerns one who is presented with an action to be evaluated, without knowing who perpetrated the action; is there an obligation to view this event with a positive perspective? The interpersonal component may pose no such obligation, as no identifiable individual will be tainted with suspicion. However, societal standards would be weakened, even if the specific actor is not known.[49]

This discussion of *dan l'khaf zekhut* as a benefit to the accused and to the one evaluating may play a role in understanding the basis for two discussions of a technical nature that appear in the responsa of R. Binyamin

---

47. *Mitzvot HaMelekh*, positive commandment 177.

48. This question is analyzed along these lines in R. Betzalel Genchersky, *Darkhei Tzedek* 3:1.

49. This analysis is also found in *Darkhei Tzedek* 5:4, and footnotes 6 and 7.

Yehoshua Zilber. The first is a consideration of whether suspecting another individual wrongly constitutes one overall prohibition or is violated every moment the incorrect belief is held.[50] From the perspective of the accused, the offense is a constantly regenerating one (and this is indeed R. Zilber's conclusion). For the one judging, however, it relates more to an overall attitude.[51] Similarly, the second responsum[52] considers whether suspicion of an entire community constitutes one violation, or one per member of the community.[53]

One technical issue to consider is whether the prohibited action is the evaluation itself or the negative opinion that ensues. That is to say, if one does judge another unfavorably, is the violation now in the past or does it continue to be infracted every moment that the position is maintained? This question is also raised by R. Litwack.

R. Yitzchak Hutner[54] notes that the Talmud[55] derives from a biblical verse that one who wrongly suspects another must seek his forgiveness. The necessity to acquire the pardon of an individual whom one has wronged is a well-established principle of halakhic social interaction; the need for an additional biblical source in this instance is to demonstrate that genuine harm is inflicted by this behavior upon the accused, above and beyond the parameters of the obligation.[56] However, in light of the above, it might be observed that an obligation to ask forgiveness is not necessarily obvious in this instance; if favorable judgment is primarily required in order to maintain social standards, failure in this area might not be an actual interpersonal offense for which one must apologize to the subject.[57]

---

50. *Responsa Az Nidbaru* 2:75.

51. R. Genchersky (*Darkhei Tzedek* 6:6, footnote 5) raises this question as well and notes that its resolution is relevant to the proper path for penitence for unfavorable judgment. After recommending that one correct his behavior by adopting a favorable evaluation, he notes that such an act may be alternatively viewed not as repentance but as ceasing to continue an ongoing offense, depending on which view is adopted.

52. Ibid., 76.

53. See also *Mishpat Tzedek*.

54. *Sefer Zikaron L'Maran Ba'al HaPachad Yitzchak*, p. 336.

55. *Berakhot* 31a.

56. See also R. Hershel Schachter, *Nefesh HaRav*, pp. 150–151.

57. It should also be noted that in the event that the subject is unaware that he was suspected, it is highly questionable if it is appropriate to inform him in order to

These various perspectives may affect the preferences for proper evaluation of the unsavory individual. Should the primary focus of the imperative of favorable judgment be the dissipation of conflict within society, then it is understandable that this approach would be productive toward all individuals, even if the *halakhah* also recognizes the right to protect oneself from the less trustworthy ones with an assumption of some degree of guilt.

However, if the fundamental goal is the preservation of social standards, then the reverse may be indicated when dealing with individuals known to be unscrupulous. A justification of their behavior may quickly lead to their adapted moral standards permeating the community. Thus, the condemnation of their behavior is more consistent with upholding the values of the community than is its favorable evaluation.[58] This is indicated as well by a comment of R. Moshe Shternbuch,[59] quoting the Satmar Rebbe, that defending wicked individuals is permissible, but only in private, so the masses will not learn to imitate their behavior. As such, *dan l'khaf zekhut* in all cases remains a laudable trait in Torah scholars, as these learned individuals are safeguarded from deleterious influences.

V. Weighing Societal Factors

After the proper precautions have been taken, however, it seems that there is a place for generous evaluation of all individuals. A popular interpretation of the *Mishnah* in *Pirkei Avot* focuses on a detail of the language used.[60] In formulating the obligation to be *dan l'khaf zekhut*,

---

seek forgiveness (see the discussion concerning *lashon hara* on pp. 153–154. Indeed, it is possible that the Talmud's statement in this context is referring only to an instance in which the subject was aware of the suspicion; see *Darkhei Tzedek*, ch. 6, footnote 7.

58. A similar, but inverse, interpretation is found in R. Shmuel Yudaikin's *Divrei Shalom* 4:12.

59. *Moadim U'Zmanim* 7:192.

60. This interpretation is found in the works of many commentaries to *Pirkei Avot* (1:6), among them R. Yehudah Aryeh Leib of Ger, *Sefat Emet*; R. Yitzchak Meir of Ger (*Chiddushei HaRim*) cited in *Pardes Yosef*, *Leviticus* 13:3; R. Gedalyah Felder, *Yesodei Yeshurun*; R. Menachem Frankel-Teomim, *Be'er HaAvot*; R. Natan Gestetner, *L'Horot Natan*; R. Ya'akov Yehoshua Belcrovitz, *Tiferet Yehoshua*; R. Zelig Pribelsky, cited in *MiShel Avot*.

the object of this endeavor is identified not merely as *kol adam*, "every person," but *kol ha-adam*, translatable as "all of the person." This is taken to mean that judgment should focus not merely on the incident at hand but on the entire individual, taking into careful account the circumstances of his life, the hardships and tribulations imposed upon him, and the influences guiding his weltanschauung. R. Menachem Mendel Schneersohn, the Lubavitcher Rebbe,[61] notes in this context that the *Mishnah*'s other topics are relevant: "Make for yourself a teacher, acquire a friend, and *hevei dan et kol ha-adam l'khaf zekhut*." The social and educational framework must be taken into account in judging each individual. R. Moshe Sofer[62] observes that maintaining a spotless reputation before the suspicious community is more difficult than remaining innocent in the eyes of God, and thus a compassionate judgment is called for.

The role of mitigating factors within the scope of this imperative is the topic of a responsum by R. Natan Gestetner.[63] He considers the question of whether one who assumes that another has transgressed inadvertently, rather than not at all, has fulfilled his responsibility in this regard. Further, one who chooses to believe that the other has sinned and repented, as opposed to never having committed any wrong-doing, is also subject to discussion. In his analysis, the relative severity and status of the relevant concepts are taken into account.[64]

Developing a generosity of spirit in the estimation of others is valuable towards the harmonization of society and the maintenance of communal standards, as well as cultivating an instinct of altruism and kindness that is ultimately self-reflective. Indeed, the Talmud[65] promises, "He who judges others favorably, he himself is judged favorably." The *Shittah Mekubetzet*[66] comments on the seeming lack of necessity for God to employ this principle; as all is revealed before Him, Heavenly justice needs no evaluative guidelines. The truth is, however, that all fair

---

61. *Biurim L'Pirkei Avot*; see also *Milei D'Chasiduta* to *Pirkei Avot*.
62. *Responsa Chatam Sofer* 6:59.
63. *Responsa L'Horot Natan* 8:13.
64. See also *D'var Moshe* to *Pirkei Avot* and *Mishpat Tzedek*.
65. *Shabbat* 127a.
66. *Nedarim* 40a, s.v. *D'lo likra*.

judgments are cognizant of factors both blatant and latent. When generosity of assessment is the norm on Earth, Divine retribution that considers these elements will not lead to God being challenged as unjust. However, if this trait is foreign to human society, it will not be appreciated when practiced Above.[67] R. Yehudah Loew of Prague (the Maharal)[68] makes a similar observation concerning the prohibitive correlate of the obligation to be *dan l'khaf zekhut*, the transgression of *chosheid bik'shairim*, suspecting the innocent.[69] The Talmud warns that one who does so will be "bodily afflicted," *lokeh b'gufo*.[70] R. Moshe Sofer[71] questions the propriety of this penalty, noting that tradition holds that Heavenly retribution does not begin with physical punishment. The Maharal explains that no punishment is involved; rather, the cycle of suspicion an individual initiates will ultimately ensnare the instigator in its consequences. It thus falls to society and to the individual to ensure that generosity and understanding dictate the policies of interpersonal assessment.

---

67. See also R. Yechiel Moshe Epstein, *Be'er Moshe*, *2 Samuel* 12:7 (pp. 464–465); R. Chaim Shmuelevitz, *Sichot Mussar*, 5733 #28; R. Chaim Kanievsky, *Orchot Yosher*, p. 18; R. Betzatel Genchersky, *Darkhei Tzedek*, p. 15.

68. *Gur Aryeh*, *Deuteronomy* 19:19, and *Chiddushei Maharal*, *Shabbat* 97a.

69. See also R. Chaim Friedlander, *Siftei Chaim, Moadim*, vol. 1, pp. 243–244, and R. Ya'akov Levinson, *Responsa HaTorah V'HaMadda*, pp. 107–109.

70. *Shabbat* 97a. R. Yehudah HaChasid, *Sefer Chasidim* 1088, considers this prohibition to obtain specifically when the suspicion is verbalized; see also R. Shmuel David Katz Friedman, *Milei D'Chasiduta* to *Sefer Chasidim*, p. 35.

71. *Chiddushei Chatam Sofer* to *Shabbat*.

NINE

Hello, Good Morning, and How Are You? Greetings in Jewish Law

I. The Obligation of Proper Greetings

The languages of civilization abound with words and phrases used for the purposes of greeting one another, evidence of a universal custom as old as culture itself, automatic and instinctual upon any encounter with one's closest friend or with a barely recognizable acquaintance. These expressions can be casual or formal, jocular or grave, as varied and diverse as the circumstances that dictate the meetings between men. Within *halakhah*, however, these utterances take on far greater significance, being not merely the rote execution of a social convention but the fulfillment of a Torah imperative.

While not expressly found as a biblical commandment, the greeting
of others is given space in several places in the Torah's narrative.
R. Menachem Kasher[1] considers the reference to Moshe's welcoming of
his father-in-law Yitro,[2] at which time "each inquired about the other's
well-being," as the most explicit indication that this behavior is to be imi-
tated. Other such recorded instances include Yaakov's inquiry concerning Lavan:[3] "and he said to them, 'Is it well with him? [hashalom lo] and
they answered, 'It is well' [shalom]"; as well as Yosef's words to his brothers upon their arrival in Egypt:[4] "and he inquired after their welfare
[vayishal lahem lishalom], and he said, 'Is your elderly father, of whom
you spoke, at peace?'"

If the biblical references are not phrased in the imperative, it may
nonetheless be that an obligation exists from a comparable source. The
verse in Psalms[5] states, "Ask for peace, and pursue it [bakkesh shalom
virodfeihu]." According to R. Yitzchak Abohab,[6] this verse constitutes an
obligation to greet others, bearing the status of a commandment midivrei
kaballah, "from tradition."[7] This designation identifies commandments
that are found in the Bible, but in the Nevi'im or the Ketuvim rather than
the Chumash, the Pentateuch.[8] These precepts are essentially rabbinical,
in that they do not stem from a Divine utterance, but their scriptural
source raises their status. According to some, mitzvot in this category are,
for certain purposes, treated with the severity of biblical commandments.[9] It should also be noted that it seems from the commentary of

---

1. Torah Shleimah to Parshat Yitro, in Ha'arot.
2. Exodus 18:7. See R. Yechezkel Cohen, Imrei Yechezkel to Exodus; for a
lengthy discussion of the implications of this meeting, see R. David Kwiat, Sukkat
David to Exodus.
3. Genesis 29:6.
4. Genesis 43:27.
5. 34:15.
6. Menorat HaMa'or, Neir 6, Klal 2, Chelek 1, and Perek 2.
7. The Sefer Chareidim (35:19) agrees that verse contains an obligation midivrei
kaballah, but considers the subject to be shalom in the sense of the state of peace as
opposed to shalom as a greeting.
8. Other examples include: the fast days commemorating the destruction of the
Beit HaMikdash (Zechariah 8:19); the mitzvot of Purim (Esther 9:21–22); and Kavod
and Oneg Shabbat (Isaiah 58:13).
9. This is the often quoted position of R. Aryeh Leib of Metz, Turei Even,
Megillah 5b, s.v. Chizkiyah; however, others disagree. See chapter 4, footnote 55.

Rabbeinu Asher[10] that one who takes an oath not to greet another places himself in violation of "You shall not hate your brother in your heart."[11]

In any case, the Talmud is unequivocal in relating to the proper greeting of others as an obligation.[12] "R. Chelbo said in the name of R. Huna: whoever knows that his friend is in the habit of greeting him, he must precede him in initiating the greeting, as it states, 'Ask for peace, and pursue it'; and if the other does greet him first, and he does not return the greeting, he is called a thief, as it states,[13] 'It is you who have ravaged the vineyard, that which was robbed from the poor is in your houses.'"[14] Rashi[15] explains the inference: as the poor have nothing to be stolen from them, the only "robbing" that is possible is their unreciprocated greeting.[16]

Thus, the Talmud seems to identify two manifestations of recommended greetings: the ideal of initiating the salutation, and the indispensable act of returning one. The first appears to be a laudable trait rather than an obligation, as it is not recorded as such in the halakhic codes.[17] However, the implication of the *Shulchan Arukh* (*Orach Chaim* 415:1) is that greeting a friend who returns from a journey is a 'mitzvah.' The *Mishnah Berurah*[18] understands this as a fulfillment of the commandments of asking 'shalom' and of "*k'vod habriyot*" (human dignity). The Rambam[19] does include the habit of taking the lead in the amenities among the qualities required of a Torah scholar; the Meiri[20] notes further that scholars make it a practice to offer greetings of

10. *Peirush HaRosh, Nedarim* 65b.

11. *Leviticus* 19:17; note, however, the more expansive interpretation in R. Yisrael Ya'akov Kanievsky's *Kehilot Ya'akov* 10:54 and *Birkat Peretz, Parshat Kedoshim*.

12. See R. Chanokh Padwa, *Responsa Cheshev HaEphod* 3:30:4.

13. *Isaiah* 3:14.

14. *Berakhot* 6b.

15. s.v. *Gezeilat Ha'ani*.

16. See also R. Yehudah Leow, *Netivot Olam, Netiv HaShalom*, ch. 2. For a different approach to the linguistic derivation, see R. Yaakov Emden, *Hagahot Ya'avetz*, and R. Yonatan Shteif, *Chadashim Gam Yeshanim* to *Berakhot*.

17. See R. Yehudah Assad, *Responsa Yehudah Ya'aleh* 9, and R. Yisrael Ya'akov Vidavski's *Sefer Amirat Shalom K'Hilkhata*, p. 63.

18. 415:3, citing the *Terumat HaDeshen, Magen Avraham*, and *Chayyei Adam*, and see also *Shaar HaTziyyun*, #9.

19. *Mishneh Torah, Hilkhot Deiot* 5:7.

20. *Gittin* 62a.

substantial length. Indeed, one such scholar, R. Yochanan b. Zakai, is singled out for praise in the Talmud[21] because "he never allowed anyone to precede him in initiating a greeting, not even a heathen in the marketplace."[22] Although the Talmud introduces the concept of initiating the greeting in reference to one who "knows that his friend is in the habit of greeting him," R. Yisrael Ya'akov Vidavski[23] suggests that this need not be interpreted solely on a personal level. Rather, any environment in which all comers are customarily welcomed automatically is subject to these guidelines. The *Yalkut MeAm Loez*[24] writes that when one encounters an individual who is wont to greet him, beating him to the punch is an obligation; to all others, such behavior is not mandatory but is praiseworthy.[25] R. Shmuel Edels[26] recommended emphasizing the first group, because a stranger may fail to return the greeting, and thus risk being labeled "a thief."[27] R. Moshe Rosmarin[28] suggests that even this concern may only be in effect if some reason exists to believe that the stranger will not respond. In addition to the goodwill engendered by initiating the greeting, this gesture is understood by many commentators[29] to also be indicative of modesty; as the pleasantries will be exchanged anyway, not waiting for the other to come to him is an act of humility.

R. Yehudah Loew of Prague, the Maharal,[30] writes that the obligation to offer warm greetings extends especially to a wicked person, lest this

21. *Berakhot* 17a; see R. Meir Dan Plotzki, *Kli Chemdah, Parshat V'Zot HaBrakhah*, and R. Yissakhar Ber Eilenberg, *Responsa Be'er Sheva* 59.

22. See *Shulchan Arukh, Yoreh Deah*, 148:9 and *Darkhei Teshuvah*. See also R. Hillel Posek, *Responsa Hillel Omer, Yoreh Deah* 66.

23. *Sefer Amirat Shalom K'Hilkhata*, p. 64.

24. *Avot* 4:14.

25. Note *Iyyun Ya'akov* to *Ein Ya'akov, Berakhot* 6b, who does not seem to recognize any distinction.

26. *Chiddushei Aggadot L'Maharsha, Berakhot* 6b.

27. See also R. Akiva Eiger, *Gilyon HaShas, Gittin* 66a; R. Yosef Sharbitner, *Pe'ar Yosef* to *Berakhot*; and R. Yitzchak Arieli's *Einayim L'Mishpat*. R. Ephraim Greenblatt (*Responsa Riv'vot Ephraim* 2:43) understands the Rambam's position (*Hilkhot Deiot* 5:7) to be different, as per R. Menachem Krakowski's *Avodat Melekh*. On the distinction between people familiar and not familiar, see *Turei Zahav, Yoreh Deah* 148:6. See also R. Yosef Chaim Sonnenfeld, *Responsa Salmat Chaim* 915–917.

28. *D'var Moshe* to *Pirkei Avot* 4:224.

29. See, for example, R. Aharon b. Yehudah HaLevi, *Chasdei Avot*, and R. Moshe Outz Meri, *Ahavat Shalom* to *Pirkei Avot* 4:20.

30. *Derekh HaChaim, Pirkei Avot* 4:14.

individual become hardened in his ways further.[31] True, some reluctance is found in sources regarding the amiable welcome of wicked people;[32] however, it appears from the Talmud Yerushalmi[33] that this refers specifically to the moment a transgression is taking place, when such a gesture may be misinterpreted as encouragement. However, very often the opposite reaction may be more likely; the friendship extended by an upstanding citizen may inspire repentance.[34] Indeed, the *Derekh Eretz Zuta* identifies this practice as the method of Aharon HaKohen in inspiring righteous behavior in others.

II. The Format of Greetings

In regards to responding to the salutation, the Talmud[35] indicates that using a double language is appropriate. The *Midrash* implies that the purpose is to maintain some element of initiative even when returning a greeting.[36] In this spirit, R. Yisrael Bruna records the custom of using a more inclusive expression, such as responding to "Good Morning" with "Good Year."[37] To the phrase *shalom aleikhem*, the well-known response is *aleikhem shalom*. While the reason for this may be purely grammatical, the *Ta'amei HaMinhagim*[38] quotes other explanations. One of these is so that it should be clear that the second party is responding and not beginning the process, so that an onlooker who hears only the second should not suspect the first party of refusing to

---

31. See also R. Ephraim Greenblatt, *Responsa Riv'vot Ephraim* 3:590:10, and R. Mordechai Moshe Laufer, in *Har HaMelekh* 4:175–177.

32. See Zohar, *Vayishlach* 171b; *Miketz*, p. 205; *Exodus*, p. 23; *Va'era*, p. 23b; *Sefer Chasidim* 51; and R. Reuven Margolios's *Mekor Chesed* at length; *Agra D'Pirka* 165; *Ta'amei HaMinhagim*, p. 547; R. Aharon Levine, *HaDrash V'HaIyyun*, *Deuteronomy*, *Ma'amar* 107; *Sefer Amirat Shalom K'hilhata*, p. 68; and *Mitzvat HaEtzah*, p. 351. It may be that the status is not applicable in modern times; see R. Avraham Yeshayah Karelitz, *Chazon Ish*, *Yoreh Deah* 1 and 2, and R. Yisrael Meir Kagan, *Sefer Ahavat Chesed*. For other sources, see Introduction, footnote 69.

33. *Shevi'it* 4:3 and 5:4 and *Avodah Zarah* 4:10; see also *Maharash Cirilo* to *Shevi'it* and *Korban HaEdah, Gittin*, ch. 5.

34. See *Sefer Amirat Shalom K'Hilkhata*, p. 68.

35. *Gittin* 62a; see also *Bamidbar Rabbah* 21:1.

36. See also R. Yosef Shalom Weinfeld, in *Otzerot Yerushalayim*, 65:1035–1039.

37. *Responsa Mahari Bruna*.

38. P. 502.

answer. Another reason is quoted in the name of the *Sefer Ge'ulat Yisrael.*[39]

Whatever the format, it seems that a greeting may not be ignored. Even in those instances when salutations are inappropriate, as discussed further on, some response is still necessary to one that is offered, albeit in a hushed and subdued manner.[40] All other times, however, the response should be commensurate with the enthusiasm of the greeting; as R. Ephraim Greenblatt[41] and R. Shlomo Aviner[42] observe, a bland nod or an uninterested grumble may not be considered sufficient reaction to an effusive welcome.[43] The *Iyyun Ya'akov*[44] remarks that the existence of strife among acquaintances is no excuse for failing to initiate a greeting and certainly not for refusing to respond to one. R. Tzvi Elimelekh of Dienov[45] comments that on the contrary, in such an instance it is all the more necessary to take the first step in offering greetings in order to hasten a reconciliation.[46] However, this does call into question the youthful behavior of the brothers of Yosef, who "could not speak with him for *shalom.*"[47] R. Shimshon Raphael Hirsch[48] therefore suggests that any overtures would be negatively interpreted.

---

39. As will be discussed later, *shalom* is one type of Divine Name. Therefore, one should be careful not to begin a phrase with this word, as the Talmud recommends (*Nedarim* 10b), for fear it will not be completed and God's name will be uttered in vain. Therefore, *aleikhem shalom* is a more appropriate response than its inverse. The initiator, however, can use the phrase *shalom aleikhem* with confidence he will finish, as the Talmud states: "He who precedes his friend in offering his greeting, his life and peace are increased." See also *Razin D'Orayta*, p. 4, and *Ta'amei Mitzvot* of R. Menachem Rikanti.

40. See *Amirat Shalom K'Hilkhata*, p. 66.

41. *Responsa Riv'vot Ephraim* 2:43.

42. *Am K'Lavi* 356, citing *Chesed L'Alafim* 150:8.

43. See also *Devarim Nechmadim* to *Proverbs* 11.

44. *Berakhot* 6b.

45. *Maggid Ta'alumot*, p. 59.

46. See also R. Gedalya Felder, *Yesodei Yeshurun*, *Pirkei Avot* 4:20.

47. *Genesis* 37:4.

48. *Biur* to *Chumash*; see *Amirat Shalom K'Hilkhata*, pp. 67–68.

III. Greetings in the Name of God

The Talmud[49] relates that it was decreed that greetings should be made using the name of God and that the Heavenly court agreed to this.[50] Whether this took place at the time of Boaz,[51] whom the Talmud identifies with this practice,[52] or was later enacted by the Hasmoneans, is a matter of some analysis.[53] R. Yehudah Assad[54] assumes this to have been instituted by Ezra.[55] The Meiri[56] explains that the reasoning behind this innovation was to make clear from whence all peace comes. This was especially necessary in light of the erosion of faith caused by the activities of the Sadducees, apparently the motivation for the enactment.[57] This preceded considerations of the inappropriate use of God's name; as the *Mishnah* cites, "It is a time to do for God, they have nullified your Torah."[58] Rashi,[59] however, implies that the fundamental concern was the spreading of peace in this era, a goal apparently encouraged by the emphasis provided by the use of God's name.[60]

The scope of the enactment is not immediately clear. Rashi[61] presents two possibilities as to whether it became obligatory to use the Divine Name in salutations,[62] or just that one who does so need not fear that

---

49. *Berakhot* 54a.

50. *Makkot* 23b.

51. As is the clear impression in *Midrash Rut Rabbah* 4:5.

52. As per *Megilat Rut* 2:4. See, in the journal *VaY'lakket Yosef*, vol 13: #s 76, 97, 103, 115, and 129.

53. See *Sefer HaMikhtam* to *Berakhot*.

54. *Responsa Yehudah Ya'aleh* 9. See also R. Yisrael Shepansky, in *Ohr HaMizrach* 113:107–111.

55. See also commentary of R. Shmuel Strashoun (Rashash), *Bava Kamma* 82a.

56. *Berakhot* 63a.

57. This is also the cause of other innovations mentioned in the *Mishnah*; see *Chiddushei HaRitva, Makkot* 23a, and R. Ya'akov ben Aharon of Karlin, *Kehilat Ya'akov* to *Berakhot*.

58. *Psalms* 119:126.

59. *Berakhot* 54a, s.v. *V'Omer*.

60. See also R. Shepansky, pp. 111–112. For a rather innovative theory as to the reasoning of the enactment, see R. Avraham Pollack in the journal *VaY'lakket Yosef*, vol. 6, no. 173.

61. *Makkot* 23b, s.v. *vish'elat shalom bishaim*. (This commentary is actually not written by Rashi, but by his student R. Yehudah b. Natan.)

62. R. Yitzchak Chajes, *Siach Yitzchak* to *Makkot*, assumes this to be the case.

he is taking God's Name in vain.[63] In either case, empirical evidence will immediately indicate that modern practice does not usually involve pronouncing God's Name in the normal mode of greeting. This discrepancy between talmudic law and modern custom is explained by the authorities in one of two ways. The first is that the enactment was temporary and is no longer in effect; in fact, the lack of reference to this notion in the Rambam's *Mishneh Torah* is accordingly noted.[64] This is the position of R. Chaim Yosef David Azulai[65] and others.[66] The second approach is that the essence of the enactment is fulfilled when care is taken to use the word *shalom*, which itself has Divine connotations.[67] Additionally, R. Yechiel Moshe Epstein[68] offers a more homiletically oriented take on the entire concept: the enactment was not primarily that greetings should be offered *with* the Name of God, but for the *sake* of the Name of God. That is to say, it must be realized that greeting others is not a mere social ritual but a profound religious act.

By such process the greeting of others became akin to pronouncing the Holy Name, in particular when the word *shalom* is used.[69] This

---

63. See R. Yosef Epstein, *Mitzvat HaEtzah*, pp. 348–349, 351; R. Shlomo Aviner, *Am K'Lavi* 356; and R. Natan Gestetner, *Natan Piryo* to *Makkot*.

64. See R. Ephraim Zalman Margoliyos, *Responsa Beit Ephraim*, *Even HaEzer* 86 and R. Yitzchak Hecht, *Responsa Sha'arei Kodesh* 1:171. R. Shepansky suggests that the Rambam felt that the thrust of the enactment was the greeting itself, a concept he does indeed record (*Hilkhot Deiot* 5:7).

65. *Petach Einayim, Yoma* 39a.

66. See R. Yitzchak Weiss, *Responsa Siach Yitzchak* 39, and R. Joseph B. Soloveitchik, cited in the journal *Mesorah* 6:33.

67. *Shabbat* 10a. See Rambam's *Peirush HaMishnayot* to *Berakhot*. The *Responsa Beit Ephraim* explicitly relates the Divinity of the word *shalom* to the enactment; note also commentary of the Arukh to *Makkot*. For a discussion of current practice in relation to this enactment, see Akiva Raz in *Sefer Avnei Shlomo, Even Shlomo* pp. 240–241. R. Shepansky suggests that the above question of whether the enactment constituted an obligation, or a permission in light of the prohibition to use God's Name in vain, is related to the issue of whether the practice became to use God's Name directly or the word *shalom* to connote Divinity. If the enactment came to permit something, its subject must be something previously forbidden, that is, the usage of God's Name in a direct sense.

68. *Be'er Moshe, Judges* 6:12 (p. 188).

69. See also R. David Oppenheim, *Responsa Nishal L'David*, *Orach Chaim* 8, and R. Yehoshua Binyamin Krupnai's discussion in *Kovetz Zikaron L'R. Yosef Chaim Shneur Kotler*, pp. 208–212.

affects the treatment of greetings in *halakhah* in a number of ways.[70] For one, it is forbidden to pronounce *shalom* in any place deemed inappropriate to say God's Name.[71] R. Yosef Engel[72] raises the question of whether this is because the act of offering greetings is now a sanctified act or because the very word *shalom* itself is considered holy. Relevant to that latter possibility, the *Tosafot*[73] consider the word to possess the status of a name that may not be erased, although Rabbeinu Asher[74] apparently disagrees.[75] R. Assad notes that the latter position is also that of the Rambam.[76] The Rama[77] recommends that an incomplete spelling be used when writing letters, to avoid problems of disrespectful treatment.[78] R. Shabtai HaKohen records that most are not of the custom to be careful for this stringency.[79] Some authorities were hesitant to allow using *shalom* to greet a bareheaded man, as he will then respond despite his lack of the necessary attire to do so;[80] nonetheless, R. Ovadiah

---

70. As to the status of non-standard designations of the Divine Name (*kinuyyei hashem*) in general, see *Responsa R. Akiva Eiger* 25 and R. Chaim Ozer Grodzinski, *Responsa Achiezer* 3:32.

71. *Shabbat* 10a and *Tosefta, Berakhot*, ch. 3, per *Judges* 6:24; see *Kessef Mishneh, Hilkhot Kriat Shema* 3:5; R. Yissakhar Shlomo Teichtal, *Responsa Mishneh Sakhir*, vol. 2, *Orach Chaim* 15; R. Eliezer Cohen, *Siach Kohen* 9; and *Responsa Sha'arei Kodesh* 2:79.

72. *Gilyonei HaShas* to *Shabbat*, based on *Responsa HaRadbaz* 1:220. See also *Ta'amei HaMinhagim*, p. 302.

73. *Sotah* 10a.

74. *Responsa HaRosh* 3:15.

75. This is implied also by the *Magen Avraham*, *Orach Chaim* 85:3; see *Machatzit HaShekel*; R. Shabtai HaKohen, *Nekudat HaKesef*, *Yoreh Deah* 277; and R. Yerucham Ciechanowicz, *Torat Yerucham* 4.

76. Note also the analysis of *Sha'arei Teshuvah*, *Orach Chaim* 84:2 and *Pitchei Teshuvah*, *Yoreh Deah* 276; R. Yosef Rosen, *Tzofnat Pa'aneach* to *Mishneh Torah*, *Mahadurah Tinyana*, p. 63; and R. Ya'akov Wehl, *Ikvei Aharon Pesher Davar*, *Gittin* 296.

77. *Yoreh Deah*, 276:13.

78. See also R. Mordechai Leib Charney, *Responsa Imrei Shalom* 46.

79. *Siftei Kohen*, *Yoreh Deah* 276:16.

80. See R. Chaim Chizkiyahu Medini, *Sdei Chemed, Kuntres HaKlallim, Ma'arekhet Ha-alef, Ot* 313, citing the *Sefer Mor V'Oholot*, p. 5. R. Medini also discusses these topics in *Ma'arekhet Aleph* 113, *Pe'at HaSadeh* 110, and *Mikhtav L'Chizkiyahu*.

Yosef[81] and R. Aharon Rosenfeld[82] are lenient, fearing such reluctance will be misinterpreted as unfriendliness. So, too, R. Moshe Shternbuch[83] feels that strictly speaking, there is no reason for concern. The *Talmud Yerushalmi*;[84] recommends distinguishing between greetings to Jews and to non-Jews in usage of the word *shalom*, an idea apparently rejected by the *Talmud Bavli*.[85]

IV. Prohibitions Related to Greetings, and the Lessons Within

In spite of the tremendous emphasis placed on providing proper greetings, there are numerous occasions when salutations are inappropriate. An understanding of these instances and their significantly varying applications, as well as other details of this area of *halakhah*, necessitates an analysis of the conceptual makeup of the phrases and the multiple functions they serve. To this end, R. Joseph D. Epstein[86] identifies several elements that are present, or may be present, when a salutation is expressed.

When the effort is taken to welcome another individual, this person enjoys an elevation of status, a boost in his personal estimation. On the most basic level, as R. Shlomo Aviner[87] points out, taking the effort to say hello to someone conveys the message, "I have time for you." In a more elaborate formulation, the greeting process can become a display of honor toward the recipient. It is in this vein that offering a greeting to a human being before praying to God in the morning[88] can be considered inappropriate.[89] Accordingly, this behavior is criticized primarily

---

81. *Yalkut Yosef.*

82. *Responsa Minchat Aharon* 2:199.

83. *Responsa Teshuvot V'Hanhagot* 1:12.

84. *Gittin* 5:5.

85. See *Gittin* 62a and *Tosafot*, s.v. *Atrata*; see also *Responsa Yehudah Ya'aleh* 9.

86. *Mitzvat HaEtzah*, p. 353.

87. *Am K'Lavi* 356.

88. Whether this law is relevant to the afternoon and evening prayers as well is the topic of an analysis by R. Ephraim Greenblatt (*Riv'vot Ephraim* 1:63); he concludes that it is applicable only to the mornings.

89. *Berakhot* 14a; *Tur* and *Shulchan Arukh, Orach Chaim* 89. See R. Ya'akov Reisher, *Responsa Shvut Ya'akov* 2:22; R. Yechezkel Landau, *Tziyyun L'Nefesh Chayah* to *Berakhot*; R. Betzalel Stern, *Responsa B'Tzel HaChokhmah* 5:71 and 73; and R. Aharon Rosenfeld, *Responsa Minchat Aharon* 1:19.

when one goes to the house of another to offer greetings, an overt act of homage, before prayers.[90] This is explicit in Rashi's language:[91] "When one is supposed to be involved in the honor of Heaven, it is forbidden to become involved in the honor of humans."

However, it should be noted that another element exists to this prohibition, that of avoiding the danger of forgetting to pray altogether. For this purpose, the Ra'avad[92] advocates utilization of alternative types of greetings, to serve as a reminder that prayer still awaits.[93] The length of time devoted to the greeting may also be a factor.[94] This topic must be carefully analyzed, for, as R. Shmuel Baruch Ohayoun observes,[95] one who is unnecessarily stringent in this area may violate the aforementioned prohibition of rejecting a greeting.

Nonetheless, once prayer has begun, various personal considerations do allow interruptions for the sake of greetings.[96] These factors differ in weight and, consequently, in the nature of interruption that is allowed, as far as the point in the prayer service and whether the greeting is an initiation or a response.[97] The first such recognized consideration is *yirah*, normally translated as "fear," which allows greetings even in the middle of the *Shema*. Rashi interprets this factor as fear for one's life; others disagree, noting such a concern would permit any violation and merit no special mention here. As such, the Rosh translates the term as

---

90. Ibid.; so, too, leniencies exist depending on the nature of the greeting used; note also *Pri Megadim, Mishnah Berurah,* and *Kaf HaChaim, Orach Chaim* 89l; *Orchot Chaim* 89:8; *Da'at Torah, Orach Chaim* 89:2; *Elyah Rabbah, Orach Chaim* 66:2, citing *Tashbetz* 246; and *Responsa Teshuvot V'Hanhagot* 1:71.

91. *Berakhot,* ibid., s.v. *Chadlu lachem min ha-adam.*

92. Cited in *Chiddushei HaRashba, Berakhot,* ibid.

93. See also *Pri Megadim, Orach Chaim* 89 and *Orchot Chaim.*

94. See *Chiddushei HaRitva* to *Berakhot.* See also R. Mordechai Willig, *Am Mordechai* 10.

95. *Responsa Halikhot SheBa* 1.

96. *Berakhot* 13a. See R. Ya'akov of Karlin, *Responsa Mishkenot Ya'akov, Orach Chaim* 83. As to whether these interruptions are permitted or actually obligated, see at length, R. Avraham Yitzchak HaKohen Kook, *Tov Roei* to *Berakhot.* See also R. Yekutiel Yehudah Rosenberger, *Responsa Torat Yekutiel, Mahadurah Kama, Orach Chaim* 46, and R. Eliyahu Ragoler, *Responsa Yad Eliyahu* 1:13 and 3:3.

97. The *Tosafot (Bava Kamma* 73b, s.v. *Ki)* suggest that avoiding the "theft" inherent in returning a greeting is a fundamental motivation behind rabbinical sanction of these interruptions.

the halakhic *mora,* or "awe," accorded to parents and *rebbeim.*[98] R. Yoel Sirkes[99] argues, noting that such awe is generally passive in nature, and upholds the position of Rashi, which is shared by the Rambam. The Meiri modifies it slightly to mean fear for any kind of harm. The other consideration is *kavod,* "honor," which justifies interrupting between blessings; Rashi understands this as referring to a dignified individual, while the Rambam[100] applies it to halakhic recipients of *kavod,* such as parents.[101] Despite these dispensations, R. Yisrael Meir Kagan[102] notes that current social understandings generally obviate the need to interrupt prayer for greetings.

Another detail of the element of offering respect with a greeting is that it must be done within certain conventions. Not every manner of addressing a distinguished individual is suitable; the Talmud[103] warns that greeting one's *rebbe*[104] in a cavalier manner may be inappropriate.[105] Thus, the *Shulchan Arukh*[106] places certain limitations on tone and style to be used.[107]

Another function of exchanging *shalom* is the concurrent increase in the sense of friendship and peace among men.[108] It is in this sense that the mention of God's Name is most called for, as per the words of the Meiri cited earlier, in order that the source of all harmony be apparent. The verse observes,[109] "As face to face in water, so does one man's heart

---

98. See also *Chiddushei HaRashba* and *Tur, Orach Chaim* 65.

99. *Bayit Chadash* to *Tur.*

100. See *Kessef Mishnah, Hilkhot Kriat Shma* 2:15.

101. See *Elyah Rabbah* 66:1.

102. *Mishnah Berurah,* 66:2.

103. See *Berakhot* 27b, *Shabbat* 89a, and *Yerushalmi Berakhot* 2:1.

104. Or perhaps all individuals of greater scholarship (see Rif to *Berakhot,* and *Ma'adanei Yom Tov,* and *Magen Avraham* 66:2) or age (see *Ma'adanei Yom Tov* 3).

105. See R. Shimon Gabel, *Kli Golah, Ta'anit* 20b.

106. *Yoreh Deah* 242:16.

107. See also R. Yitzchak Sternhill, *Kokhvei Yitzchak* to *Yerushalmi Berakhot* 2:1, at length; R. David Shperber, *Responsa Afarkasta D'Anya,* 1:104; and R. Yitzchak Hecht, *Sha'arei Kodesh* 2:181. See also R. Elazar Eidan, in the journal *Ohr Torah,* vol. 33, #142, pp. 845–848.

108. See, for example, R. Natan Gestetner, *L'Horot Natan* to *Pirkei Avot* 4:69, and R. David HaKohen Sikili, *Responsa Kiryat Chanah David,* vol. 1, *Likutim* 31.

109. *Proverbs* 27:19.

to another." Rashi explains,[110] the attitude of the first is reflected by those he encounters; an enthusiastic welcome will receive an equivalent response.

Depending on the intent, the objective of a greeting may go further than a general contribution to social unity, and is more specifically geared toward the deepening of particular bond joining two individuals. It is this type of inquiring of *shalom* that a man is enjoined from proffering toward a married woman.[111] Consequently, when there is a reason to believe the woman is not well and a genuine investigation into her health is intended, the *Responsa Avnei Mishpat*[112] feels there is no prohibition. In modern contexts, halachic authorities have assumed that in general, greetings offered to women are devoid of romantic intent.[113]

Another element present within the unsolicited salutation is perhaps also relevant to the previous instance, that of endearing oneself to the recipient. The Rambam[114] explicitly notes this as a goal of initiating greetings: "so that people will be satisfied with him."

Additionally, a greeting offered contains an aspect common to an act of kindness; one returned is part of the courtesy of gratitude. Thus, a person who is known to greet the other deserves, by rights, to have the same done to him; and when a salutation is offered unsolicited, it constitutes an act of generosity toward the recipient. It is with this perspective that the possibility that an out-of-the-ordinary welcome to one who has lent money to the greeter may be considered a form of nonmonetary interest.[115]

---

110. *Yevamot* 117a, s.v. *verabbanan.*

111. See *Kiddushin* 70b and Rashi, and *Shulchan Arukh, Even HaEzer* 21:6. See also Meiri, *Berakhot* 24a; *Responsa Sha'ar Ephraim* 116; R. Yitzchak Weiss, *Responsa Minchat Yitzchak* 8:126, and, at length, *Responsa B'Tzel HaChokhmah* 5:49–51.

112. Cited in *Otzar HaPoskim, Even HaEzer* 21:3.

113. See R. Moshe Shick, *Responsa Maharam Shick, Even HaEzer* 53, and R. Yosef Shalom Elyashiv, *Kovetz Teshuvot* 2:20:4, based on *Tosafot, Kiddushin* 82a, s.v. *hakol*, in a different context. See also R. Shamai Kehat Gross, *Responsa Shevet HaKehati* 5:227.

114. *Mishneh Torah, Hilkhot Deiot* 6:7; see also *Responsa Yehudah Ya'aleh* 9.

115. See *Bava Metzia* 75a; *Talmud Yerushalmi, Bava Metzia* 5:8; and *Shulchan Arukh, Yoreh Deah* 160:11.

Attention to the phraseology used by the Talmud reveals a basic duality inherent to the exchanging of *shalom*. On the one hand, the gesture serves as an inquiry into the person's welfare; hence the term *sh'eilat shalom*, "asking" *shalom*. Additionally, the phrase *notein shalom*, "giving" *shalom*, is also found.[116] The latter phrase has the connotation of bestowing a blessing on the recipient, offering him one's best wishes for happiness and success.[117] R. Eliezer of Papo writes that when pronouncing the word *shalom*, one's intention should be, "It should be His will that peace be with you."[118] A very real manifestation of this concept is found in the Talmudic recommendation for an individual who has dreamed he was excommunicated and fears the ominous implications. He is to sit at the crossroads and offer *shalom* to ten passersby.[119] Rabbeinu Nissim[120] explains the value of this course of action: "And through that they will respond to him, *shalom*, this will protect him from affliction."

Identifying these components is important in considering the prohibition of *sh'eilat shalom* to a mourner, or to anyone on the fast of Tisha B'Av, when all Jews are in a state of mourning.[121] To a tormented individual, freshly anguished by a painful loss, an inquiry into his *shalom* can only be inappropriate; as the Talmud states, he is far from being *sharui b'shalom*, "in a state of peace."[122] However, an offering of wishes for happier times, or an expression of a social convention, may not be uncalled for;[123] a distinction between certain modern greetings and the Talmudic *sh'eilat shalom* is evident already in the Rama.[124] Along these lines,

---

116. See, for example, *Berakhot* 14a.

117. Interestingly, R. Shabtai Kohen (*Peirush HaShakh LaTorah, Exodus* 18:7) ascribes the meaning of a blessing to the term *sh'eilat shalom*, understanding the term to be a request that the recipient attain and maintain a state of *shalom*. Compare also the position of R. Avraham Bornstein, *Responsa Avnei Nezer, Yoreh Deah* 474:1 with that of his questioner, and see *Chiddushei Maharsha, Shabbat* 89a, and *Responsa B'Tzel HaChokhmah* 5:49.

118. *Pele Yoetz, Erekh HaBerakhot*.

119. *Nedarim* 8a.

120. *Peirush HaRan*, s.v. *viyahev*.

121. *Moed Katan* 15a, 21b.

122. See R. Eliyahu Levine, *Divrei Shirah* to *Ben HaMeitzarim/Aveilut/Kaddish* 17.

123. Note, however, the opposite understanding found in *Sefer Amirat Shalom K'Hilkhata*, p. 59, footnote 6, and p. 60, footnote 8.

124. *Yoreh Deah* 381:1; note his words in *Darkhei Moshe, Orach Chaim* 89, and see *Be'er Heitev, Yoreh Deah* 385:2. See also *Chiddushei HaRitva, Moed Katan* 27b,

R. Tzvi Pesach Frank[125] allows a handshake and a blessing for long life, as does R. Raphael Evers.[126] However, many authorities take a different approach and forbid all greetings.[127] Additionally, R. Avraham Weinfeld[128] suggests that during the initial *shivah* period, an imperative of "silence" is applicable, warranting stringency despite the nature of the greeting.

Far from being a mere social convention or an instinctive grunt, the words expressed upon meeting another are packed with multiple levels of spiritual significance. Each greeting carries the potential to affect the balance of holiness in society in countless ways. The *Derekh Eretz Zuta* records God's promise, that "he who loves *shalom* and pursues *shalom*, offers *shalom* and responds with *shalom*, the Holy One, Blessed be He, will bequeath to him this world and the next."

---

and *Leket Yosher* (customs of the author of the *Terumat HaDeshen*), p. 110. See R. Shlomo Leib Tabak, *Responsa Teshurat Shai* 2:173.

125. *Responsa Har Tzvi, Yoreh Deah* 290.

126. *Responsa V'Shav V'Rapha* 62. See also R. Shraya Deblitsky, *Otzerot Yerushalayim* 28:447.

127. See R. Yisrael Meir Kagan, *Mishnah Berurah* 554:41; *Elyah Rabbah* 554:21; *Responsa B'Tzel HaChokhmah* 5:72; and R. Yosef Chaim Sonnenfeld, *Responsa Salmat Chaim* 618 and 620–621 (note also 619).

128. *Responsa Lev Avraham* 95.

To Forgive is Divine, and Human: The Bilateral Obligation of Forgiveness

I. The Obligation to Ask Forgiveness

It is abundantly clear that the halakhic view places great import on influencing the individual's interaction with others in society. The relationship of man to his fellow stands as a formidable component of any Jew's spiritual record, an irreplaceable element of one's overall standing. It is thus not surprising that any reckoning of one's religious status is considered incomplete if lacking a thorough analysis of this interaction, along with whatever methods are necessary to rectify any aberrations or disturbances that may arise within this context. The Talmud introduces this concept clearly in the course of a discussion of the laws of Yom Kippur. The Day of Atonement effects forgiveness for all transgressions, under the appropriate circumstances and accompanying devices. Nonetheless, we are told: "Sins that are between man and God, Yom Kippur atones for them; Sins that are between man and his fellow, Yom Kippur will not atone until he appeases his fellow."[1]

This notion, the imperative to attain *mechilah*, forgiveness, from an aggrieved party, is more innovative than it may initially seem.[2] While impositions upon the rights of others constitute a significant portion of prohibited behaviors, the necessity to beg the pardon of the victim is by no means obvious. It might equally have been assumed that just as God issued commands as to the behavior of one individual toward another, He, too, serves as the aggrieved party Who must forgive when these commands are trod upon. The very fact that this role is placed in the hands of the human being reflects profoundly upon the halakhic recognition of the individual as an independent entity, presiding over the circumstances of his standing with others and of theirs with him.

Through this reality the oppressor becomes subject to the mercy of his victim, the expiation of his sins contingent upon the good graces of those who have suffered at his hands. The *Pri Megadim*[3] explains that the control of the offended party extends beyond the damage incurred to him personally. The Talmud's statement that interpersonal violations are not atoned for without *mechilah* is absolute; even to the extent that these same actions are to be considered for whatever reason an affront against God, He, too, will not grant His pardon prior to the attainment of that of the aggrieved person.[4] R. Shmuel Germaizin[5] puts forward a more extended version of this position; as suggested earlier, every transgression against man by definition contains an aspect of rebellion against God.[6] Attaining the forgiveness of man is a prerequisite to being excused

---

1. *Yoma* 85b; see *Mishneh Torah* 2:9 and *Shulchan Arukh, Orach Chaim* 606:1.

2. Although some did consider this idea self-evident; see *Shlom Yerushalayim*, cited in R. Nachum Kahana's *Orchot Chaim* 606:1.

3. *Mishbetzot Zahav, Orach Chaim* 606.

4. See also *K'tzeh HaMatteh* to *Matteh Ephraim* 606, citing *Birkei Yosef*.

5. Quoted in *Pri Chadash*, ibid. Note Rashi, *Leviticus* 5:21; see also *Kerem Shlomo* in *Orchot Chaim*.

6. See also *Pri Megadim* in *Eishel Avraham, Orach Chaim* 156; *Sefer Me'irat Einayim, Choshen Mishpat* 272:10; R. Moshe Schick, *Maharam Schick Al Sefer*

for the offense against God present in every sin. This formulation goes further in dealing not only with multileveled transgressions, as does the *Pri Megadim*, but also by identifying two elements automatically in every interpersonal wrongdoing.[7] Moreover, the Vilna Gaon[8] and others claim that no transgressions at all are forgiven until forgiveness is asked of offended people.[9]

Thus, the acquisition of *mechilah* fulfills a vital goal, the securing of a pardon from the party empowered to grant it. However, it seems that the actual role of the request for forgiveness encompasses more than this. While the consent of the aggrieved individual is indispensable for spiritual housekeeping, indications exist that additional elements are present in the necessity of appeasing the offended.

II. The Problem of Unrequested Forgiveness

Were a waiver of claims the only goal of the process, it would follow that if the victim would forgive of his own initiative, without waiting for his oppressor to seek his pardon, the latter gesture would become redundant. Nonetheless, many authorities who concern themselves with this issue indicate that a request for forgiveness is necessary even if the other party has already excused the offense. R. Binyamin Yehoshua Zilber, among others, maintains that the obligation to seek *mechilah* is operative regardless.[10] However, R. Yehoshua Ehrenberg is inclined to believe that unrequested forgiveness is enough.[11]

HaMitzvot 272; *Torat Chaim, Bava Kamma* 90a; R. Yosef Babad, *Minchat Chinnukh* 364; R. Elchanan Wasserman, *Kovetz Ha'arot, Biurei Aggadot* 7:7; R. Moshe Yechiel Epstein, *Be'er Moshe* to *Genesis*, p. 39; R. David Cohen, *V'Im Tomar* 2:503; and R. Gedalya Felder, *Yesodei Yeshurun, Avot* 4:1.

7. See R. Yosef Shaul Nathanson's *Responsa Shoel U'Meishiv, Mahadurah Revia* 3:64, for support for this position. See also *Peirush HaRif* to *Ein Ya'akov, Binyan Ariel*, and R. Chaim Pilagi's *Birkat Moadekha L'Chaim, Teshuvah Drush* 15, all cited in R. Shlomo Wahrman's *Orot Yemei HaRachamim* 37.

8. See *Siddur HaGra*; see also R. Chaim Yosef David Azulai, *Birkei Yosef*, and R. Ya'akov Chaim Sofer, *Kaf HaChaim, Orach Chaim* 606.

9. See R. S. T. Shapira, *Meishiv Nefesh* to *Hilkhot Teshuvah* 2:31. Note, overall, his discussions in 30:43.

10. *Responsa Az Nidbaru* 2:65.

11. *Responsa D'var Yehoshua* 5:20.

A story related by the Talmud[12] is cited by those who agree with R. Zilber as support for their position. Rav had been offended by a certain butcher, and, following the passage of some time, they had still not reconciled. As Yom Kippur was approaching, Rav took pains to make himself available to the butcher so that the latter may apologize. R. Yitzchak Blazer[13] observes that in doing so, Rav was engaging in a form of *imitatio Dei*, as God also brings Himself closer to facilitate repentance during the Ten Days of Penitence between Rosh Hashanah and Yom Kippur.[14] That aside, the very necessity of accessibility on the part of Rav is troubling; as he is clearly prepared to forgive and forget, there should be no need for the butcher to ask. It seems, then, that the act of apologizing is integral to the forgiveness granted on Yom Kippur.[15] Similarly, R. Eliezer Ginsberg[16] writes that the *mechilah* would be ineffectual, lacking genuine penitence on the part of the sinner.

This element is relevant to another issue of concern among authorities. Yom Kippur, mentioned as a motivation to seek *mechilah*, is seemingly superfluous; if an offense has been committed, forgiveness must be sought irrespective of the time of year. R. Ephraim Zalman Margoliyos, in his classic collection of the laws relevant to the High Holy Day period, *Matteh Ephraim*,[17] writes that this is, of course, the case; however, Yom Kippur is noted as the final deadline for this obligation. R. Pinchas A. Z. Goldenberger[18] suggests an approach in line with this. If an interpersonal violation is committed, pardon must be sought immediately; nonetheless, if the victim bears no grudge, then this action is of less necessity. However, the impending arrival of Yom Kippur imposes an additional requirement of obtaining *mechilah* that is not suspended in the event of unsolicited forgiveness.[19]

---

12. *Yoma* 87a.
13. *Kokhvei Ohr* 5.
14. *Isaiah*, ch. 58, as per *Yevamot* 49a.
15. See also R. Shlomo Zalman of Volozhin's *Toldot Adam*.
16. *V'Atah B'Rachamekha HaRabim, Hilkhot Teshuvah* 2:9.
17. *Matteh Ephraim*, 606.
18. *Responsa Minchat Asher* 3:32.
19. See the similar interpretation in R. Moshe Shternbuch, *Responsa Teshuvot V'Hanhagot* 2:285.

This added element may explain the reluctance of many authorities to allow reliance on the prayer composed by R. Avraham Danzig, the *Chayyei Adam*, known as *tefillah zakkah*.[20] In this invocation, recited by many immediately before the onset of Yom Kippur, all nonmonetary grievances are forgiven. As such, the widespread adoption of this prayer should render the requests for *mechilah* obsolete. Nonetheless, this has not been the view of many decisors. As R. Meir Isaacson[21] observes, while the prayer plays a valuable role in strengthening the resolve to genuinely forgive others, the latter's obligation to actually apologize is not at all diminished. Along similar lines, R. Zilber[22] advises against depending on the nightly recitation found in the Talmud[23] in the name of Mar Zutra, "I forgive all who have anguished me" (noting further that it is usually pronounced without much thought). However, in another responsum,[24] he does acknowledge the *tefillah zakkah* as a last resort, but only in an instance where the aggrieved party cannot be reached.

III. The Focus on the Process

Thus, it seems that the appeal for forgiveness accomplishes a goal above and beyond the absolution of the victim. R. Zilber provides a technical spin in his formulation, writing that the obligation is the request itself, and the aim of attaining the pardon of the offended party is only a method of measuring what degree of apology is necessary. Many rabbinic scholars felt that the operative element is the embarrassment experienced by the aggressor who comes, hat in hand, to beg forgiveness; it is this act itself that effects atonement.[25] The Talmud[26] states as much: "Whoever commits a sin, and is embarrassed of it, he is forgiven all of his transgressions."[27] R. Shlomo Wahrman[28] suggests that it is

---

20. See *Chayyei Adam, Klal* 144.
21. *Responsa Mevaser Tov* 2:55.
22. *Responsa Az Nidbaru* 7:65.
23. *Megillah* 28a.
24. *Responsa Az Nidbaru* 8:68.
25. See R. Yosef Cohen, *Be'eri BaSadeh* to *Hilkhot Teshuvah*; and R. Mordechai Carlebach, *Chavatzelet HaSharon al haTorah, Genesis* pp. 722–725.
26. *Berakhot* 12b.
27. See also *Hasagot HaRa'avad, Hilkhot Teshuvah*.

contrary to the nature of the hardhearted sinner to admit wrongdoing to his victim; in conquering his nature, he earns his pardon.[29]

Interestingly, while forgiveness without the formality of the request is apparently insufficient, a case for the reverse circumstance is found in the writings of R. Shlomo Luria.[30] His discussion centers around a traditional procedure of appeasement, which involved the guilty individual standing before the congregation and declaring, "I have sinned against God and against this man." The confession for the offenses against God, preceding that for the crime against man, seems premature; it has already been established that Heavenly forgiveness comes only after human forgiveness. R. Luria suggests that once the offender has shown his willingness to beg the absolution of his victim and commenced the process, even though he has not actually received the pardon of the wronged individual, God's reprieve is forthcoming.

More so, even if the attempt at forgiveness is not successful, some authorities feel that the effort is sufficient.[31] The *Pri Chadash* explains in this manner the fact that the offender is not obligated to make his application more than three times.[32] The existence of an exemption after a certain point indicates that the process is more the concern than the result.

The element of subordination in the seeking of forgiveness comes into play as well in considering the issue of the effectiveness of a request for *mechilah* carried out by a third party. R. Baruch Rakovsky[33] notes that the lack of confrontation results in a limited sense of submission, and to that effect cites the *Derekh HaMelekh*[34] as discouraging such a practice; although the *Yefei Mareh* allows it, cited approvingly by the *Matteh Moshe*

---

28. *Orot Yemei HaRachamim* 37.

29. See also *Moadim U'Zmanim* 1:54, at length.

30. *Yam Shel Shlomo, Bava Kamma* 8:49.

31. See R. Yitzchak Sorotzkin, *Gevurat Yitzchak* to *Hilkhot Teshuvah*.

32. As to whether this is an exemption or a prohibition, compare *Bayit Chadash* and *Pri Chadash*; see also *Sefat Emet, Yoma* 87. Many of the commentaries to *Shulchan Arukh* maintain there is no prohibition as long as no "disgrace to the Torah" is involved; see R. David Ariav, *L'Reakha Kamokha*, vol. 3, sec. 3, ch. 4, *Nir L'David* 575, and R. Mordechai Eliyahu, in his *Bein Adam L'Chaveiro*, p. 38.

33. *Birkat Avot*, 62.

34. *Hilkhot Teshuvah* 2:9.

and skeptically by the *Pri Chadash*. The *Pele Yo'etz*, however, does warn against letting the stigma of embarrassment deter one from seeking *mechilah*, allowing that a messenger or a letter are preferable alternatives to bypassing this requirement.[35]

Another concept drawing relevance from this idea is that cited by the Gaon of Vilna[36] in the name of the *Midrash Tanchuma*: "If he has gone to appease him, and the latter has not accepted, what should he do? R. Shmuel says, Let him bring ten individuals, and form a line, and say to them, there was a quarrel between me and my friend, and I tried to appease him, and he did not accept . . . and God will see that he lowered himself, and he will have compassion." Here, too, the embarrassment experienced by this public confession is integral to the atonement.[37] To this end, R. Yosef Chaim ben Eliyahu[38] questions whether it is necessary that the ten be men, as is required for communal prayer, or perhaps women are equally effective. He analyzes whether the publicity will be diminished, and whether equal embarrassment is felt in front of different social groups, in deciding the issue. R. Yechiel Michel Epstein, however, understands the role of the *minyan* differently;[39] the purpose is to evoke the Divine presence, and thus to encourage forgiveness.[40]

This notion of personal redemption through the process of apology may also explain a difficult phrase in the Rama. After recording the admonition to an offended individual not to cruelly refuse forgiveness, the Rama adds that *mechilah* "may be withheld if it is for the good of the sinner."[41] The meaning behind this is suggested by R. Yisrael Meir

---

35. See also R. Mordechai Eliyahu in his *Bein Adam L'Chaveiro*, p. 39.

36. *Biur HaGra, Orach Chaim* 606.

37. See also commentary of the Mordechai, *Yoma* 8:723. R. Mordechai Eliyahu, in his *Bein Adam L'Chaveiro* (p. 38), also mentions the submission as the operative factor in effecting the atonement, but implies the motivation for this particular ritual is to avoid "suspicion" among the public that the offender had not attempted to obtain forgiveness.

38. *Responsa Rav Pe'alim* 63.

39. *Arukh HaShulchan, Orach Chaim* 606:4.

40. See also the analysis of both possibilities in R. Shamai Kehat Gross, *Responsa Shevet HaKehati* (5:104).

41. *Orach Chaim* 606:1; see *Nezirut Shimshon* in *Orchot Chaim*, and R. Ya'akov Yichizkiyah Fish, *Titten Emet L'Ya'akov*, p. 195. The source for the Rama's ruling is discussed in detail by R. Natan Nota Kahana, *Responsa Divrei R'nanah*, 2.

Kagan:[42] the more the oppressor finds it necessary to appeal for absolution, the greater his sense of submission and thus his atonement. R. Epstein, however, notes that such an attitude is more theoretically noted than practically recommended.[43]

IV. The Ultimate Goal

In any case, it might be suggested that an additional function is contained within the imperative of seeking *mechilah*, beyond the sense of submission that accompanies the ordeal. Even after an individual who has suffered at the hands of another forgives his oppressor, the scars of the offense remain. It is comparable to one who has incurred physical injury and pardons his attacker; although the assailant receives his absolution, the painful effects of his violence are left in full force. The imperative of seeking *mechilah* is as much the appeasement as the forgiveness.[44] It is possible for the latter to exist without the former; the emphasis on process as well as result is to ensure that both are obtained.[45] Thus, the *Shulchan Arukh* rules that an unsuccessful attempt at reconciliation must be followed by a second, and then a third; and, as the commentators on the *Shulchan Arukh* observe, each time employing a different method of self-ingratiation, earnestly attempting to find the one that succeeds.

Apparently, this, too, is a prerequisite for achieving atonement on Yom Kippur: that harmonious relationships among men must resume, that strife and discord be eliminated. This idea is explicit in the *Pirkei D'Rav Eliezer* (ch. 15), where it is stated that at the time of Yom Kippur,

---

42. *Mishnah Berurah* 606:9.

43. *Arukh Hashulchan, Orach Chaim* 606:2. See also the comments of his son, R. Baruch Epstein, *Torah Temimah, Genesis* 20:17, and R. Yosef Cohen, *Ikvei HaSadeh* to *Hilkhot Teshuvah*. R. Mordechai Eliyahu in his *Bein Adam L'Chaveiro* (p. 40), recommends that even in such an instance, the offended party should forgive the offender in his heart, only maintaining an outward appearance of rigidity.

44. For an interesting discussion of certain aspects of this concept, see R. Yedidiah Monsonigo, *Responsa D'var Emet* 18.

45. Interestingly, R. Mordechai Carlebach (*Chavatzelet HaSharon al haTorah, Genesis*, pp. 645–646) recognizes this distinction, but assumes that appeasement generally precedes a waiver of claims (and he then proceeds to analyze this waiver). See also R. David Cohen, *Birkat Ya'avetz*, vol. 1, pp. 57–59.

Samael argues for the defense of Israel, noting their similarity to the ministering angels. Among the comparisons is "What is true of angels? There is peace between them, so too Israel." This argument is so compelling that God forgives the Jewish people their sins. R. Yechiel Michel Epstein identifies this idea as being behind the practice of asking *mechilah*, the conduit to peace. The *Midrah* states similarly: "Great is peace, for at a time when the Jewish people are united, even if they have worshipped idols, God forgives them."[46]

In this spirit, Rashi[47] notes that a show of reconciliation is as valuable as expressing the forgiveness: "If he hugged him and kissed him, there is no *mechilah* greater than this."[48] However, absent some such display, some verbal forgiveness must be expressed.[49]

This notion is similarly manifest in a homiletic observation of R. Moshe Sofer.[50] Addressing his followers between Rosh Hashanah and Yom Kippur, he commented, "In the time when the *Beit HaMikdash* stood, we do not find that there was an obligation for every Jew to seek *mechilah* from his friend on the eve of Yom Kippur. For the nature of the sacrifices is to bring closer the hearts of men, and to make peace among them on their own."[51]

R. Baruch Leizerofsky[52] notes the difference of expression that is found in various talmudic sources; in one, the process of attaining *mechilah* is called a "request";[53] in another,[54] it is "appeasement." These two descriptions appear to address specifically the twin goals of the process: the seeking of absolution and the bringing about of reconciliation.

---

46. *Tanchuma, Parshat Tzav* 7, and *Bereishit Rabbah* 38:6; see *Bamidbar Rabbah* 11:7; *Derekh Eretz Zuta*, ch. 9; *Sefer Mitzvot Katan* 8; *Sefer Charedim*, ch. 7; *Peirush HaGra* to *Proverbs* 26:20 and 29:22; and *Torah Temimah* 19:6. See *Birkat Ya'avetz* (ibid., pp. 59–60) for a different formulation of this idea.

47. *Responsa Rashi* 245.

48. See also an analysis of this position in R. Carlebach's *Chavatzelet HaSharon al haTorah*, ibid., pp. 644–646 and p. 718.

49. See *Responsa Mishpetei Shmuel* 119. See also R. David Binyamin Brezacher, in the journal *Kol Torah*, vol. 20, pp. 68–69.

50. *Derashot Chatam Sofer, Shabbat Shuvah.*

51. See also R. Fishel Avraham Mael, *Shivtei Yisrael*, pp. 484–487.

52. *Responsa Ta'am Baruch* 21.

53. *Bava Kamma* 92a.

54. *Yoma* 85b.

If the goal of asking *mechilah* is more reconciliation than a technical release of claims, it may follow that in determining the need for a request, the focus is more on the disturbance of interpersonal equilibrium than on the act of transgression itself. The Rambam, in discussing the imperative of *mechilah*, includes theft among the offenses necessitating such action.[55] However, elsewhere in his code,[56] he comments about such a person who has damaged the property of another: "Once he has paid the damages, he is forgiven." The implication is that no request is necessary. R. Avraham De Boton[57] suggests that the distinction is due to the fact that theft benefits the perpetrator, while damaging property does not; thus, the former offense is more of a deliberate affront; while the latter, technically a crime, is less likely an intentional impingement.[58] Thus, it is assumed that theft causes a greater rift between men and is therefore more subject to requiring *mechilah*.

For this reason, the Butchacher Rav[59] wrote that although ordinarily forgiveness should be sought immediately at any time of the year, one valid reason does exist for intentionally delaying it until just before Yom Kippur. If the passage of time preceding the request will contribute to the healing, if the more deliberate scheduling will lend greater permanency to the reconciliation, that justifies a postponed appeasement.[60] Along similar lines, R. Yechezkel Levenstein[61] cautioned against issuing perfunctory, less than sincere pardons.[62]

---

55. *Mishneh Torah*, *Hilkhot Teshuvah* 2:9. Compare *Sha'arei Teshuvah* 1:44 and 4:18.

56. *Hilkhot Choveil U'Mazik* 5:9.

57. *Lechem Mishneh*, *Hilkhot Choveil U'Mazik*.

58. R. Brezacher, *Kol Torah*, *ibid.*, pp. 66–67, offers support for this suggestion; see, however, the *mafteach* of R. Shabtai Frankel to *Mishneh Torah*, citing *Ma'aseh Rokeach; Darkhei David*, *Bava Kamma* 92a; *Tosafot Yom HaKippurim*, *Yoma* 85b, s.v. *aveirot*; and *Responsa Shtei HaLechem* 15, who disagree. See also R. Y. M. Charlap, *Beit Zvul*, *Bava Kamma* 5; R. Zalman Uri, in the journal *HaPardes*, vol. 35, no. 5:21–22 (45); and R. Zevulun Zaks, in the journal *Moriah*, vol. 24, no. 3–4, p 114–8. On asking forgiveness for theft, see R. Alon Avigdor, *Responsa Adnei Paz* 28.

59. *Eishel Avraham*; see *Orchot Chaim* 606:2.

60. See R. Chaim David Weiss' *Responsa VaYa'an David* 1:26.

61. Cited in R. Avraham Tobolsky's *Hizharu B'Khvod Chaveirkhem*, p. 99.

62. See also R. Shammai Ginzberg, *Imrei Shammai*, pp. 90–91.

VI. Counterproductive Apologies: the Dispute Between R. Y. M. Kagan and R. Yisrael Salanter

In this light, one must also take into consideration those circumstances in which a request for *mechilah* would do more harm than good. R. Yoel Sirkes[63] writes that in apologizing, one is required to specify the offenses of which one is aware, rather than mouthing a general confession lacking any recognition of the particular manner in which harm has been done to the other. In this vein, R. Yisrael Meir Kagan, in his classic work on the laws of *lashon hara* (malicious gossip),[64] rules that one who has spread damaging information about another must seek his forgiveness, basing his comments on those of Rabbeinu Yonah.[65] R. Yisrael Lipkin (Salanter), revered founder of the modern *Mussar* movement, disagreed, noting that this would require informing the victim, who was until now blissfully ignorant. In inflicting emotional pain, such a gesture would be manifestly counterproductive.[66] R. Binyamin Yehoshua Zilber[67] was of the opinion that R. Kagan would certainly agree that the victim should not be informed of negative talk against him that he is unaware of;[68] it is only when he knows of the gossip but not the source that he would advocate confession.[69] Similarly, R. Shlomo Aviner[70] writes that *lashon hara* that has "succeeded" in having a negative effect must be owned up to, but that which has not is better left alone.[71] R. Yochanan Segal Vosner[72] proposes that

63. *Bayit Chadash.*

64. *Chafetz Chaim*, part 1, *Klal* 4:12.

65. *Sha'arei Teshuvah, Sha'ar* 3:207.

66. It is said that R. Lipkin withheld his approbation of R. Kagan's work out of concern for this issue. See R. Eliyahu Lopian, *Lev Eliyahu*, vol. 1, p. 108, and *Meorot HaGedolim* 141.

67. *Responsa Az Nidbaru* 8:68. A similar suggestion is made by R. Yisrael Isser Hertzog in the journal *HaDarom* 52:62–67.

68. See also *Sh'eilat Shmuel*, in *Orchot Chaim.*

69. Earlier authorities did make exception for situations that would be embarrassing to the victim; see *Magen Avraham, Orach Chaim* 606:1, and *Machatzit HaShekel*; note also *Elyah Rabbah.*

70. *Am K'Lavi* 1:181.

71. See also R. Yitzchak Ben Shoshan, *Responsa Toldot Yitzchak* 1:29.

72. *Responsa Chayei HaLevi* 3:100. Note, in *Chafetz Chaim, Be'er Mayim Chaim* 48.

R. Kagan was referring to a situation in which the offense would have eventually become known to the victim, and thus it is better heard from the antagonist than from anyone else. R. David Binyamin Brezacher[73] suggests that anguish to the victim is sufficient reason to dispense with asking *mechilah*, but that the embarrassment of the offender is not.

When seeking *mechilah* and specifying the offense is indeed contraindicated, options still exist. The first is to ask for a general forgiveness, without identifying a particular wrongdoing. This does tend to arouse suspicion, and in this vein R. Wahrman offers another approach to explain the relationship between requesting *mechilah* and Yom Kippur. Ordinarily, it is difficult to ask forgiveness without naming a crime; however, on the eve of Yom Kippur, when everyone is asking *mechilah* of everyone else, it is expected and raises no questions. This approach is found also in the writings of R. Moshe Shternbuch,[74] and to some extent in those of R. Avraham Erlanger,[75] who also suggests that this may be one situation in which it is preferable to rely on the *zakkah* prayer. R. Ahron Soloveichik[76] suggests that in the instance of *lashon hara*, in place of begging absolution, it is appropriate to disperse information that will counteract the negative effects of the gossip; in this case, such action is more consistent with increasing harmony than seeking the victim's pardon.

VII. The Obligation of the Victim

Further, it is with this perspective that some motive can be offered for the victim to initiate the process that is the responsibility of the aggressor. R. Aviner[77] considers the case of a man whose acquaintance burst

---

73. *Kol Torah, ibid.*, pp. 67–68.

74. *Moadim U'Zmanim* 1:54. See also the discussion of this in R. Mordechai Babad, *Minchat Machvat* 2:132.

75. *Ma'or HaSha'ar* to *Sha'arei Teshuvah*.

76. *Parach Mateh Aharon, mada*, pp. 186–189. The dispute between R. Kagan and R. Lipkin is recounted in detail here; see also, pp. 86–88. This is part of a longer discussion as to the function and mechanism of *teshuvah* and *mechilah*. R. Soloveichik suggests a similar notion in a different context as well, that of when the precise victim is unknown (p. 197).

77. *Noam*, vol. 25, pp. 202–213.

into his home and behaved in an offensive manner. After being removed from the premises, the intruder developed a grudge that remained powerful for months afterward, avoiding all interaction with this man, even as Yom Kippur loomed closer. R. Aviner advised the man that even though the blame lies with the aggressive individual, it is still recommended that he take the initiative in asking *mechilah*, as that is the only way reconciliation will be forthcoming. Thus, while forgiveness flows primarily from the victim to the oppressor, appeasement may go in either direction when indicated.[78]

Therefore, we find, not surprisingly, that *mechilah* is formulated as an obligation not only for the offender to seek but also for the aggrieved party to bestow. The Mishnah[79] warns that one who refuses to forgive is call *akhzari*, "cruel." The Meiri explains that he is apparently unconcerned about the punishment that will befall the now-penitent individual who wronged him. Such callousness is not befitting a descendant of Avraham, cited by the Talmud as the model of forgiveness. The text of the *Mishnah* as found in the Talmud Yerushalmi states the *halakhah* as a prohibition, noting the source for the *halakhah* that "one may not be cruel and refuse to forgive."[80] The necessity for harmonization demands that the imperative of *mechilah* be bilateral; granting forgiveness is as mandatory as requesting it.[81] In this light, some authorities discuss the status of those who swear in anger never to forgive. It is possible that this is considered an oath in violation of the Torah and is thus null and void.[82] Rabbeinu Asher, the *Rosh*,[83] rules that a father who forbids his

---

78. See also *Sefat Emet, Yoma* 87b, s.v. *ikpid; Piskei Teshuvot, Orach Chaim* 606:1; R. Mordechai Eliyahu, *Bein Adam L'Chaveiro*, p. 38.

79. *Bava Kamma* 92a.

80. See also *Mishneh Torah, Hilkhot Teshuvah* 2:9, and *V'Atah B'Rachamekha HaRabbim*.

81. Although there are specialized instances in which it is permissible to maintain some type of grudge; an analysis of these cases can be found in the journal *Torat HaAdam L'Adam*, vol 4, pp. 283–291.

82. R. Yoel Sirkes, *Responsa HaBach HaChadashot* 46, considers this possibility and rejects it on technical grounds. See also *Responsa Rashi* 245; *Responsa Geonei Batrai* 40; and R. Yosef Engel, *Gilyonei HaShas, Pesachim* 4a, and *Yoma* 87a.

83. *Responsa HaRosh, Klal* 15:5.

son to forgive a penitent adversary is commanding a violation of the Torah and thus forfeits his parental right to honor.

Concerning the perspective of the victim, R. David Ariav[84] (referencing the writings of R. Joseph Epstein) relates an analytical theory of the nature of forgiveness that parallels the above theories concerning asking for *mechilah*. This theory builds on a difference in wording between the commentaries of Rashi and the Meiri in interpreting a Talmudic passage discussing forgiveness (*Bava Kamma* 92a). In Rashi's understanding, the forgiveness is needed because the victim "worries" (present tense) about his suffering; while in the Meiri's rendering, the issue is that the victim "worried" (past tense) over his suffering.

While apparently a narrow distinction, this theory builds upon the difference to create two models of forgiveness. One is an emotional reality, the dissipation of bad feeling; this goal is indicated by Rashi, who looks for forgiveness to undo a current state of "worrying." Such an interpretation is consistent with the aforementioned position of Rashi in his responsa that any show of reconciliation is sufficient. The second, that of the Meiri, refers to a past situation, which may not have any current presence; thus, it is best compared to a monetary claim, that forgiveness removes as a "waiver."

R. Ariav notes that examining whether *mechilah* is to be viewed as an emotional reconciliation or as a release of debt is helpful for considering a number of hypothetical queries. Among them: Does one need to apologize for anguish that has been forgotten? Is forgiveness effective if the victim expresses absolution, but does not genuinely feel it? Is there a formal language for granting *mechilah*? What if a victim forgives quickly for a semi-forgotten offense, and then later regrets, after recalling the acute pain that was felt? What if forgiveness was granted under false pretenses, for example to one who claims an intentional slight was unintended? What if the victim grants a perfunctory, general *mechilah*, in response to a unspecific request (as is common on the eve of Yom Kippur), not realizing that the perpetrator actually committed a genuine offense for which significant appeasement would be needed (as with the above discussion concerning *lashon hara*)?

---

84. *L'Reakha Kamokha*, vol. 3, *Kuntres haBiurim*, 7.

Further, some of his hypotheticals build upon the notion of the rules of monetary law governing the *mechilah* process, if such an inference can be drawn from the Meiri. Can *mechilah* be revoked? If a victim forgives mentally, but does not express it, can he deny forgiveness later, when asked? Can a child (who is not empowered to release monetary debts) fully express *mechilah*, or must the offender wait until the victim attains majority? R. Ariav's essay weighs all of these questions, and concludes[85] that it is evidently crucial for the victim to take into account the necessity of both approaches, and to clearly express forgiveness, while at the same time doing his utmost to create an inner reality that is consistent with that expression.

The relationship between men serves as a barometer of their standing before Heaven. As the *Mishnah*[86] states, "What is the right course that a man should choose for himself? One which is an honor to the one doing it, and honorable to him from men." Any time the social equilibrium is disrupted, repairing the rift becomes a spiritual necessity of utmost urgency.

---

85. In the following essay, #8.
86. *Avot* 2:1

CHAPTER

ELEVEN

One Strike and You're Out: Hitting and Raising a Hand in Violence

I. The Prohibition of Physical Violence

Almost all societies, certainly in modern times, have strictures against unprovoked violence toward another person. It is no surprise that the *halakhah* is no exception, looking severely askance at one who would deign to strike another. A biblical injunction imposes itself on this behavior, prohibiting in an illuminating context the act of hitting another. Under the proper circumstances, the rabbinical court was forced at times to administer lashes to certain transgressors. The Torah prescribes forty of these lashes, and by rabbinical interpretation the number is thirty-nine.[1] Simultaneous to the instruction of this procedure is a

---

1. *Makkot* 22b.

prohibition not to allow the number of lashes to be exceeded by any small degree. "Forty [lashes] shall you strike him," states the Torah, but "*lo yoseif, pen yoseif l'hakkoto*—do not add, lest you hit him addition-ally."[2] As the Rambam observes,[3] if it is forbidden to strike a convicted felon, already deserving of lashes, even one extra time, certainly an assault on an innocent individual is inconceivable.[4] The Rambam cites the first half of the phrase, *lo yoseif*,[5] as the basis of the prohibition; to the *Tur* and the *Shulchan Arukh*,[6] the second phrase, *pen yoseif*, is the source. Rabbeinu Bachya[7] was of the opinion that the verse contains two injunc-tions, both of which are violated when one person strikes another.

It should be emphasized at the outset that the subject here is not the inflicting of an injury, the restitution for which occupies an entire chap-ter of the Talmud[8] and substantial further analysis. The reference is only to the action of hitting, regardless of whether any bodily harm was actu-ally experienced. Thus, it is encoded in *Shulchan Arukh*:[9] "One who strikes his fellow violates a prohibition, and is subject to the penalty of lashes." The action is forbidden independently of the damage it may incur, and as such R. Ya'akov Weil discusses at length the penitence that must be undertaken for this behavior.[10]

Partaking in such conduct is not excused easily in *halakhah*. As R. Shammai Kehat Gross[11] observes, citing Rabbeinu Asher,[12] even if one curses the parents of another, a popular method of provocation in modern society, it is not permissible to respond with violence. Nonetheless, there is some avenue of defense for one who loses control

---

2. *Deuteronomy* 25:3.
3. *Mishneh Torah, Hilkhot Choveil U'Mazik* 5:1.
4. On this derivation, see *Netivot Olam* to *Kitzur Sefer Mtizvot Gadol* (*Smag*), and, at length, R. Avraham Price, *Mishnat Avraham* to *Smag*.
5. See *Arukh L'Neir, Sanhedrin* 2:13.
6. *Choshen Mishpat* 420; see *Sefer Meirat Einayim*. See also R. Aharon David Goldberg, *Shirat David* to *Exodus* 2:13.
7. Commentary to the Torah, *Deuteronomy* 25:3.
8. The eighth chapter of *Masekhet Bava Kamma*, 83b-93a.
9. *Choshen Mishpat* 420:1–2.
10. *Responsa Mahari Veil* 28 and 87.
11. *Responsa Shevet HaKehati* 3:319.
12. *Orchot Chaim* 82.

in the heat of conflict. R. Yair Bachrach[13] notes the existence of two mitigating factors in this instance. The first, of course, is the element of self-defense that is involved. The second is less obvious; this line of defense bases itself on the reduced level of self-control that exists when one is under attack and is fueled by physical provocation. This concept, *chom levavo*, or "heat of his heart," provides some degree of excusability to the violent response.[14] Still, R. Bachrach emphasizes that this is only applicable to a reaction toward a physical offensive, not verbal attacks.[15] Moreover, even when that element is present, justification is subject to the approval of the local custom, rather than being a unilateral element of Jewish law.[16] R. Ya'akov Ariel observes that even one who strikes back in the "heat of his heart" may still be culpable if the original strike against him came from a justified figure authorized to use force to maintain order.[17] Whether one may use violence to evict an unwanted individual who enters his home (assuming, of course, he does not pose a danger) is a matter of some debate.[18]

II. Raising the Hand in Threat of Violence

However, the previous discussion of one person who strikes another actually exists on a level at least one beyond that of the boundary of the *halakhah*. Even before contact is made with the victim, certainly before any bodily harm has been incurred, Torah law has been seriously transgressed. The Talmud warns,[19] "Resh Lakish said He who raises his

---

13. *Responsa Chavvot Yair* 65:2.

14. See also R. Yisrael Grossman, *Responsa Netzach Yisrael* 15.

15. Compare R. Shlomo Luria, *Yam Shel Shlomo, Bava Kamma* 8:42, who concedes some measure of reduced culpability, but with the prohibition still no less in effect, in the instance of one who reacts violently to verbal provocation. See chapter 7, p. 105, n.43.

16. See R. Joseph D. Epstein's analysis of this concept in his *Mitzvot HaShalom*, pp. 173–177.

17. *Responsa B'Ohalah Shel Torah* 1:4:6.

18. Compare *Shulchan Arukh, Choshen Mishpat* 4:1, with ibid., 421:6, and see *Bava Kamma* 48a, *Mishneh Torah, Hilkhot Sanhedrin* 2:12 and *Lechem Mishneh*; Meiri, *Bava Kamma* 27b; *Arukh HaShulchan, Choshen Mishpat* 421:9; R. Seymour Turk, *Responsa Pri Malkah* 77; and R. Shlomo Aviner, in the journal *Noam* 25:202–213.

19. *Sanhedrin* 58b.

hand to strike another, even though he has not actually struck him, is considered wicked."[20] This is grounded in a biblical quotation: Moshe, when coming upon two men facing physical combat, acted to halt the conflict. To one of the pair, whom the Torah names "The Wicked One," Moshe asks, "Why would you strike your friend?"[21] The verb tense used indicates that no blows had yet been inflicted; nonetheless, the display of intent was sufficient to earn the label "wicked."[22]

The Talmud continues its criticism of even a threatening gesture. R. Zeiri, in the name of R. Chanina, calls the perpetrator of such behavior "a sinner," and adduces textual proof for his position. Further positions cited call into question the appropriateness of allowing such an individual to retain possession of his hands.[23] According to some, these last measures are examples of extralegal initiatives afforded to rabbinical courts at their discretion.[24] In any event, it thus emerges that there exists a transgression prior to the act itself of striking; any commencement of physical aggression, regardless of its outcome, is subject to a biblical prohibition.

Some authorities find the existence of this law surprising, noting that in *halakhah* intent is never considered an action in itself to incriminate; crimes that are planned but not carried out carry no label of guilt.[25] Further, if no blow is actually completed, no injury whatsoever is inflicted, and thus the offense would seem to be avoided entirely; thus, any possibility that this should be included among actions that are prohibited because they violate the law to some degree, though lacking in the specifications necessary for punishment (*chatzi shiur*),[26] is difficult to

---

20. See also *Midrash Tanchuma, Korach* 8.

21. *Exodus* 2:13.

22. It also appears from Moshe's assumption that no excuse would have been acceptable; see R. Yosef Yehudah Leib Sorotzkin, *Meged Yosef* to *Exodus*.

23. Whether this last comment is meant to refer to one who raises his hand or rather to one who actually hits (as well as how literally it is to be taken) is subject to some ambiguity; see Rashi to *Sanhedrin; Responsa Maharam MiRotenberg* (Prague) 81; *Responsa HaRitva* 131; *Responsa Rivash* 151; R. Yitzchak Arieli, *Einayim L'Mishpat, Sanhedrin* 58b; R. Menachem Chakham, *Z'hav Menachem*, vol. 1, *Choshen Mishpat* 50; R. Ya'akov Chaim Sofer, *Yechi Yosef* 15:15; and R. Shlomo Zalman Braun, *Shearim Metzuyanim B'Halakhah* to *Sanhedrin*.

24. See, for example, R. David Sinsheim, *Yad David* to *Sanhedrin*.

25. *Kiddushin* 39b.

26. *Yoma* 74a.

support. R. Aharon Grossman[27] puts forth the theory that the prohibition is protective in nature, and it and the stigmas attached in the Talmud are for the purpose of preventing the threat of bodily harm from being actualized.[28] R. David Ariav[29] questions whether the reason for the prohibition is rooted in an actual intent to harm (a reason supported by R. Chaim Kanevsky[30]) or perhaps because of the fear that is instilled, a violation of the prohibition of *ona'at devarim*.[31] If it is the latter, he suggests, the prohibition would only be incurred if the potential victim was aware of the gesture.

It might be further suggested, however, that the prohibition is not merely designed to prevent further transgression but rather speaks to the declaration of an attitude. A person who raises his hand in threat of striking another has severely altered the tone of interaction, indicating that he is prepared to introduce violence into the equation. The civil relationship between human beings has been disrupted, lowered to an animalistic conflict in which physical violence is not an anathema. Such corruption of the standards of behavior constitutes an independent prohibition.[32]

It may be for this reason that such an individual finds himself disqualified for testimony, as is true of all who have the status of "wicked."[33] Although R. Shlomo of Lublin[34] quotes R. Moshe Mintz that, despite the prohibition, the threatening individual may still serve as a witness, the Rama rules[35] that a person who raises his hand against another, while biblically fit to testify, is nonetheless excluded on a

27. *V'Darashta V'Chakarta*, pp. 120–122.

28. The feasibility of specific biblical laws being commanded primarily in order to protect other laws (often the role of rabbinical enactments) has been established by R. Yosef Engel, *Lekach Tov* 8, and R. Moshe Sofer (Erlau), *Responsa Yad Sofer* 26; see also *Ittur Sofrim* to *Yad Sofer*.

29. *L'Reakha Kamokha* vol. 3, ch. 2, *Nir L'David* 71.

30. In rulings printed in the back of the above cited volume, #43.

31. See chapter 1, pp. 19–25.

32. On the extent to which this prohibition is distinct from that of striking, see R. Aharon Soloveichik, *Parach Mateh Aharon*, *Mada* p. 6.

33. R. Ya'akov Chaim Sofer, *Yechi Yosef*, ibid., suggests that the two opinions in the Talmud as to whether a person who raises his hand in violence is called "sinner" or "wicked" are actually dealing with this issue.

34. *Responsa Maharash MiLublin* 89.

35. *Choshen Mishpat* 34:4.

rabbinical level. R. Yehoshua Falk explains,[36] citing the Mordechai, that
although the prohibition is indeed biblical, as it is not subject to punishment by lashes, it does not disqualify testimony on a biblical level.
R. Shmuel Rozovsky,[37] however, assumes that if the exclusion is not
biblical, it must be that the status of "wicked" is not either, and the
verse is cited merely as an allusion (*asmachta*). Nonetheless, it was the
opinion of R. Yoel Sirkes, in his commentary to the *Tur*,[38] not only that
there is an exclusion from testimony, but that it is indeed biblical as is
the implication of the Rambam in his *Sefer HaMitzvot*,[39] and is the position of R. Yehoshua DiTrani.[40] Further, R. Ya'akov Veil wrote that even
the threatening gesture does in fact earn the punishment of lashes.[41]
Using this *halakhah* as a basis, the third Lubavitcher Rebbe,
R. Menachem Mendel, considers whether a ritual slaughterer guilty of
such behavior should be removed from his position.[42] Further, it seems
to be the position of at least R. Yehudah HaChasid[43] that a ban of
excommunication enacted on those who strike others[44] applies also to
a person who raises his hand to do so. Apparently, display of this attitude enters one into a category of those adhering to a reduced standard
of moral guidelines.

III. Other Types of Hitting

Focusing primarily on the mindset indicated by the violent individual
informs the discussion of several applications of the prohibition.
R. Shimon Sofer[45] considers the widespread practice of friends slapping
one another in a playful manner. Stealing as a practical joke is prohib-

---

36. *Sefer Me'irat Einayim*; see also *Urim* 34:4.
37. *Chiddushei R. Shmuel* to *Sanhedrin* 12.
38. *Bayit Chadash, Choshen Mishpat* 34.
39. Prohibition 300.
40. *Responsa Maharit, Even HaEzer* 43; note the objection of R. Yosef Shaul
Nathanson, *Responsa Shoel U'Meishiv, Mahadura Tinyana*, vol. 2, no. 70.
41. *Responsa Mahari Veil* 28.
42. *Responsa Tzemach Tzedek, Choshen Mishpat, Sha'ar HaMiluim* 15.
43. *Sefer Chasidim* 49.
44. See *Shulchan Arukh, Choshen Mishpat* 420:2, and *Sefer Me'irat Einayim* 4.
45. *Responsa Hitor'rut Teshuvah*, vol. 4, *Choshen Mishpat* 33.

ited;[46] the Rambam[47] believes this is to avoid becoming accustomed to theft. Such a concern may equally apply to hitting in jest. Likewise, stealing to benefit the victim—who will profit from the penalties paid—is also forbidden; thus, the excuse that the hitting is to display affection may not help.[48] R. Moshe Feinstein,[49] R. I. A. Friedman,[50] and R. Isser Yehudah Unterman,[51] however, permit this, for reasons to be explained later.

A similar issue is that of one person who gives another permission to strike him. The early authority R. Yitzchak b. Sheshet[52] takes it as a given that while one may decline to accept compensatory damages for an injury,[53] such release is impossible in relation to the basic prohibition. This opinion is shared by R. Shneur Zalman of Liadi, the first Lubavitcher Rebbe,[54] R. Yair Bachrach,[55] R. Chaim Chizkiyahu Medini,[56] and R. Meir Dan Plotzki.[57] R. Binyamin Yehoshua Zilber[58] assumes that one has no right to waive on his own behalf protection against being hit, for "his life is not his property." R. Feinstein, despite his leniency on this issue, also forbids this. R. Yosef Babad,[59] however, does believe that this is an area in which the victim has some autonomy, and if he allows or requests another individual to strike him, that person violates no prohibition. Earlier, R. Aryeh Leib of Metz[60] and R. Levi ibn Chaviv[61] assumed this to be the case as well.

---

46. *Bava Kamma* 61b.

47. *Mishneh Torah, Hilkhot Geneivah* 1:2.

48. This reasoning is also found in R. Chaim Chizkiyahu Medini, *Sdei Chemed, Ma'arekhet Heih* 4, citing *Chesed L'Alafim* 156:21 and *Yafeh L'Leiv* 156:9.

49. *Responsa Iggerot Moshe, Orach Chaim* 3:78.

50. In the journal *Torat Eretz Yisrael* 4:3/4.

51. *Responsa Shevet MiYehudah*, vol. 1, *Mahadurah* 2, p. 439. R. Unterman's responsum deals with the sport of boxing.

52. *Responsa HaRivash* 484.

53. *Bava Kamma* 93a. This depends somewhat on the language used; see Rashi and *Tosafot*.

54. *Shulchan Arukh HaRav, Hilkhot Nizkei HaGuf* 4.

55. *Responsa Chavvot Yair* 163.

56. *Sdei Chemed, Ma'arekhet Ha-Alef, Klalim* 40.

57. *Chemdat Yisrael, Ner Yisrael* 79.

58. *Responsa Az Nidbaru* 9:49.

59. *Minchat Chinnukh, Mitzvah* 48, no. 2.

60. *Turei Even, Megillah* 27a, s.v. *Im Tomar*.

61. *Responsa Maharalbach, Kuntres HaSmikhah*, p. 60b.

These concerns are affected significantly by a phraseology found in the Rambam's *Mishneh Torah*. In formulating the prohibition against striking another, which he discusses together with wounding the other, he seems to add a specification to the nature of the hitting. However, the precise nature of this stipulation is somewhat unclear, due to variant texts.[62] According to one version, the strike must be *derekh bizayon*, "in a humiliating fashion." The alternate reading is *derekh nitzayon*, or "in a manner of quarreling."[63] In either case, one gets the impression that hitting of a benevolent nature, such as playfully, or with the other's permission, may not be included within the prohibition.[64]

However, it should also be pointed out that some, such as R. Joseph B. Soloveitchik,[65] question the Rambam's limitations, in light of at least two talmudic sources. One records the prohibition upon an individual to wound himself.[66] While it is certainly possible to do so in a humiliating manner, it is difficult to imagine quarreling alone. Thus, at least one of

---

62. Note R. Moshe Troyesh's *Orach Meisharim* 3:1.

63. R. Unterman (*Responsa Shevet MiYehudah* 3:2; 21:2) discerns a similar intention in the words of the *Hagahot Asheri, Bava Kamma* 1:20. See also R. Yehudah Assad, *Responsa Yehudah Ya'aleh*.

64. Despite the fact that R. Yitzchak b. Sheshet (Rivash), as noted above, does not feel that giving permission removes the prohibition against hitting, R. Unterman suggests that he may nonetheless agree with the Rambam's qualifications. The topic of the case in his discussion involves someone who borrows money under the understanding that if he does not pay off the debt, the lender is allowed to beat him. The Rivash forbids such an arrangement, thus not recognizing an individual's ability to waive the right not to be beaten. However, in this instance, the beating, although agreed to, would certainly be querulous. However, if the hitting is truly friendly, it may be that even the Rivash would allow it. This is similar to the position of R. Moshe Feinstein mentioned above.

Along the lines of the discussion of the Rivash, R. Shlomo Yosef Zevin takes up the question of how a Jewish *Beit Din* would address the situation depicted in Shakespeare's *The Merchant of Venice* (*L'Ohr HaHalakhah*, pp. 310-336). In that play, Shylock demands a pound of flesh from Antonio, as the latter had agreed to in the event of defaulting on a loan from the former. In his essay, R. Zevin considers the question of whether one may allow another to harm him, the issue of *nitzayon/bizayon* (see below), and general issues of one's ownership, or lack of ownership, over one's body. R. Zevin observes that although Shylock's wishes have been taken to reflect negatively on Jews, in actuality, a genuine Jewish *Beit Din* would never have even entertained the positions taken seriously by the [albeit fictional] Venetian court.

65. In the journal *Mesorah* 2:22.

66. *Bava Kamma* 91b.

the versions of the Rambam's words appears difficult. Further, the prohibition of wounding is also discussed in the context of surgery, where separate sources are adduced to permit it.[67] Medical treatment, one would assume, would not fulfill the requirement of either text.

In response to these objections, some authorities suggest that the Rambam's language is to be interpreted differently. His actual words read, "And not only one who wounds, but rather all who hit a decent person in Israel,[68] whether child or adult, whether man or woman, in a manner of *nitzayon/bizayon*, he violates a prohibition . . ." It might be that wounding, inflicting an actual injury to the body, is prohibited in all instances, with no exception made automatically for those that are self-inflicted or for surgical purposes. Such bodily harm is easily observable and thus definable. However, hitting in a non-injurious manner occupies territory that is somewhat murkier; as is evident by the aforementioned discussions, it is possible to do so in a completely non-offensive fashion, and perhaps this should be permitted. Therefore, some kind of standard is required in order to establish the offensive mode of hitting while leaving room for the innocuous.[69]

It must be emphasized that, as the Mordechai[70] points out, a person who would strike his wife is not only in violation of the aforementioned prohibitions, but he has committed additional prohibitions as well. The Talmud commands that a man show his wife "honor more than to himself."[71] Certainly, physical violence tramples this concept as well as

---

67. *Sanhedrin* 84b.

68. On this phrase, see *Hagahot Chadashot* of R. Yehoshua Tzeitlish to *Sefer Mitzvot Katan* 84.

69. Suggestions along these lines appear in *Chemdat Yisrael, Sdei Chemed, Ma'arekhet Ha-Alef, Klalim* 40, and in R. Eliezer Menachem Mann Shach, *Beit HaMidrash* to *Mishneh Torah*. Also, in particular reference to self-injury, the comments of R. Tzvi Schapira, *Tzivyon HaAmudim* to *Sefer Mitzvot Katan* 84:1, are consistent with this theory. However, R. Unterman explicitly assumes that the Rambam's qualifications are to be applied to wounding as well, and he responds to the problems in a different manner (*Responsa Shevet MiYehudah* 1:2, pp. 442–443). See also R. Uri Jungreiss, the journal *Torat HaAdam L'Adam*, vol. 4, p. 119. Note as well the comment of R. Shlomo Zalman Auerbach printed in the journal *Mevakshei Torah*, vol. 4, #20, p. 151.

70. *Ketubot* 5:186, quoting Rabbeinu Simchah. Note *Responsa Terumat HaDeshen* 218, and *Sdei Chemed, Ma'arekhet Heih* 5, at length.

71. *Yevamot* 62b and *Sanhedrin* 76b.

many other relevant prohibitions.[72] Thus, such behavior is considered to be even more egregious and to be dealt with most severely.[73] R. Meir of Rothenberg[74] writes that the individual who would strike his wife must be excommunicated and punished with all means available to society. The *Agudah*[75] adds that the husband must give his sworn assurance that he will immediately cease this behavior and, if he does not, he must release his wife from the marriage and pay the full value of her *ketubah*.[76] The permissibility, or advisability, of corporal punishment toward one's own children is a separate topic, beyond the scope of this discussion; R. Avraham Halevi[77] considers those issues at length.[78]

The prevention of violence, both injurious and not, is a priority of civilization as a whole. Within the framework of *halakhah*, it is imperative that even the suggestion of physical confrontation be recognized as inconsistent with acceptable interaction.

---

72. This is codified by the Rama in *Even HaEzer* 154:3.

73. See *Be'er HaGolah* to *Even HaEzer* and *Piskei Batei Din HaRabbaniyim* 12, pp. 80–86, 91–92.

74. *Responsa Maharam MiRotenberg* (Prague) 81.

75. P. 121b.

76. See also R. Eliezer Papo, *Pele Yoetz, Ma'asekhet Haka'ah,* and *Pitchei Teshuvah, Even HaEzer* 154:8.

77. *Responsa Even Chein,* vol. 1, pp. 217–281.

78. See also *Responsa Hitor'rut Teshuvah, Choshen Mishpat* 32, in *Ikvei Sofer,* and R. Yosef Chaim Sonnenfeld, *Responsa Salmat Chaim* 524.

CHAPTER

TWELVE

The Love-Hate Relationship: Love and Hatred

I. The Love Imperative

One of the most well-known principles of religious thought is a verse that appears in *Parshat Kedoshim*: "Love your neighbor as yourself."[1] The centrality of this ideal in Jewish theology, unmistakably evident in popular discussion, is expressed formally by R. Akiva, who stated simply, "This is a great principle in Torah."[2] The *Sefer HaChinnukh*[3] locates this "greatness" in the fact that many other principles of inter-personal relations derive from this one. Allowing a genuine love for one's fellow to flourish will automatically lead to an attention to those other commandments that govern the interactions between people; thus, this commandment serves as the backbone of Jewish societal law.

---

1. *Leviticus* 19:18.
2. *Torat Kohanim* and *Talmud Yerushalmi, Nedarim* 9:5.

Recognizing this primacy, the famous kabbalist R. Yitzchak Ashkenazi (Arizal) recommended that prior to praying, one express the acceptance upon himself of particular attention to this commandment.[4]

This love is thus an actual biblical commandment and transcends the sense of affection that is often felt between two people on an instinctual level. R. Yitzchak Hutner[5] writes that it is integral to the fulfillment of this precept that the feeling of love derive from the realization of the shared brotherhood of the Jewish people, rather than from an appreciation of any personal qualities.[6] This is not meant to imply that humanity as a whole is outside the imperative of love; certainly one is obligated to cultivate a concerned sense of care and compassion toward all people.[7] In fact, it may be with this in mind that Ben Azai responded to R. Akiva's famous comment with what he considered to be an even more encompassing verse, "This is the book of the descendants of Adam, on the day that God created man, He made them In the likeness of God,"[8] whose subject is apparently all of humanity.[9] However, the unique familial connection creates a special bond among Jews. So, too, this commandment gains strength as the kinship increases.[10] In this sense, the Talmud[11] suggests that the same verse applies in a more intense manner when referring to one's wife.

---

3. *Mitzvah* 243.

4. See R. Yochanan Segal Vosner, *Responsa Chayyei HaLevi*, *Yoreh Deah* 74:14; R. Asher Anshel Katz, *Shemen Rosh*, vol. 2, p. 569; R. David Ariav, *L'Reakha Kamokha*, p. 181, *Nir L'David* 268; and R. Ovadiah Yosef, *Anaf Etz Avot* to *Pirkei Avot*, 5:17.

5. *Pachad Yitzchak* to *Pesach* 8:1 and 29:2.

6. On the connection between love and shared peoplehood, see also, in R. Avraham Bick, ed., *Ba'ayot Aktualiyot L'Ohr HaHalakhah*, R. Shlomo Yosef Zevin, pp. 79–80, and R. Joseph B. Soloveitchik, pp. 126–127.

7. See the extensive discussion of this point in R. Shlomo Shneider, *Responsa Divrei Shlomo* 2:121.

8. *Genesis* 5:1.

9. See, for example, R. Shlomo Goren, in the journal *Ohr HaMizrach*, vol. 1 no. 1:10. See also R. Dov Rosenthal, *Divrei Yosher* to *Pirkei Avot*; R. Shmuel Yitzchak Hillman, *Ohr HaYashar*, *Parshat Kedoshim*; R. Uri Langer, *Ohr HaMitzvot* 206; and R. Shimshon Chaim Nachmeni, *Toldot Shimshon*, *Avot* 1:12.

10. See R. Yosef Patzanovsky, *Pardes Yosef*, *Leviticus* 19:17, as well as *Maharatz Chayes*, *Shabbat* 31a, in contrasting the views of R. Akiva and Ben Azai. See also *Anaf Etz Avot* to *Pirkei Avot*, 2:15.

11. *Kiddushin* 41a, *Niddah* 17a.

II. Understanding "*Kamokha*"

The term *kamokha*, "as yourself," appears somewhat daunting; the investment one has in oneself is a powerful reality that is hard to parallel.[12] R. Shlomo Goren[13] suggests that the reference is to a specific category of love, as distinct from the usage of that word in other contexts. The love for God is one that requires a complete submission to Him; His needs are paramount and above any human affections. The love for God is thus certainly not as that for oneself but as that for greater than oneself. In contrast, when one expresses love toward, for example, an object or a food, he refers not to a bond of identity with that thing, but rather is stating that that object fulfills one's needs and is in fact subservient to the one who loves. The love for fellow Jews, then, is thus differentiated from both of these in that it is a love in which neither party is in a context of service to the other or exalted beyond the other but, rather, each loves the other on the level that one does oneself. Another homiletic suggestion is that just as one manages to love oneself, despite one's flaws and shortcomings, so too the perceived deficiencies of another do not justify withholding love from him.[14]

In addition to the challenge of "*kamokha*," many find it difficult to know how to react to a commandment that seems to address itself to an emotion, demanding "love" toward another. In reality, though, this commandment is interpreted on a level that is more outwardly demonstrable. The Talmud[15] renders it into Aramaic as *mah d'alakh sni l'chavr'kha lo ta'avid*—"That which is hateful to you, do not do to others." Thus, many understand the commandment in this manner, as focused on refraining from negative behavior toward another.[16] As the

---

12. See, among others, R. David Shlomo of Sraka, *Arvei Nachal*, and R. Yuval Yosef Ordentlich, *P'ninei Nefesh*, to *Leviticus*.

13. In *Ohr HaMizrach*, ibid. See also R. Yosef Aryeh Petrover, *Divrei Yosef* to *Leviticus*.

14. Cited by R. Yosef Schwartz, in his *Misped V'Kinah* (printed in the back of the bound editions of the journal *VaY'lakket Yosef*, vol. 9).

15. *Shabbat* 31a. See also *Bereishit Rabbah*, 24:7.

16. See *Chiddushei Maharsha* and *Maharatz Chayes* to *Shabbat*; note the translation of R. Yonatan b. Uziel. See also R. Zalman Sorotzkin, *Oznayim LaTorah* to *Leviticus*, who suggests this issue is behind the difference between R. Akiva and Ben Azai. Note also *Pri Megadim*, *Eishel Avraham*, *Orach Chaim* 156, and R. Raphael Silber, *Marpei L'Nefesh* 2:44:2.

Ramban[17] explains, it is problematic to obligate a person to attend to the needs of others on a level equal to the attention he gives to his own needs, or "as himself." A similar comment is made by *Tosafot*.[18] Beyond the practical challenge of such absolute magnanimity, the Talmud[19] has explicitly recognized that a person must give precedence to his own vital necessities, as is stated "your life comes first."

Another reason it might be assumed that the commandment is focused on avoiding the negative is suggested by R. Moshe Avigdor Amiel.[20] Were a person to limit his service to others to that which he wishes for himself, it is possible that severe discrepancies could exist between an individual and other members of society, sharply curtailing his sense of communal responsibility. Therefore, the Torah left it for other *mitzvot* to describe the parameters of such service, while this verse focuses on restricting harmful activity.[21] R. Joseph D. Epstein[22] suggests that even the previously cited authorities would agree that this imperative demands active behavior as well; however, the commandment is only

---

17. Commentary to *Leviticus*.

18. *Sanhedrin* 45a, s.v. *Bror*. The Talmud, referring to an individual being executed, notes that it must be carried out in a humane manner because of "Love your neighbor as yourself" (see also *Ketubot* 37b). In this context, *Tosafot* explain that the needs of a living person cannot possibly be taken as equal to one's own; thus, when the Talmud mentions this commandment in an active sense, it is specifically in dealing with the needs of one no longer living.

19. *Bava Metzia* 62a. The context is a discussion of two individuals stranded in a desert, while one of them has a quantity of water sufficient to sustain only himself; thus, Ben P'tura and R. Akiva disagree as to whether or not the one with the water is obligated to give all or part of it to the other. R. Akiva, whose opinion is authoritative, rules that the water should be kept by the owner, for while he must be concerned for the life of the other, "his life comes first."

20. *L'Nevukhei HaTekufah*, *Sha'ar* 2:32. See also R. Meir Leibush Malbim, *HaTorah V'HaMitzvah*, and R. Ya'akov Kaminetsky, *Emet L'Ya'akov*, to *Parshat Kedoshim*.

21. However, such a limitation might then be present in regards to negative behavior as well; in fact, the Rash and the Ra'avad, early commentators to the *Torat Kohanim*, understand this to be the reason for Ben Azai's preference of the verse "This is the book of the descendants of Adam . . ." See also *Da'at Z'kenim L'Ba'alei HaTosafot* to *Parshat Kedoshim*. Note also R. J. David Bleich's comments further on. For other interpretations of the differences between Ben Azai and R. Akiva, see R. Avraham Gumbiner, *Zayit Ra'anan* to *Torat Kohanim*, and *Sefer HaRa'avan* 37. See, at length, R. Natan Gestetner, *L'Horot Natan* to *Leviticus*.

22. *Mitzvot HaMussar*, pp. 211–214.

demonstrably transgressed when a person allows harm to befall his fellow. In this spirit, R. Meir Halevi[23] and R. Shlomo Luria[24] attributed to this verse the injunction against damaging another's property.[25] Within this general understanding, performing any act that one would not wish upon oneself places one in defiance of this commandment.[26] Contemporary authors have included examples such as eavesdropping in this category.[27] R. Natan Gestetner[28] rules that every moment behavior in violation of this commandment is continued, an additional violation is incurred[29]. However, there is some discussion as to whether one violates this commandment if the behavior is motivated by innocent, non-malicious concerns.[30]

Another possibility existing among commentaries may be that the commandment contains two branches: one, a prohibitive function, as described above, as well as an active element, that commands an emotional "love," but does not necessarily obligate behavior.[31] Yet another possibility, consistent with the words of the Ramban, would assert that

23. *Yad Ramah, Bava Batra* 2:107.

24. *Yam Shel Shlomo, Bava Kamma* 10:23.

25. Interestingly, while the Torah clearly establishes the rules for remuneration of property damages, the precise source prohibiting the infliction of these damages is less obvious. R. Meir Auerbach, *Imrei Binah, Choshen Mishpat, Hilkhot Eidut* 33, discusses this verse as a possibility. See also Rabbeinu Yonah's commentary to *Pirkei Avot* 1:1, s.v. *Moshe*; Rabeinu Asher, *Responsa HaRosh, Klal* 108:10; R. Eliyahu of Vilna, *Biur HaGra, Choshen Mishpat* 155:8; R. Shmuel Strashoun, *Chiddushei Rashash, Ketubot* 18; R. Yoav Yehoshua Weingarten, *Chelkat Yoav, Choshen Mishpat* 20; R. Yisrael Ya'akov Kanievsky, *Kehilot Ya'akov, Bava Kamma* 1; R. Moshe Sofer, *Responsa Chatam Sofer, Yoreh Deah* 241; R. Baruch Ber Leibowitz, *Birkat Shmuel, Bava Kamma* 2; R. Aryeh Zev Gurwicz, *Rashei She'arim* to *Bava Kamma* 1; R. Avraham Yitzchak HaKohen Kook, *Responsa Orach Mishpat, Choshen Mishpat* 26; and R. Joseph B. Soloveitchik in the journal *Mesorah*, 7:56.

26. See, however, *Orach Mishpat*, ibid.

27. See R. Aharon Grossman, *Responsa V'Darashta V'Chakartav*, 1, *Yoreh Deah*, 46.

28. *Responsa L'Horot Natan* 4:129. See also his commentary to *Pirkei Avot* 1:9, where other practical applications of this commandment in the monetary arena are discussed. Note also *Orach Mishpat*, ibid.

29. See also the discussion of R. David Ariav, the journal *Torat HaAdam L'Adam*, vol. 4, pp. 101–4.

30. See R. Uri Jungreiss, in the journal *Torat HaAdam L'Adam*, vol. 4, pp. 118–32.

31. This view may be associated with the *Yereim* (*Sefer Yereim HaShalem*, 224) and the *Chinnukh* (see note 34).

the commandment addresses itself to an attitude of generosity toward another, concerning oneself with another's welfare with the same care one has for one's own (rather than obligating one to actually provide that welfare to the same degree as he acquires his own).[32]

To the Rambam, however, this imperative apparently takes on a more active nature. In his *Mishneh Torah*[33] he codifies this commandment as requiring "that each person love every individual of Israel as himself, as it says, 'love your neighbor as yourself'; therefore, he must speak his praise, and worry about his money as he worries about his own and wishes for his own honor."[34] In his *Sefer HaMitzvot*,[35] he adds that as an aspect of this love, "and whatever will be in his control, if he wants it for himself, I want it also; and whatever I want for myself, I want[36] for him as well."[37] In addition, the Rambam also traces to this imperative a biblical commandment to engage in acts of loving kindness.[38] However, he considers the specific examples that he lists, visiting the sick, comforting mourners, and so forth, to be rabbinic incarnations.

As noted, though, adopting an affirmative commandment in this instance is difficult due to the seemingly unattainable nature of

---

32. See the analysis of the Ramban's position by R. Yechiel Neuman, in the journal *Torat HaAdam L'Adam*, vol. 4, pp. 79–80. Note also the words of the *Divrei Chaim*, R. Chaim Sanzer, cited by R. Naftali Halberstam, in the journal *Ohr Yisrael* (1:3 p. 188–189), and note as well the author's expansions and supports of the cited comments.

33. *Hilkhot Deiot* 6:3. See also *Targum Onkelos* to *Leviticus*, and R. Eliyahu of Vilna, *Biur HaGra to Torat Kohanim*.

34. It is noteworthy that the *Sefer HaChinnukh* (prohibition 219) combines a language similar to that of the Rambam with the phraseology of the Talmud in *Shabbat* ("that which is hateful to you . . ."). Note also *Sefer Mitzvot Katan* 8. See R. Ezriel Ciment, *Mitzvot HaMelekh*, positive commandment 8. See also R. Neuman, in the above cited article, pp. 89–90.

35. Positive commandment 206.

36. R. Chaim Heller, in his edition of *Sefer HaMitzvot*, also includes "and whatever I hate for myself, or for one close to me, I will hate for him as well."

37. The *Chizkuni*, in his commentary, appears to adopt a position similar to that of the Rambam. However, as R. Moshe Miernik (in the journal *Torat HaAdam L'Adam*, vol. 4, p. 63) observes, the language allows for a slight differentiation: the Rambam commands love, and the behavior emanates from that emotion; the Chizkuni understands the behavior to be the actual interpretation of the commandment.

38. *Hilkhot Aveil* 14:1.

"*kamokha*," making the Rambam's position surprising. The Netziv,[39] sensitive to this, suggests that the Rambam does not mean to obligate one to do for another as he would do for himself; rather one should do for another as one would want that other to do for them. R. Yisrael Meir Lau,[40] combining the Rambam's words about acts of kindness with the Netziv's suggestion, posits that the affirmative requirements of this commandment are all rabbinical in obligation, and, because of the rule of "your life comes first," the rabbis were limited to a formulation like that of the Netziv.

Some contemporary authors[41] suggest that perhaps the Rambam perceives a two-tiered commandment. One element, the prohibitive one, is absolute and mandatory. The second, the active component, is voluntary in nature. Known in halachic terminology as a *mitzvah kiyumit* (as contrasted with a *mitzvah chiyuvit*), this category would indicate that behavior in this area is a fulfillment of the goal of the commandment, without being mandatory in nature. (In other words, declining to behave in this manner would not incur any guilt or implications of negligence.) As is noted by proponents of this theory, adopting such an interpretation of the Rambam's position would leave the practical difference between his opinion and that of other authorities very narrow, if at all existent.[42]

R. J. David Bleich[43] explains that the comments in *Mishneh Torah* and those in *Sefer HaMitzvot* are to be taken as a sort of progression. In its essence, the imperative of loving one's neighbor is centered on treating another as one would oneself, as he writes in *Mishneh Torah*. However, that has some limitations, in that one may not wish for oneself, were one in a comparable situation, that which one's friend feels he currently needs. Therefore, he adds in *Sefer HaMitzvot* that it is incumbent on the

---

39. *Ha'amek Davar* to *Leviticus*.

40. *Responsa Yachel Yisrael* 3:31.

41. See, in the journal *Torat HaAdam L'Adam*, vol. 4, R. Moshe Miernik (pp. 60–77), and R. David Ariav (pp. 96–98), who adduces evidence from the writings and citations of the Chazon Ish, R. Yehoshua Leib Diskin, and R. Chaim Kanievsky.

42. See, however, R. Miernik's qualification in footnote 10 of his article.

43. In *Y'kara D'Chaim* (memorial volume for R. Chaim Ya'akov Goldvicht), pp. 85–89.

individual to strive to develop this sensitivity to another's concerns, so that they become identical with his own, at which point they will become a part of the central obligation of love. However, as this may not automatically be the case, the Rabbis found it necessary to specifically command visiting the sick, comforting mourners, and the like, in the event that a person may feel that were he sick or bereaved, he would not want visitors. If this individual has not yet developed the complete sense of mutual identification, his sense of love will not yet motivate him to take up these activities; thus, a rabbinic command is needed.[44]

R. Eliyahu Bakshi Doron[45] uses this concept of an ongoing development within this commandment to explain the Rambam's comment that one must express one's love to the other by "speaking his praise."[46] The Torah commands love not just in relation to one's fellow but also toward God. In delineating this commandment,[47] the Rambam writes that the development of that love comes through the study of, and the involvement in, His Torah and His creations. By focusing on the Divine majesty, one nourishes one's love for God. So, too, speaking the praises of one's fellow man will foster a sense of brotherly respect and love.[48]

R. Sh'ar Yashuv Cohen[49] focuses on this comparison as well and suggests that both commandments of love are representative of the principle that often the Torah directs a *mitzvah* at the emotions by working through actions.[50] It is indeed true that one cannot be ordered how to feel; thus, all such imperatives that have such aspirations are centered on performable actions, as a means to an end. In this spirit is the comment

---

44. See also R. Moshe Shternbuch, *Moadim U'Zmanim* 5:346, and R. Yitzchak Shmuel Schechter, *Responsa Yashiv Yitzchak*, 3:31.

45. *Responsa Binyan Av* 3:78, and in the journal *Torah SheB'Al Peh* 36:33–40.

46. See also, on this point, R. Boruch D. Povarsky, *Bad Kodesh al HaTorah*, vol. 2, pp. 71–73.

47. *Sefer HaMitzvot*, positive commandment 3.

48. R. Shraga Feivel Shneebalg, *Responsa Shraga HaMeir* 1:1, discusses this at length. This idea need not be viewed as differing from R. Hutner's aforementioned words that the love must be due to shared peoplehood; rather, one refers to the motivation for love, the other to the process of developing it.

49. In *Torah SheB'Al Peh* 36:45–57.

50. This is a recurring theme in the halakhic thought of R. Joseph B. Soloveitchik; see chapter 7, footnote 74, p. 112, note 80.

of the *Derekh Eretz Zuta*: "If you wish to attach yourself to love of your fellow, you should [involve yourself in actions that are] in his benefit."[51]

Thus, the imperative of love demands that, at a minimum, one be protective of another to the extent that one is of oneself, if not actually requiring that one foster another with the same level of active attention, a position also with substantial support. R. Ya'akov Tzvi Mecklenberg[52] lists a number of practical manifestations, some of which are explicitly included in other commandments, and others whose primary home is this verse.[53] Among these are displaying genuine affection; giving respectful treatment; seeking other's best interests; feeling sincere empathy; showing expressions of friendship and joy in greeting one another; giving the benefit of the doubt;[54] providing financial, physical, and practical assistance; and taking care not to express, or to feel, condescension.

R. David Cohen,[55] in his discussion of obligations emanating from this commandment, offers another suggestion as to why R. Akiva terms the imperative "a great principle in Torah." He notes a fundamental distinction between interpersonal commandments and those that are between Man and G-d. The latter category tends toward absolute rules, while interpersonal laws are often situational and those given to exceptions. The reason for this is that the "principle" of "Love your neighbor as yourself" stands as an overarching concept, rather than a specific law, and exists to provide a goal point that will affect the ultimate application of all the laws that relate to it.

III. The Sin of Hatred

Paralleling this commandment, actually one verse earlier, is its negative correlate, "You shall not hate your brother in your heart."[56] The param-

---

51. See also *Orchot Tzaddikim, Sha'ar HaAhavah*, and R. Chaim Shmuelevitz, *Sichot Mussar*.

52. *HaK'tav V'HaKabballah* to *Leviticus*.

53. See also R. Shaul Wagshal, *Orchot Yesharim* 11.

54. Note also the implication of R. Eliezer of Metz, *Sefer Yereim* 39; *Yesod V'Shoresh HaAvodah, Sha'ar Avodat HaLev*, ch. 8; and R. Moshe Yechiel Elimelekh of Libertov, *VaYomer Moshe, Parshat Kedoshim*.

55. *Birkat Yaavetz*, vol. 1, pp. 45–52.

56. *Leviticus* 19:17.

eters of this prohibition, particularly in relation to the positive commandment, are a matter of some discussion.[57]

The Rambam[58] interprets the verse in a manner specific to its words.
That is to say, the prohibition is geared toward hatred that is hidden
"within the heart," as implied in the Talmud;[59] overt acts of distaste are
considered to be violations of "love your neighbor."[60] In this spirit, the
Rambam elsewhere recommends that someone who finds himself to be
harboring a dislike for another should discuss his feelings with that
person and attempt to come to a reconciliation;[61] so, too, the *Chizkuni*[62]
considers this to be an integral part of this prohibition. According to the
Ramban, however, at least in one of two positions that he quotes, and
others,[63] any type of hatred violates this prohibition.

The word "hatred" itself is a somewhat vague, and usually emotion-
ally charged, term. R. Chaim b. Attar[64] understands it as a "distancing
in the heart" and claims that any degree of such separation is a violation
of the prohibition. R. Yaakov Etlinger[65] describes a "hatred of the heart"
as a controlled reaction to a negative stimulus, which can equally be controlled to remove from the heart, as per the commandment. This is distinct from a "hatred of the soul," which is instinctual.[66]

The Talmud[67] states that it is possible to violate this prohibition by
means of a vow. According to most commentators,[68] this refers to the

---

57. See R. Yosef Engel, *Gilyonei HaShas, Kiddushin* 41a.

58. *Sefer HaMitzvot*, prohibition 302.

59. See *Arakhin* 16b, as well as *Torat Kohanim* to *Kedoshim* 4.

60. See *Targum* of R. Yonatan b. Uziel and *Sefer Mitzvot Katan* 17. Note
R. Naftali Tzvi Yehudah Berlin, *Harchev Davar* to *Deuteronomy* 22:3. See
R. Raphael Yosef Chazan, *Responsa Chikrei Lev, Yoreh Deah* 80.

61. *Mishneh Torah, Hilkhot Deiot* 6:6. See also commentary of R. Shimshon
Raphael Hirsch to the Torah, and R. Menachem Krakowski, *Avodat Melekh* to
Hilkhot Deiot.

62. Commentary to *Leviticus*.

63. See, for example, *Sheiltot D'Rav Achai Gaon* 33.

64. *Ohr HaChaim* to *Leviticus*.

65. *Responsa Binyan Tziyyon HaChadashot* 75.

66. See also R. Yitzchak Isaac Hertzog, *Responsa Heikhal Yitzchak* 2. All of
these manners of hatred are related in *Mitzvot HaShalom*, pp. 70–81.

67. *Nedarim* 65b.

68. Such as the Ritva, the Meiri, and the *Nimmukei Yosef*.

standard vow forbidding another from benefiting from the one taking the vow. The Rosh understands this vow to be one against greeting the other;[69] possibly, this is based on the statement of the Talmud elsewhere[70] that a "hater" is one who, out of animosity, does not converse with the other for a three-day period. It is possible that these positions may indicate somewhat the type of activities forbidden by this injunction.[71] However, it should be noted that the vow itself may be incidental to the prohibition; Rashi[72] implies that the vow is a result of violating this injunction, while the Ritva writes that the vow, if kept, will lead to its transgression.

R. Yisrael Meir Kagan[73] points out that this prohibition does not cease if one merely stops hating the other. Just as a person who steals must return the stolen property in order to undo the damage he has caused, so, too, a person who has hated another must take active steps to remove the hatred from his heart and prevent its recurrence.

The context of this prohibition is that of the commandment to provide effective rebuke to one who has sinned on some level. Thus, it might be suggested that this factor is contributory to determining the prohibition; in fact, Rashi understands the intent of the verse to be warning against hatred shown during the course of rebuke.[74] Some commentaries[75] understand the implication to be that when one person has wronged someone else, the victim should bring the matter to his attention rather than nursing a hatred against the offender. Others[76]

---

69. See also *Responsa Orach Mishpat, Choshen Mishpat* 26, at length.

70. *Sanhedrin* 27a. See also *Responsa Maharil Diskin, K'tavim* 20.

71. As R. Dov Menashe Septimus (quoted in *V'Im Tomar* 3:1103) observes, this may challenge the Rambam's position somewhat.

72. This commentary was actually not written by Rashi himself.

73. *Ahavat Chesed,* ch. 4. R. Kagan discusses this *mitzvah* throughout this work, as well in his *Chafetz Chaim, Petichah,* and *Hilkhot Lashon Hara* 4:3, and in his *Mishnah Berurah, Orach Chaim* 156.

74. See a discussion of his and other positions in R. Yisrael Ya'akov Kanievsky, *Kehilot Ya'akov* to *Makkot* 16 (in older editions).

75. Such as the Chizkuni mentioned earlier, in line with the Rambam in *Hilkhot Deiot;* see also Ramban and Rashbam.

76. See, for example, commentaries of *Pa'aneach Raza* and the *Tur* to the Torah.

understand the context to be that of a person deserving of rebuke for a sin against God, while some apply the verse to either instance.[77]

IV. Permissible Hatred?

The interplay between rebuke and the prohibition of hatred is a complicated one, and thus so is the relationship of the latter prohibition, as well as the commandment of love, with an individual who has sinned to the extent he has earned the label "wicked' (*rasha*). This is further complicated by the usage of the words "your brother" and "your fellow" in the relevant verses, terminology that has at times been interpreted as exclusive of those whose behavior has, possibly, created a degree of spiritual alienation.[78] Nonetheless, many authorities[79] assumed that these commandments are in full effect even when dealing with a *rasha*, based on strong talmudic indications. However, there exists as well substantial opinion that a *rasha* is excluded from these *mitzvot*, and this has significant textual support as well.[80] Further, some sources indicate that not only may a *rasha* be hated, but that this is appropriate.[81]

Many authorities suggest that a reconciliation can exist between these positions and the relevant sources, talmudic and otherwise.[82] The First Lubavitcher Rebbe, R. Shneur Zalman of Liadi,[83] rules in an apparently paradoxical manner that a person can only hate someone

---

77. See R. Yosef B'khor Shor, and *Sefer Yereim* 195.

78. For essays on this topic, see, for example, R. Ephraim Greenblatt, *Responsa Riv'vot Ephraim* 2:198:1; R. David Ariav, *L'Reakha Kamokha*; and R. Joseph D. Epstein, *Mitzvot HaShalom*.

79. See, for example, *Avot D'R'Natan*, ch. 16; *Yad Ramah, Sanhedrin* 52a; *Chiddushei Maharsha, Sanhedrin* 59a; *Tosafot, Pesachim* 113a; *Mishneh Torah, Hilkhot Rotzeach* 13:14.

80. See *Tosafot, Bava Metzia* 32b; *Sefer HaChinnukh* 80; *Hagahot Maimoniyot, Hilkhot Deiot*, ch. 6; Rama, *Choshen Mishpat* 272, and *Siftei Kohen, Sefer Meirat Einayim*, and *Biur HaGra*; and *Hagahot Mishneh L'Melekh*. See also R. Yosef Hochgelerntner, *Mishnat Chakhamim*, prohibition 5; *Responsa Shraga HaMeir* 6:12:1; and R. Moshe Ariel Weinberg, *Dibrot Ariel* to *Arakhin* 3. Note the limitations found in R. Moshe Feinstein, *Dibrot Moshe, Bava Metzia, Ha'arah* 77.

81. See *Pesachim* 113b (and note *Gilyonei HaShas*) and *Magen Avraham, Orach Chaim* 156. Note the interpretation of R. Elchanan Wasserman, *Kovetz He'arot* 655 (70 in other editions).

82. See also R. Moshe Troyesh, *Orach Meicharim* 3:1.

83. *Tania*, ch. 32. See also R. Chaim Shmuelevitz, *Sichot Mussar*.

whom he is close to, and who is beloved to him. However, a person who is estranged will only be pushed further, and thus must not be hated; the hatred must be limited to those who are loved. The blatant contradiction of love and hate within one person requires explanation. R. Aryeh Leib Heller,[84] in a different context, observes that while goodness is a fundamental element of a person, sin never is; rather, it is a foreign element, introduced into the soul temporarily. Thus, the individual himself must always be loved; hatred is only allowed toward the sinful intrusion, an external aspect distinct from the person himself. Far from a mere homiletic device, this position is evident in the words of the Abarbanel and is held in practice by such later authorities as R. Avraham Yitzchak HaKohen Kook,[85] R. Avraham Grodzenski,[86] R. Eliyahu Bakshi Doron,[87] R. Shlomo Wahrman,[88] R. Yehudah Gershuni,[89] R. Aharon Soloveichik,[90] and others.[91]

This approach may explain a comment of *Tosafot*[92] that appears to support hatred of a *rasha*. The Talmud is discussing the *mitzvah* of *te'inah u'prikah*, assisting a struggling individual with the loading and unloading of packages. Surprisingly, precedence is given in this area to a "hated" individual, rather than to a friend, in order to help subjugate this deleterious instinct toward hatred.[93] *Tosafot* question how a hated person

---

84. Introduction to *Shev Shmat'ta*.

85. Quoted by R. Shlomo Goren in *Ohr HaMizrach* 1:1 and R. Yisrael Schepansky in *Ohr HaMizrach*, vol. 51, pp. 173–176.

86. *Torat Avraham*, pp. 156–157.

87. *Responsa Binyan Av*, ibid.

88. In the journal *HaDarom* 63:78 82, and in *Orot HaShabbat* 13.

89. In *Kol Tzofayikh*, pp. 327–329.

90. *Parach Matteh Aharon, Madda*, p. 78.

91. See, for example, R. Asher Anshel Katz, *U'L'Asher Amar* to *Leviticus*; R. Shimon Gable, *Sofrei Shimon* to *Berakhot* 31a; and R. Moshe Aharon Teichman, in *Har HaMelekh*, vol. 6, *Hilkhot Deiot* 6:3, pp. 157–168, at length. Note also the discussion of R. Norman Lamm, *Halakhot V'Halikhot*, pp. 149–159. See also R. Simchah Rabinowitz, *Piskei Teshuvot*, vol. 6, ch. 156, p. 320–321.

92. *Pesachim* 113b, s.v. *Shera'ah*. See R. Shammai Kehat Gross, *Responsa Shevet HaKehati* 3:86, and R. Moshe Gross, *Nesiat Kapayim K'Hilkhata*, pp. 142–144.

93. See also the comment of Meiri, *Yoma* 75a: "One should never allow his hatred to restrain him from benefiting his fellow in any manner that he can benefit him."

can exist, in light of the prohibitions against such attitude,[94] and suggest that the subject is a sinner who should be hated.[95] If that is the case, and the hatred is appropriate, then the question becomes why the Talmud would recommend a method to minimize it. The answer given is that hatred has a tendency to grow and, if it is not quelled, may develop into a *sinah gemurah*, an "absolute hatred."[96] The difference between "hatred" and "absolute hatred" seems somewhat undefined. Based on this theory, some of its proponents suggest that the initial hatred, that which is permissible, refers to the isolated loathing of sin in and of itself. "Absolute hatred," however, is directed at the person himself, and this, apparently, is always unacceptable.[97]

Further, even if one does not accept this theory, the possibility of hating a *rasha* is most likely of extremely limited relevance. In order to attain the status of "wicked," one must reject rebuke.[98] The offering of

94. It is also possible that the meaning is "one who hates" rather than "is hated"; see R. Baruch Epstein, *Torah Temimah*, *Exodus* 23:37, and R. Yaakov Moshe Feldman, *Meshivat Nefesh*.

95. In contrast to the position of *Tosafot* to *Bava Metzia*, 32b, s.v. *Lakhof*.

96. See, however, R. Moshe Sofer, *Torat Moshe*, *Parshat Mishpatim*. See also the discussion of R. Avraham Weinfeld in the journal *Chakhmei Lev*, vol 5, p. 71–74.

97. See also a different interpretation in R. David Cohen, *Birkat Yaavetz*, vol. 2, pp. 47–50.

98. See *Sefer HaMitzvot Katan* 17; *Responsa Maharam Lublin* 13; R. Ephraim Erdit, *Matteh Ephraim* to *Mishneh Torah*; R. Amram Blum, *Responsa Beit She'arim*, *Orach Chaim* 69 (see, however, R. Yosef Shwartz, *Responsa Ginzei Yosef* 107:4; his interpretation, though, seems difficult in the language of the Talmud and is without support from any other authorities); R. Shlomo HaKohen of Vilna, *Responsa Binyan Shlomo*, *Choshen Mishpat* 63; and, in the journal *Techumin*, R. Avraham Sherman (1:311) and R. Avraham Wasserman (21 pp 180–188).

99. *Arakhin* 16b. Proper application of rebuke is extremely complex and beyond the scope of this discussion, see also *Nimmukei Yosef*, *Yevamot* 65b; *Sefer Yereim* 37; R. Moshe of Coucy, *Sefer Mitzvot Gadol*, positive commandment 11; *Mishneh Torah*, *Hilkhot Deiot* 6:7, and *Derekh HaMelekh*; R. Avraham Tzvi Eisenstadt, *Pitchei Teshuvah*, *Yoreh Deah* 157:5; R. Yosef Babad, *Minchat Chinnukh* 239; R. Moshe Shick, *Responsa Maharam Shick*, *Orach Chaim* 303; R. Avraham Bornstein, *Responsa Avnei Nezer*, *Yoreh Deah* 461:15; R. Shalom Mordechai Schwadron, *Responsa Maharsham* 6:48; R. Yoel Teitlbaum, *Responsa Divrei Yoel* in several places; R. Shimon Krasner, *Nachalat Shimon* to *1 Samuel* 1:5; R. Joseph B. Soloveitchik, in the journal *Mesorah* 8:55; R. Shimon Greenfeld, *Responsa Maharshag* 1:43 and 2:125; R. Avraham ben Mordechai, *Responsa Ginnat Veradim*, *Orach Chaim*, *Klal* 3; R. Tzvi Ungstein in *Responsa Mekadd'shei Hashem* 2:79 and

rebuke in a proper manner is an extremely difficult and sensitive task, requiring a skill the Talmud indicates cannot be found in modern times.[99] Thus, for all practical purposes, the concept of *rasha* may be an irrelevant one. As such, many of this century's greatest authorities have ruled that the status is indeed inapplicable.[100] R. Meir Simchah of Dvinsk[101] offers perhaps the most far reaching version of this theory, suggesting that the last time it was possible to hate a *rasha* was back in the desert, before the sin of the golden calf. Since then, no Jew is on secure enough moral footing to hate another for his spiritual or ethical failings.

Thus, it seems that very little room is left in this day and age for any hatred whatsoever of one's fellow Jew. Rather, the twin commandments mandating love and forbidding hatred combine to engender within the halakhically sensitive soul a genuine concern, respect, and affection for each and every member of the family.

1:124 in *D'var Tzvi*; R. Shimon (Eiger) Sofer, *Responsa Hitor'rut Teshuvah*, vol. 3, *He'arot* to *Shulchan Arukh* 608; R. Avraham Shmuel Binyamin Sofer, *Responsa K'tav Sofer, Even HaEzer* 47; R. Shlomo Fisher, *Beit Yishai* 10; R. Avraham David Horowitz, *Responsa Kinyan Torah B'Halakhah* 5:59; R. Avraham Erlanger, *Birkat Avraham, Beitzah*, p. 93, and *Bava Metzia*, p. 161; R. Yosef Roth, *Siach Yosef* 12; R. Yochanan Segal Vosner, *Responsa Chayyei HaLevi* 1:95:5: R. Ya'akov Traube, *Responsa Avnei Ya'akov* 206; R. Yehudah Polatchek, *Responsa Meged Yehudah* 36; R. Yosef Sharbit, *Responsa Orchot Yosher, Choshen Mishpat* 1; R. Menashe Silber, *Responsa Moznai Tzedek* 28; R. Chaim Sofer, *Responsa Machaneh Chaim* 2:21; R. Moshe Dov Wolner, *Responsa Chemdat Tzvi* 2:81; R. Avraham Binyamin Silverberg, *Responsa Maharab* 47; *Responsa Beit Shearim* 181; R. Ezra Basri, *Responsa Sha'arei Ezra* 103 and 128; R. Leib Baron, *Responsa Yismach Chaim* 31; *Responsa Binyan Av* 3:4:2; R. Dov Eliezerov, *Responsa Shoeli Tziyyon* 1:5; R. Yosef Chaim Sonnenfeld, *Responsa Salmat Chaim* 816–819; *Responsa Shraga HaMeir* 6:94 and 8:63:1; R. Baruch Rakovsky, *Birkat Avot* 25; *Responsa Sha'arei Torah* 6; R. Yehudah Herzl Henkin, *Responsa Bnai Banim* 2:27; and R. Menachem Mendel Schneerson, *Responsa Admor MeChabad* 60 and 68. For book-length treatments of this topic, see R. Yoel Schwartz, *Hokheach Tokheach*, and R. Hillel David Litwack, *Mitzvat HaTokhachah*.

100. This position is most well-known as that of the *Chazon Ish*, R. Avraham Yeshayah Karelitz, and it exists in whole or in part in the writings of the aforementioned authorities, as well as those of R. Yaakov Etlinger, R. Akiva Eiger, R. Chaim Ozer Grodzinski, R. Sh'ar Yashuv Cohen, R. Shmuel Vosner, R. Avraham Tovolsky, R. Joseph D. Epstein, R. Moshe Tzuriel, R. Ephraim Moshe Korngut, and many others. For a more complete listing, see Introduction, pp. xxvii–xxviii, footnotes 87–89.

101. *Meshekh Chokhmah, Deuteronomy* 22:4.

THIRTEEN

When Push Comes to Shove: Aggressiveness and Insensitivity toward Others

I. Piety Through Aggression

The enthusiastic performance of God's commandments gives central structure to the life of a Jew, motivating his decisions and infusing significance into the broad spectrum of his daily activities. Essential to the sacred mission of the committed adherent of halakhah, the active pursuit of spiritual opportunities is a fundamental element of the serious religious personality. The accomplishment of realizing any one of the Torah's imperatives is an eternal one, transcending any value measurable in temporal terminology. While the Talmud assigns restitution of ten gold pieces to anyone who has had a *mitzvah* "stolen" from him,[1] his actual loss in metaphysical terms is, of course, incalculable.

---

1. *Chullin* 87a.

It is thus perhaps to be expected that some measure of aggressive tendencies may enter the behavior of one focused on spiritual attainments, particularly in those instances when the resources or opportunities relevant to a given *mitzvah* are limited. When faced with competition in attempting to secure the circumstances necessary for the fulfillment of certain commandments, a defensive or even combative instinct may rise to the surface. Such inclinations give the impression of honorability; if religious accomplishments are to be esteemed, can their enthusiastic, or even assertive, pursuit be reasonably neglected? The crowded arena of religious activity, lovingly described by the Talmud,[2] finds itself the site of increased intensity, often in the form of an apparently noble self-interest. It is not a great distance to imagine the actual imposition of a physical element, perhaps in the form of the bodily pushing of others, for example, into the fray.

However, such a conclusion, along with its accompanying logic, is categorically rejected in a sweeping statement by R. Avraham Gumbiner, writing in his authoritative commentary to the *Shulchan Arukh*, *Magen Avraham*.[3] The Rama, discussing the laws governing communal prayer, rules that no individual may lead the congregation against the will of the members.[4] The *Magen Avraham* anticipates the reaction of those who would be inclined to defy the wishes of the community, feeling that the spiritual bounty to be gained from representing the congregation in prayer would outweigh any reluctance he feels toward contradicting their desires. He states, simply and broadly, "One is not to quarrel over any *mitzvah*."

His source for this principle is a statement that appears a number of times in the Talmud, initially in reference to the division of the *lechem hapanim* among the *kohanim*. After describing the limited quantity available for distribution in proportion to the number of *kohanim*, we are told of the competition that ensued in pursuit of this *mitzvah*. Although many

---

2. See *Berakhot* 6b, *Agra d'kallah duchka*, "the reward earned for attending the Torah lecture is in accordance with [the enduring of] the crowding." For an emphasis of the positive elements of this situation, see R. Yosef Chaim ben Eliyahu, *Responsa Torah L'Shmah 38.*

3. *Orach Chaim* 53:26.

4. *Orach Chaim* 53:22, citing the *Responsa Binyamin Ze'ev* 183.

kohanim edged to the forefront, the Talmud notes, "*V'hatznu'im moshkhim et y'deihem*—and the modest ones (i.e. the refined ones) would draw back their hands."[5]

R. Shmuel Halevi of Kellin, in his *Machatzit HaShekel*, expresses difficulty in understanding the *Magen Avraham*'s basis for extrapolating from this passage to all *mitzvot*, observing that in the case in the Talmud it would be impossible for every *kohen* to acquire a quantity sufficient for the *mitzvah* of eating sanctified foods. The implication of the *Tosfot Y'shanim* and Rashi (*Yoma* 39a) is that had it been possible to do so, there would have been no "drawing back of the hands."[6] He concedes, however, that any occasion falling short of a complete *mitzvah* certainly cannot justify quarrelling and further restricts his objection to the *Magen Avraham*'s position by suggesting that even if there were a complete quantity accessible, it may be that the only reason hands were not retracted was because it was unclear a quarrel would ensue. If a quarrel is inevitable, however, he seems ready to concede to the *Magen Avraham* that even an actual *mitzvah* does not warrant such involvement. A similar objection is noted by R. Moshe Sofer.[7]

Many authorities rise to defend the *Magen Avraham* against even the modified limitations of the *Machatzit HaShekel*. R. Shimon Greenfield[8] comments that the interpretation of the Talmud's description of the "modest" in a noncomprehensive manner is difficult in light of the repetition of this statement elsewhere,[9] in an instance dealing with a complete *mitzvah*.[10] R. Shlomo Reizner observes that even the *Magen*

---

5. See also *Be'er Heitev* and R. Gedalyah Felder, *Gilyonei Yeshurun, Yoma* 39a.

6. See also R. Eliezer Zusman Sofer's glosses to R. Yaakov Alpandari's *Responsa Mutzal Me'Eish* 51, and R. Meshulam Roth's *Responsa Kol Mevasser* 2:28.

7. *Hagahot* to *Shulchan Arukh, Orach Chaim* 53, as well as *Responsa Orach Chaim* 49 and *Kovetz Teshuvot* 3.

8. *Responsa Maharshag* 3:16.

9. *Chullin* 133a.

10. This touches on a broader issue, that of whether a *mitzvah* performed on a quantity less than that usually required constitutes any kind of a meaningful action. See R. Chaim Mordechai Margolios, *Shaarei Teshuvah, Orach Chaim* 475 and 482; R. Moshe Yehoshua Yehudah Leib Diskin, *Responsa Maharil Diskin, Psakim* 4; R. Yitzchak Blazer, *Responsa Pri Yitzchak* 217 and *Anaf Pri*; R. Avraham Bornstein, *Responsa Avnei Nezer, Orach Chaim* 383; R. Yosef Babad, *Minchat Chinnukh* 6 and 144; R. Chaim Halberstam, *Responsa Divrei Chaim, Orach Chaim* 1:25; R. Chaim

Avraham deals not with a personal obligation but rather with an individual's performance of a communally relevant religious task. Even though, in the aforementioned incident of eating sanctified foods, an insufficient quantity does bear some significance, acquiring a complete portion is certainly preferable in theory. If so, it would stand to reason that it is advisable to grab as much as possible in order to achieve this goal. The very fact that the example of the "modest" is presented, contradicting such a notion, bears out the truth of the *Magen Avraham*'s position.[11]

R. Ya'akov Ariel[12] notes, however, that the *Magen Avraham*'s words are not referring to a situation where the religious needs will go unfulfilled; rather, his position is addressed toward those who would fight over their own opportunity to be the one to perform the *mitzvah*.

In any event, the margin of disagreement is minor; the *Magen Avraham*'s admonition against quarrelling over *mitzvot* is applicable, even according to his detractors, to anything short of a complete, genuine *mitzvah* obligation, and perhaps even then if a quarrel is a definite outcome. R. Ovadiah Yosef[13] quotes the *Magen Avraham* without noting

---

Chizkiyahu Medini, *Sdei Chemed, Ma'arekhet Chet Klal* 13; *Orchot Chaim* 475; R. Yoav Yehoshua Weingarten, *Responsa Chelkat Yoav, Yoreh Deah* 39; R. Natan Nota Landau, *Responsa Knaf R'nanah* 75; R. Yosef Engel, *Responsa Ben Porat* 38 and Lekach Tov 3; R. Yehoshua Babad, *Responsa Sefer Yehoshua* 24; R. Yosef Patzanofsky, *Pardes Yosef*, vol. 2, p. 379; R. Avraham HaKohen, *Responsa VaYashev Avraham, Orach Chaim* 39; R. Shmuel Engel, *Responsa Maharash Engel* 369; R. Shraga Feivel Shneebalg, *Responsa Shraga HaMeir* 3:11 and 87; R. Shlomo Avraham Rzechte, *Responsa Bikkurei Shlomo, Orach Chaim* 29; R. Moshe Duber Rifkin, *Tiferet Tziyyon* 3; R. Mordechai Winkler, *Responsa Levushei Mordechai*, vol. 2, *Orach Chaim* 84; and R. Ze'ev Zitikovsky, in the journal *HaDarom* 52:62–67. In particular reference to *mitzvot* of eating sanctified objects, see R. Moshe Sofer, *Responsa Chatam Sofer, Orach Chaim* 49 and 146; and R. Eliyahu Bakshi Doron, *Responsa Binyan Av* 3:8:4. R. Greenfield suggests this may underlie the dispute between the *Magen Avraham* and the *Machatzit HaShekel*.

11. *Ginzei Chaim, Orach Chaim* 53:9. R. Yitzchak Motchen, in the journal *Otzerot Yerushalayim* 34:542 also supports the *Magen Avraham*'s position. See also *Likutei He'arot* to *Responsa Chatam Sofer, Orach Chaim* 49, for a detailed explanation of the *mitzvot* relevant to eating sanctified foods, and the relevance of this analysis to this talmudic passage.

12. *Responsa B'Ohalah Shel Torah*, vol. 1, 4:5. R. Ariel points out that this distinction is also in the *Mishnah Berurah* 53:5.

13. *Responsa Yabbia Omer*, vol. 7, *Orach Chaim* 23:4.

any dissent, instead recording the approving citation of his words in the *Knesset HaG'dolah*,[14] and by R. Chaim Yosef David Azulai in *Emet L'Ya'akov*,[15] and *L'David Emet*.[16]

The underlying logic is immediately evident. "Its ways are ways of pleasantness, and its paths are paths of peace." The imposition of an aspect of overt aggressiveness, of violence of body or of spirit, is contradictory to the fundamental essence of *halakhah*. It is inimical to the basic values contained in *mitzvot* to suggest that their pursuit is recommended even at the expense of one's sense of interpersonal equilibrium. Note the language of R. Yosef Karo, in a different context:[17] "One should not use the trait of obduracy [*azzut*] at all, even for a matter of *mitzvah*."

A pleasant interaction with others serves as more than a social nicety; it is a fundamental principle of *halakhah*. "One's manner should always be acceptable to the people," states the Talmud.[18] R. Avraham Yitzchak HaKohen Kook[19] notes, based on the Rambam's formulation of this concept, that this appears to be a function of the sanctification of God's Name. The *Mishnah* states further, "Which is the path that a man should choose? That which is glorious for his Creator and glory to him from the people"[20] and "One whom people are satisfied with, the Creator is satisfied with him."[21] We are instructed to greet all others with a cheerful countenance,[22] and the Rambam and Rabbenu Yonah understand this as an imperative to conduct all dealings with others in a manner that is consistent with harmonious interaction.[23]

Thus, the very introduction of an environment of combativeness into the arena of spiritual behavior is anathema to the halakhic spirit. This is certainly true when it comes to communal activities in which the individual hopes his heightened participation will reap additional merit for

---

14. Number 153.
15. *Mitzvot Sefer Torah* 3.
16. 2:3.
17. *Beit Yosef, Orach Chaim* 1. See also *Mishnah Berurah*.
18. *Ketubot* 17a.
19. *Tov Roei* to *Ketubot*.
20. *Pirkei Avot* 2:1.
21. *Pirkei Avot* 3:10.
22. *Pirkei Avot* 1:15.
23. See *Darkhei Noam* of R. Shaul Wagshal, chs. 1 and 2.

him; in these instances the loss engendered by the belligerence will easily outweigh any benefit. R. Ovadiah Yosef expresses this directly, advising a family fractured by dissension on the issue of a proper memorial for a beloved relative, writing that the soul of the deceased will profit much more from harmony among his family than from any specific gesture marred by dispute. R. Reizner and R. Ya'akov Davidson[24] make similar comments. Further, R. Moshe Dov Wolner[25] observes that these concepts are found in the Talmud in relation to the consumption of sanctified foods, an area of *halakhah* that specifically mandates dignity in its details. This translates itself most particularly to the parallel topic of leading in prayer, which is often the source of much debate on the communal level.

This is certainly not to deny the primacy of one's own concerns in the quest for religious accomplishments and the resources necessary. In fact, R. Moshe Feinstein,[26] in discussing prioritization regarding the time and materials available for *mitzvot*, applies the position of R. Akiva in a well-known dispute with one Ben P'tura.[27] The Talmud discusses the case of two men traveling in a desert, one of whom holds a container of water sufficient only for himself. While Ben P'tura felt that the water should be divided between them, so that "one should not watch the death of his friend," R. Akiva taught that the one with the water should drink it, for "your life takes precedence over that of your friend." R. Feinstein writes that this policy of R. Akiva is relevant not only to physical necessities but to spiritual ones as well, expressing astonishment at a contradictory indication in the works of the *Chatam Sofer.*[28] Nonetheless, this refers only to maintaining for oneself that which is already in one's possession; surely, R. Akiva would not instruct the unlucky traveler to wrest the water bottle away from its owner or to otherwise acquire it in an inappropriate manner. So, too, the recognition of

---

24. *Hilkhot Derekh Eretz.*
25. *Responsa Chemdat Tzvi* 2:3.
26. *Responsa Iggerot Moshe, Even HaEzer,* vol. 4, 26:4.
27. *Bava Metzia* 62a.
28. See also *Sha'arei Teshuvah, Orach Chaim* 482:1; R. Natan Gestetner, *Natan Piryo* to Chanukah, p. 79; R. Yehoshua Segal Deutsh, *Beit HaLachmi al HaTorah,* vol. 2, p. 11.

personal primacy in *mitzvot* cannot be construed as license for unduly aggressive behavior.

The Rambam enters these concerns into his halakhic codification, specifically in his treatment of the edible gifts to which *kohanim* are entitled. "A *kohen* should not grab the gifts," he writes,[29] "nor should he ask for them verbally; rather, if he is given them with dignity, he should take them. And when there are many people in the slaughterhouse, the modest draw back their hands, while the gluttons take." The reserved manner appropriate for *kohanim* is emblematic of the proper conduct in all things.[30]

II. Personal Space

The consideration offered toward the personal space of another is displayed as well in the Ramban's commentary to the Torah,[31] discussing the incident of Yosef and the wife of Potifar. Rebuffing her advances, Yosef hurriedly leaves, allowing his outer garment to remain in her hands, a falsely incriminating clue that would have been better retrieved. Surely Yosef, a man of strength, would have had little trouble wresting the coat from her hands. Nonetheless, the honor he granted his master's wife mandated against such aggressiveness. The Ramban thus instructs on a fundamental ingredient of respect; an act of invasion into another's personal space, to intrude into one's grasp in the manner necessary to forcibly retrieve an object, is incompatible with an attitude of honor toward that individual.[32]

A respect for personal territory also flows from the imperative of loving one's fellow. R. Ephraim Greenblatt[33] comments that of the angels we find that they "give, out of love, permission to one another,"

---

29. *Mishneh Torah, Hilhot Bikkurim* 9:22.

30. For an interpretation more specific to the laws of gifts of the *kohanim*, see R. Yechiel Michel Charlop's *Torat Chof Yamim*.

31. *Genesis* 39:12.

32. See also R. Simcha Mordechai Ziskind Broide, *Sam Derekh: HaYashar VeHaTov*, pp. 96–7, who discusses this comment of the Ramban and adduces other incidents to establish that such sensitivity was emblematic of the behavior of Yosef in Egypt.

33. *Responsa Riv'vot Ephraim* 3:520.

the implication is that allowing another to have individual space is a reflection of love.[34]

Another element is relevant to the allocation of limited tools of spiritual ascent. The entity of a line or queue in which people wait in an orderly fashion is not a construct external to the halakhic system. Dr. Itamar Warhaftig, writing in the journal *Techumin*,[35] offers an extensive treatment of the issues impacting the contravention of these lines. The Talmud contains the basis for the principle that those who arrive first possess the rights to priority of attention.[36] Another relevant talmudic concept is that of acknowledging the moral priority in acquiring ownerless property to one who has clearly begun attending to it (*ani ha-m'happekh b'charara*).[37] Dr Warhaftig goes as far as considering the assessment of monetary remuneration for the "theft of time."[38]

III. Damaging Other's Property in Pursuit of a Mitzvah

Unfortunately, the enthusiasm felt toward religious activities may at times siphon energy away from the attention paid to the needs of others. At first glance, the Talmud seems to acknowledge this and to forgive it somewhat. The discussion is of one who, in the course of hurrying on a Friday afternoon to prepare for *Shabbat*, damages the property of another. He is relieved of the obligation to pay for the damage he causes because his actions have the status of *ratz bir'shut*, that is, "running with permission."[39] The implication is that the involvement in a *mitzvah* activity absolves him of the responsibility for his carelessness.

R. Yair Bachrach[40] explains that this is a misinterpretation of the text. Even if religious involvement could reduce the level of guilt, the most it

---

34. R. Greenblatt's comments, however, deal more directly with professional territory than with personal physical; nonetheless, a parallelism is assumed.

35. Vol. 12, pp. 124–132.

36. *Sanhedrin* 8a, with *Meiri*.

37. *Kiddushin* 59a. Further talmudic support for respecting lines is offered by R. Tzvi Shpitz, *Responsa Mishpetei HaTorah*, #8.

38. On related topic, see also, in the journal *Techumin* (vol. 22), articles by R. Yitzchak Zvi Oshinsky (pp. 334–341) and R. Yitzchak Arama (pp. 342–344). See also R. Yaakov Yeshaya Bloi, *Pitchei Choshen*, vol. 4, ch. 15, #3.

39. *Bava Kamma* 32a.

40. *Responsa Chavvot Yair* 207.

could do is convert the status of the action to that of an unavoidable accident, called *onus*. That would be unhelpful in this instance, as even damages incurred by an individual completely against his will are nonetheless his burden financially. Rather, the variable here is the responsibility of the owner to protect his own property. Belongings left exposed outdoors are understood to be more prone to destruction, and this does mitigate somewhat the guilt of the one who damages it. Similarly, on a Friday afternoon, it is to be expected that people will be hurrying in the streets; hence, it is incumbent upon the owner of possessions to be aware of the heightened danger they risk when outside. Thus, there is no principle exempting those involved with *mitzvot* from the consequences of their actions; rather, there is merely a greater onus of protection on the times when the populace in general is distracted by such things.[41]

R. Avraham Yafeh-Shlesinger expresses a similar rejection of the former assumption.[42] While R. Aharon David Grossman cites a comment of R. Moshe Sofer[43] disputing a portion of R. Bachrach's reasoning in the specific instance he deals with, his correspondent, R. Tzvi Shpitz, argues that R. Bachrach's position is nonetheless normative.[44] As he observes, "It will develop, [otherwise] . . . that all those walking in public will have to protect themselves from people running, for perhaps they are running to prayer or to synagogue, or to a wedding, or to a *brit* or the like, and that would be a matter of great astonishment." However, it might be inferred from the writings of R. Yehoshua Baumol and R. David Horowitz that they do recognize some degree of extenuation when a *mitzvah* is involved, although the impact to this particular instance is debatable.[45]

---

41. A similar reasoning is considered, although he concluded differently, by R. Yonatan Binyamin Goldberger, *Responsa Avnei Cheifetz* 1:59.

42. *Responsa Be'er Sarim* 1:10.

43. *Chiddushei Chatam Sofer, Shabbat* 21b.

44. *Responsa V'Darashta V'Chakarta, Choshen Mishpat* 18 and 19. See also his *Mishpetei HaTorah* 1:10.

45. They discuss the practice of fasting when a Torah scroll falls, assuming it to be an atonement for the sin of treating the scroll carelessly. What, however, would happen if the scroll fell during the performance of a *mitzvah*, such as rejoicing on

R. Yisrael Grossman,[46] discussing damage done during a Purim celebration, considers another talmudic text that indicates leniency for one who, while rejoicing in a *mitzvah* (in the Talmud's case, it is the celebration of Sukkot) causes bodily or material harm.[47] Once again, it becomes clear that this is due to the widespread awareness of the exuberant mood of the festival and the correspondingly intensified need to protect one's property. As the Rama[48] quotes from earlier authorities,[49] "Since their custom is [to act in a dangerous manner] they are exempt," that is to say, the exculpation is rooted only in the familiarity of the victims with the risks of their situation. Nonetheless, the Rama adds[50] that the courts are within their bounds if they choose to enact penalties regardless. Further, R. Grossman concludes that despite any theoretical exemption, it is highly appropriate for the responsible party to offer some restitution. R. Binyamin Yehoshua Zilber[51] adds, based on the *Magen Avraham*,[52] that also relevant to leniencies on Purim is the fact that in the interest of allowing celebrations to go unfettered, those involved generally forgo their monetary rights that would otherwise inhibit the rejoicing. To this end, R. Yoel Sirkes distinguishes between minor damages and more significant losses.[53]

Simchat Torah (the subject of discussion of R. Baumol's *Responsa Emek Halakhah* 2:9) or the public lifting of the Torah (R. David Horowitz's *Responsa Imrei David* 115)? The apparent assumption is that the Talmud's category of "running with permission" is one that reduces the culpability of those involved in *mitzvot*; see also *Responsa Minchat Aharon* 384 and *Responsa Shevet HaLevi* 5:4. The extent that this would be relevant to the above is unclear.

46. *Responsa Netzach Yisrael* 15.
47. *Sukkah* 45a.
48. *Choshen Mishpat* 378:9.
49. *Mordechai, Sukkah* 2:742; *Tosafot, Rosh, Agudah, Sukkah* 45a.
50. Citing *Terumas HaDeshen, Psakim* 210.
51. *Responsa Az Nidbaru* 9:49.
52. *Orach Chaim* 695:7.
53. See *Mishnah Berurah* 695:7. Note also the discussion of R. David Shperber, *Responsa Afarkasta D'Anya* 1:148; and of R. Alter Gilrenter, in the journal *HaEmek*, vol. 64, pp. 16–20.

IV. Disturbing Sleep for a Mitzvah

The reading of R. Bachrach and of those in agreement with him further emphasizes the admonition not to allow the zeal for spiritual accomplishment to compromise one's commitment to the needs of others. Another issue taken up by halakhic authorities is also of interest. The prohibition against disturbing the sleep of another is branded with the stigma of theft (*gezel sheinah*)[54]. Often, an individual enjoying a peaceful slumber is at risk of missing the appointed times for prayer. Does this warrant the disturbing of his rest?

R. Moshe Shternbuch[55] is reluctant to allow this except in cases of clear biblical obligation, without prior indication that this would be in consonance with the wishes of the recumbent individual. R. Aharon Rosenfeld concurs,[56] ruling that he should be woken up if a biblical *mitzvah* is at risk, but to do so for a rabbinical one requires an estimation of his wishes.[57] R. Raphael Evers is stricter with those who fall asleep wearing tefillin, which is forbidden.[58] R. Shimon Sofer[59] considers an act of greater premeditation: altering another's alarm clock in order to create a situation in which he will wake up earlier for prayer. This also involves issues of dishonesty, and R. Sofer's conclusion is to recommend against this course of action.[60]

This discussion deals entirely with circumstances in which the pursuit of a spiritual imperative gives rise to the possibility of mitigating gestures of aggressiveness and disrespect against another, and it is clear that these excuses nonetheless fall far short. It need not be said that absent these largely invalid exculpations, any failings in this area are incomprehensible.

---

54. See chapter 1, p. 21 and in note 119.

55. *Responsa Teshuvot V'Hanhagot* 2:50.

56. *Responsa Minchat Aharon*, vol. 3, *Orach Chaim* 180.

57. His discussion focuses on a person who has fallen asleep accidentally and thus has the status of being a transgressor against his will (*onus*).

58. *Responsa V'Shav V'Rapha* 1: 2. See also R. Yochana Segal Vosner, *Responsa Chayyei HaLevi* 3:45:13.

59. *Responsa Hitor'rut Teshuvah, Orach Chaim* 36.

60. On dishonesty in *mitzvot*, see R. Ya'akov Yichizkiyahu Fish, *Titten Emet L'Ya'akov, Responsa* 4.

FOURTEEN

Created in His Image: Concerns for Human Dignity

I. Halakhic Concessions for Human Dignity

The concern for personal dignity is one that influences much of daily behavior. The desire to avoid embarrassment and degradation impacts heavily on the decision to partake in or abstain from a given activity, usually overwhelming even such formidable opponents as the desire for material gain or personal gratification. However, the performance of *mitzvot* is the highest calling and the noblest goal; it might be assumed, then, that if necessary the individual's self-consciousness must bow to the demands of his spiritual obligations.

It therefore emerges somewhat unexpectedly that this is not unilaterally the case. "Great is human dignity [*k'vod habriyot*]," states the

Talmud, "so much so that it overpowers a prohibition of the Torah."[1] The magnitude of this proclamation comes as a surprise, and the Talmud notes the apparently contradictory verse, "There is no wisdom, no understanding, no counsel in opposition to God."[2] The prohibition mentioned is then identified as that of "You shall not deviate . . . ,"[3] the admonition to heed the words of the sages, possibly the biblical source for rabbinical authority.[4] It emerges, then, that concerns for human dignity take precedence over rabbinical commandments.

Further, even biblical principles do not indiscriminately obtain when challenging the dignity of man. Following a discussion of the principles involved, the Talmud concludes that a biblical precept can at times bow to *k'vod habriyot*, provided no actual prohibition will actively be transgressed; that would create a desecration of God's Name, in violation of the aforementioned verse. Thus, the deviation from Torah law must be passive, or *shev v'al ta'aseh*.[5]

In the course of this discussion, additional dispensations are uncovered. The commandment to return lost objects is suspended if the mission will be considered degrading to the one who spots the object; for example, an elderly individual who is not accustomed to such searching is exempt.[6] The Talmud rejects utilizing this idea, derived from a bibli-

---

1. *Berakhot* 19b; *Shabbat* 81b and 94a; *Megillah* 3b; and *Eiruvin* 41b.

2. *Proverbs* 21:30.

3. *Deuteronomy* 17:11.

4. The actual relationship between this verse and rabbinic enactments is a matter of dispute between the Rambam (*Mishneh Torah, Hilkhot Mamrim* 1:2, *Sefer HaMitzvot, Shoresh* 3) and the Ramban (glosses to *Sefer HaMitzvot*). See *Lechem Mishneh*; *Derashot HaRan*; *Zohar HaRakia*; R. Shimon Shkop, *Sha'arei Yosher* 1:7; R. Elchanan Wasserman, *Kuntres Divrei Soferim*; R. Eliezer Deutsh, *Chelkat Hasadeh, Ar'ah D'Rabannan* 61; and R. Shimon Eiger, *Responsa Hitor'rut Teshuvah*. Note R. Hillel Posek, *Responsa Hillel Omer, Yoreh Deah* 103.

5. *Berakhot* 20a. It is somewhat unclear whether or not the Rambam recognizes this category. See R. Nechemiah Gunzberg, *Responsa Divrei Nechemiah* 51; R. Yosef M. Baumol, in the *Sefer Yovel L'Khvod HaGrid Soloveitchik*, pp. 157–192; and R. Ya'akov Greenwald, in the journal *VaY'lakket Yosef*, vol. 5, no. 163, and vol. 6, no. 68, and the response of R. Moshe Neirenberg in vol. 6, no. 12. Note also R. Natan Horowitz, *Responsa Meorot Natan*, p. 4.

6. R. Yitzchak Blazer considers whether the term *zaken*, used in the Talmud, refers to a Torah scholar or to any individual of advanced years (*Responsa Pri Yitzchak* 1:53). See also R. Zalman Nechemiah Goldberg, in the journal *Moriah*

cal verse,[7] to serve as the source for the larger concept of laws that step aside for concerns of dignity, noting that as a monetary matter, rather than a more ritually oriented *mitzvah* or prohibition, it creates its own category.[8] Thus, three categories that bow to dignity emerge directly from the text of the Talmudic passage: rabbinic law, passive biblical law, and monetary law.[9]

It should also be noted that according to many authorities, human dignity is not to be interpreted as Jewish dignity; all human beings merit this prioritization, as the phrase itself suggests. R. Shimon Sofer[10] considers this to be the opinion of the Rambam in his *Mishneh Torah*[11] and rules accordingly, as does R. Aharon Lichtenstein.[12] R. Yisrael Shepansky[13] and R. Dov Rosenthal[14] note that this conclusion is the logical extension of the fact that concerns of dignity stem from the creation in the Divine image,[15] a fact true of all of mankind.[16] R. Natan Leiter[17] and R. Yitzchak Sternhill[18] also consider this possibility, although they do not rule conclusively.

(Vol 22, #1/2, p. 115–116), for a nuanced understanding of this concept; see also his analysis printed in the journal *Tzohar* (*"Ohel Baruch"* volume, pp. 328–331). On ascending levels of respect to various types of individuals, see R. Moshe Troyesh, *Orach Meisharim* 4:2.

7. *"Vihitalamta mehem*—and hide yourself from them" (*Deuteronomy* 22:1). The Talmud derives that on certain occasions it is appropriate to hide oneself (*Berakhot* 19b).

8. See *Responsa Divrei Nechemiah* 52; *Responsa Zera Avraham, Yoreh Deah* 17; and R. Yosef Nechemiah Kornitser, *Responsa R. Yosef Nechemiah* 124.

9. As to whether these dispensations are biblical or rabbinical in origin, see *Pri Megadim*, in *Mishbetzot Zahav* 312:1; R. Mordechai Farhand, *Petach HaShearim*, p. 169; and R. Yisrael Shepansky, in *Ohr HaMizrach*, vol. 33, nos. 3–4:219.

10. *Responsa Hitor'rut Teshuvah* 1:39.

11. *Hilkhot Sanhedrin* 24:9.

12. In the journal *Machanayim* (new series) 5:8–15. Note his extensive discussion of this detail, and his analysis of various types of dignity.

13. *Ohr HaMizrach*, ibid., p. 228.

14. *Divrei Yosher* to *Pirkei Avot* 1:12.

15. Note R. Malkiel Tannenbaum, *Responsa Divrei Malkiel* 1:67 and 3:82.

16. As per *Tiferet Yisrael* and *Tosafot Yom Tov, Avot* 3:14. Note also Ramban, in his commentary to *Chumash, Deuteronomy* 21:22, and R. Moshe Rosmarin, *D'var Moshe, Pirkei Avot* 3:140. See also R. Avraham Geiser, in the journal *Derekh Eretz Dat U'Medinah*, pp. 159–165.

17. *Responsa Me'orot Natan* 97.

18. *Kokhvei Yitzchak*, vol. 3, p. 9, *Kuntres K'vod Melakhim* 4. See also the discussion in R. Elyakim Dvorkes, *B'Shvilei HaParshah*, p. 93.

R. Naftali Amsterdam, in a letter to R. Yitzchak Blazer (also known as R. Itzeleh Peterburger), writes that to qualify for the classification of *k'vod habriyot* the matter must be one of objective degradation for at least the majority of individuals.[19] In this respect, the dignity referred to is that of mankind, rather than of any individual. Along these lines, R. Shimon Gabel[20] explains that it is for this reason that one is not asked to dispense with one's dignity for the sake of the *mitzvah*; no single person can make that decision. R. Blazer, responding to R. Amsterdam in one of a lengthy series of responsa on the topic[21], writes to prove the existence of a subjective standard.[22] Nonetheless, R. Eliyahu Bakshi Doron, former Sefardi chief rabbi of Israel, argues that an observable, albeit individual, humiliation must be present; one's internal, emotional biases may be halakhically relevant, but under other categories.[23]

II. Controversial Categories

Beyond the Talmud text itself, three additional categories, disputed among the commentaries, may be found. A specific word in another verse teaches that the injunction against a *nazir* or *kohen gadol* involving himself with a dead body, even for the funeral of relatives, is suspended in the instance of an individual who passes away with no family to attend to his proper burial (*met mitzvah*).[24] The concern for the dignity of the deceased takes precedence over the prohibition of a *nazir* or *kohen gadol* coming into contact with a dead body.[25] This is at least the understanding of *Tosafot*,[26] who explain that although an active prohi-

---

19. See also *Responsa Divrei Malkiel*, ibid.

20. *Sofrei Shimon, Berakhot* 20a.

21. The two rabbis were among the foremost students of R. Yisrael Lipkin (Salanter).

22. *Responsa Pri Yitzchak* 1:53, 54. See also R. Yisrael Meir Kagan, *Mishnah Berurah* 13:12, and R. Baruch Weiss, *Birkhot Horai* 32:66.

23. *Responsa Binyan Av* 2:56. See also R. Shepansky, pp. 223–225.

24. "*V'la-achoto*—for his sister" (*Numbers* 6:7). "For his sister he may not defile himself, but for a *met mitzvah* he may."

25. That it is a consideration for human dignity rather than the commandment of burial that overcomes the prohibition is proven by R. Meir Simchah HaKohen of Dvinsk, *Ohr Sameach, Hilkhot S'machot* 3:8.

26. *Berakhot* 19b, s.v. *Omrat*.

bition is involved, protecting the purity of a *kohen gadol* is less severe than most transgressions, for it is a prohibition relevant only to a portion of the population (*lav sh'eino shaveh lakol*), a categorization bearing some leniency. It is thus more susceptible to being overcome by concerns of dignity. Likewise, the status of a *nazir* is subject to abrogation by a rabbinical scholar (*efshar b'sheailah*).[27] Rashi, however, is of a different view; a *met mitzvah* is not included within the category of the prohibition in the first place, and thus no explanation is necessary for the dispensation.[28] Thus, according to *Tosafot*, biblical prohibitions that are somehow weakened, such as those that do not apply to the entire populace or those that can be removed by rabbinic decision, create yet another category suspended for concerns of human dignity, while Rashi apparently does not recognize this category.

A second disputed category may be discovered in the difference between two of the great halakhic codifiers of the medieval era. Bowing to the active nature of the offense, the *Talmud*[29] rules that someone who discovers a forbidden mixture in his clothing (*shatnez*) must remove the garment immediately, even in a public place, despite the ensuing embarrassment. Rabbeinu Asher, the *Rosh*, limits the range of this law, in the process adding yet another category to the growing list of those areas of *halakhah* that step aside in respect to human dignity. According to the text in his possession, one is only required to disrobe in public if the mixture is found *b'bigdo*, in his garment, as opposed to a situation in which he realizes that his companion is inadvertently wearing *shatnez*. Only if he discovers it himself, and is thus knowingly so attired, is he required to sacrifice considerations of *k'vod habriyot*; however, if the wearer himself is unaware and is thus transgressing without his own knowledge (*b'shogeg*), *k'vod habriyot* still prevails. Thus, it emerges that even an active biblical law can be violated for the sake of human dignity, as long as the transgression is unintentional.

---

27. See R. Avraham Tzvi Klein, in the journal *VaY'lakket Yosef*, vol. 2, no. 7.

28. *Berakhot* 20a, s.v. *shev v'al ta'aseh shani*. See R. Amram Blum, *Responsa Beit She'arim* 112. On these issues of the process of deferral, see, at length, R. Baruch Frankel-Teomim, *Baruch Ta'am, Din Aseh Docheh Lo Ta'aseh, Din* 5, chs. 1–8.

29. *Berakhot* 20b.

However, it is clear from the Rambam that he does not agree to this innovation. His text contains no distinction as to the wearer and the discoverer; any *shatnez* discovered must immediately be removed, regardless of the intent or lack thereof.[30] Thus, a dispute exists between the Rosh and the Rambam as to the status of an inadvertent transgression, the Rosh allowing it to continue if concerns for dignity require it, with the Rambam dissenting.[31]

R. Aryeh Leib of Metz[32] challenges the Rosh's position, noting a counterindicative passage in the Talmud.[33] In response, many authorities[34] suggest a revamped understanding of the Rosh's position. The focus is not in reality on the inadvertent transgressor and the severity, reduced or otherwise, of his action; rather, it is on the discoverer of the *shatnez*, and on the question of his obligation to inform the former of the situation. While an obligation exists to prevent another Jew from sinning, if the latter is acting unintentionally, this obligation, according to the Rosh, is only rabbinical.[35] As such, it is overlooked if *k'vod habriyot* mandates it.

Either understanding of the Rosh, if his position is accepted, impacts significantly upon the *halakhah*, allowing one to refrain from informing an unsuspecting other of his transgression if the alternative is humiliation. One discussion to address this issue is that of R. Yechezkel Landau.[36] The case was of a young man who had had an affair with his mother-in-law, and now wishes to repent. He had queried as to whether he was required to inform his father-in-law, for the latter is obligated to divorce his unfaithful wife. As they were a distinguished family, this course of action would cause significant embarrassment. If the Rosh is

---

30. *Mishneh Torah, Hilkhot Kilayim* 10:29.

31. See R. Mordechai Benet, *Responsa Gedulat Mordechai* 27 and 28 (in *Har Hamor*). See also R. Ya'akov Yeshayah Bloi, *Malbushei Yesha* 1:12, 13.

32. *Sha'agat Aryeh* 58; see also R. Shmuel Dertzinsky, *Ohel Moshe*.

33. *Menachot* 38a.

34. See R. Yoel Sirkes, *Bayit Chadash*; *Responsa Goren David, Yoreh Deah* 32; and *Responsa Maharash Engel* 8:210.

35. R. Eliyahu Bakshi-Doron ties this detail to a larger analysis of the obligation to prevent another from sinning (*l'hafrish me'issura*); see *Responsa Binyan Av* 2:54.

36. *Responsa Noda B'Yehudah, Mahadurah Kamma, Orach Chaim* 35.

indeed correct, perhaps the father-in-law might be allowed to remain ignorant and continue living with his wife, avoiding humiliation. R. Landau, after considering this issue, concludes stringently, but suggests a plan in which the embarrassment can be circumvented.[37] However, R. Chaim Halberstam[38] and R. Shmuel Engel[39] are lenient, for other reasons.[40]

Another case to be affected is that of a woman who, in her more promiscuous youth, had become pregnant; now, as a reformed and happily married adult, she has given birth to her husband's first child. The husband is anxious to perform the ritual of redemption of the firstborn (*pidyon haben*), unaware that his wife's past makes it unnecessary. Although allowing him to remain uninformed will result in a fraudulent ceremony and an unwarranted blessing, perhaps, in accordance with the Rosh, *k'vod habriyot* may indicate such a course. This situation, apparently more common than one would imagine, is taken up by a number of authorities.[41]

The Rama[42] adopts the position of the Rosh in discussing a *kohen* who is asleep in bed, undressed, when someone passes away in the same building, rendering the dwelling unfit for habitation by a *kohen*. Although the *kohen* must leave immediately, the Rama allows the newsbringer to ask him to dress first, and only when he is properly covered to inform him that he must leave the building.[43]

---

37. He observes that while the husband and wife must cease their intimate relationship, there is no need to actually divorce; at their advanced age, they presumably have no desire to marry others. Thus, the public need not know.

38. *Responsa Divrei Chaim* vol. 1, *Orach Chaim*, 35.

39. *Responsa Maharash Engel* 8:210.

40. See also R. Yitzchak Shmuel Schechter, *Responsa Yashiv Yitzchak* 5:34.

41. R. Shimon Greenfeld, *Responsa Maharshag* 3:65; R. Ovadiah Yosef, *Responsa Yabbia Omer*, vol. 8, *Yoreh Deah* 32; R. Eliyahu Bakshi-Doron, *Responsa Binyan Av* 2:54. See chapter 6, p. 93.

42. *Yoreh Deah* 372:1.

43. This ruling is based upon the *Terumat Hadeshen* (284), who does require the *kohen* to leave immediately if he learns of the death before he can dress. R. Yehoshua Babad (*Responsa Sefer Yehoshua* 1,63) questions this stringency (as do R. Yair Bachrach, *Responsa Chavvot Yair*, and R. Meir Eisenstadt, *Responsa Panim Meirot*) in light of the opinion of *Tosafot*, cited above, that the purity of *kohanim*, being a prohibition of limited application, does bow to *k'vod habriyot*. (In fact, Rabbi Yechezkel Landau, in his *Tziyyun L'Nefesh Chayah* to *Berakhot* 20a, writes

A third controversial category can be developed from a dispute found in the writings of later decisors, one that will hinge explicitly on understanding the process by which human dignity exerts its halakhic priority.

III. Explaining the Priority of Dignity: the *Mechilah* Theory

It thus bears determining, then, the mechanism by which the maintenance of personal self-respect overpowers religious obligations.[44] One of the previously listed categories, that of monetary matters, may provide a crucial clue. R. Moshe Sofer[45] explains that the relevant concept here is that of *mechilah*, of "forgiving" that to which one is entitled. Certainly, an individual has a number of personal rights granted to him by the Torah; among these is having his lost property returned to him. Nonetheless, it is presumed that no Jew would stand on his rights if it meant degradation to another. Thus, it can be assumed that an implicit *mechilah* is in effect in such instances, allowing the concern for human dignity full attention.

With this foundation, R. Sofer continues, an extrapolation may be made to the supercession of rabbinical precepts as well. Although the honor due to the Talmudic authorities mandates obedience to their dictates, they forgive the obligations of their own honor in favor of that of the individual, much as does the possessor of monetary rights.[46] The Tzanzer Rebbe, Rabbi Chaim Halberstam, in a similar analysis[47] observes that

---

that the position is tenable only according to Rashi and therefore rules leniently in his *Dagul MeR'vavah* to *Shulchan Arukh.*) R. Babad suggests that perhaps the embarrassment, taking place at night in a residential area, is minor (*gnai katan*) and further suggests that the element of the obligation of burial is necessary for leniency; this may be somewhat at variance with the words of the *Ohr Sameach* cited earlier. See also R. Avraham Shmuel Binyamin Sofer, *Responsa K'tav Sofer, Yoreh Deah* 169, and R. Yoav Yehoshua Weingarten, *Responsa Chelkat Yoav, Mahadurah Tinyana* 9. Note, as well, R. Aharon Soloveichik, *Od Yisrael Yosef Bni Chai* 28.

44. See, for example, R. Eliyahu Ragoler, *Responsa Yad Eliyahu* 2:3.

45. *Chiddushei Chatam Sofer* to *Shabbat*. See also R. Chaim Kanievsky, *Derekh Emunah, Kilayim* 10:136.

46. See Rashi to *Berachot* 19b, and note also R. Avraham Bornstein, *Responsa Avnei Nezer, Orach Chaim* 392:8. See, as well, the analysis of R. Moshe Shmuel Schapiro in the journal *Tzohar* ("*Ohel Baruch*" volume, pp. 477–479).

47. *Responsa Divrei Chaim* vol. 1, *Orach Chaim*, 35.

while the authority of the sages may indeed stem from biblical origins, as their mandates are not explicitly identified in the Torah no desecration to God's Name is incurred by their violation. Hence, the path is clear for the rabbis to step aside and allow dignity to take precedence.[48]

R. Halberstam takes this further and suggests adding yet another category to this list. Just as rabbinical commandments are overridden by dint of their lack of overt reference, so, too, even genuine biblical commandments that are not explicitly expressed, or principles transmitted to Moshe at Sinai, may also be treated in that manner. This last extension was considered insufficiently grounded for the Munczaczer Rebbe, R. Chaim Elazar Shapiro, who does endorse the initial thesis.[49] Nonetheless, R. Shmuel Engel, in his responsa,[50] does support this innovation, noting that it exists also in the work *Limmudei Hashem*, who explains in this manner an unusual ruling of the Rambam.[51]

Thus, it may be that the precedence of human dignity over monetary matters and rabbinical commandments is a function of *mechilah*.[52] It consequently seems indicated that this also plays a role in explaining the inclusion of passively violated biblical concepts in these categories. To actively flout God's will (or explicit will, according to the Tzanzer Rebbe) is a desecration of His Name and at variance with "There is no wisdom, no understanding, no counsel in opposition to God." However,

---

48. See also R. Nissim Gerondi, *Derashot HaRan, Drush* 5, *Nusach* 2, that the rabbis did not demand adherence to their words in a situation of *k'vod habriyot*, and Rashbatz, *Zohar HaRakia, Sefer HaMitzvot Shoresh* 1, who writes that it was built into the original rabbinical enactments that they should not apply when challenging *k'vod habriyot*. R. Meshulam Shinker, in the journal *BiNetivot Yam* 6:192–199, discusses this issue, noting that a ramification of whether or not the enactments were made at all in situations of *k'vod habriyot* is the question of whether there is any value to being stringent in these areas.

49. *Responsa Minchat Elazar* 1:24:1.

50. *Responsa Maharash Engel* 8:209.

51. The Rambam writes that someone who is in the process of shaving and hears that his father has passed away may continue, despite the restrictions of mourning (in this instance, biblically mandated in the Rambam's opinion), to avoid the embarrassment of appearing half-shaven. As the imperative to observe mourning rituals is not explicit, even if indeed biblical, that may explain his position. See also *Responsa V'Darashta V'Chakarta*, vol. 3, *Orach Chaim* 7:4.

52. R. Joseph D. Epstein advances a different theory concerning the common denominator of these aspects; see *Mitzvot HaMussar*, pp. 169–180.

where this is not the case, it seems possible that God Himself forgives some of His honor for the sake of that of His creations.[53] An extreme example of this can be found in a midrashic comment on God's destruction of the donkey of Bilam. This was out of consideration for Bilam's honor; a living example of his inferiority to his own donkey would be the source of considerable embarrassment.

An understanding of this phenomenon is somewhat challenging. It is not difficult to see that as people are creations in the Divine image, honor and respect shown to a human being translates to his Creator.[54] Nonetheless, it could also be assumed that the honor of God Himself would be inclusive of all such gestures, and thus has no purpose in deferring to that of the Creation, at best a secondary representation. Certainly Bilam, an almost paradigmatic example of opposition to God's will, is an unworthy recipient of honor, in light of the testament to God's majesty that would be evident in the miracle of a speaking animal.

The key may lie in a paradox that exists within the concept of honor. The great ethicists[55] point to an inconsistency in the behavior of vain individuals. With an exaggerated sense of self-worth, they feel little regard for the status of others. Nonetheless, were this really the case, the very honor and adulation they so prize would be worthless. Of what value is the esteem of an insignificant person? Thus, they are forced to consider other individuals worthy, only to the extent necessary to accept their praise. Thus, receiving honor is only possible if it is first ceded somewhat to those from whom it is desired.

It might be suggested that this is the message of the statement in *Pirkei Avot*, "Who is honored? He who honors others."[56] Not only is someone who is respectful to others worthy of such treatment himself, as the *Mishnah* states openly, but further it is only possible for a person to receive honor if he first accords it to others, deeming them appro-

---

53. On this possibility, see *Kiddushin* 32a, and R. Natan Gestetner, *L'Horot Natan* to *Pirkei Avot* 4:1.

54. Note one of many such discussions in R. Avraham Tobolsky's *Hizaharu Bikh'vod Chaveirkhem*, pp. 85–86, citing R. Yechezkel Levenstein.

55. See, for example, R. Eliyahu HaKohen of Izmir, *Shevet Mussar*, ch. 43.

56. *Avot* 4:1.

priate sources of expressions of esteem. As Rabbeinu Yonah comments, "All honor that one shows to people, he is showing to himself."

Perhaps this may contribute to understanding God's *mechilah* of His honor from His creations. The very concept of honor is one that is built upon *mechilah*, and is fed by its utilization; showing honor to another ultimately strengthens the latter's ability to appropriately reciprocate. Thus, all respect shown to human beings reflects onto God in two ways; first, in that He is their Creator, and second, in that it allows them the authority to respect Him in a meaningful manner.[57]

R. Ya'akov Davidson suggests an additional idea as well.[58] God's relationship to His creations contains the dual roles of Father and King. As a Father, His compassion for His children entreats Him to dispense with standing on His honor, on their behalf. However, in the role of King this is impossible; as opposed to a father, "A King who waives his honor, his honor is nevertheless not waived."[59] The result of this conflict is a sort of compromise; certain elements are forgiven, such as passive violations, but others cannot be, such as active disobedience to the Torah's dictates.

Thus, it may be that the fundamental operating element in the overriding of other principles for the sake of human dignity is that of *mechilah* by the possessor of monetary rights; by the rabbinical sages; and, to some extent, by God Himself.

IV. The "Values Clash" Theory

Alternatively, the explanation may be somewhat more prosaic. The concern for human dignity is a religious value like others; when irreconcilably placed in conflict, it is understood that one must prevail over the other. Whether or not *k'vod habriyot* is indeed dominant will depend in each instance on the severity of its competition.[60]

---

57. A similar theory is advanced in R. Simcha Mordechai Ziskind Broide, *Sam Derekh: HaYashar VeHaTov*, pp. 91–2.

58. *Hilkhot Derekh Eretz*, ch. 13.

59. *Kiddushin* 32b, *Ketubot* 17a, *Sotah* 41b, and *Sanhedrin* 19b.

60. See also R. Tzvi Shimshovitch, in the journal *Kuntres Kol Sofer* 5754:46–51.

In this area, the distinction between active and passive deviations from Torah law is instructive. This is a differentiation found elsewhere in *halakhah*, namely in the authority of the Rabbis, under certain circumstances, to mandate disobedience to a biblical imperative,[61] as well as the financial strain imposed.[62] The reasoning for this distinction is the topic of much discussion.[63] A number of possibilities suggest themselves. In some respects, an active transgression is considered more severe than one passive in nature; thus, the differentiation may be qualitative in essence.[64] If one indeed understands the precedence of *k'vod habriyot* to stem from its attaining higher priority in a clash of values, this variance in stringency is certainly relevant to determining which consideration shall emerge as primary. An analysis along these lines is suggested by R. Yisrael Ya'akov Kanievsky, the Steipler Gaon.[65]

Alternatively, it may be that the distinction is not due to severity but to the nature of action itself. When faced with a conflict in which any action taken will have negative consequences, either for the purposes of human dignity or for other religious values, the safest course of behavior may be to abstain from any visible[66] activity. From some standpoint, this approach is palatable to one who favors an understanding based on *mechilah*. While an active transgression is a desecration of God's Name, forgiving the performance of an obligation is more readily acceptable when warranted.

---

61. *Yevamot* 90b.

62. In the opinion of the Rama (*Orach Chaim* 556) the Talmud's limit of one-fifth of one's resources (*Ketubot* 50b) is relevant only to obligations and not prohibitions; the Vilna Gaon, however, dissents (*Biurei HaGra, Yoreh Deah* 157). See also R. Chanokh Eigesh, *Marcheshet* 43.

63. See R. Elchanan Wasserman's *Kovetz He'arot* 69 and *Kuntres Divrei Sofrim, Petichah HaKollelet* of the *Pri Megadim*, and R. Ya'akov Etlinger's *Bikkurei Ya'akov* 556.

64. See R. Mordechai Yaffe's *Levush Malkhut* (*Orach Chaim* 556); R. Yair Bachrach, *Responsa Chavvot Yair* 139; *Responsa Rivash* 387; R. Chaim Chizkiyahu Medini, *Sdei Chemed, Ma'arekhet HaLamed Klal* 107; *Responsa Minchat Shai* 20, based on the commentary of the Ramban to the Torah; and R. Shimon Pollack, *Responsa Shem M'Shimon* 1:12.

65. *Kehilot Ya'akov* to *Berakhot* (10) and *Shevuot* (26) [new editions]. See also the *Kovetz He'arot* cited above, whose central concept is quoted by R. Kanievsky.

V. Applications of the Two Theories

Thus, the two above theories serve as possible models to explain the three categories in the Talmud, and as well shed light on the different sides in the three controversial categories. The issue argued by Rashi and *Tosafot*, that of "weakened" prohibitions, is illuminated by these possibilities. If the core issue is the conflict, with biblical prohibitions remaining supreme, the position of *Tosafot* may be understood: when a prohibition for some reason assumes a lower status, it may no longer retain the primacy given to undiminished prohibitions. Alternatively, if the issue is one of *mechilah*, employed in all instances other than active disgraces against God's authority, then no distinction should be made for a "weakened" prohibition; it remains an active offense. Thus, the position of Rashi, who appears not to accept this category.

This range of options is perhaps demonstrable in another dispute among *rishonim*, the above mentioned difference between the Rambam and the Rosh concerning inadvertent transgressions. Here, too, the two options seem relevant. If the conflict between Torah law and human dignity is adjudicated on the basis of severity, a violation performed without intent is surely of a lesser degree of offense, and perhaps the position of the Rosh is indicated in recognizing such a distinction. Alternatively, if the priority is avoiding an active infraction and the accompanying desecration of God's Name, the actual perpetrator of the action may not be consequential, as in the Rambam's view.[67]

Likewise, the question debated by the *Divrei Chaim* and his detractors, if a category can be created for non-explicit prohibitions, is also affected, as discussed above.

VI. Further Applications

In this light, a comment of *Tosafot* is particularly informative. The Talmud[68] discusses the responsibility of an esteemed Torah scholar to

---

66. See *Torah Temimah, Genesis* 28:23.

67. R. Akiva Sofer suggests a completely different interpretation of the Rambam; see *Responsa Da'at Sofer* 106. See also R. Yitzchak Avraham Twersky, in the journal *Beit Yitzchak* 24:441–446.

68. *Shevuot* 30b.

appear before a court presided over by rabbis of a lesser stature, thus compromising his own prestige, and concludes that there is such an obligation.[69] The *Tosafot*[70] observe that to fail to appear would be passive in nature, and thus considerations of his honor should precede those of his testimony. Two answers are offered, both of which, if accepted into *halakhah*, significantly adapt the parameters of the concept under discussion.

The first suggestion is that although *k'vod habriyot* may indicate deferring performance of a religious obligation, this is only in the event of a significant humiliation (*g'nai gadol*); when the diminishment to one's honor is minor (*g'nai katan*), however, the *mitzvah* prevails. The Ramban presents conflicting impressions in his writings as to his acceptance of this principle.[71]

The second possibility is that the assumption of passivity in this instance is misleading. Following the incorrect judgment that will occur as a result of the missing testimony, active transgressions against the Torah will take place, albeit at the hands of another. Thus, even though the scholar himself will not perform an action, this case cannot be treated as passive and thus *k'vod habriyot* considerations are secondary.

The two approaches in *Tosafot* parallel, to an extent, the possible rationales for treating passive violations differently. If one assumes that these instances are more susceptible to being ruled by considerations of dignity because of a reduced severity, then it follows that a concurrent evaluation should be made of the degree of humiliation involved, to more properly judge which should prevail. In such a context, a distinction between major and minor degradation is more readily understood.

---

69. For modern applications of this concept, see *Responsa Chatam Sofer, Choshen Mishpat* 162, and R. Yosef Sharbit, *Responsa Orchot Yosher, Choshen Mishpat* 3. The whole discussion, they emphasize, refers to a scholar testifying, as opposed to defending allegations against himself personally, to which he certainly must respond. On these issues of testimony, see R. Aryeh Leib of Metz, *Gevurot Ari, Yoma* 74a, s.v. *Limiutei*; R. Aryeh Leib HaKohen, *Shev Shmat'ta* 7:1; and R. Raphael Schapiro, *Torat Raphael* 3:31.

70. S.v. *aval issura*.

71. See *Responsa Pri Yitzchak* 1:26.

Alternatively, if the priority given to avoiding active transgressions stems from the egregiousness of a visible act in opposition to Torah law, it may not be relevant that the act is being performed by another. Since some individual will commit an actual misdeed, the overall situation is governed by that reality.

Another general issue may trace itself back to the central mechanism governing the relationship between *k'vod habriyot* and the laws that conflict. When indeed human dignity does prevail, what becomes the status of the overtaken *halakhah*? It might be assumed that it is completely removed (*hutrah*), no longer to be taken into consideration as long as dignity is at stake. Alternatively, it may be that the *halakhah* remains firmly in place, merely suspended for the necessity of avoiding humiliation (*d'chuyah*).[72] To whatever extent both can be accommodated, this must be done.

If *mechilah* is indeed employed, it might be suggested that the prohibition or obligation has been completely "forgiven,"[73] stepping away as a consideration. Alternatively, if a conflict of values is forcing one to be upheld at the expense of the other, it would seem that license to deviate from *halakhah* is only as far as *k'vod habriyot* necessitates it absolutely.[74]

R. Hershel Schachter, focusing on rabbinical prohibitions, suggests that they are completely removed from consideration but for other reasons.[75] Citing R. Joseph B. Soloveitchik, he writes that the concern for another's dignity constitutes an absolute obligation between two people, similar to a monetary obligation. As such, the Rabbis have no permission to interfere with this relationship by instituting a law that would obstruct it. However, as he observes, this explanation applies only to the dignity needs of another; deviations for the purpose of one's own honor require a different explanation.[76]

---

72. R. Yosef Engel (*Gilyonei HaShas, Berakhot* 19b) assumes this is certainly the case.

73. See, for example, R. Nachum Eizenstat's *Avnei Shoham*, pp. 50–51.

74. See *Responsa L'Horot Natan* 4:36.

75. *B'Ikvei HaTzon*, pp. 88–89.

76. See R. Yonatan Eibshutz, *Urim V'Tumim* 28, as well as *Menachot* 38a and *Responsa Pri Yitzchak* 1:26.

The relevance of this question is significant. On the purely spiritual level, R. Yair Bachrach[77] considers the effect upon the soul, questioning whether a transgression committed for the sake of human dignity must be followed by some form of atonement. He concludes that this is called for, indicating that while the needs of *k'vod habriyot* are often paramount, the halakhic price paid is nonetheless not discounted without another thought.[78]

R. Meir Simchah HaKohen of Dvinsk[79] considers two issues that also are related. The first is that of whether one is permitted to perform an active gesture of honor to a king in violation of *halakhah*, when the gesture's absence would not be considered a humiliation. The question of whether the Torah concept steps aside only because of the concern of avoiding human degradation, or instead flows from the forgiving of the honor of God or of the Rabbis in favor of that of the individual, is fundamental to this exploration.

His second issue is the permissibility of sewing garments of honor on the intermediate days of a festival, when such work is normally forbidden. He responds to this question by advancing a principle. *K'vod habriyot* can only allow the prohibited when the transgression will alleviate the challenges to dignity at the same time as the violation is occurring (*b'idna*). Deviating from the Torah now in order to prevent some future embarrassment cannot be countenanced. This rule of simultaneity is common to areas of *halakhah* in which one value prevails over another in conflict with it; the implication, then, is that this evaluation is present here as well.

R. Yechezkel Landau, in the aforementioned responsum concerning the adulterous son-in-law, adds another rule to this system. One of his reasons for advocating informing the father-in-law of the situation is that otherwise, he would live the rest of his life in violation. Even assuming a concern of *k'vod habriyot*, a transgression is allowed only if it will constitute a temporary deviation from *halakhah*. However, to allow an

---

77. *Responsa Chavvot Yair* 2:36.
78. See also R. Yosef Yedid HaLevi, *Responsa She'erit Yosef* 2:6.
79. *Ohr Sameach, Hilkhot Yom Tov* 6:14.
80. See R. Yehudah Polatchek, *Responsa Meged Yehudah* 55 and 157.

infraction to continue permanently cannot be sanctioned.[80] This limitation suggests that the prohibition is not totally forgiven but merely concedes to human dignity out of necessity.

R. Shlomo Kluger[81] discusses another such element, that of the degree of responsibility the individual carries for his own situation. If a challenge to one's dignity is a result of one's own negligence (*p'shiah*), perhaps this impacts on his right to ask the Torah to bear the costs of his dereliction. Such a conclusion would imply again that the overlooking of *halakhah* comes only as a result of an irreconcilable conflict; the individual's complicity in creating his situation detracts from the weight of his concerns.[82]

Slightly different, but related, is the question posed by R. Akiva Eiger.[83] His analysis concerns the degree to which one must evaluate all the options available. The case in question concerns a man whose *tallit* has become invalid, and thus unfit for wear, just prior to morning services. To sit in synagogue without a *tallit* would be embarrassing, and to wear this garment with invalid fringes would actually only be a passive violation of the obligation to attach proper fringes. Thus, it would seem clear that he is permitted to wear this *tallit*. However, another option also exists; he can pray at home, without a *tallit*, avoiding both embarrassment and the wearing of an unqualified garment. While certainly it is normally preferable to pray with the community, perhaps such considerations must be sacrificed to avoid a conflict between the fundamental *halakhah* and human dignity. Once again, it becomes significant to query the nature of the relationship between *halakhah* and dignity. If the *halakhah* is forgiven, it might not be necessary to search for alternative results; for example, in this case, why compromise the quality of prayer when the issue of the *tallit* is no longer a concern. However, if the point of Torah law is deferred but nonetheless operative, it is worthwhile to attempt to find an option that more fully allows a balance of the values involved.[84]

---

81. *Chokhmat Shlomo* to *Orach Chaim* 13.

82. See also R. Avraham Steinberg, *Responsa Machzeh Avraham, Orach Chaim* 2; *Orach Meisharim* 4:1; and R. Shimon Gabel, *Sofrei Shimon, Berakhot* 20b.

83. *Chiddushei R. Akiva Eiger, Orach Chaim* 13.

84. See also R. Yehoshua Friedlander, *Responsa Avnei Yoshpe* 1:77.

A question raised by R. Yaakov Orenstein[85] goes further toward determining the nature of this relationship. We are aware that *k'vod habriyot* can often overwhelm an imperative of *halakhah*. What, however, if the considerations of dignity challenge not one, but two or more points of law? Does *k'vod habriyot* defeat all opposition, undaunted by quantitative realities? If the law is indeed forgiven, it may not matter that this *mechilah* needs repeated utilization. Alternatively, if human honor merely prevails in conflicts, it is not to be assumed that it will continue to dominate when its rival is doubled or tripled. Along these lines, the *Pri Megadim*[86] interprets the Talmud's giving precedence to *k'vod habriyot* over *milah* and the Passover sacrifice as applying even to both of those together, while many authorities may disagree.[87]

As the theoretical underpinnings continue to be analyzed, the issues in *halakhah* are consequentially illuminated and defined accordingly. Even the Talmud's seemingly outdated permission to carry rocks on *Shabbat* to a lavatory for personal purposes[88] has become the basis of extensive discussion of modern implications.[89] As the ongoing analysis of Jewish law struggles with the delicate balance of God's laws and the dignity of His creations, one message emerges that is beyond doubt or the need for any further definition. If such fundamental values as the strict adherence to *halakhah* and Torah can incorporate into themselves the imperative of human dignity and honor, granting its accommodation such priority, anything less in the more mundane elements of daily existence is inconceivable.

---

85. *Yeshuot Ya'akov, Orach Chaim* 3:12.
86. *Shoshanat HaAmakim, Klal* 6.
87. See R. Schepansky, p. 219.
88. *Shabbat* 81a-b.
89. See R. Shraga Feivel Shneebalg, *Responsa Shraga HaMeir* 8:22:1; R. Shammai Kehat Gross, *Responsa Shevet HaKehati* 3:129; *Responsa Avnei Yoshpe* 1:77; R. Yosef Yedid HaLevi, *Responsa She'erit Yosef* 2:6; R. Raphael Blum, *Responsa Birkhot Shamayim* 1:106; R. Avraham Amram Meisels, *Responsa VaYa'an Avraham* 31; and R. Yosef Chaim Moskowitz, in the journal *Beit HaTalmud L'Hora'ah, Kovetz Shve'ei*, pp. 51–58.

List of Sources Cited

Dates and cities listed refer to one edition, not necessarily the first or the most recent. Some dates are approximated from the Hebrew dates. An indented listing is a commentary to the work listed immediately before it.

A. THE BIBLE AND COMMENTARIES

These works are arranged as commentaries to the Torah and/or *Nevi'im* and *K'tuvim*.

Arvei Nachal. R. David Shlomo of Sraka (eighteenth/nineteenth century). Jerusalem: *Pe'er HaChasidut*, 1966. Also authored *Levushei S'rad* to *Shulchan Arukh*.

Ashdot HaPisgah. R. Chaim Pardes, Tel Aviv: Makhon Yad Mordechai, 1986.

Ateret Yirmiyahu. R. Eliezer Friedman, Montreal, Canada, 1986.

Ba'al HaTurim. R. Ya'akov ben Asher, author of the *Tur* (see Section F). Printed in standard editions of the *Mikraot G'dolot* printings of the Torah.

Bad Kodesh. R. Boruch D. Povarsky (contemporary). Oral discourses edited by students. B'nei Brak: Yeshivat Ponevez, 2001.

Be'er Moshe. R. Yechiel Moshe Epstein (1889–1971), Ozharover Rebbe. To the Torah and the *Nevi'im*. Tel Aviv: *Keren L'Hotza'at Sifrei Aish Dat*, 1986.

Beit Yitzchak Al HaTorah. R. Yitzchak Shmelkes (see Section G). Jerusalem: *Makhon Torat Chakhmei Polin, Makhon Yerushalayim*, 1986.

Binyan David al haTorah. R. Dov Berish Meisels (1814-76). Vajda: Ohel, 1941.

Birkat Peretz. R. Yisrael Ya'akov Kanievsky. Bnei Brak, 1971 (see *Kehilot Ya'akov*, Section D).

B'Shvilei HaParshah. R. Elyakim Dvorkes (contemporary). Halakhic essays arranged according to the weekly portion. Jerusalem: Makhon Hilchati Aktuali Derekh Eliezer Sh'Al Yedei Mercaz Torani Chomat Yerushalayim, 2002.

B'khor Shor. R. Yosef ben Yitzchak (twelfth century) of Orleans, a student of the Tosafist Rabbeinu Tam. Jerusalem, 1983.

Chanukkat HaTorah. R. Yehoshua Heschel (1595–1663) of Krakow, Jerusalem: *Melekhet Machshevet*, 1995.

Chavatzelet HaSharon al haTorah. R. Mordechai Carlebach. Jerusalem, 2004.

Chiddushei HaLev. R. A. Chenakh Leibowitz. *Rosh Yeshivah* of Yeshivas Chafetz Chaim in Forest Hills, Queens, NY. Prepared by his students. Jerusalem and Forest Hills, 1987.

Chizkuni. R. Chizkiyah ben Manoach. Vilna, 1880.

Da'at Zekenim MiBa'alei HaTosafot (see Tosafot Section B). In *Mikraot G'dolot* editions.

Degel Machaneh Ephraim. R. Moshe Chaim Ephraim (ca. 1740–1800) of Sudylkow. Jerusalem: Mir, 1994.

Divrei Shaul. R. Yosef Shaul Nathanson (see *Responsa Shoel U'Meshiv*, Section C). Lemberg: Avraham Nissan Zeiss, 1875.

Divrei Yosef. R. Yosef Aryeh Petrover. Petach Tikvah, 1991.

Emet L'Ya'akov: Iyyunim B'Mikra. R. Ya'akov Kaminetsky (1891–1986). Edited by Daniel Yehudah Neustadt. New York: *Makhon Emet L'Ya'akov,* 1990. *Rosh Yeshivah* of Yeshivah U'Mesivtah Torah VoDa'ath, Brooklyn, NY. His talmudic lectures have also been published in volumes of the same name, *Emet L'Ya'akov.*

Gevurot Yitzchak. R. Yitzchak Sorotzkin. Halakhic discussions arranged according to the *parshiyot* of the Torah. 2 volumes. Wickliffe, Ohio: Telshe Yeshivah, 1994. Also authored *Rinat Yitzchak* to the Torah and other works under the title *Gevurot Yitzchak,* including one to *Mishneh Torah Hilkhot Teshuvah* (see Section E).

Gur Aryeh. R. Yehudah Loew (see *Maharal,* Section D).

Ha'amek Davar and *Harchev Davar.* R. Naftali Tzvi Yehudah Berlin (1817–1893). Known as the *Netziv,* he was *Rosh Yeshivah* of the Yeshivah of Volozhin and also authored *Ha'amek Shealah* to the *Sheiltot D'Rav Achai Gaon, Meromei Sadeh* to the Talmud, and *Responsa Meishiv Davar* (see individual listings), as well as other works.

HaDrash V'HaIyyun. R. Aharon Levine. Rav of Reisha, Poland. Jerusalem, 1982.

HaKtav VeHakabbalah. R. Ya'akov Tzvi Mecklenberg (1785–1865). Frankfort, 1880. Chief Rabbi of Koenigsberg, Germany.

HaTorah V'HaMitzvah. R. Meir Leibush Malbim (1809–1879). New York: Torath Israel Publishing Co., 1950.

Ibn Ezra. R. Avraham Ibn Ezra (d. 1167). Printed in standard *Mikraot G'dolot* editions.

Imrei Boruch. R. Boruch Simon (contemporary). Rosh Yeshiva at Rabbi Isaac Elchanan Seminary. 2004.

Imrei Chen. R. Yehudah Heschel Levenberg. Lakewood, NJ, 1996. Also authored volumes of the same name on other topics.

Imrei Yehudah. R. Yehudah Horowitz (d. 1981) Jerusalem, 1994.

Ish MiBeit Levi. R. Pinchas Katz. Tel Aviv, 1990. Portions of lectures given at the Kollel *Tiferet Zekenim Levi Yitzchak* of *Beit K'nesset Geulat Yisrael,* Tel Aviv.

Ketz HaMizbeach. R. Chaim Kasar. Jerusalem: Keren Shem Tov, 1985. Printed together with *Responsa HaChaim V'HaShalom*.

Kli Chemdah. R. Meir Dan Plotzki (1867–1928) Petach Tikvah: *Yeshivat Lomza*, 1996. Student of *Avnei Nezer*, he also authored *Chemdat Yisrael* (see Section C).

K'tav Sofer Al HaTorah. R. Avraham Shmuel Binyamin Sofer. Tel Aviv: Sinai, 1966 (see Section G).

Lev Aryeh. R. Aryeh Leib Hoshki. Kiryat Yoel: Broch, 1991.

L'Horot Natan. R. Natan Gestetner (see Section G).

Maharil Diskin Al HaTorah. R. Moshe Yehoshuah Yehudah Leib Diskin (see Section G).

Ma'or VaShemesh. R. Kalonymous Kalman Epstein (d. 1823) of Krakow, Jerusalem: *Makhon Pe'er HaSefer*, 1993.

Marpei L'Nefesh. R. Raphael Silber. Brooklyn, NY, 1994 (see Section F).

Meged Yosef. R. Yehudah Leib Sorotzkin. Brooklyn, NY: Meisels, 1987.

Merish BaBirah. R. Shmaryahu Shulman (contemporary) of Queens, NY. New York, 1989. Author of many works, such as *Sukkat Shalem* to the tractate *Sukkah*, commentaries to the *mishnayot* of *Masekhet Rosh HaShanah* and *Mishneh Torah Hilkhot Kiddush HaChodesh*; *Be'er Sarim* (talmudic essays) and *Shomer HaPetach* to *Pitchei Teshuvah Hilkhot Nedarim*. He also brought many earlier works into publication.

Meshekh Chokhmah. R. Meir Simchah HaKohen of Dvinsk. Jerusalem, 1974 (see *Ohr Sameach*, Section E).

Minchat Ani. R. Ya'akov Ettinger (see *Binyan Tziyyon*, Section G).

Minchat Asher al haTorah. R. Asher Weiss. (contemporary). Jerusalem: Machon Minchat Asher. Genesis, 2003; Exodus, 2004.

Nachal Kedumim. R. Chaim Yosef David Azulai (see *Petach Einayim*, Section D). Jerusalem, 1967.

Nachalat Shimon. R. Shimon Krasner. Halakhic essays arranged as a commentary to the Nevi'im. Brooklyn, 1978.

Nachalat Tzvi. R. Elazar Yehudah Leib Pinter. Israel, 1997.

Nitzanei Nisan. R. Nisan Hameiri. Bnei Brak, 1983.

Noam Elimelekh. R. Elimelekh of Lisensk (1717–1787). Jerusalem: *Makhon Zikhron Yehudah*, 1987.

Ohel Ya'akov. R. Ya'akov Kranz (ca. 1740–1804) of Dubno, Jerusalem: *Yerid HaSefarim*, 1980. Known as the *Maggid* of Dubno, he was famed for his parables.

Ohr HaChaim. R. Chaim ben Moshe Attar (1669–1743). In standard *Mikraot G'dolot* editions.

Oznayim LaTorah. R. Zalman Sorotzkin (1881–1966). Known as the Lutzker Rav, he also authored *Moznayim L'Mishpat.*

Pa'aneach Raza. R. Yitzchak ben Yehudah HaLevi (thirteenth century). Comments of the tosafists. Jerusalem, 1965.

Panim Yafot. R. Pinchas HaLevi Horowitz (1730–1805). Author of *Sefer Hafla'ah* to the tractate *Ketubot* and *Sefer HaMakneh* to *Kiddushin*, and rebbe of *Chatam Sofer.* Also wrote notes to the Talmud and *Shulhan Arukh.*

Pardes Yosef. R. Yosef Patzanofsky. Commentary to *Bereishit, Shemot*, and *Vayikra*, containing citations from sources in all areas of Torah study. Loch, 1900. R. David Avraham Mandelbaum (contemporary) printed a new edition of this work, adding to it his own *Pardes Yosef HaChadash* to *Bamidbar* and *Devarim*, maintaining the eclectic style of the original and entitling the set *Pardes Yosef HaShalem.*

Peh Kadosh. R. Yitzchak of Volozhin (1779–1849). Jerusalem: *Makhon Moreshet HaYeshivot*, 1994.

Perush HaGra to Mishlei. R. Eliyahu of Vilna (see *Biur HaGra*, Section F). Petach Tikvah: *Yeshivat Ohel Yosef*, 1985.

Perush HaShakh LaTorah. R. Shabtai HaKohen (see *Siftei Kohen*, Section F).

Pirkei Torah. R. Mordechai Gifter (b. 1916). Jerusalem, 1973. *Rosh HaYeshivah* of Telshe Yeshivah of Wickliffe, Ohio.

P'ninei Nefesh. R. Yuval Yosef Ordenlich (contemporary). Bnei Brak, 1990.

Rabbeinu Bachya. R. Bachya ben Asher (d. 1340). Kabbalist and student of Rashba. Amsterdam, 1746. Annotated edition, ed. R. Charles Chavel, Jerusalem: *Mossad HaRav Kook*, 1974.

Ramban. R. Moshe ben Nachman (1194–1270) of Verona, Italy. Also authored *Chiddushim* to the Talmud and many other works. In standard *Mikraot G'dolot* editions.

> *Karan P'nei Moshe.* R. Moshe Greenes. Far Rockaway, NY: *Makhon L'Mechkarei Torah B'Amerika,* 1988.

Rashi. R. Shlomo ben Yitzchak (Yitzchaki) (1040–1105) of Troyes, France. Printed in most Hebrew editions of the Torah. Preeminent biblical and talmudical commentator; also authored responsa.

> *Mizrachi.* R. Eliyahu Mizrachi (Re'em) (1450–1525) of Constantinople. Also authored responsa.

> *Siftei Chakhamim.* R. Shabsi Bass (1641–1718). In standard *Mikraot G'dolot* editions.

Sefat Emet. R. Yehudah Aryeh Leib Alter (1847–1905), Rebbe of Ger.

Shemen Rosh. R. Asher Anschel Katz (see *Ul'Asher Amar*). Brooklyn: *Yeshivat Beit Asher Sambethali,* 1989.

Shirat David. R. Aharon David Goldberg. Wickliffe, Ohio: Telshe Yeshivah, 1993.

Targum Yonatan ben Uziel. In standard *Mikraot G'dolot* editions.

Teivat Gomeh. R. Yosef Teomim (see *Pri Megadim,* Section F).

Tiferet Yehonatan. R. Yonatan Eibshutz (d. 1764). Tel Aviv: Asher, 1985. One of the foremost authorities of his time, he also authored *Kreiti U'Pleiti, Urim V'Tumim* (see Section F), *Ya'arot D'vash* (see Section J), as well as several other biblical commentaries, such as *Ahavat Yehonatan* and *Nefesh Yehonatan.* Recently, his novellae to the Talmud were also printed.

Torah Shlemah. R. Menachem Kasher (b. 1895). A multi-volumed compilation of commentaries to the Torah. Jerusalem: Torah Shlemah Institute, 1938. Also authored *Responsa Divrei Menachem.*

Torah Temimah. R. Baruch Epstein (1860–1942), Biblical commentary intended to display the unity of Oral and Written Torahs, citing most talmudic and midrashic passages relevant to verses and adding a commentary analyzing the relationship. New York: Hebrew Publishing Co., 1925. Also authored the biblical commentary *Tosefet Brakhah,* and *Baruch She'amar* to *Pirkei Avot* and a prayerbook.

Meshivat Nefesh. R. Ya'akov Moshe Feldman of Los Angeles, CA. A Critical Commentary–Corrective and Supplemental to the *Torah Temimah*, with Indices of Topics and Authorities Cited. Brooklyn, NY, 1982. Also authored *Areshet S'fateinu* and other works.

Torat Moshe. R. Moshe Alshikh (1508–1600). Amsterdam, 1777. A student of R. Yosef Karo (author of the *Shulchan Arukh*), he also authored responsa (see Section C), *Marot HaTzovot* and *Rommimut Keil.*

Torat Moshe. R. Moshe Sofer (see *Chatam Sofer*, Section G).

Ul'Asher Amar. R. Asher Anschel Katz (1881–1974). Brooklyn, NY: Yehoshuah Katz, 1983. Also authored responsa.

VaYomer Moshe. R. Moshe Yechiel Elimelekh (d. 1941) of Libertov. Jerusalem: *Makhon Ginzei Maharitz Sh'Al Yedei Chasidei Bialya*, 1985.

V'Darashta V'Chakarta. R. Aharon Yehudah Grossman. Jerusalem, 1995. Also authored responsa.

R. Yehudah Assad Al HaTorah (see Section G).

Yismach Moshe. R. Moshe Teitlbaum (1759–1841).

Zera Shimshon. R. Shimshon Chaim Nachmeni (d. 1779). Jerusalem: Wagshal, 1990. Also authored *Toldot Shimshon* to *Pirkei Avot* (see Section K).

B. THE TALMUD AND COMMENTARIES—*RISHONIM*

The following commentators wrote on the Talmud and lived in the medieval era, preceding the *Shulchan Arukh.*

Agudah. R. Alexander Suslin HaKohen (d. 1349) of Frankfurt.

Ma'or HaGadol. R. Zerachiah HaLevi (1125–1186). A critique of the *Rif* (see further on). Printed in standard editions of the Vilna Talmud.

Meiri. R. Menachem ben Shlomo HaMeiri (1249–1316), of Provence, France. Talmudic comments in *Chiddushei HaMeiri* and *Beit HaBechirah.*

Milchamot HaShem. R. Moshe ben Nachman (*Ramban*, see Section A). Commentary to the *Rif.* In standard Vilna editions.

Mordechai. R. Mordechai ben Hillel HaKohen (1240–1298) of Germany. In Vilna editions.

Nimmukei Yosef. R. Yosef ibn Chaviv (fifteenth century). Commentary to the *Rif*. In Vilna editions.

Ra'avad. R. Avraham ben David (see Section E). Commentary to the *Rif* and to *Torat Kohanim*.

Rambam, Perush Mishnayot. R. Moshe ben Maimon (see Section E). Commentary to the *Mishnah*. In Vilna editions.

R. Yeshayah Pick. Rav of Breslau.

Ramban. R. Moshe ben Nachman (see Section A).

Ran. Rabbeinu Nissim Gerondi (1290–1375) of Barcelona. Also authored *Derashot HaRan*. His comments are written directly to the Talmud as well as to the code of the *Rif*. In Vilna editions.

Rash. R. Shimshon of Santz (d. 1215). Commentary to the *Mishnah* (*Zeraim* and *Taharot*), printed in the Vilna Talmud.

Rashba. R. Shlomo ben Aderet (1235–1310) of Barcelona. Also authored many volumes of responsa.

Rashi. R. Shlomo ben Yitzchak (see Section A). Printed alongside the text in standard Vilna editions.

Rif. R. Yitzchak Al Fasi (1013–1103) of Fez, Morocco. Authored a code of the halakhically relevant portions of the Talmud.

Ritva. R. Yom Tov ben Ishbilli (1250–1330). Also authored responsa.

Rosh. Rabbeinu Asher ben Yechiel (1250–1327), Germany. Code to halakhically relevant sections of the Talmud, and running commentary to *Masekhet Nedarim*. Father of the *Tur*.

Shiltei Gibborim. R. Yehoshua Boaz; commentary to the *Rif* and the Mordechai.

Shittah Mekubetzet. Opinions of many *rishonim*, compiled by R. Betzalel Ashkenazi (d. 1592).

Tosafot. Talmudic comments of eleventh- and twelfth-century French and German scholars, printed alongside the text in the Vilna Talmud.

Yad Ramah. R. Meir ben Todros HaLevi Abulafia (1170–1244).

C. CODES OF *MITZVOT* AND HALAKHIC CODES OF *RISHONIM*

Halakhot G'dolot. R. Shimon Kayyara (ninth century Babylonia).

Kol Bo. R. Aharon HaKohen (fourteenth century) of Luneil.

Ohel Mo'ed. R. Shmuel Gerondi ben Meshulam (fourteenth century).

Sefer Charedim. R. Elazar ben Moshe Azkiri. Jerusalem, 1981.

Sefer Chasidim. R. Yehudah HaChasid (1150–1217) of Regensberg Jerusalem: Mossad HaRav Kook, 1964.

> *Brit Olam.* R. Chaim Yosef David Azulai (see *Petach Einayim*, Section D). In above edition.

> *Mekor Chesed.* R. Reuven Margolios (see *Margoliot HaYam*, Section D). In above edition.

> *Milei D'Chasiduta.* R. Avraham David Wahrman. New York: R. Shmuel David Katz Friedman, 1995.

> *Mishnat Avraham.* R. Avraham Price of Toronto, Ontario. Toronto. *Yeshivat Torat Chaim*, 1955.

Sefer HaChinnukh. Anonymous, but believed to be R. Aharon HaLevi of Barcelona.

> *Maharam Shick Al Sefer HaMitzvot.* R. Moshe Shick (see Section G).

> *Minchat Chinnukh.* R. Yosef Babad (1800–1875) of Tarnopol.

>> *Shittah Mekubetzet L'Minchat Chinnukh.* R. Shmuel Eliezer Rolnick. Collection of later authorities who commented on positions of the *Minchat Chinnukh.* Jerusalem, 1990.

>> *Minchat Tzvi.* R. Tzvi Zesherovsky. Brooklyn, 1990.

Sefer HaEshkol. R. Avraham ben Yitzchak (ca. 1110–1179) of Narbonne. Tel Aviv, 1964.

> *Nachal Eshkol.* R. Tzvi Binyamin Auerbach (in above edition).

Sefer HaMitzvot L'R. Sa'adiah Gaon. R. Sa'adiah Gaon (882–942).

> *Biur.* R. Yerucham Fishel Perlow (1846–1934). Three volumes, Jerusalem: *Keter: Keren Sefarim Toraniyyim*, 1973.

Sefer HaMitzvot L'Rambam. R. Moshe ben Maimon; printed with most editions of the *Mishneh Torah.*

Chemdat Yisrael. R. Meir Dan Plotzki (see *Kli Chemdah*, Section A). Contains two sections, *Ner Mitzvah* and *Torah Ohr*. Pietrkov, 1903.

Derekh Mitzvotekha. R. Yehudah Rosanes. Printed in *Parashat Derakhim* (see Section N).

Marganita Tava. R. Aryeh Leib Zittel Horowitz (eighteenth century).

Mitzvot HaMelekh. R. Ezriel Cziment. Chicago, IL, 1992.

Ner L'Maor. R. Elyah Kushelevsky (b. 1909). Jerusalem, 1969,

Ohr HaMitzvot. R. Uru Langer. Brooklyn: Faster Press, 1963.

R. Chaim Heller. Footnoted edition. Pietrkov: M. Tzederboim, 1914.

Ramban. R. Moshe ben Nachman (see Section A). In standard editions. Includes additional *mitzvot* the Rambam omits.

Zohar HaRakia. R. Shimon ben Tzemach Duran (1361–1444). Also authored *Responsa Tashbetz* (see Section C) and *Magen Avot* to *Pirkei Avot* (see Section K).

Sefer Mitzvot Gadol. R. Moshe of Coucy (early thirteenth century). Known as the *Smag*, this work is divided into two sections, *Lavin* (prohibitions) and *Essin* (positive commandments).

Brit Moshe. R. Moshe Chaim Weiss of Klein-Varden. Brooklyn: A. Samet, 1959.

Dina D'Chayai. R. Chaim Benveniste (see *K'nesset HaG'dolah*, Section F). Jerusalem, 1970.

R. Isaac Stein. R. Isaac Stein (1420–1495) of Regensherg. Student of *Terumat HaDeshen* (see Section G).

Mei Kama. R. Elyakim Shulsinger. Jerusalem, 1989.

Mishnat Avraham. R. Avraham Price. Three volumes, Toronto: *Yeshivat Torat Chaim*, 1972.

R. Yehudah Zak. In *Makhon Yerushayim* edition, Jerusalem, 1993.

Sefer Mitzvot Katan. R. Yitzchak ben Yosef (d. 1280) of Corbell. Also known as the *Smak* and *Amudei HaGolah*.

Hagahot Chadashot. R. Yehoshua Zeitlish of Shklov, in *Tzivyon HaAmudim* edition, Jerusalem, 1965.

Imrei Yehosef. R. Chaim Yehosef Ralbag. Brooklyn, NY.

Sefer Yereim. R. Eliezer of Metz (ca 1115–1198). A discussion of the mitzvot following the listings of R. Yehudai Gaon and the *Ba'al Halakhot G'dolot,* divided into seven *amudim* (pillars). Also known as the *Re'em.* A French tosafist and student of Rabbeinu Tam.

> *Saviv LiReav.* R. Aharon Walkin (1865–1942) of Pinsk, Lithuania. Pinsk, 1935, and New York, 1961. Also authored *Responsa Z'kan Aharon* and *Birkat Aharon* to the Talmud.

> *Toafot Re'em.* R. Avraham Abba Schiff. Vilna, 1891.

> *Tosefet Ahavah.* R. Shmuel Aharon Rabin. Jerusalem: Wagshal, 1984.

Sheiltot D'Rav Achai Gaon. R. Achai MiShabcha (680–760).

> *Ha'amek Shealah.* R. Naftali Tzvi Yehudah Berlin (see *Ha'amek Davar,* Section A).

Ta'amei HaMitzvot. R. Menachem ben Binyamin Rikanti (thirteenth/ fourteenth century). London: *Makhon Otzar HaChokhmah,* 1962.

D. TALMUD COMMENTARIES–*ACHARONIM*

Commentaries to the Talmud written in the centuries after the Shulchan Arukh.

Am Mordechai. R. Mordechai Willig (contemporary). To the tractate *Berakhot. Rosh Yeshivah* and *Rosh Kollel* at Yeshiva University in New York and Rav of Young Israel of Riverdale, NY.

Arukh L'Ner. R. Ya'akov Etlinger. Novellae to several tractates, Jerusalem, 1962 (see *Binyan Tziyyon,* Section G).

Bartenura. R. Ovadiah of Bartenura (ca. 1450–1510). Commentary to the *Mishnah,* printed in standard editions of the *Mishnah.*

Be'er Ya'akov. R. Chaim Ya'akov Arieli, Bnei Brak, 1977.

Be'erot Mayim. R. Moshe Mordechai Shteger. Jerusalem: *Mifal Torat Chokhmei Polin, Makhon Yerushalayim,* 1994.

Beit Zvul. R. Ya'akov Moshe Charlap. Jerusalem: *Hotza'ah Midrash Gavohah L'Talmud Beit Zvul,* 1960.

Birkat Avraham. R. Avraham Erlanger. Jerusalem, 1973. To several tractates. *Maggid Shiur* at *Yeshivat Kol Torah*, Jerusalem.

Birkat Shmuel. R. Baruch Ber Leibowitz. Analytical essays to several tractates of the Talmud. New York, 1972. A student of R. Chaim (Brisker) Soloveitchik, he was the *Rosh Yeshivah* of the Yeshivah of Kaminetz.

Chadashim Gam Yeshanim. R. Yonatan Shteif (1877–1958) of Brooklyn, NY. To the tractates *Berakhot, Pesachim,* and *Chullin*. Brooklyn: Rabenu Jonathan Shteif Library Foundation, 1959. Also authored Responsa.

Chamra V'Chayai. R. Chaim Benveniste. To *Massekhet Sanhedrin*.

Chasdei David. R. David Shmuel Pardo (1710–1790). Commentary to the *Tosefta*. Liorna Nella Stampia di Giorgi, 1776.

Chatam Sofer. R. Moshe Sofer (see Section G).

Chiddushei R. Reuven. R. Reuven Grozovsky (1888–1958). New York, 1964.

Chiddushei R. Shimon Yehudah HaKohen. R. Shimon Yehudah Shkop (1860-1939). Also authored *Sha'arei Yosher*.

Chiddushei R. Shlomo. R. Shlomo Heiman (1886–1944), *Rosh Yeshivah* of Yeshivah U'Mesivtah Torah VoDa'ath of Brooklyn, NY. NY: Otzar HaSeforim, 1975.

Chiddushei R. Shmuel. R. Shmuel Rozovsky. Talmudic lectures; printed in several versions. *Maggid Shiur* at Yeshivat Ponevezh in B'nei Brak. Also authored halakhic essays, printed in the volume *Zikhron Shmuel*.

Chiddushei R. Ya'akov Emden (see *S'h'eilat Ya'avetz*, Section G).

Chiddushim U'Biurim. R. Shmuel Greenman. To several tractates, and to topics of *Orach Chaim*. Bnei Brak, 1983.

Darkhei David. R. Mordechai David Levin. Jerusalem: R. Ya'akov Moshe Karlinsky, 1959.

Dibrot Ariel. R. Moshe Ariel Weinberg. To *Masekhet Arakhin*. Bnei Brak, 1996.

Dibrot Moshe. R. Moshe Feinstein (see *Iggerot Moshe*, Section G).

Einayim L'Mishpat. R. Yitzchak Arieli (1894–1974), Rosh Yeshivah in Merkaz HaRav, Jerusalem. Talmudic commentary to *Berakhot, Nedarim,*

Kiddushin, Bava Batra, Sanhedrin, and *Makkot,* summarizing the positions of earlier commentaries and codes, and adding novellae. Jerusalem, 1947.

Even Yisrael. R. Yisrael Y. Piekarski. To the first chapter of *Massekhet Yevamot.* New York, 1948. *Rosh Yeshivah* of *Yeshivat Tomkhei T'mimim* (Lubavitch).

Gevurot Ari. R. Aryeh Leib Gunzherg of Metz. To the tractates *Yoma, Ta'anit,* and *Makkot* (see *Sha'agat Aryeh,* Section G).

Gilyon HaShas. R. Akiva Eiger (1761–1837) (see Section G). A terse talmudic commentary containing questions and references.

Gilyonei HaShas. R. Yosef Engel (see *Atvan D'Orayta,* Section G).

Griz. R. Yitzchak Ze'ev Soloveitchik. To the talmudic tractates related to the order of *Kodashim.* Known as the Brisker Rav, he was the son of R. Chaim (Brisker) Soloveitchik and also authored *Chiddushei Maran Riz HaLevi* to *Mishneh Torah.*

Ikvei Aharon Pesher Davar. R. Ya'akov Wehl. Brooklyn, 1993. To several tractates, also authored *Haggadat Ki Yishalkha Binkha.*

Iyyim Ba Yam. R. Aharon Yosef Rosen. New Square, NY, 1991.

Kehilat Ya'akov. R. Ya'akov ben Aharon (d. 1844) of Karlin. Vilna: Romm, 1847.

Kehilot Ya'akov. R. Yisrael Ya'akov Kanievsky (d. 1985) of B'nei Brak, Israel. Known as the "Steipler Gaon" (after the town of Hornsteiple), he authored *Sha'arei Tevunah* in his youth, and his *Kehilot Ya'akov,* originally a ten-volume collection of essays, was later rearranged, revised, and expanded according to the tractates of the Talmud. Also authored *Birkat Peretz* to the Torah (see Section A) and served as a *Rosh Yeshivah* in the Yeshivah of Novardok.

Keren Orah. R. Yitzchak of Karlin. Israel: *Orayta,* 1977.

Kli Golah. R. Shimon Gabel (d. 1986). Printed together with his halakhic commentary *Sofrei Shimon.* Brooklyn, NY, 1989.

Korban Ha'Edah. R. David Fraenkel (1707–1762). To the *Talmud Yerushalmi.*

Kovetz He'arot. R. Elchanan Bunim Wasserman (1875–1941). Essays to the tractate *Yevamot.* A student of R. Yisrael Meir Kagan and *Rosh Yeshivah* of the Yeshivah of Baranovitz

Kovetz Shiurim. R. Elchanan Wasserman. Portions of talmudical lectures. See *Kovetz Hearot.*

Maharal, Chiddushei Aggadot. R. Yehudah Leow (1525–1609). Known as the Maharal of Prague, he was the author of many halakhic and philosophical works, including *Netivot Olam, Derekh Chaim,* and *Gur Aryeh.*

Maharsha, Chiddushei Aggadot, and Chiddushei Halakhot. R. Shmuel Eidels (1555–1631).

Margoliyot HaYam. R. Reuven Margolios (b. 1889). To the tractate *Sanhedrin.* Also authored *Brit Olam* and several other works.

Meromei Sadeh. R. Naftali Tzvi Yehudah Berlin (see *Ha'amek Davar,* Section A).

Minchah Charevah. R. Pinchas ben Yeshayahu (1887–1969). To *Massekhet Sotah.* Jerusalem, 1967.

Mishnat Moshe. R. Moshe Blau (b. 1909). Jerusalem, 1972.

Natan Piryo. R. Natan Gestetner. To several tractates, and sections of *Shulchan Arukh.* Bnei Brak, 1980 (see *L'Horot Natan,* Section G).

Ohr HaYashar. R. Shmuel Yitzchak Hillman (d. 1953). Multivolume work actually covering the Bible, both Talmuds, and the *Mishneh Torah.* Jerusalem, 1977.

Petach Einayim. R. Chaim Yosef David Azulai (1724–1806). Known as *Chida* and author of *Birkei Yosef* and many other works, including *Chaim Sha'al* and *Shem HaGedolim.*

P'nei Yehoshua. R. Ya'akov Yehoshua (1680–1756). Sudylkov, 1834. Subtitled *Apei Zuta* ("small face") to differentiate from the *Responsa P'nei Yehoshua* of his grandfather.

Ramat Shmuel. R. Shmuel Halevi Yafeh (1884–1953). Jerusalem, 1968.

Rashash. R. Shmuel Strashoun (1794–1872) of Vilna. Printed in standard Vilna editions of the Talmud.

Roshei She'arim. R. Aryeh Leib Gurwicz. Talmudic lectures. Gateshead, 1979. The title translates to "Heads of Gates," a reference to the Yeshivah of Gateshead, England, where he served as *Rosh Yeshivah.* Also authored the talmudic commentary *Arza D'Bei Rav.*

Sha'ar Yosef. R. Chaim Yosef David Azulai. To *Massekhet Horayot* (see *Petach Einayim*).

She'arim Metzuyanim B'Halakhah. R. Shlomo Zalman Braun. Also authored a four-volume commentary of the same name to R. Shlomo Gantzfried's *Kitzur Shulchan Arukh.*

Siach Yitzchak. R. Yitzchak Chajes. Jerusalem, 1992.

Sofrei Shimon. R. Shimon Gabel (see *Kli Golah*, listed earlier).

Tiferet Ya'akov. R. Ya'akov Gesuntheit (1816–1878). To the *Masekhtot Chullin* and *Gittin.* Jerusalem, 1970.

Tiferet Yisrael. R. Yisrael Lipshutz (1782–1860), of Danzig, Poland. Commentary to the *Mishnah.*

Torat Chaim. R. Chaim ben Shabtai (1555–1647) of Salonika, Greece.

Torat Ze'ev. R. Ze'ev Dov Tzitzik. To *Massekhet Zevachim.* Zikhron Meir: R. M. M. Shulsinger, 1985.

Tosafot Yom HaKippurim. R. Moshe Chaviv (1654–1696), commentary to the eighth chapter of the tractate *Yoma.* Also authored *Yom Teruah* to *Rosh HaShanah* and *Kappot T'marim* to *Sukkah.*

Tosefot Yom Tov. R. Yom Tov Lipman Heller (1579–1860). Commentary to the *Mishnah.*

Tov Roei. R. Avraham Yitzchak HaKohen Kook (1865–1935). Beit El, Israel: *Makhon Beit El*, 1987. First Ashkenazic Chief Rabbi of modern Israel and preeminent figure of Modern Religious Zionism.

Turei Even. R. Aryeh Leib Gunzberg of Metz. To the tractates *Rosh HaShanah, Megillah,* and *Chagigah* (see *Sha'agat Aryeh*, Section G).

Tziyyun L'Nefesh Chayyah. R. Yechezkel Landau. Lemberg, 1876 (see *Noda B'Yehudah*, Section G).

Yad David. R. Yosef David Sinsheim (1745–1812), Jerusalem. *Makhon Yerushalayim*, 1983.

Yam Shel Shlomo. R. Shlomo Luria (1510–1574) Prague, 1715. Known as *Maharshal*, he also authored the talmudic commentary *Chokhmat Shlomo.*

Yefei Mareh. R. Shmuel Yafeh ben Yitzchak Ashkenazi of Berlin. To the *Talmud Yerushalmi.*

Zayit Ra'anan. R. Avraham Gumbiner (see Magen Avraham, Section F). To *Midrash Rabbah.*

E. THE RAMBAM'S MISHNEH TORAH AND COMMENTARIES

R. Moshe ben Maimon (1135–1284), known as the Rambam or as Maimonides, authored a codification of the laws in the Talmud, entitled *Mishneh Torah,* or *Yad HaChazakah.* The latter name is a reference to the organization of the work, which is arranged in fourteen volumes (the numerical value of the word *Yad* is fourteen). The following works are commentaries to the Rambam's code.

Adnei Yad HaChazakah. R. Adoniyahu Kraus. Jerusalem, 1970.

Avi Ezri. R. Eliezer Menachem Mann Shach. First appeared in four editions (*mahadurot*) and later was consolidated into one four-volume set. Jerusalem, 1948. *Rosh Yeshivah* of the Ponevezh Yeshivah, Bnei Brak, Israel.

Avodat Melekh. R. Menachem Krakowski. To *Sefer Madda.* Jerusalem: Mossad HaRav Kook.

Be'er Miriam. R. David Yitzchak Mann (contemporary). To *Hilkhot Melakhim.* Kfar Chasidim, Israel, 1981.

Beit HaMidrash. R. Eliezer Menachem Mann Shach. See *Avi Ezri.*

Da'at Yisrael. R. Yisrael Frankforter of Paris. To *Hilkhot Deiot.* New York: Mendelsohn Press, 1990.

Derekh Emunah. R. Chaim Kanievsky (see *Orchot Yosher,* Section J). Three volumes, to *Seder Z'raim.* Bnei Brak, 1984.

Derekh HaMelekh. R. Dov Kohen Rappaport. Lemberg, 1892.

Divrei Yirmiyahu. R. Yirmiyahu Loew (1814–1874). Muncacz: Bleier, 1875.

Gevurot Yitzchak. R. Yitzchak Sorotzkin (see Section A). To *Hilkhot Teshuvah.*

Hagahot Maimoniot. R. Meir HaKohen (thirteenth century), Rottenberg. Student of Maharam of Rottenberg.

Har HaMelekh. 7 volumes of essays from different authors. Kiryat Malachi, Israel: *Nachalat Har Chabad,* 1986.

HaRambam L'Lo Stiyah Min HaTalmud. R. Binyamin Ze'ev Benedict. Lectures on the *Mishneh Torah.* Jerusalem: *Mossad HaRav Kook,* 1985. Rav of Achuzah, Israel

Hasagot HaRa'avad. R. Avraham ben David (1120–1197) of Posquieres. Also authored commentaries to the *Rif* and the *Sifra,* and the *Ba'alei HaNefesh* to the laws of *Niddah.* In standard editions of the *Mishneh Torah.*

Introduction to Mishneh Torah. R. Isadore Twersky (1930–1997). New Haven and London: Yale University Press, 1980. Talner Rebbe and professor at Harvard University.

Kessef Mishneh. R. Yosef Karo (see *Shulchan Arukh,* Section F). In standard editions of the *Mishneh Torah.*

Kiryat Sefer. R. Moshe MiTrani. New York, 1966.

Lechem Mishneh. R. Avraham de Baton. Also authored *Responsa Lechem Rav* (see Section G). In standard editions.

LiTeshuvot HaShanah. R. Yisrael Yosef Rappaport. To *Hilkhot Teshuvah.* Bnei Brak, 1986.

Maggid Mishneh. R. Vidal Yom Tov (d. 1370) of Tolosa. In standard editions.

Ma'aseh Rokeach. R. Masud Rokeach (1690–1768).

Masa Bnei Kehat. R. Shammai Kehat Gross (see *Shevet HaKehati,* Section G).

Mateh Ephraim. R. Ephraim Erd. Saloniki, 1791.

Mayim Chaim. R. Chizkiyah de Silva (see *Pri Chadash,* section F).

Meishiv Nefesh. R. S. T. Shapira. *Hilkhot Teshuvah.* Bnei Brak, 1986.

Mirkevet HaMishneh. R. Shlomo of Chelm (d. 1781).

Mishnat Chachamim. R. Yosef Hochgelertner. To *Sefer Madda.* Jerusalem, 1970.

Mishnat Ya'akov. R. Ya'akov Nissan Rosenthal. Haifa, 1986.

Ohr Sameach. R. Meir Simchah of Dvinsk (1843–1926). Also authored *Meshekh Chokhmah* (see Section A).

Parach Mateh Aharon. R. Aharon Soloveichik. *Sefer Madda*. Jerusalem, 1997. *Rosh Yeshivah* of Yeshivah Brisk of Chicago and at Yeshiva University in New York. His thoughts have been printed in English as *The Warmth and the Light* and *Logic of the Heart, Logic of the Mind* (Genesis Jerusalem Press).

Sefer HaTeshuvah: Be'eri BaSadeh; Ikvei HaSadeh. R. Yosef Cohen (contemporary). A two-volume work to *Hilkhot Teshuvah*, including several differently named commentaries by the author. Rabbinical court judge in Jerusalem. A grandson of R. Tzvi Pesach Frank (see *Responsa Har Tzvi*), he authored the commentary *Har'rei Kodesh* that appears with his grandfather's recorded discussions of the festivals, *Mikraei Kodesh*.

Tzofnat Pa'aneach. R. Yosef Rosen (see Section G).

V'Atah B'Rachamekha HaRabbim. R. Eliezer Ginsberg (contemporary). To *Hilkhot Teshuvah*. Brooklyn, 1992.

Yad HaK'tannah. R. Dov Berish Gottlieb (eighteenth century). To *Madda, Ahavah*, and *Z'manim*. New York: *Va'ad L'Haramat Keren HaYeshivot*, ca. 1950.

Yad Peshutah. R. Nachum Rabinowitz. Jerusalem: *Birkat Moshe*, 1987. *Rosh Yeshivah* of *Yeshivat Birkat Moshe*, Ma'ale Adumim, Israel.

Yad Yisrael. R. Yisrael Avraham Abba Krieger (1879–1931). Brooklyn: Krieger Publications, 1985.

Yedaber Shalom. R. Shalom Dov Ber Wolpe (contemporary), Kiryat Gat, Israel, 1987.

F. THE *TUR* AND *SHULCHAN ARUKH* AND COMMENTARIES

R. Ya'akov ben Asher (ca. 1270–1340; son of the Rosh; see Section B) of Germany and Toledo, Spain, authored a codification of Jewish law entitled the *Arba'ah Turim* (the "four rows"; see Exodus 28:17), so named as it is divided into four sections: *Orach Chaim*, covering daily life, prayer, and festivals; *Even HaEzer*, on marital law; *Choshen Mishpat*, on civil law; and *Yoreh Deah*, covering the remaining areas of Jewish law, such as kashrut, *niddah*, mourning, vows, and other topics. Two centuries later, R. Yosef Karo (1488–1575), who authored the commentary *Beit Yosef* to the *Turim* (as well as *Kessef Mishneh* to *Mishneh Torah*), earned the title "the *Mechaber*" ("the Author') with his *Shulchan Arukh* ("set table"), which followed the organization of the *Turim* and took into account the rulings of the *Rif*, the Rosh, and the Rambam. However, the rulings are reflective primarily of the Sephardic background of their author, a fact rectified by R. Moshe Isserles (1520–1572), known as the Rama and author of *Darkhei Moshe* to the *Turim*, who wrote glosses, known as *Mappah* ("tablecloth"), to the *Shulchan Arukh*, representing Ashkenazic practice. Together with the Rama's glosses, the *Shulchan Arukh* has become accepted as the standard text of Jewish law, and the titles listed below are commentaries to that work (or the *Turim*, when indicated as such).

Artzot HaChaim. R. Meir Leibush Malbim, (see *HaTorah V'HaMitzvah*, Section A). To parts of *Orach Chaim*. Jerusalem: S. A. Krishevsky, 1959.

Arukh HaShulchan. R. Yechiel Michel Epstein (1829–1908), comprehensive code on all sections of the *Shulchan Arukh*, adding *Arukh HaShulchan HeAtid* to those areas not covered (ritual impurity, laws of agriculture relevant only in the land of Israel, sacrificial order, etc.). Warsaw, 1900–1912. Rav of Novardok and father of *Torah Temimah* (see *Responsa B'nei Banim* 2:8, for a citation of the halakhic authority R. Yosef Eliyahu Henkin concerning the special qualities of this code).

Bayit Chadash (Bach). R. Yoel Sirkes (1561–1640), Poland. Commentary to the *Tur*; also author of responsa (see later entries) and talmudic emendations. Rav of Belz, Brest-Litovsk, and Krakow, and father-in-law of *Turei Zahav*.

Be'er HaGolah. R. Moshe Rivkes of Vilna. In standard editions.

Be'er Heitev. R. Yehudah ben Shimon Ashkenazi (eighteenth century). Amsterdam, 1742.

Be'er Heitev. R. Zechariah Mendel (d. 1706). Commentary digest of earlier authorities. Rav of Belz, Poland.

Beit Shmuel. R. Shmuel Phoebus (1650–1700). In standard editions.

BikkureiYa'akov. R. Ya'akov Etlinger (see *Binyan Tziyyon*, Section G). To *Hilkhot Lulav*; usually printed with *Arukh L'Ner* (Section D).

Birkei Yosef. R. Chaim Yosef David Azulai. Lemberg, 1774 (see *Petach Einayim*, Section D).

Biur HaGra. R. Eliyahu ben Shlomo Zalman (1720–1797). Towering scholar known as the *Gaon* of Vilna, or *Gra* (an acronym for *Gaon R. Eliyahu*). Author of more than eighty works.

Chatam Sofer. R. Moshe Sofer (see Section G).

Chazon Ish. R. Avraham Yeshayah Karelitz (1878–1953), B'nei Brak, Israel. This seven-volume halakhic work actually combines the sections of the Talmud and the *Shulchan Arukh* and defies easy categorization. Bnei Brak, 1958. Also authored *Emunah UBitachon.*

Chelkat Michokek. R. Moshe Lima (1605–1658) of Brisk. In standard editions.

Chiddushei R. Akiva Eiger (see section G). Compiled in several editions, printed in various editions of the *Shulchan Arukh.*

Chokhmat Shlomo. R. Shlomo Kluger (see *HaElef L'kha Shlomo*, Section G).

Da'at Torah. R. Shalom Mordechai Shwadron (1835–1911), Galicia. To *Orach Chaim* (4 volumes, with some responsa. Brooklyn, NY: *Heikhal HaSefarim*, 1982) and part of *Yoreh Deah*. Also authored *Responsa Maharsham.*

Dagul MeRevavah. R. Yechezkel Landau (see *Noda B'Yehudah*, Section G). In standard editions.

Drishah and Prishah. R. Yehoshua Falk (1555–1614), of Lublin, Poland, and Lemberg, Germany. Commentaries to *Tur*. Also author of *Meirat Einayim* to *Shulchan Arukh.*

D'var Tzvi. R. Tzvi Hirsch of Abironav. To *Orach Chaim*. Vilna: Romm, 1880.

Eishel Avraham (Butchach). R. Avraham David Wahrman (1771–1840), of Butchach, Ukraine. Commentary to *Shulchan Arukh* Orach Chaim.

Elyah Rabbah. R. Elyah Schapiro (1660–1712) of Prague. Commentary to *Orach Chaim*. Jerusalem: *Pe'ar Ha Torah.*

Ginzei Chaim. R. Shlomo Reizner (ca. 1840–1933). To *Orach Chaim.* Jerusalem: *Morashah L'Hanchil,* 1990.

Kaf HaChaim. R. Ya'akov Chaim Sofer (1870–1939) of Baghdad and Jerusalem. Commentary to *Orach Chaim* and *Yoreh Deah.*

Ketzot HaChoshen. R. Aryeh Leib HaKohen Heller. To *Choshen Mishpat.* Also authored *Avnei Miluim* (to *Even HaEzer*) and *SHEV SHMAT'TA* (see Section N).

Knesset HaG'dolah. R. Chaim Beneviste (1603–1673). Jerusalem: *Keren l'Hotza'at Kol Sifrei Knesset HaG'dolah,* 1970.

Levush Malkhut. R. Mordechai Yaffe (1535–1612), Author of several works, all known as the *Levushim.*

Magen Avraham. R. Avraham Gumbiner (1637–1683) Poland. In standard editions.

Machatzit HaShekel. R. Shmuel HaLevi of Kellin. In standard editions.

Magen Gibborim. R. Mordechai Ze'ev Ettinger (1804–1863). To *Orach Chaim.* Otzar HaSefarim, 1969.

Marpei L'Nelesh. R. Raphael Silber of Brooklyn, NY. Four volumes of commentary to *Orach Chaim.* Brooklyn, 1959.

Matteh Ephraim. R. Ephraim Zalman Margolios. To the laws of the *Rosh HaShanah–Yom Kippur* period (see *Responsa Beit Ephraim,* Section G). Brooklyn, NY: *Kol Aryeh* Research Institute, 1973.

K'tzeh HaMatteh. R. Chaim Tzvi Ehrenreich. In above edition. Also authored *Responsa Kav HaChaim.*

Meirat Elnayim. See *Drishah.*

Mishnah Berurah. R. Yisrael Meir Kagan (1838–1933) of Radin. Commentary to the *Orach Chaim* section of the *Shulchan Arukh,* evaluating the positions of earlier authorities and arriving at conclusions. Includes the more in-depth *Biur Halakhah* and the *Sha'ar HaTziyyun,* listing sources. One of the preeminent moral authorities of the late eighteenth and early nineteenth centuries, he authored *Chafetz Chaim* (a name he came himself to be identified with) and *Ahavat Chesed* (see individual listings) as well as many other works, including *Likkutei Halakhot,* a three-part commentary to the talmudical order *Kodashim,* written in the style of *Mishnah Berurah.*

Mitzvot Ra'ayah. R. Avraham Yitzchak HaKohen Kook. Comments to *Shulchan Arukh* and other halakhic works. Jerusalem: *Mossad HaRav Kook*, 1970.

Netivot HaMishpat. R. Ya'akov Loerbaum of Lisa. To *Choshen Mishpat.* Author of several works, including *Chavvot Da'at, Derekh Chaim, Beit Ya'akov, Torat Gittin, Emet L'Ya'akov, Mekor Chaim,* and others.

Orchot Chaim. R. Nachman Kahana (1861–1904) of Spinka. A compilation of the views of earlier authorities, with commentary, to *Orach Chaim.* Two volumes. Jerusalem: *Keter,* 1982.

Otzar HaPoskim. A multivolume compendium of the positions of decisors concerning *Shulchan Arukh Even HaEzer.* Jerusalem: Otzar HaPoskim Institute, 1962.

Pitchei Teshuvah. R. Avraham Zvi Eisenstadt (1813–1868), of Kovno. Summary of responsa arranged according to the order of *Shulchan Arukh.*

Pri Chadash. R. Chizkiyah de Silva (1659–1698). In many standard editions. Also authored *Mayim Chaim* to *Mishneh Torah* (see Section E).

Pri Megadim. R. Yosef Teomim (1727–1792). Supercommentary to *Shulchan Arukh* commentaries, including *Aishel Avraham* to *Magen Avraham* and *Mishbetzot Zahav* to *Turei Zahav.* Author of several other works, such as *Teivat Gomeh, Petichah HaKolelet, Shoshannat HaAmakim,* and *Matan S'kharan Shel Mitzvot* (see individual listings), and *Responsa Megadim.*

Sha'arei Teshuvah. R. Chaim Mordechai Margolios of Dubno, to *Orach Chaim.* In standard editions.

Shulchan Arukh HaRav. R. Shneur Zalman of Liadi (1745–3813). First Rebbe of Lubavitch (Chabad) and author of the *Tania.*

Siftei Kohen (Shakh). R. Shabtai HaKohen (1621–1662) In standard editions. Also authored a commentary to the Torah,

Tiv Kiddushin. R. Aryeh Leib Tzinz (ca. 1773–1833). Jerusalem, 1969.

Turei Zahav (Taz). R. David ben Shmuel HaLevi (1586–1667) of Krakow, Poland. Also authored a commentary to the Torah.

> *Nekudat HaKessef.* Responses of R. Shabtai HaKohen (*Shakh*) to the comments of the *Turei Zahav.*

Urim V'Tumim. R. Yonatan Eibshutz (see *Tiferet Yehonatan,* Section A). To *Choshen Mishpat.*

Yad Shaul. R. Yosef Shaul Nathanson (see *Shoel U'Meishiv,* Section G).

Yeshuot Ya'akov. R. Ya'akov Meshulam Orenstein (1775–1839) of Galicia. NY: R. Chaim Zimmerman, ca. 1950.

G. COLLECTIONS OF RESPONSA AND HALAKHIC AND TALMUDIC ESSAYS

The following works are either responsa, written to answer halakhic inquiries, or collections of essays on topics of halakhic and talmudic analysis. The titles of the works of responsa are generally preceded by the term *She'alot U'Teshuvot* ("Questions and Answers"), translated in the text as Responsa and omitted in this listing.

Achiezer. R. Chaim Ozer Grodzenski (1863–1940). Three volumes. Vol. 1, Vilna, 1922; vol. 3, New York, 1946. Chief Rabbi of Vilna and leading halakhic authority of the pre-World War II era.

Admor MeChabad. R. Menachem Mendel Schneersohn (1902–1994), Crown Heights, Brooklyn, NY. Brooklyn: Kehot (*Karnei Hod Torah*) Publication Society and *Kollel Avrekhim* of *Beit HaKnesset U'Beit Midrash Tzemach Tzedek,* 1987. Seventh Rebbe of Lubavitch (Chabad). His ideas are also printed in the form of *Sichot, Chiddushim L'Shas,* and *Biurim L'Pirkei Avot.*

Adnei Paz. R. Alon Avigdor. Rosh HaAyin, 1995.

R. Akiva Eger. R. Akiva Eger (1761–1837) of Eisenstadt, Austria, and Posen, Poland. Two volumes of responsa. New York, 1945. One of the leading halakhic authorities of his time, he also authored glosses to *Shulchan Arukh,* as well as the talmudic works *Chiddushim, Drush V'Chiddush,* and *Gilyon HaShas.*

Alshikh. R. Moshe Alshikh (see *Torat Moshe,* Section A).

Am K'Lavi. R. Shlomo Aviner. Jerusalem, 1983.

Aseh L'kha Rav. R. Chayim David Halevi (1924–1998). Tel Aviv: HaVa'ad L'Hotza'at Kitvei HaGarchad HaLevy, 1976. Sefardic Chief Rabbi of Tel Aviv.

Ateret Moshe. R. Moshe Natan Nota Lemberger. Two volumes, to topics pertaining to *Yoreh Deah*. Bnei Brak, 1990.

Atvan D'Orayta. R. Yosef Engel (1859–1920). Collection of essays on talmudic topics,. also authored *Gilyonei HaShas, Responsa Ben Porat*, and *Lekach Tov* (see individual listings), as well as several other works, such as *Tziyyunim L'Torah, Gevurot Shemonim, Beit HaOtzar, Shivim Panim L'Torah, Otzerot Yosef, Chosen Yosef*, and *Shivah D'Nechamta*.

Avkat Rokhel. R. Yosef Karo. Author of the *Shulchan Arukh*; see Section F.

Avnei Chefetz. R. Yonatan Binyamin Goldenberger. Brooklyn, NY, 1989.

Avnei Mishpat. R. Shlomo Reisner of Pelstein. Galicia. 1902.

Avnei Nezer. R. Avraham Bornstein (1839–1910). Four volumes, Pietrkov, 1926. Rebbe of Sochatchov, Poland; also authored *Eglei Tal* to *Hilkhot Shabbat*. Innovator of a distinct style of talmudic analysis continued by such students as *Chelkat Yoav, Kli Chemdah* (see individual listings), *Torat Michael* (R. Michael Forshlager), and *Eretz Tzvi* (R. Tzvi Hirsch Frimer, Kozaglover Rav).

Avnei Shoham. R. Nachum Eizenstat (contemporary), of Oak Park, Michigan, and Boston, Massachusetts. Collection of essays on talmudic topics. Union City, NJ, 1986. Also authored a volume on the festivals.

Avnei Ya'akov. R. Ya'akov Yechiel Traube. Brooklyn, 1982.

Avnei Yoshpe. R. Yehoshua Friedlander. Kiryat Moshe, Kiryat Ono: Yeshivat Beit Eliyahu, 1988.

R. Avraham B'no Shel HaRambam. R. Avraham HaNagid (1186–1237), son of the Rambam. Also authored *HaMaspik L'Ovdei HaShem, Birkat Avraham, Ma'asei Nissim*, and *Milchamot HaShem*.

Az Nidbaru. R. Binyamin Yehoshua Zilber. Fourteen volumes. Bnei Brak, 1969. Also authored several volumes of *mussar*, some anonymously.

Bach (Chadashot). R. Yoel Sirkes (see Section F).

Baruch Ta'am. R. Baruch Frankel-Teomim (late eighteenth–early nineteenth century) of Leipnick, Moravia.

Be'er Avraham. R. Avraham Yeshayah Savitz. Lakewood, NJ, 1991.

Be'er Chaim Mordechai. R. Chaim Mordechai Roller (1868–1946). Tel Aviv: *Makhon L'Hotza'at Sefarim U'Kitvei Yad Shel Gedolei Romaniah,* 1976.

Be'er Sarim. R. Avraham Yafeh Shlesinger (contemporary). Four volumes. Jerusalem: *Chemed,* 1990.

Be'er Sheva. R. Yissakhar Ber Eilenberg (d 1623). Jerusalem, 1982.

Be'ero Shel Avraham. R. Avraham Shitrit. (contemporary) Petach Tikvah, 2003.

Beit Av. R. Elyakim Shlezinger. London: *Yeshivat HaRamah,* 1985.

Beit Ephraim. R. Ephraim Zalman Margolios (1762–1828). Brody, Russia.

Beit Shearim. R. Amram Blum (1834–1907). Brooklyn, NY: Makhon Mishneh Halakhot G'dolot, 1979.

Beit Ya'akov. R. Ya'akov ben Shmuel of Tzoizmir. Dinerport, 1696.

Beit Yishai. R. Shlomo Fisher. Jerusalem, 1987.

Beit Yitzchak. R. Yitzchak Shmelkes (1828–1906). Premszl, 1875, and New York: Makhon L'Cheker Ba'ayot HaYahadut HaChareidit, 1958.

Ben Porat. R. Yosef Engel. Responsa (see Atvan D'Orayta).

Besamim Rosh. Attributed to the Rosh (see Section B). Jerusalem, 1984.

Bikkurei Shlomo. R. Shlomo Avraham Rzechte. Two volumes. Pietrkov: S. Belchakovsky, 1844.

B'ikvei HaTzon. R. Herschel Schachter (contemporary). Halakhic essays. Jerusalem: *Beit HaMidrash D'Flatbush,* 1997. *Rosh Yeshivah* and *Rosh HaKollel* at Rabbi Isaac Elchanan Theological Seminary, Yeshiva University, in New York; he also authored talmudic essays under the title *Eretz HaTzvi,* as well as *Nefesh HaRav* (see Section N) and is one of the editors of the journal *Mesorah* (see Section L).

Binyamin Ze'ev. R. Binyamin Ze'ev (sixteenth century) of Arta. Jerusalem: Yad HaRav Nissim, 1988.

Binyan Av. R. Eliyahu Bakshi-Doron. Three volumes. Haifa, Israel, 1983. Sefardic Chief Rabbi of Israel.

Binyan Shlomo. R. Shlomo HaKohen of Vilna. Vilna, 1809.

Binyan Tziyyon. R. Ya'akov Etlinger (1798–1871) of Altona, Denmark. Rebbe of R. Shimshon Raphael Hirsch. Also authored *Arukh L'Ner* and *Bikkurei Ya'akov* (see individual listings).

Birkhat Avot. R. Baruch Rakovsky. Halakhic essays, many concerning the Forefathers and Pre-Sinaitic Judaism in general. Jerusalem, 1990.

Birkhat Shlomo. R. Chaim Shlomo Abrahams (contemporary). Brooklyn, NY; HaMatik Printing, 2000. Also authored a similar volume in the same genre under the title *Divrei Shlomo.*

Birkhat Ya'avetz. R. David Cohen (contemporary). Rabbi of Cong. Gevul Yaavetz, Brooklyn, NY. Brooklyn, NY: Mesorah Publications, Vol. 1, 1986: Vol. 2, 1997.

Birkhot Shamayim. R. Raphael Blum of Bedford Hills, NY. Two volumes. Kashuer Rebbe.

B'nei Banim. R. Yehudah Herzl Henkin (contemporary) of Beit Shean, Israel. Three volumes. Jerusalem, 1981.

B'Ohelah Shel Torah. R. Ya'akov Ariel (contemporary). Machon haTorah V'HaAretz, 1997.

Brit Ya'akov. R. Baruch Mordechai Livshitz (1809–1885). Jerusalem, 1970.

B'Tzeil HaChokhmah. R. Betzalel Stern (d. 1989) of Vienna, Melbourne, Australia, and Jerusalem. Six volumes. Jerusalem, 1967.

B'Yitzchak Yikkarei. R. Avigdor Neventzal. Jerusalem: *Yeshivat Imrei Yosher, Torat Kohanim Sh'AlY'dei Aggudat Atarah L'Yoshnah*, 1987. Rav of the Old City of Jerusalem.

Chacham Tzvi. R. Tzvi Ashkenazi (1660–1718). Rav of Amsterdam, Netherlands, and other cities. Father of R. Ya'akov Emden.

Chakal Yitzchak. R. Yitzchak Isaac Weiss (1875–1944) of Spinka. Brooklyn, NY: 1990.

Chatam Sofer. R. Moshe Sofer (1763–1830). Responsa to the four sections of *Shulchan Arukh* and additional volumes. Vienna, 1855. Rav of Pressburg and one of the leading halakhic authorities of his time, he became the son-in-law of R. Akiva Eiger and ancestor to a long line of rabbinic scholars, beginning with his son *K'tav Sofer.* Also authored *chiddushim* to the Talmud and *Shulchan Arukh*, and *Torat Moshe* to the Torah.

Likkutei He'arot. A summary of comments to the *Responsa Chatam Sofer*, prepared by the *Makhon L'Hotza'at Sefarim V'Cheker Kitvei Yad Al Shem haChatam Sofer.* Jerusalem, 1979.

Chatan Sofer. R. Shmuel Ehrenfeld (1835–1883).

Chavalim BaN'imim. R. Yehudah Leib Graubart (1862–1937) of Toronto. Pietrkov: S. Pinsky, 1901.

Chavvot Yair. R. Yair Chaim Bachrach (1638–1702), Rav of Worms, Germany. Lemberg, 1896.

Chayyei HaLevi. R. Yochanan Segal Vosner (contemporary). Three volumes, Montreal, 1986.

Chazon Nachum. R. Nachum Weidenfeld (1874–1939). New York, 1951, and Jerusalem: *Yeshivat HaGaon MiTshebin Kokhav MiYa'akov,* 1993.

Chelkat HaSadeh. R. Eliezer Deutsh (1850–1916) of Bonyhad, Hungary; printed together with his *Responsa Pri HaSadeh.*

Chelkat Yoav. R. Yoav Yehoshua Weingarten (1847–1922) of Kinsk. Responsa, including the *Kava D'Kashyata,* a collection of 103 talmudic questions that has on its own inspired several books responding to its challenges. Edited, footnoted, and indexed by R. David Avraham Mandelbaum. Jerusalem: *Makhon L'Hantzachat Moreshet Chakhmei Polin,* 1997.

Chemdat Tzvi. R. Moshe Dov Wolner, Ashkelon, 1973.

Chesed L'Avraham. R. Avraham Teomim. Jerusalem, 1967.

Cheshev HaEphod. R. Chanokh Padwa of London, England. Three volumes. Jerusalem, 1963.

Chikrei Lev. R. Raphael Yosef Chazan (1741–1820). Jerusalem: *Makhon Chikrei Lev,* 1981.

Da'at Sofer. R. Akiva Sofer (1877–1959). Jerusalem, 1965.

Darkhei Shalom. R. Yechiel Michel Leiter. Vienna, 1932.

Derekh Y'sharah. R. Yitzchak Yedidiah Frenkel (b. 1913). Two volumes. Tel Aviv: Y. Y. Frenkel, 1981.

Divrei Chaim. R. Chaim Halberstam (1793–1876). Sanzer Rebbe, Lemberg, 1875.

Divrei Maikiel. R. Malkiel Zvi Tannenbaum of Lomza, Poland. Seven volumes. Vilna, 1901.

Divrei Moshe. R. Moshe Halberstam. Jerusalem, 1993.

Divrei Nechemiah. R. Nechemiah Gunzberg. Bnei Brak: *Yahadut*, 1978.

Divrei Ohr. R. Yitzchak Hershkowitz (contemporary) Brooklyn, 1993

Divrei R'nanah. R. Natan Note Kahana (d. ca. 1650). Brooklyn, 1984.

Divrei Shalom. R. Shmuel Yudaikin (contemporary). Halakhic essays and sources. Five volumes. Bnei Brak, 1989.

Divrei Shirah. R. Elyah Levine (contemporary). Volume dealing with *Bein HaMeitzarim/Aveilut/Kaddish*. Netanya, Israel: Orayta, 1988. Author of several volumes of the same name, halakhic essays on topics such as the festivals, *challah*, *agunot*, and the *sh'mittah* year.

Divrei Shlomo. R. Shlomo Abraham (contemporary). Talmudic Essays. Brooklyn, NY, 1996.

Divrei Shlomo. R. Shlomo Shneider (d. 1995) of Monticello, NY. 3 volumes. Brooklyn, NY, 2000.

Divrei Yatziv. R. Yekutiel Yehudah Halberstam, Sanz-Klausenberger Rebbe. Netanya: *Makhon Shefa Chaim*, 1996.

Divrei Yissakhar. R. Yissakhar Berish of Bendin. Pietrkov, 1910.

Divrei Yoel. R. Yoel Teitlbaum. First Satmar Rebbe. Brooklyn, NY: *Yerushalayim* Publishing, 1981.

D'var Emet. R. Yehudah Monsonigo. Jerusalem: *Makhon Bnei Yissakhar*, 1990.

D'var Shmuel. R. Shmuel Abuhab (d. 1694). Jerusalem, 1967.

D'var Yehoshua. R. Yehoshua Ehrenberg (b. 1904) of Tel Aviv. Jerusalem, 1970.

Emek Brakhah. R. Aryeh Pomerantzik (1908–1942). Tel Aviv, 1971. A student of R. Yitzchak Ze'ev Soloveitchik (see *Griz*, Section D), he also authored *Torat Zeraim* on the agricultural laws.

Emek Halakhah. R. Yehoshua Baumol (b. 1880). New York, 1934, and Jerusalem, 1976.

Etz Erez. R. Tzvi Tannenbaum of Chelsea, Mass. 3 volumes. 1981

Even Chen. R. Avraham Halevi. Two volumes. Jerusalem: *Ohr haDerekh,* 1991.

Even Y'kara. R. Binyamin Aryeh Weiss (1842–1912). Brooklyn, NY, 1989.

R. Ezriel. R. Ezriel Hildesheimer (1820–1899) of Eisenstadt and Berlin. Tel Aviv, 1969. Founder of Hildesheimer Rabbinical Seminary.

Gedulat Mordechai. R. Mordechai Benet (1731–1829). Chief Rabbi of Moravia. Printed in *Har HaMor.* Also author of *Parashat Mordechai.*

Geonei Batrai. Collection of responsa. *Turka,* 1764.

Ginnat Veradim. R. Avraham ben Mordechai HaLevi (ca. 1650–1712). Chief Rabbi of Cairo.

Ginzei Yosef. R. Yosef Shwartz. New York: *Chevrah Mefitzei Torah,* 1989.

Goren David. R. Aharon David Daitsch (1812–1878). Two volumes, Jerusalem: P. Kalman, 1994.

HaElef L'kha Shlomo. R. Shlomo Kluger (1785–1869), of Brody, Russia. Also authored *Responsa Tuv Ta'am VaDa'at, Responsa U'Bacharta BaChaim,* and *Chokhmat Shlomo* to *Shulchan Arukh.*

Halakhah L'Moshe. R. Moshe Naiman. Printed together with *Shut Nir L'David,* responsa of the author's father, R. David Naiman. Jerusalem, 1981.

Halakhot V'Halikhot. R. Norman Lamm. Talmudic lectures. Jerusalem: *Mossad HaRav Kook,* 1990. Chancellor and Rosh HaYeshiva of Yeshiva University.

Halikhot SheBa. R. Shmuel Baruch Ohayoun (b. 1906). Tel Aviv: Arzi, 1972.

Har Tzvi. R. Tzvi Pesach Frank (1873–1960). Responsa to *Orach Chaim* and *Yoreh Deah,* with a section on *Z'raim* (agricultural law). Chief Rabbi of Jerusalem; his ideas appear as well in the multivolumed *Mikraei Kodesh,* and other works, such as *Hadrat Kodesh* and *Mikdash Melekh,* and glosses to later works such as *Minchat Chinnukh* and *Ohr Sameach.*

HaTorah V'HaMadda. R. Ya'akov Levinson of Brooklyn. New York, 1932.

Heikhal Simchah. R. Simchah Rosenberg (contemporary). Brooklyn, NY, 1979.

Heikhal Yitzchak. R. Yitzchak Isaac HaLevi Hertzog (1888–1959). To *Even HaEzer.* Jerusalem, 1967. Ashkenazic Chief Rabbi of Israel. Recently, responsa in other areas of *halakhah*, as well as essays, were printed in several volumes under the title *Kol Kitvei HaGri Hertzog*.

Heshiv Moshe. R. Moshe Teitibaum (1759–1841). New York: Tamar, 1946.

Hillel Omer. R. Hillel Posek. Tel Aviv: Bar Yehudah, 1956.

Hitor'rut Teshuvah. R. Shimon (Eiger) Sofer (1850–1944). Four volumes, accompanied by the commentary *Ikvei Sofer* of the author's grandson R. Akiva Menachem Sofer. Jerusalem: *Makhon Chatam Sofer*, 1990. Grandson of *Chatam Sofer* and son of *K'tav Sofer*.

Iggerot Moshe. R. Moshe Feinstein (1895–1986) of Luban, Poland, and New York, NY. Eight volumes of responsa, beginning in 1961, New York. Considered one of the leading authorities of the late twentieth century, he was *Rosh Yeshivah* of Mesivta Tiferet Yerushalayim in the Lower East Side of Manhattan and also authored *Dibrot Moshe* to several volumes of the Talmud.

Imrei Binah. R. Meir Auerbach. Jerusalem, 1869. Kalisher Rav of Jerusalem.

Imrei David. R. David Horowitz of Stanislav. New York: E. Grossman, 1966.

Imrei Shalom. R. Mordechai Leib Charney. St. Louis, MO: Quality Press, 1943.

Imrei Tzvi. R. Tzvi Domb. Bnei Brak, 1994.

Keren L'David. R. Eliezer David Greenwald (1868–1928). Brooklyn, 1981.

Kinyan Torah BaHalakhah. R. Avraham David Horowitz of Strassburg, France, and later a rabbinical court judge in Jerusalem. Eight volumes.

Kiryat Chanah David. R. David HaKohen Sikili. Jerusalem, 1935.

K'naf R'nanah. R. Natan Neta Landau (1843–1906). Brooklyn, 1979.

Kokhvei Yitzchak. R. Yitzchak Sternhill of Baltimore, MD. Three volumes. Brooklyn: Balshon, 1979.

Kol Aryeh. R. Avraham Yehudah Schwartz (1824–1883). Brooklyn, NY: *Chevra Mefitzei Torah MiMishpachat Kol Aryeh*, 1983.

Kol Mevasser. R. Meshulam Roth (1875–1963). Member of Israeli Chief Rabbinate Council and halakhic advisor to the Chief Rabbinate and Supreme Rabbinical Court.

Kol Tzofayikh. R. Yehudah Gershuni. Jerusalem, 1980. Also authored *Shittah Mekubetzet L'Massekhet Pesachim, Mishpat HaMelukhah*, and other works.

Kovetz Teshuvot. R. Yosef Shalom Elyashiv (contemporary) Collected writings. 3 volumes. Jerusalem, 2000.

K'tav Sofer. R. Avraham Shmuel Binyamin Sofer (1815–1871). Pressburg, 1873. Son of the *Chatam Sofer*, he also authored *chiddushim* to the Torah and to the tractate *Chullin*.

Lechem Rav. R. Avraham de Baton (see *Lechem Mishneh*, Section F).

Lekach Tov. R. Yosef Engel. Collection of talmudic essays (see *Atvan D'Orayta*).

Lev Aryeh. R. Aryeh Leib Grosnas. London, 1958. Rabbinical court judge in London.

Lev Avraham. R. Avraham Weinfeld. Monsey, NY: *Keren Yeshuah*, 1977.

Lev Chaim. R. Chaim Pilaggi (d. 1869). Saloniki, 1823. Author of several other works of responsa, including *Nishmat Kol Chai*.

Levushei Mordechai. R. Mordechai Winkler (b. 1844). Toltshoshtal, 1912.

L'Horot Natan. R. Natan Gestetner (contemporary) of Bnei Brak, Israel. Ten volumes of responsa. Bnei Brak, 1973. Also authored many other works, such as commentaries of the same name to the Torah and *Pirkei Avot* (see individual listings) and the festivals, and *Natan Piryo* to tractates of the Talmud and sections of the *Shulchan Arukh*. A descendant of R. Akiva Eiger, he has also brought to print writings of that scholar.

Livnei Binyamin. R. Avraham Shmuel of Wolkowysk. Warsaw: Shmuel Engelband, 1869.

Machaneh Chaim. R. Chaim Sofer (1823–1886). Pressburg, 1882, and Jerusalem, 1963.

Machazeh Avraham. R. Avraham Steinberg. New York, 1964.

Maharam Lublin. R. Meir ben Gedalyah (1588–1616) of Lublin.

Maharam Mintz. R. Moshe Mintz (1435–1485) of Poland and Germany. Krakow, 1637.

Maharam MiRotenberg. R. Meir ben Baruch HaLevi (1320–1390) of Rottenberg. Berlin, 1891. Rebbe of the Rosh and the Mordechai.

Maharam Shick. R. Moshe Shick (1807–1879). Muncacz, 1881. Rav of Chust and student of *Chatam Sofer.*

Maharash Engel. R. Shmuel Engel. Seven volumes. Bardiov, 1926.

Maharash MiLublin. R. Shlomo of Lublin. Brooklyn: Hershkowitz, 1978.

Mahari Bruna. R. Yisrael Bruna (1400–1481), of Germany. Student of *Mahari Veil* and *Terumat HaDeshen.* Salonika, 1798.

Mahari Veil. R. Ya'akov Veil (d. 1455). Venice, 1523.

Maharil Diskin. R. Moshe Yehoshua Yehudah Leib Diskin (1818–1898). Jerusalem: *Chedvat Yisrael,* 1911. Rav of Brisk.

Maharit. Joseph of Trani. Lemberg, 1861.

Maharalbach. R. Levi ibn Chaviv (1483–1545). Known for his opposition to the renewal of the original process of *semikhah* in the sixteenth century.

Maharshag. R. Shimon Greenfeld of Bisenmitali, Hungary. Three volumes, Brooklyn, 1973.

Maharshal. R. Shlomo Luria (see *Yam Shel Shlomo,* Section D).

Maharsham. R. Shalom Mordechai Shwadron (see *Da'at Torah,* Section F).

Maharashdam. R. Shmuel Di Medina (1506–1589). Rav of Salonica, Greece, and cities in Turkey.

Maor HaChaim. R. Meir Chaim Unger (1905–1958). With footnotes *Meorot Natan* by R. Natan Gestetner (see *L'Horot Natan*). Jerusalem, 1960.

Marcheshet. R. Chanokh Eigesh (b. 1864) of Vilna. Two volumes. Jerusalem, 1968. A third volume containing previously unpublished writings was added later.

Matzav HaYosher. R. Shneur Zalman Dov Anusishky. Originally published in 1881, reprinted New York: Goldenberg, 1991.

Meged Yehudah. R. Yehudah Meshulam David Polatchek. Brooklyn, 1994.

Me'il Tzedakah. R. Yehudah Lansdorfer (1678–1712). Sedilkov, 1835.

Menuchat Moshe. R. Moshe Natan Nota HaLevi Yungreis. Muncacz: Shmuel Zanvil Kahana, 1905.

Mekad'shei HaShem. A collection of responsa by various authorities compiled by R. Tzvi Hirsch Meisels, who added a commentary, *D'var Tzvi.*

Meorot Natan. R. Natan Goldberg; edited by his grandson, R. Natan Horowitz. New York: Shulsinger Bros., 1944.

Meorot Natan. R. Natan Leiter. Pietrkov, 1927.

Merkachat B'samim. R. Shmuel Greenberger. New York: Y. Lichter, 1992.

Meshiv Davar. R. Naftali Tzvi Yehudah Berlin. Warsaw, 1849 (see *Ha'amek Davar*, Section A).

Mevasser Tov. R. Meir Isaacson. Staten Island, NY, 1976.

Mima'amakim. R. Ephraim Oshry. New York, 1959. This work of responsa, the title of which translates as "out of the depths," relates the author's rulings as Rav of Kovno during the Holocaust years.

Minchat Aharon. R. Aharon Rosenfeld. Monroe, NY, 1983.

Minchat Asher. R. Pinchas A. Z. Goldenberger. Forest Hills, NY, 1976.

Minchat David. R. David Rozenberg of Monroe, NY. Four volumes. Brooklyn, 1979.

Minchat Elazar. R. Chaim Elazar Schapiro (1871–1937). Muncaczer Rebbe; also authored *Ot Chaim V'Shalom* and other works. Son of the author of *Darkhei Teshuvah* to *Yoreh Deah.*

Minchat Shai. R. Avraham Tzvi Shor. New York, 1990.

Minchat ShIomo. R. Shlomo Zalman Auerbach (1910–1995). Jerusalem: *Sha'arei Ziv,* 1986. *Rosh Yeshivah* of *Yeshivat Kol Torah* of Jerusalem and considered one of the leading authorities of his time. Also authored *Meorei Esh* to the laws of electricity on *Shabbat,* and *Ma'adanei Aretz.*

Minchat Yitzchak. R. Yitzchak Weiss (1902–1989). Ten volumes of responsa. London, 1955. Rabbinical court judge in Manchester, England, and later Rav of *Edah HaChareidis* in Jerusalem.

Mishkenot Ya'akov. R. Ya'akov of Karlin. Jerusalem: *Keren Orah,* 1960.

Mishnat Sakhir. R. Yissakhar Shlomo Teichtal (b. 1885). *Va'ad L'Hotza'at Kitvei HaM'chabber,* 1974.

Mishnah Shlemah. R. Shlomo Gross. Rabbinical court judge of Belzer Chasidim of Boro Park, Brooklyn, NY. Jerusalem, 1991.

Mishnat Avraham. R. Avraham Price (see Section C).

Mishnat Binyamin. R. Avraham Binyamin Silverberg. Rav of Pittsburg, PA. NY: Moinester Publishing, 1948.

Mishpetei HaTorah. R. Zvi Shpitz, 3 vols. Jerusalem, 1998.

Mishpetei Ouziel. R. Ben Zion Meir Chai Ouziel (1880–1954). Sephardic Chief Rabbi of Israel. Tel Aviv, 1935, and Jerusalem, *Mossad HaRav Kook,* 1964.

Mishpetei Shmuel. R. Shmuel ben Moshe. Viencia: Daniel Zaniti, 1599.

Moznai Tzedek. R. Menashe Silber (contemporary). Brooklyn, 1987.

Mutzal M'Eish. R. Ya'akov Alpandri (1650–1738). Glosses by R. Eliezer Zusman Sofer. Brooklyn, 1964.

Nachal Yitzchak. R. Yitzchak Elchanan Spector (1817-1896), Rav of Kovno. *Hotza'at Chaim U'Brakhah,* 1976.

Netivot Adam. R. Mattityahu Deutsch (contemporary). Jerusalem, 2001.

Netzach Yisrael. R. Yisrael Grossman. Jerusalem, 1986.

Nishal L'David. R. David Oppenheim. Jerusalem: *Makhon Chatam Sofer,* 1975.

Noda BiYehudah. R. Yechezkel Landau (1713–1793). Responsa according to the four sections of the *Shulchan Arukh,* in two editions, *Mahadura Kama* and *Tinyana.* Vilna, 1904. Rav of Prague and a leading authority of his time, he also authored *Dagul MeRevavah* to *Shulchan Arukh* and *Tziyyun L'Nefesh Chayyah* to the Talmud.

Ohalei Tam. R. Tam ibn Yahya (d. 1542). Printed in *Tumat Yeshanim.* Venice, 1622.

Ohr Avraham. R. Avraham Strok. Monsey, 1982.

Ohr Gadol. R. Yerucham Yehudah Leib Perlman. Jerusalem: *Makhon Yerushalayim, Mifal Torat Chakhmei Lita,* 1987. Known as the "Minsker Gadol," he also authored a commentary to *Mishnayot* by the same name.

Ohr HaMeir. R. Meir Shapiro (1887–1933). Reprinted in a two-volume edition, edited by R. David Avraham Mandelbaum, *Makhon L'Hantzachat Moreshet Chakhmei Lublin,* 1996. *Rosh Yeshivah* of *Chakhmei Lublin* and founder of the *Daf Yomi* program.

Ohr Yechezkel. R. Ephraim Moshe Korngut. *Makhon Ohr Yechezkel, Beit Midrash L'Mishpat HaHalakhah,* 1994.

Orach Mishpat. R. Avraham Yitzchak HaKohen Kook (1865–1935). Jerusalem: *Mossad HaRav Kook,* 1979.

Orchot Yosher. R. Yosef Sharbit of Ashkelon, Israel. Two volumes. Jerusalem, 1975.

Panim Me'irot. R. Meir Eisenstadt (1670–1744) of Eisenstadt.

Parashat Mordechai. R. Mordechai Benet (see *Gedulat Mordechai*). Sighet: Vieder, 1889.

Pe'er HaDor. R. Moshe ben Maimon (see Section E).

Piskei Teshuvah. R. Avraham Piotrokovski of Lodz, Poland 1933.

Pri Malkah. R. Seymour Turk (contemporary). San Jose, CA. Cong. Am Echad and Beis Hamidrash Kesser Torah.

Pri Yitzchak. R. Yitzchak Blazer (1837–1907). K'far Chasidim, Israel: *Yeshivat K'nesset Chizkiyahu,* 1975. Known as R. Itzele Peterburger, he was a leading disciple of R. Yisrael Salanter and was equally renowned for accomplishments in *halakhah* and in *mussar* (see *Kokhvei Ohr,* Section J).

Radbaz. R. David ben Zimra (1479–1573), Chief Rabbi of Egypt. Warsaw, 1862. Also authored commentary to *Mishneh Torah.*

Rama. R. Moshe Isserles (see Section F). Edited by R. Asher Siev. Jerusalem, 1971.

Rama MiPanu. R. Menachem Azariah of Panu (1548–1620). Kabbalist. Italy. Venice, 1600.

Ramban, Teshuvot Meyuchasot. (see section A).

Rashba. R. Shlomo ben Aderet (see Section B).

Rashi. R. Shlomo ben Yitzchak (see Section A).

Rav Pe'alim. R. Yosef Chaim ben Eliyahu (1834–1909). Four volumes. Jerusalem, 1905, and *Siach Yisrael,* 1994.

Ritva. R. Yom Tov ben Ishbili (see Section B).

Rivash. R. Yitzchak ben R. Sheshet (1326–1407) of Barcelona, Spain.

Riv'vot Ephraim. R. Ephraim Greenblatt (contemporary) of Memphis, Tenessee. Twelve volumes.

Rosh. R. Asher ben Yechiel (see Section B).

Salmat Chaim. R. Yosef Chaim Sonnenfeld (1848–1932). Rav of *Edah HaChareidis* of Jerusalem. B'nei Brak, 1982.

Sefer HaPardes. R. Shlomo Yitzchaki (Rashi; see Section A). Bnei Brak: *Yahadut,* 1980.

Sefer Yehoshua. R. Yehoshua Heschel Babad (1754–1838) of Tarnipol, Jerusalem, 1991.

Seridei Eish. R. Yechiel Ya'akov Weinberg (d. 1966). Jerusalem: *Mossad HaRav Kook,* 2003.

Sha'agat Aryeh. R. Aryeh Leib Gunzberg (1695–1785) of Metz. Also authored *Turei Even* and *Gevurot Ari* to tractates of the Talmud.

> *Ohel Moshe.* R. Shmuel Avigdor HaLevi Dertzinsky of Volozhin and Glosses to several later authorities. Jerusalem, *Mossad HaRav Kook,* 1939.

Sha'ar Ephraim. R. Ephraim of Vilna. Jerusalem, 1981.

Sha'arei Deah. R. Chaim Yehudah Leib Litwin. Originally printed in 1878; reprinted in New York by B. Cohen

Sha'arei Ezra. R. Ezra Basri. Jerusalem, *Sukkat David,* 1978.

Sha'arei Kodesh. R. Yitzchak Hecht. Two volumes. Jerusalem, 1977. Contains a large number of responsa dealing with the sanctity of the Divine Name and related topics.

Shalmei Simchah. R. Simcha Elberg. Five volumes, largely dealing with the festivals. Brooklyn, NY: Balshon, 1964. Longtime editor of the journal *HaPardes* (see Section L).

She'erit Yosef. R. Yosef Yedid HaLeyi (1867–1930). Brooklyn: Sh. Yedid, 1976.

She'erit Yosef. R. Shlomo Wahrman (contemporary). Seven volumes of talmudic and halakhic essays. Far Rockaway, NY, 1977. Also authored *Orot HaShabbat, Orot Yemei HaRachamim* (see Section H), and *Orot HaPesach.*

Sh'eilat Ya'avetz. R. Ya'akov Emden (1697–1776) of Altona. Altona, 1739. Also authored *chiddushim* to the Talmud and *Mor U'Ketziah* to *Shulchan Arukh.*

Sh'eilat Yitzchak. R. Yitzchak Ohlboim. Prague, 1931.

Shem Aryeh. R. Aryeh Leibush Balhuvar (nineteenth century). Jerusalem: *Makhon Chatam Sofer,* 1970.

Shem MiShimon. R. Shimon Pollack. Satmar, 1932.

Shemesh Tzedakah. R. Shimshon Morpugo (1681–1740) of Ancona.

Shevet HaKehati. R. Shammai Kehat Gross (contemporary), of *Khal Machzikei HaDas* (Belz), Israel. Five volumes. Jerusalem: Orayta, 1987.

Shevet HaLevi. R. Shmuel HaLevi Vosner (contemporary). Bnei Brak, 1969.

Shevet MiYehudah. R. Isser Yehudah Unterman (1886–1964). Ashkenazic Chief Rabbi of Israel. Jerusalem: *Mossad HaRav Kook,* 1994.

Shoel U'Meishiv. R. Yosef Shaul Nathanson (1810–1875), of Lemberg. Brooklyn, NY: *Harrirei Kodesh,* 1994. Also authored *Yad Shaul* to *Shulchan Arukh* and *Divrei Shaul* to the Torah.

Shraga HaMeir. R. Shraga Feivel Shneebalg of Stamford Hill, London, England. Eight volumes. Bnei Brak: Friedman, 1972. Also authored *Beit Pinchas* to the Torah and other works.

Shtei HaLechem. R. Moshe Chagiz (1671–ca. 1750). Jerusalem, 1970.

Shvut Ya'akov. R. Ya'akov Reisher (1670–1733). Lemberg: Salant, 1897. Rav of Prague and other cities.

Siach Kohen. R. Eliezer Cohen. Tel Aviv, 1980.

Siach Yitzchak. R. Yitzchak Weiss (d. 1942). Jerusalem: *Mifal Moreshet Yahadut Hungariya, Makhon Yerushalayim,* 1994.

Siach Yosef. R. Yosef Roth. Halakhic essays. Bnei Brak, 1992. An earlier volume of the same name deals with *Massekhet Niddah.*

Siftei Ani. R. Menachem Mendel Schneebalg, Rav of Congregation Machzikei HaDas, Manchester, England. Bnei Brak: Friedman, 1993.

Sofer HaMelekh. R. Meir Tzvi Bernfeld. Zikhron Meir, Bnei Brak, 1975.

Ta'am Baruch. R. Baruch Leizerofsky of Philadelphia, Pennsylvania. Brooklyn Balshon, 1979.

Tashbetz. R. Shimon ben Tzemach Duran. Amsterdam, 1739. See *Zohar HaRakia,* Section C.

Tehillot David. R. David Betzalel Klein. Rav of Yesodot, Israel. Two volumes. Yesodot, 1992.

Terumat HaDeshen. R. Yisrael Isserlein (1390–1460) of Germany.

Teshurat Shai. R. Shlomo Leib Tabak (1832–1908). Sziget, 1905, and NY: Grossman, 1960.

Teshuvot V'Hanhagot. R. Moshe Sternbuch (contemporary) of Johannesberg, South Africa, and Har Nof, Jerusalem. Three volumes. Jerusalem, *Netivot HaTorah V'HaChesed,* 1986. Author of several works, such as *Ta'am V'Da'at* to the Torah; *Mo'adim U'Z'manim* (see Section H); *P'shat V'HaIyyun* to the Talmud; and other works.

Tiferet Tziyyon. R. Moshe Duber Rivkin. Talmudic essays. Brooklyn, NY: *Tiferet Tziyyon,* 1975.

Toldot Yitzchak. R. Yitzchak Ben Shoshan, Bnei Brak, 1980.

Torah LiShmah. R. Yosef Chaim ben Eliyahu. Jerusalem, 1976. See *Responsa Rav Pe'alim.*

Torat Chaim. R. Chaim Abelson. Jerusalem, 1985.

Torat Chesed. R. Shneur Zalman of Lublin. Warsaw, 1883.

Torat Chof Yamim: Siftei Chaim. R. Yechiel Michel Charlop. Talmudic essays. Jerusalem: *HaKeren L'Hadfasat Kitvei R. Yechiel Michel Charlop Al*

Y'dei Kollel Chof Yamim Midrash Gavohah L'Talmud Beit Zvul, 1988. Another volume is subtitled *Sefer Zikaron*.

Torat Raphael. R. Raphael Schapiro of Volozhin. Jerusalem: Yeshivat Volozhin, 1995.

Torat Yekutiel. R. Yekutiel Ya'akov Rosenberger. Two editions (*Kama* and *Tinyana*). Jerusalem, 1980.

Torat Yerucham. R. Yerucham Ciecanaowitz. New York: Twersky Bros., 1951.

Tzemach Tzedek. R. Menachem Mendel (1789–1866). Third Rebbe of Lubavitch (Chabad). Brooklyn: Kehos, 1976.

Tzitz Eliezer. R. Eliezer Yehudah Waldenberg. Twenty-one volumes, beginning Jerusalem, 1944.

Tzofnat Pa'aneach. R. Yosef Rosen (1858–1936) of Dvinsk, known as Rogatchover Gaon. Responsa in several editions. Also authored commentaries to the Torah and to the *Mishneh Torah*.

U'Bacharta BaChaim. R. Shlomo Kluger. Brooklyn, NY: M. Finkelstein, 1960. See *HaElef L'kha Shlomo*.

VaYa'an Avraham. R. Avraham Amram Meisels. Brooklyn, 2001.

VaYa'an David. R. Chaim David Weiss. Printed together with *VaYechi Yosef* to the laws of prohibited interest. Jerusalem, 1992.

VaYashev Avraham. R. Avraham Hakohen (1897–1931). Israel, 1989.

VaYashev Moshe. R. Moshe Ze'ev Zoger Jerusalem, 1986.

V'Darashta V'Chakarta. R. Aharon David Grossman.

V'Shav V'Rapha. R. Raphael Evers of Amsterdam Holland. Jerusalem: Fischer, 1994.

Yabbia Omer. R. Ovadiah Yosef (1920–). Former Sephardic Chief Rabbi of Israel. Eight volumes of responsa. Jerusalem: *Yeshivah Gedolah Porat Yosef, Mossad HaRav Kook*. Also authored *Shut Yechavveh Da'at, Yalkut Yosef*, and other halakhic works.

Yachel Yisrael. R. Yisrael Meir Lau (contemporary). Three volumes, including one on medical matters. Jerusalem, 1982. Former Ashkenazic Chief Rabbi of Israel.

Yad Eliyahu. R. Eliyahu ben Shmuel (d. 1735) of Lublin. Brooklyn: *Makhon Hotza'at Sefarim Atikim*, 1982.

Yad Eliyahu. R. Eliyahu Ragoler (1794–1849). *T'nuah L'Hafatzat Torah*, 1969.

Yad Sofer. R. Moshe Sofer of Erlau. Jerusalem: *Makhon L'Hotza'at Sefarim V'Cheker Kitvei Yad Al Shem HaChatam Sofer*, 1981.

Ittur Sofrim. R. Yochanan Sofer. Printed in the above edition.

Yagel Ya'akov. R. Chaim Mordechai Ya'akov Gottleib (d. 1936). Brooklyn, NY, 1988.

Yashiv Moshe. R. Moshe Turetsky. Recording rulings of R. Yosef Shalom Elyashiv, a contemporary leading Israeli authority. Gateshead, England, 1989.

Yashiv Yitzchak. R. Yitzchak Shmuel Schechter (contemporary). 8 volumes, Kiryat Sanz, Netanyah: Machon Yashiv Yitzchak, 1998.

Yechi Yosef. R. Ya'akov Chaim Sofer. Jerusalem, 1991.

Yehudah Ya'aleh. R. Yehudah Assad (1797–1866). Rav of Rete and Semnitz. Pressburg, 1880, and Bnei Brak, 1985. Student of R. Mordechai Benet.

Yeriot Shlomo. R. Shlomo Yehudah Leib Levitan.

Yismach Chaim. R. Leib Baron (b. 1912), Montreal Canada: Torah Study Center, 1986.

R. Yosef Nechemia. R. Yosef Nechemiah Kornitser of Krakow. Bnei Brak: Yeshivat Ohel Yosef, 1986.

Zecher Yehosef. R. Zechariah Stern (1831–1903). Warsaw: Boimberg, 1860.

Zera Avraham. R. Avraham Loftiber, son-in-law of R. Meir Simchah HaCohen of Dvinsk. One volume of halakhic novellae and one volume of correspondence with R. Menachem Ziemba.

Z'hav Menachem. R. Menachem Chakham. Israel, 1989.

Zikhron Betzalel. R. Elazar Kahanov. Jerusalem: *Makhon HaRav Frank, Mifal Cheker Halakhah*, 1992.

Zikhron Yehudah. R. Yehudah ben HaRosh (1280–1349). Berlin, 1846.

H. WORKS OF *HALAKHAH*

Avnei Gazit. R. Yisrael Yosef Bronstein (contemporary) Laws pertaining to the Sanhedrin. Jerusalem, 1998.

Ba'ayot Aktualiyot L'Ohr HaHalakhah. R. Avraham Bick, ed. Responses of halakhic authorities to R. S. Z. Shragai. Jerusalem: *Mossad HaRav Kook,* 1993.

Birkhot Horai. R. Baruch Weiss (contemporary). To the laws of *birkat kohanim.* Jerusalem, 1994.

Chayyei Adam. R. Avraham Danzig (1748–1820), Vilna. Work of *halakhah* relevant to *Orach Chaim* section of *Shulchan Arukh.* Also authored *Chokhmat Adam* to *Yoreh Deah.*

Hokheach Tokhiach. R. Yoel Schwartz (contemporary). To the laws of rebuke. Jerusalem: *Devar Yerushalayim,* 1991.

Imrei Shammai. R. Shammai Ginzberg (contemporary). To the laws of the festivals. NY, 1993.

L'David Emet. R. Chaim Yosef David Azulai (see *Petach Einayim,* Section D). To *Hilkhot Sefer Torah.* Jerusalem: *Yeshivat Ohr VaDerekh, Merkaz L'Moreshet Yisrael,* 1986.

Leket Yosher. R. Yosef ben Moshe (1420–1490) of Bavaria. Practices of the *Terumat HaDeshen.* Berlin, 1903.

Magen Tzvi Sefer Kedushat HaAretz. R. Baruch Magence of St. Louis, MO. Essays on topics related to the Land of Israel. Jerusalem, 1979.

Malbushei Yesha. R. Yaakov Yeshayah Bloi (contemporary) of Jerusalem. A treatment of the laws of shatnez (forbidden mixtures in garments). Jerusalem: *Va'ad Tzibburit LiM'niat Mikhsholim B'Shatnez,* 1991. Author of numerous halakhic works, including the eight-volume *Pitchei Choshen* to *Choshen Mishpat, Netivot Shabbat, Brit Yehudah* to the laws of prohibited interest, and *Chovat HaDar* to the laws of *mezuzah* and *menorah.*

Minchat Eliyahu. R. Eliyahu Mann. To *Hilkhot Tefillin, Sefer Torah, Mezuzah* and *Tzitzit.* Bnei Brak, 1975.

Mishpetei HaTorah. R. Zvi Shpitz (contemporary). Responsa to Actual Questions in Monetary and Interpersonal Law. 3 volumes. Jerusalem, 1998.

Mo'adim UZ'manim. R. Moshe Sternbuch (see *Teshuvot V'Hanhagot,* Section G). Nine volumes. On the festivals. Jerusalem.

Nesiat Kappayim. R.Yitzchak Fishberg. To the laws of *birkat kohanim.* Bnei Brak, 1996.

Nesiat Kappayim K'Hilkhata. R. Moshe Gross. To the laws of *birkat kohanim.* Jerusalem, 1994.

Od Yisrael Yosef B'ni Chai. R. Aharon Soloveichik (see *Parach Mateh Aharon,* Section E). To the laws of mourning. Chicago, IL. Yeshivas Brisk, 1993.

Orot HaShabbat. R. Shlomo Wahrman. An Analytical Study of Various Topics of Talmudical Law Pertaining to *Shabbat.* NY: Mendelsohn Press, 1996 (see *She'erit Yosef,* Section G).

Orot Y'mei HaRachamim. R. Shlomo Wahrman. An Analytical Study of Various Topics of Talmudical Law Pertaining to the High Holidays. NY: Fink Graphics, 1994.

Ot Chaim V'Shalom. R. Chaim Elazar Schapiro (see *Minchat Elazar,* Section G).

Pe'at HaShulchan. R. Yisrael ben Shmuel (d. 1839) of Shklov. To the laws pertaining to the Land of Israel. Jerusalem: *Pardes,* 1958. Student of the Gaon of Vilna.

Pidyon HaBen K'Hilkhato. R. Gedalyah Oberlander. Brooklyn, 1993. Laws of "Redemption of the first-born."

Pitchei Choshen. R. Yaakov Yeshaya Bloi (contemporary). Laws pertaining to the *Choshen Mishpat* section of Shulchan Arukh. 8 volumes, Jerusalem: Yeshivat Ohel Moshe Diskin, 1983,

Sdei Chemed. R. Chaim Chizkiyahu Medini (1832–1904) of Constantinople. Extensive ten-volume collection of halakhic essays, including citations of many contemporaries of the author.

Yalkut Yosef. R. Ovadiah Yosef (see *Yabbia Omer,* Section G). Prepared by R. Yitzchak Yosef. Jerusalem, 1985.

I. WORKS OF *HALAKHAH* DEVOTED TO TOPICS OF INTERPERSONAL RELATIONSHIPS

Ahavat Chesed. R. Yisrael Meir Kagan. Discussion of the laws of loving-kindness. Warsaw, 1888 (see *Mishnah Berurah*, Section F).

Amirat Shalom K'Hilkhata. R. Yisrael Ya'akov Vidavski (contemporary). A treatment of the imperative to greet one another in *halakhah* and *aggadah.* Jerusalem: *Even Yisrael*, 1989.

Bein Adam L'Chaveiro. R. Mordechai Eliyahu (contemporary), former Sefardi Chief Rabbi of Israel. Collected rulings.

Chafetz Chaim. R. Yisrael Meir Kagan. Classic work to the laws prohibiting gossip *(lashon hara)*, (see *Mishriah Berurah*, Section F).

Chovat HaShemirah. R. Yisrael Meir Kagan. To *lashon hara.* Warsaw: Wiedza, 1920.

Dan L'Khaf Zekhut. R. David Kog'ah (contemporary). Treatment of the laws of judging one another favorably.

Darkhei Noam. R. Shaul Wagschal (contemporary). Jerusalem, 1992.

Darkhei Tzedek. R. Betzatel Genchersky (contemporary). A treatment of the laws relating to judging others favorably. Tifrach, 2002.

Erekh Appayim. R. Avraham Yellin. A treatment of the laws pertaining to anger. Jerusalem, 1963.

Hilkhot Derekh Eretz. R. Yaakov Davidson. Two volumes. A discussion of principles relating to interpersonal relationships as suggested in various passages throughout *Shulchan Arukh Orach Chaim* and its commentaries. New York, 1991.

Hizaharu BiKhvod Chaveirkhem. R. Avraham Tovolsky. "A Collection of Statements of *Chazal, Rishonim,* and *Achronim,* Concepts, Ideas, Illuminations and Information Concerning the Quality of One Who Is Careful with the Honor of People, and the Disgrace of Those Who Insult and Anguish Them." Part of *Tikkun Sidrat HaMiddot*, a series of books, all by the author, devoted to the clarification of details pertaining to the proper implementation of principles of interpersonal behavior. Bnei Brak: Yeshivat Ohel Yosef, 1981.

Kodesh Yisrael. R. Avraham Yosef Ehrman. Essays on laws of interpersonal relationships, printed together with *Halikhot Olam*, a compilation of the relevant laws. Bnei Brak, 1996.

K'tzet HaShemesh BiGvurato. R. Avraham Tovolsky. Part of *Tikkun Sidrat HaMiddot* (see *Hizaharu Bikhvod Chaveirkhem*, mentioned earlier); this volume concerns the prohibitions against revenge and taking a grudge, and the obligation of forgiveness. 1979.

L'Reakha Kamokha. R. David Ariav (contemporary) A treatment of laws pertaining to interpersonal relations. Includes rulings of R. Chaim Kanievsky. 3 volumes. Jerusalem, 2000.

MiDvar Sheker Tirchak. R. Hillel David Litwack. A treatment of the laws of the prohibitions against falsehood. Brooklyn, NY, 1978.

MiDvar Sheker Tirchak. R. Avraham Tovolsky. Part of *Tikkun Sidrat HaMiddot*; this volume concerns the prohibitions against falsehood.

Mishpat Tzedek. R. Hillel David Litwack. A discussion of the laws of judging others favorably. Brooklyn, NY, 1997.

Mitzvat HaEtzah. R. Joseph D. Epstein. Studies and Insights into the Legal Ramifications of the Torah Precept of Offering Good Counsel, as Well as Its Psychological and Behavioral Aspects in Light of the Talmud and Jewish Religious Ethics. New York Torath HaAdam Institute, 1983.

Mitzvot HaBayit. R. Joseph D. Epstein. A Guide to the Jewish Way of Life in the Family: The Home; Its Social, Educational, and Economic Aspects, in Light of Halakhic Ethics and Tradition, Compiled from the Talmud, Code of Jewish Law and Responsa, with Critical Notes and Interpretations; A Manual for Rabbinic Counseling. Two volumes. New York: Torath HaAdam Institute 1966.

Mitzvot HaLevavot. R. Mordechai Lichtenstein (b. 1865). Brisk: A. Handler, 1924.

Mitzvot HaMusar. R. Joseph D. Epstein. Torah Precepts in Ethics: Introductory Essays on the Theory of Halakhic Ethics; Discources in *Halakhah* Revealing the Preceptual Obligatory Aspects of Ethics; Observations in Psychological Situations in Light of Halakhic Analysis. Vol. 1 of the series of *Mitzvot HaMusar*. New York: Torath HaAdam Institute, 1973.

Mitzvot HaShalom. R. Joseph D. Epstein. A Guide to the Jewish Understanding of Peace and Harmony in Interpersonal and Communal

Life in Light of Torah; A Compendium of Essays and Selections from the Talmud, Code of Jewish Law and Responsa, with Critical Notes and Interpretations. New York: Torath HaAdam Institute, 1969 (second edition, 1987).

Mitzvot HaShem. R. Yonatan Shteif (see *Chadashim Gam Yeshanim*, Section D). Contains one section on faith and one on interpersonal relationships. Monsey, 1980.

Niv S'fatayim. R. Nachum Yavrov. Essays on the laws of falsehood. Brooklyn, NY, 1980.

Orach Meisharim: Shulchan Arukh L'Middot. R. Moshe Troyesh. Sources and commentary concerning matters relevant to the development of character traits. Megenze, 1878.

Orchot Yesharim. R. Shaul Wagshal. Gateshead, England, 1982.

Sefer Limmud L'Hilkhot Bein Adam L'Chaveiro: Lo Tisna Et Achikha Bilvavekha. R. Zvi H. Weinberger and R. Boruch A. Heifetz. Textbook for the study of Torah laws concerning the relations of man to his fellow man, volume 1: "Do not hate your brother in your heart," including Part 1: source material quoted with notes, summaries, and charts; Part 2 halakhic essays, including a digest of earlier halakhic authorities with original research clarifying the laws and their details, with a section of short stories from daily life to illustrate the application of the laws. Safed, Israel: Machon "Toras Haodom–L'odom," 1995.

Sha'arei Ona'ah. R. Hillel David Litwack A discussion of the laws prohibiting verbal oppression. New York, 1979. Also including an English translation, "Gates of the Oppressed."

Shalom Yihyeh. R. Yosef Avraham Heller (contemporary). A treatment of the laws pertaining to the imperative of peace and the prohibitions against dispute. Brooklyn, NY, 1989.

Titten Emet L'Ya'akov. R. Ya'akov Y'chizkiyah Fish. A treatment of the laws of falsehood, including responsa by the author and a section of responsa of earlier authorities. Jerusalem, 1981.

Yisrael HaKedoshim. R. Hillel David Litwack A discussion of the laws relevant to the prohibitions against taking revenge and bearing a grudge. New York, 1984.

J. WORKS OF MUSAR AND PHILOSOPHY

The following titles include works of ethical instruction and inspiration, as well as those of philosophy and homiletic discourses.

Agra D'Pirka. R. Tzvi Elimelekh (1785–1841) of Dynow. Chasidic discourses. Brooklyn, NY: Meisels, 1984.

Al HaTeshuvah. R. Joseph B. Soloveitchik (see *Shiurim L'Zekher Abba Mari,* Section N). Discourses on repentance. Edited by R. Pinchas Peli. Jerusalem: *Histadrut HaTziyyonit HaOlamit.*

Chibur HaTeshuvah. R. Menachem ben Shlomo HaMeiri (see Section B). Essay on repentance. Edited by R. Avraham Schreiber. NY, 1950.

Da'at Chokhmah U'Musar. R. Yerucham Levovitz. Brooklyn: Da'as Chochma Umussar Publications, 1966. *Mashgiach* of the Mir Yeshivah of Jerusalem.

Derashot Chatam Sofer. R. Moshe Sofer (see Section G). Expository discourses.

Derashot HaRan. Rabbenu Nissim Gerondi (see Section B). Essays on fundamental beliefs of the Jewish religion. Jerusalem, 1959.

Halakhot V'Halikhot. R. Mordechai Hakohen. Essays. Jerusalem: *Yad Ramah, Makhon L'Erkhei Yisrael V'Eretz Yisrael,* 1975.

Iggeret HaMusar. R. Yisrael Salanter (see *Ohr Yisrael,* further on). Printed in some editions of Mesilat Yesharim (see later in this section).

Iggeret HaTeshuvah. Rabbenu Yonah. Printed in many editions of *Sha'arei Teshuvah* (see later in this section).

Kad HaKemach. R. Bachya Ben Asher. Discourses on faith and on mitzvoth. Constantine, 1515.

Kokhvei Ohr. R. Yitzchak Blazer. Jerusalem, 1974 (see *Pri Yitzchak,* Section G).

Lev Eliyahu. R. Eliyahu Lopian (1876–1970). Jerusalem: *Va'ad L'Hotza'at Kitvei Maran,* 1983.

LiNevukhei HaTekufah. R. Moshe Avigdor Amiel (1882–1945), rav of Tel Aviv. Subtitled *Pirkei Histak'lut B'Mahut HaYahadut.* Brooklyn, NY, 1980. Published as well in an English version, *Light for an Age of*

Confusion. Jerusalem: The Rabbi Amiel Library, 1996. Also authored *Derashot El Ami* and the three-volume *HaMiddot L'Cheker HaHalakhah*, among other works.

Ma'alot HaMiddot. R. Yechiel ben Yekutiel Anav (thirteenth century). Jerusalem: Eshkol, 1968.

Ma'amarei HaRa'ayah. R. Avraham Yitzchak HaKohen Kook (1865–1935). Discourses. Jerusalem. *Hakeren Al Shem Goldah Katz,* 1984.

Menorat HaMa'or. R. Yitzchak Abuhab (fourteenth century). Jerusalem: *Makhon HaMidrash HaMevuar,* 1988.

Mesilat Yesharim. R. Moshe Chaim Lutzatto (1707–1746), of Padua, Italy. Known as Ramchal, he was a kabbalist and author of several works of *mussar.* Tel Aviv: Netzach, 1958.

Moreh Nevukhim. R. Moshe ben Maimon (see Section E).

Netivot Olam. R. Yehudah Loew (see *Maharal,* Section D).

Ohr Yisrael. R. Yisrael Lipkin (1810-1883) of Salant. Jerusalem: *Beit HaMusar,* 1992. Founder of the *Musa*r movement.

Orchot Tzaddikim. Unknown (fourteenth century).

Orchot Yosher. R. Chaim Kanievsky. Discussion of talmudic and midrashic statements concerning matters of "fear of Heaven, good character traits, Torah, prayer, and faith." Bnei Brak, 1997. The son of the Steipler Gaon (see *Kehilot Ya'akov,* section D), he is the author of many works including *Nachal Eitan* (to the laws of *eglah arufah*), *Siach HaSadeh, Shoneh Halakhot* to *Shulchan Arukh Orach Chaim, Derekh Emunah* to *Mishneh Torah Sefer Z'raim,* and commentaries to the *Talmud Yerushalmi* and *Massekhtot K'tannot.*

Pachad Yitzchak. R. Yitzchak Hutner (1905–1980). Philosophical essays arranged according to the festivals, with a volume of "letters and writings." Brooklyn: *Mossad Gur Aryeh,* 1960. *Rosh Yeshivah* of the Yeshivah Chaim Berlin in Brooklyn, New York, and the *Kollel Gur Aryeh.* In his youth, he authored *Torat HaNazir to Mishneh Torah, Hilkhot Nezirut.*

Pele Yoetz. R. Eliezer Papo (1785–1827). Jerusalem: *Kerem Shlomo,* 1962.

Reishit Chokhmah. R. Eliyahu ben Moshe deVidas (sixteenth century).

Sam Derekh: HaYashar VeHaTov. R. Simcha Mordechai Ziskind Broide (d. 2000). *Rosh Yeshiva* of Yeshivat Chevron Knesset Yisrael. An exposition of the themes emanating from the Ramban's comments to the verse of "the right and the good." Collected writings, edited by R. Yaakov Yehudah Zilberlicht. Jerusalem: *Otzar HaPoskim,* 2004.

Sefer HaMiddot (Breslov). R. Nachman (1172–1811) of Bratslav. First, and only, Bratslaver Rebbe. With footnotes by R. Natan of Bratslav.

Sha'arei Kedushah. R. Chaim Vital (1543–1620). Jerusalem: *Ahavat Shalom,* 1987.

Sha'arei Teshuvah. Rabbenu Yonah ben Avraham Gerondi (1200–1263). Classic ethical work. Also authored a commentary to the *Rif.*

Ma'or HaSha'ar. R. Avraham Erlanger. Jerusalem, 1984 (see *Birkat Avraham,* Section D).

Ohr Chadash. R. Moshe Karelitz. Bnei Brak, 1986.

Ohr HaTeshuvah. R. Reuven Melamed. Bnei Brak, 1986.

Zeh HaSha'ar. Anonymous. Bnei Brak, 1969.

Shemonah Perakim. R. Moshe ben Maimon (see Section F). Introduction to *Pirkei Avot.*

Hagahot Ya'avetz. R. Ya'akov Emden (see *Sh'eilat Ya'avetz,* Section G).

Shevet Musar. R. Eliyahu HaKohen (1650–1729) of Izmir. Jerusalem: Waldman, 1988.

Sichot Chokhmah U'Musar. R. David Kronglass. *Mashgiach* of Ner Israel Rabbinical College, Baltimore, Maryland.

Sichot Musar. R. Chaim Shmuelevitz (1901–1979). Recorded discourses from the years 1972–1974. The *Rosh Yeshivah* of the Mir Yeshivah of Jerusalem, his talmudic novellae have been printed as *Sha'arei Chaim* (to *Gittin* and *Kiddushin*).

Siftei Chaim. R. Chaim Friedlander. To the festivals. Bnei Brak, 1989.

Tania:Likkutei Amarim. R. Shneur Zalman of Liadi (see *Shulchan Arukh HaRav,* Section F). A classic of *Chassidut* in general and Chabad (Lubavitch) *Chassidut* in particular. Brooklyn: *Otzar HaChassidim,* 1956.

Tomer Devorah. R. Moshe Cordevero (1522–1570). New York: *Hotza'at Shoshanim,* 1960.

Torat Avraham. R. Avraham Grodzenski (ca. 1882–1943). Jerusalem, 1963.

Tzidkat HaTzaddik. R. Tzadok HaKohen of Lublin (1823–1900). Bnei Brak: *Hotza'at Yahadut*, 1966. Author of many works of chasidic philosophy, including *Pri Tzadik* to the Torah.

Ya'arot D'vash. R. Yonatan Eibshutz (d. 1764). Expository discourses. Bnei Brak. *Hotza'at Chokhmah Umusar*, 1964.

Yesod V'Shoresh HaAvodah. R. Alezander Susskind ben Moshe (d. 1973) of Grodno. Bnei Brak: *Makhon L'Hotza'at Sefarim Chasdei Chaim*, 1987.

K. COMMENTARIES TO PIRKEI AVOT

The talmudic tractate *Avot* (part of Seder *Nezikin*) is particularly relevant to issues of interpersonal relationships, the following titles are commentaries to that tractate.

Ahavat Shalom. R. Moshe Outz Meri. Jerusalem: *Hotza'at Yeshuah ben David Salem*, 1988.

Anaf Etz Avot. R. Ovadiah Yosef (see *Yabbia Omer*). Jerusalem: Machon Maor Yisrael, 2001

Ateret Mordechai. R. Michael Fisher. London, 1953.

Be'er Avot. R. Menachem Mendel Frankel-Teomim. Philadelphia: *Va'ad Keren Hadfasat Sifrei HaRaMaM Frenkel-Teomim*, 1944.

Beit HaLachmi. R. Yehoshua Segal Daitsch. Brooklyn: A. G. Pollak, 1992.

Biurim L'Pirkei Avot. R. Menachem Mendel Schneersohn (see Section G). Brooklyn: Kehos, 1982.

Chasdei Avot. R. Aharon ben Yehudah HaLevi (eighteenth century). Brooklyn: *Achim Goldenberg*, 1993.

Derekh HaChaim. R. Yehudah Loew (see *Maharal*, Section D).

Divrei Binah. R. Yitzchak Ya'akov of Bialia. New York: *Va'ad Yeshivat Bialia Ohr Kedoshim*, 1975.

Divrei Yosher. R. Dov Rosenthal. Tel Aviv, 1965.

D'var Moshe. R. Moshe Rosmarin (contemporary). Jerusalem, 1977. Also authored volumes of the same name to several *massekhtot*.

Ein Chanokh. R. Chanokh Henakh of Sassov. Kiryat Yismach Moshe, 1988.

Etz Yosef. R. Chanokh Zundel. Jerusalem, 1993.

L'Horot Natan. R. Natan Gestetner. Bnei Brak, 1985 (see Section G).

Ma'aseh Avot. A compilation by R. Shalom Yisrael Direnfeld. Jerusalem, 1982.

Magen Avot. R. Shimon ben Tzemach Duran (see *Zohar HaRakia,* Section A). Lipsia: Shnois, 1855.

Me'Am Loez. R. Ya'akov Culi (1685–1732) of Constantinople. Student of *Mishneh L'Melekh*; also commented on the entire *Tanakh.*

Midrash Shmuel. A compilation by R. Shmuel Uceda (b. 1540). Jerusalem: *Makhon HaKtav,* 1988.

Milei D'Chasiduta. A compilation of chasidic interpretations by R. Yekutiel Grin. Kfar Chabad, 1985.

Mirkevet Eliyahu. R. Eliyahu of Vilna (see *Biur HaGra,* Section D). Lakewood, 1986.

MiShel Avot. A compilation by R. Moshe Levi. Bnei Brak, 1992

Nishba La'Avotekha. R. Baruch Tzvi Moskowitz. Bnei Brak: *Beit Midrash Tenuvat Baruch,* 1992.

Rabbenu Bachya (see Section A).

Rabbenu Yonah (see Section B). In standard editions of the Vilna Talmud.

Sefat Emet. R. Yehudah Aryeh Leib Alter (1847–1905), Gerrer Rebbe. Jerusalem, 1966. Also authored volumes of the same name to the Torah and the Talmud (*Mo'ed* and *Kodashim*).

Tiferet Yehoshua. R. Yehoshua Belcrovitz. Jerusalem: *Makhon Orot HaGenuzim.*

Toldot Shimshon. R. Shimshon Chaim Nachmeni. Brooklyn, 1979 (see *Zera Shimshon,* Section A).

Yesodei Yeshurun. R. Gedalyah Felder of Toronto, Canada. New York, 1991. Author of works of *halakhah* and other works of the same name.

Yismach Moshe. R. Moshe Teitlbaum (see Section A).

L. JOURNALS

Much halakhic discussion is found in periodical journals, often published by *yeshivot* or rabbinical organizations. Years listed represent the inititiation of the publication.

Am HaTorah. Torah journal of *Zeirei Agudas Yisroel* of America. 1974.

Beit Talmud L'Hora'ah. Torah journal of *Kollel Beit Talmud L'Hora'ah* of *Khal Yirei Hashem* of Brooklyn, under the presidency of R. Yechezkel Roth. 1984

Beit Yitzchak. A Publication Devoted to Studies in *Halakhah* by the *Rebbeim* and *Talmidim* [Faculty and Students] of Yeshiva University. Published by the Rabbi Isaac Elchanan Theological Seminary and Student Organization of Yeshiva. 1952.

BiNetivot Yam. Torah journal of the Lomza Yeshiva of Petach Tikvah, Israel. 1970.

Chokhmei Lev. Torah journal of Yeshivat Lev Avraham, Jerusalem.

Derekh Eretz Dat U'Medinah. A collection of essays and presentations on the topic of Judaism, Government, and Democratic values. Published by the Israeli Govt. Dept. of Education/ Beit Morasha/ Yesodot. Jerusalem, 2001.

HaDarom. Torah journal of the Rabbinical Council of America. Rabbi Charles B. Chavel, founding editor. 1957.

HaEmek. Torah journal of Beth Medrash Emek Halachah.

HaMa'ayan. Torah journal of *Poalei Agudat Yisrael*, Jerusalem. 1961.

HaMetivta. Torah journal of Yeshiva and Mesivta Torah VoDa'ath of Brooklyn, NY. 1978.

HaPardes. Rabbinical journal founded in Poland in 1913, then brought to America and edited originally by R. S. A. Pardes of Chicago, Ill., and for many years by R. Simcha Elberg (d. 1994) of Brooklyn, NY. Published by the Pardes Institute

Har HaMor. Torah journal published between 1982 and 1986 by the *Makhon HaRav Frank*, an institution dedicated to the publication of the writings of R. Tzvi Pesach Frank (see Section G).

Kerem Shlomo. Torah journal of the Bobov Kollel of Brooklyn, NY. 1975.

Kitrei Eliezer. Torah journal of Kollel Gavohah Imrei Kohen, Brooklyn, 2002.

Kol Torah. Torah journal of *Agudas Yisroel* of Europe. 1977.

Kovetz Torani of *Kollel Zikhron Shneur.* Torah journal of *Kollel Zikhron Shneur* of Monsey, NY. 1993.

Kuntres Kol Sofer. Torah journal of *Yeshivat Chatan Sofer.* 1994.

Machanayim (old edition). Journal of the Israel Defense Forces. 1948.

Machanayim (new edition). A Quarterly for Studies in Jewish Thought and Culture.

Mesorah. Journal of the Kashrut Division of the Union of Orthodox Jewish Congregations of America. Includes halakhic articles relating to *kashrut* as well as recorded ideas from the talmudic lectures of R. Joseph B. Soloveitchik. Edited by R. Herschel Schachter (see *B'ikvei HaTzon*, Section G) and R. Menachem Genack. 1989.

Moriah. A Monthly Journal for Torah, *Halacha*, & Contemporary Jewish Issues. Published by Moriah Publishing Company. 1969.

Nehorai. Torah journal of Beis Midrash Gavohah of Lakewood, NJ.

Niv HaMidrashiyah. Forum for Matters of *Halakhah*, Thought and Education; Journal of *Chug Yedidei HaMidrashiyah.* 1963.

Noam. A Forum for the Clarification of Contemporary Halakhic Problems. *Makhon Torah Shelemah*, 1958.

Ohr HaMizrach. Dedicated to Torah, People of Israel, and the State of Israel. Published jointly by the Torah Education Department of the World Zionist Organization and Mizrachi/HaPoel HaMizrachi of Canada and of America. 1954.

Ohr Torah. Torah journal of *Chevrat Ohr Torah Sh'Al Y'dei Beit Knesset Algrivah*, and the Rabbinical Organization of immigrants from North Tunisia in Israel. 1968.

Otzerot Yerushalayim. Rabbinical journal edited by R. Tzvi Markovitch of Jerusalem.

Piskei Batei Din HaRabaniyyim. Decisions of the Supreme Rabbinical Court of the Chief Rabbinate of Israel. 1950.

Sanhedrei K'tannah. Journal printed in 1973 by the *Kollel* of *Yeshivat Rabbeinu Yitzchak Elchanan,* Yeshiva University, containing articles pertaining to *Massekhet Sanhedrin.*

Sha'alei Da'at. Torah journal of *Yeshivat Sha'alvim,* Israel. 1972.

Shma'atin. Journal of the Organization of Teachers of Religious Subjects at Religious Elementary Schools. 1964.

Sinai. Mossad HaRav Kook, Jerusalem. 1937.

Techumin. Research Articles Concerning Torah, Society, and State/Halakhic Monographs Concerning the Relationship of Torah to Modern society. Published by "Zomet" (*Tzva'atei Madda V'Torah*) Alon Shvut, Gush Etzion, Israel. 1980.

Torah SheB'Al Peh. Records of the National Conference (*Kinus Artzi*), *Mossad HaRav Kook.* 1959.

Torat HaAdam L'Adam. A collection of Torah essays concerning the relationships of man to his fellow man, published by Machon Torat HaAdam L'Adam. Safed, Israel.

VaY'lakket Yosef. Torah journal printed between 1899 and 1906, containing correspondence between scholars of that time and edited by R. Yosef Schwartz of Grossvarden. Reprinted in 5 bound volumes by the *Kol Aryeh* Research Institute, Brooklyn. 1997.

M. MEMORIAL AND JUBILEE VOLUMES

Avnei Shlomo. Volume in memory of R. Shlomo Levi. Jerusalem, 1993.

Beit Abba. Volume in memory of R. Tzvi Abba Luria. Bnei Brak, 1989.

Kovetz Zikkaron L'R. Yosef Chaim Shneur Kotler. Volume in memory of the *Rosh HaYeshivah* of *Beit Midrash Gavohah* of Lakewood, NJ. Lakewood: *Ichud Talmidei Kletzk U'Beit Midrash Gavohah,* 1985.

Mazkeret Moshe: Sefer Zikkaron L'Moshe Efrati. Jerusalem, 1975.

Mevakshei Torah memorial volume for R. Shlomo Zalman Auerbach. Edited by Shalom Eliezer Rotter, Jerusalem, 1997.

MiPri Yadeha. Volume in memory of Rebbetzin Rachel Toledano. Bnei Brak, 1993.

Nehorai: L'Zecher Nishmat R. Meir Kotler. Lakewood: *Beit Midrash Gavohah*, 1980.

Nehorai: Sefer Zikaron L'R. Yosef Chaim Shneur Kotler. Lakewood: *Beit Midrash Gavohah*, 1985.

Sefer Yovel LiKhvod HaGrid Soloveitchik. Essays in honor of R. Joseph B. Soloveitchik. Jerusalem: *Mossad HaRav Kook* and New York: Yeshiva University, 1984.

Sefer HaZikaron L'Maran HaGarshab Verner Zatzal. Memorial Volume for R. Shmuel Boruch Werner of Tel Aviv. Edited by R. Yosef Buchsbaum. Jerusalem: *Makhon Yerushalayim*, 1996.

Sefer Zikaron L'Maran Ba'al HaPachad Yitzchak. Memorial volume to R. Yitzchak Hutner (see *Pachad Yitzchak*, Section J), containing unpublished novellae and biographical information. Jerusalem, 1984.

Y'kara D'Chaim. Memorial volume in honor of R. Chaim Ya'akov Goldvicht (1925–1995), founding *Rosh Yeshivah* of Yeshivat Kerem B'Yavneh. New York: American Friends of Yeshivat Kerem B'Yavneh, 1996.

N. OTHER WORKS

Abudraham. R. David ben Yosef Abudraham (fourteenth century). Commentary to the *siddur*.

Ahavat Avraham. R. Avraham Binyamin Koltonowsky of Veiroshab. Concerning the dispute as to whether cases of doubt in cases of biblical law are treated stringently biblically or rabbinically. Originally printed in 1889, reprinted, Bnei Brak: Gal Ed, 1994.

Ein HaRo'im. R. Shalom Mordechai Schwadron (see *Da'at Torah*, Section F, and *Responsa Maharsham*, Section G). Talmudic principles.

Mattan S'kharan Shel Mitzvot. R. Yosef Teomim (see *Pri Megadim*, Section F). Pietrkov, 1884.

Meorot HaGedolim. R. Chaim Ephraim Zaichyk. Biographies of major figures of the Mussar movement.

Nefesh HaRav. R. Herschel Schachter (see *B'ikvei HaTzon*, Section G). A halakhic biography of R. Joseph B Soloveitchik, including many of his positions on matters of Jewish law.

Parashat Derakhim. R. Yehudah Rosanes (1657–1727). Expositions. Jerusalem: Mekor, 1961. Also authored *Mishneh L'Melekh* to *Mishneh Torah.*

Petach HaShearim. R. Mordechai Farhand. Talmudic principles.

Petichah HaKollelet. R. Yosef Teomim (see *Pri Megadim,* Section F). Bnei Brak: Farkas, 1980.

Sha'arei Yosher. R. Shimon Yehudah HaKohen Shkop (1860–1939). New York: *Ha Va'ad L'Hotza'at Sifrei HaGaon Rabbe Shimon,* 1958.

Shev Shmat'ta. R. Aryeh Leib Hakohen (ca. 1745–1813). Brooklyn, NY, 1954.

Shiurim L'Zekher Abba Mari. R. Joseph B. Soloveitchik (1903–1993) of Boston. Talmudic lectures delivered in memory of his father, R. Moshe Soloveitchik. Known as "the Rav," he was *Rosh Yeshivah* at Rabbi Isaac Elchanan Theological Seminary and one of the most influential figures of Modern Orthodoxy. His talmudic lectures and philosophical writings have been presented in several other works as well.

Shivtei Yisrael. R. Fishel Avraham Mael. Essays on topics concerning the twelve tribes of Israel. Baltimore, 1997.

Shnei Luchot HaBrit. R. Yeshayahu Horowitz (1565–1630). Jerusalem: *Zikhron Yehudah,* 1993. Work of *halakhah* and Jewish thought.

Shoshannat HaAmakim. R. Yosef Teomim (see *Pri Megadim,* Section F). Jerusalem: Wagshal, 1994.

Siddur HaGra. A collection of the comments of R. Eliyahu of Vilna (see *Biur HaGra,* Section F). New York: *Hotza'at Kol Torah,* 1953.

Ta'amei HaMinhagim. R. Abraham J. Sperling (1851–1921). Explanations of customs. Brooklyn, NY: Torah Ohr, 1944.

V'Im Tomar. R. David Cohen (contemporary). Rabbi of Cong. Gevul Ya'avetz of Brooklyn, NY. A collection of talmudic difficulties, with sources. NY: Mesorah Publications, 1982. Author of many works, such as *Gevul Ya'avetz, Birkat Ya'avetz,* and *Shirat Ya'avetz.*

Zohar. Classic kabbalistic text attributed to R. Shimon Bar Yochai.

Glossary

agudot agudot—separate and distinct groups within the community

akhzari—"cruel one"

asmachta—a rabbinically assigned allusion; rather than actual meaning of a verse (as per the understanding of Rambam [introduction to the Mishnah], Kuzari [3:73] and Mabit [introduction to *Kiryat Sefer* ch. 1]; Ritva, however, understands and asmachta to reflect on some level the intention of the Torah itself [*Chiddushim* to *Rosh HaShanah* 17a, s.v. *Tania*]).

azzut—the trait of obduracy

b'bigdo—"in his garment"

b'dvarim—verbally

b'nei amekha—the members of your nation

b'rabbim—in public

b'shogeg, shogeg—inadvertent

beit midrash—study hall

betulta da—"this virgin"; a phrase inserted into the marriage contract when appropriate

birkat kohanim—the priestly blessing pronounced during prayer services

brit, brit milah—the covenant of circumcision

chatzi shiur—less than the required measurement for incurring punishment for a transgression or for fulfilling a commandments; lit. "half measurement"

chevrusas—study partners

Chol HaMoed—the intermediate days of the festival [of Sukkot and Passover]

chom levavo—in the heat of the moment; lit. "heat of his heart"

Chumash—the Pentateuch

d'chuyah—a laws that is suspended, as opposed to completely removed (*hutrah*)

dan l'khaf zekhut—judge favorably

darkhei shalom—ways of peace

derekh he'arah—by way of comment

derekh nitzayon in a manner of quarrelling

derekh tzachut—by way of rhetoric

edomi—"red one"

efshar b'sheilah—subject to abrogation by a rabbinical scholar *eid zomem*—one who attempts to cause harm to another by testifying falsely against him, and is exposed by others testifying that personal circumstances would have prevented his witnessing the event in question; as per Deuteronomy 19:19, the witness is subject to the same punishment he attempted to inflict on his intended victim

gehinnom—Hell

gemilat chasadim—deeds of kindness

geneivat da'at—falsely attempting to obtain the gratitude or good opinion of another

gezel sheinah—"theft" of sleep

gezerat hakatuv—by decree of the Scriptural text

gnai gadol—significant embarrassment

grama—actions that are causative rather than direct

halakhah—Jewish law

halbanat panim—causing humiliation; literally, "whitening the face" as if all the blood has been drawn out

hin tzedek—a just measure

hutrah—a law that is completely removed, as opposed to merely suspended (*d'chuyah*)

k'sh'fikhat damim—"like" murder

k'vod habriyot—human dignity

kamokha—"as yourself"

kashrut—Jewish dietary laws

kavod—honor

kefel—lit. "double"; twice the value of a stolen object, a fine paid for theft under certain circumstances *kehunah*—the priesthood; see *kohen*

kesher r'sha'im—a band of evildoers

ketubah—marriage contract

kiddush—blessing, generally said over wine, in honor of the Sabbath and Festivals

kinnui—a nickname

kohen—a member of the Jewish priesthood, i.e., a male descendant of Aaron, brother of Moses

l'hachzik b'machloket—to initiate, or aggravate, a dispute

l'shakker—to lie

lashon hara—malicious gossip

lav sh'eino shaveh lakol—a prohibition relevant only to a portion of the population

lechem hapanim—The Showbread, as in Leviticus 24:5

lo tikom—the prohibition against revenge

lo tigod'du—the prohibition against self-mutilation (Deut. 14:1) and interpreted Talmudically (*Yevamot* 14a) against "*agudot, agudot*"; see above

lot titor—the prohibition against bearing a grudge

lokeh b'gufo—to be punished corporally

lulei d'mistafina—"were that I were not afraid"

ma'avir al midotav—to forgive personal offenses; lit. "passes on his measurements", thus in usage one who does not take care to evaluate the exact degree to which another person anguishes him, but rather dispenses with such evaluations and goes on his way (as per Rashi, *Rosh HaShanah* 17a) *makkot mardut*—rabbinically (as opposed to biblically) ordained lashes; lit. "lashes of rebellion"

masekhta—tractate

mechilah—1) forgiveness; 2) a waiving of one's rights (personal or monetary)

mechzi k'shikra—having "the appearance of falsehood"; misleading behavior

met mitzvah—one who has died and has no relatives to attend to his burial, the responsibility thus becoming a *mitzvah* incumbent upon the community or anyone aware of the situation

midah megunah—a "repugnant trait"

midivrei kabbalah—a reference to principles that although not biblical, are possibly of a different status than rabbinical principles due to mention in post-Pentateuchal Scripture; lit. "from Tradition"

milei d'alma—worldly matters

milei d'Orayta—matters relating to the Torah

minyan—quorum of ten adult Jewish males required for certain religious practices

mishum shlom beito—for the sake of a peaceful household

mitkabbed biklon chaveiro—drawing honor through the humiliation of one's fellow

mitvah, mitzvot (pl.)—one of the 613 positive and negative commandments incumbent upon Jews; also a reference to rabbinic commandments

mitzvah haba'ah ba'aveirah—a commandment fulfilled through violation of a transgression (in general, disqualifying fulfillment of the commandment)

mora—awe

Mussar movement—a movement founded by R. Yisrael [Salanter] Lipkin in the nineteenth century to encourage the focused study of ethical behavior

na'ah—"pleasant"

nazir—one who has taken the Nazirite vow, and is thus subject to the prohibitions in Numbers ch. 6

nekimah—revenge

netirah—bearing a grudge

nitkavein l'hakhlimo—"he intended to humiliate him"

Noahide laws—seven commandments that apply to non-Jews as well as Jwes, i.e. prohibitions against blasphemy, theft, sexual immorality, idolatry, eating from a live animal, and the commandment of justice

notein shalom—"giving shalom"; offering a blessing, one's best wishes for happiness and peace

ona'at d'varim—"verbal," or emotional, oppression

ones—a deed or omission by compulsion

oseh ma'aseh amkha—one who behaves in a manner consistent with the standards of the Jewish nation' lit. "does the deeds of your nation"

p'shiah—negligence

pidyon haben—ritual of redemption of the firstborn

psak—halakhic ruling

ra—bad

rasha—wicked one

ratz b'rshut—one whose carelessness can be justified by the motivation for his haste; lit. running with "permission"

rebbe, rebbeim (pl.)—teacher

remiza k'dibbur—the [questionable] equation of non-verbal indication to speech, for certain intents and purposes

Ribbono Shel Olam—"Master of the Universe"; a reference to God

safek—doubt; undetermined situations

sh'eilat shalom—"asking" shalom; inquiring into a person's welfare

Shabbat—the Sabbath

Shalom—peace, as well as a greeting; also a form of God's Name

sharui b'shalom—"in a state of peace"; a mindset lacking in one who is in mourning

shatnez—a forbidden mixture of wool and linen in one's clothing

sheker—falsehood

shekhiach hezeika—a significant likelihood of danger

shelo l'vayesh—"so as not to embarrass"; the motivation cited for certain practices within halakhah

shem shafel—a "low" or derogatory name

shem tafel—a secondary name

shev v'al ta'aseh—passive behavior; lit. "sit and do not do"

shivah—seven-day mourning period

shma—a three-paragraph, biblically mandated reading that is said twice daily and begins, "Hear O Israel, the Lord is our God, the Lord is One"

shochet—ritual slaughterer

sinah gemurah—"absolute hatred"

sukkah—a temporary structure used for the Sukkot festival

tallit—four-cornered prayer shawl with fringes (tzitzit)

Tanakh—the Bible; short for *Torah* (Pentateuch), *Nevi'im* (Prophets), and *Ketuvim* (Writings)

te'inah u'prikah—lit. "loading and unloading"; physical assistance as mandated by Exodus 23:5

tefillin—passages of Torah in square boxes, to be worn on the head and arm (as per Deut. 6:8) during prayer, wrongly translated as "phylacteries"

tza'ar haguf—physical or personal anguish

yir'ah—fear or reverence

Index of Sources

Codes of Mitzvot and Halakhic Codes of Rishonim

Index of Subjects

295